# Making Room

Brendan O'Flaherty

# Making Room

## the economics of homelessness

Harvard University Press

Cambridge, Massachusetts, and London, England

Copyright © 1996 by the President and Fellows
    of Harvard College
All rights reserved
Printed in the United States of America
Second printing, 1998

First Harvard University Press paperback edition, 1998

*Library of Congress Cataloging-in-Publication Data*

O'Flaherty, Brendan.
    Making room: the economics of homelessness / Brendan O'Flaherty.
        p.   cm.
Includes bibliographical references and index.
ISBN 0-674-54342-4 (cloth)
ISBN 0-674-54343-2 (pbk.)
1. Homelessness—United States.  2. Homelessness—Canada.
3. Housing—United States.  4. Housing—Canada.  5. Housing policy—United States.
6. Housing policy—Canada.  I. Title.
HV4488.036  1996      95-40146

*To my mother, Tony O'Flaherty,*
*and to my wife, Mary Gallagher*

# Contents

# Acknowledgments

This book began when David Bloom and Richard Freeman asked me to prepare a short paper on international comparisons of homelessness as part of a National Bureau of Economic Research project on extreme poverty in wealthy, industrialized countries. Despite financial assistance from the Bureau, I have yet to complete a short paper. My debt to David and Richard—for getting me started, for not telling me to stop, and for many useful comments along the way—is very great.

So is the list of people who have contributed to the writing of this book. Many of the people I bothered in trying to dig up information are cited in the text and notes. Three I haven't cited, but their contributions were large: Hubert Williams of the Police Foundation, who made it possible for me to talk to many different police departments; and Randae Pavalov and Aloysius Siow, who provided welcome hospitality in Toronto.

In each city there were people who went out of their way to help me and whom I didn't thank adequately. For Newark: Lenny Arends, Juanita Dennis, Joe Frisina, Jane Frouton, Karen Highsmith, Firefighter William Jackson, Pat Kazimir, Evelyn Laccitiello, Klaus Mangold, Sheila Oliver, Tom Ostapiej, the late Phil Parelli, the Parrott family, Gloria Parsons, Natu Patel, Emory Pearce, Ben Quattlebaum, Ramon Rivera, Reverend Lee Schmookler, Myles Varley,

Dave Weiner, Audrey Harris West, and, especially, Tony O'Flaherty. For New York: Nancy Degnan, Patrick Gallagher, Nate Smith, and Katherine Temple. For Toronto: Paul Dowling, Susan Golets, and Gillian Kerr. For Chicago: Joyce Allen, John Appel, Jean Butzen, John Donahue, Sergeant Samuel Harris, Toni Hartrich, Audrey Le-Sondak, Stacy Patrioski, Jose Sifuentes, Michael Sosin. For London: Judi Komaki, Ali del Castillo-Freeman, Jean Drèze, Inspector Mike Goodwin, John Hills, Andy Parret, Ann Power, and Inspector Alex Sutherland.

A small army of students and research assistants helped me at Columbia: John Balestriere, Eugene Beaulieu, Sarah Kemp, Sarah Benioff, Stacey Feigenbaum, Alex Kadvan, David Kreeger, Dionne Monsanto, Joerg Oechssler, June Park, Seth Weissman, and Tomoko Yamahara. I could not have put the manuscript together without word-processing assistance from Kathleen Park Ji and the kind forbearance of the Columbia Economics Department office staff. Grete C. Gallagher went over the manuscript with great care, like pangur bán. My classes during the last few years were sometimes forced to endure tentative bits and pieces of the project; they held up well and improved the book considerably.

My debt to colleagues at the Columbia Economics Department is great; they often kept me from going astray or led me to some source of information. Their patience and encouragement were also very important to me. Harold Watts, especially, supplied me with reams of data and frequent commentary. Marj Honig and Randy Filer are the first economists I know who have given thought to homelessness; I doubt that I would have started this work without their example or continued it without their constant willingness to exchange ideas.

In the community of scholars who study homelessness, Irv Garfinkel, Kim Hopper, Bob Ellickson, and Gwen Dordick shared their time and knowledge and kept me from innumerable errors. Richard Arnott commented extensively on the manuscript and made several important contributions, not the least of which was a framework for assessing pathology explanations. Finally, I have a special intellectual debt to Christopher Jencks. Although some of my conclusions differ radically from his, it is only because Jencks framed the questions first that we can disagree about the answers. I greatly admire his book and learned a lot from it.

Michael Aronson of Harvard University Press has been an extraordinarily helpful and wise editor. To the extent that noneconomists can gather anything useful here, Mike is responsible; he turned a book for specialists into one that, I hope, is accessible to everyone.

# Making Room

# Introduction

In 1990, each of Manhattan's major transportation terminals had the population of a small apartment building. But none had any apartments. In fact, most of the terminals didn't even have a single comfortable bench on which a commuter could relax with a newspaper. At the end of the longest peacetime expansion in American history, in the financial capital of the world, hundreds—maybe thousands—of people were making the public spaces of these terminals their home, and the benches had been removed to dissuade others from doing the same.

It wasn't always like this. In 1964, researchers from Columbia University scoured four of Manhattan's major parks in order to count the homeless people sleeping there: they found one man. During the 1970s, the *New York Times* published on average fewer than four stories a year about homelessness; since 1985, the *Times* has been averaging about four stories a week.

Nor was Manhattan an aberration. Newark's transportation terminals were just like New York's, and apartment janitors on Chicago's gold coast hosed down their sidewalks early every morning just as assiduously as those on Manhattan's upper east side. Beggars dotted Toronto's streets, and over 150 people were camping each night in Lincoln's Inn Fields in London. In Hamburg, authorities estimated 400 people a night sleeping in streets and public places.

What happened? Each of these cities has a different history. In the early 1980s homelessness was declining in Europe but rising rapidly in North America. In the late eighties it was rising in Europe but probably declining in New York. A resident of Newark in 1990 was about thirty times more likely to be living on the street than a resident of Toronto. Characteristics differ too: white homeless people are rare in New York, and black homeless singles are almost unheard of in Toronto and London; Puerto Rican homeless families are rare in Newark and Chicago, but common in New York. In all of these cities, though, homelessness grew for some period during the 1980s, and in all of them it stopped being a monopoly of old white men, many of whom liked alcohol a lot.

One purpose of this book is to trace these histories and make these comparisons. But my larger goal is to explain the rise of the "new homelessness." Why did a phenomenon that fifteen years ago most people thought of as a colorful anachronism—like a World War I veterans' organization—change into a serious social problem?

The rise is puzzling. Although homelessness in the past was a phenomenon of economic depression, much of the rise in the new homelessness has occurred in relatively prosperous times. In cities where the problem is most severe, moreover, homelessness has been accompanied by rising rents for housed poor people, even though a general increase in poverty sufficient to raise homelessness should decrease rents, not raise them. On the other hand, homelessness in the United States has been accompanied by continued housing abandonment, even though gentrification pressure sufficient to force poor people out of their homes should fill up all the empty houses before it pushes anyone onto the street.

The puzzle is not unsolvable, however. I will offer a relatively simple economic explanation for the rise of homelessness. It is not a mystery or a sign of the times. It is not the product of individual afflictions like mental illness, substance abuse, or sloth. It is not the result of a dastardly plot by Ronald Reagan to end public housing or of a conspiracy by liberals to embarrass Reagan by discovering and exacerbating a problem that never really existed. The rise of homelessness is an economic phenomenon just like the rise of basketball players' salaries, the fall in computer prices, and the growth of the U.S. trade deficit with Japan: it happened because the set of opportunities available to people changed, and they changed their behavior accordingly.

In particular, I will argue that income inequality is behind the increased homelessness in North America. Income inequality went up the most in those cities with the most severe homelessness. In cities where poor people get most of their housing from richer people, a smaller middle class means a smaller supply of housing for the poor, and this in turn makes bad housing more expensive so that fewer poor people buy into it. (I will fill out this explanation in more detail and give some evidence to support it in Chapters 6 and 7.) Also I think that tenants' rights laws and the huge increase in the United States in the number of released prisoners have contributed to the rise of homelessness, but their role is both smaller and harder to document.

Policy responses also matter in explaining the volume of homelessness, partly because the fashion is to count people in shelters as homeless. Shelters do two things in this regard: they provide a place to stay for some people who would not otherwise be on the street, and they reduce the demand for bad housing and cause some of it to disappear from the market. Homelessness is an extremely difficult public-policy problem because it is so difficult to identify people who would be homeless in the absence of relief efforts; almost any humanitarian response, then, is likely to have significant side effects.

This is not an argument against humanitarian efforts: almost everybody gets vaccinated to prevent a smallpox epidemic that would kill at most 10 percent of the population—but nobody thinks that inoculating the other 90 percent is a waste or a sham (but then nobody considers the vaccinated to be in the same class as those who actually have smallpox). Does my concentration on the housing market unduly neglect the role of mental illness and substance abuse? I think not.

Consider the Sunshine Hotel, an old lodginghouse on the Bowery. It is full of alcoholics, drug users, and severely disturbed men. And it is private-market housing (as of this writing). Nothing is especially nice about the Sunshine, but it shows that this kind of housing is feasible for mentally ill people and substance abusers. Being mentally ill or a drug user or an alcoholic doesn't mean you have to live on the street or in a shelter. The overwhelming majority of severely mentally ill people and substance abusers live in conventional housing, and most of it is nicer than the Sunshine. Why some do not—why they don't all live at the Sunshine or someplace better—has to do with the housing market.

I don't argue that mental illness and substance abuse are good for anyone. People with these disabilities are likely to end up at the bottom of the list in any distribution of the good things in life—most likely to be sick, most likely to be hungry, most likely not to own much of anything. The interesting question is not who is at the bottom of the housing list, but why the bottom of the housing distribution is on the street rather than at the Sunshine, where it was thirty years ago. Many of these same people are at the bottom of the clothing market too, but they aren't naked.

One analogy to the way that I approach homelessness—and why I play down the influence of mental illness and substance abuse—is the way that economists generally approach unemployment. Less-educated people have always been more likely to be unemployed than better-educated people, but nobody thinks the Great Depression came about because suddenly people had less education. The reason is that education levels rose rather than fell in the 1930s. Because unemployment rates rose for every education group, economists pay no attention to education as an explanation for the depression.

Causality is a slippery concept. Many conditions are necessary before even the simplest of events can occur. World War II would never have happened as it did if Germany had not been allowed to rearm, or if Hitler's grandfather had never met his grandmother, or if the atomic bomb had not been invented, or if a giant meteorite had obliterated Europe in 1930, or if the bubonic plague had made human beings extinct in 1400. What we tend to do in finding "causes" or "explanations" is to link events that are novel or out of the normal course of things with necessary conditions that are also novel or out of the normal course of things. Because it seems only normal that a giant meteorite did not obliterate Europe, we don't explain World War II as a case of meteorite failure. The Great Depression might well have been avoided if education levels had skyrocketed in the late 1920s, but we don't use a normal occurrence—the slowness of educational growth in the twenties—to explain an abnormal one.

What seems natural and ordinary, however, differs among people, and even within the same observer at different times. Astronomers used to operating in the context of geological eons would find nothing unusual about a meteorite obliterating Europe. Let me illustrate with a personal story, the only one in this book. One of my uncles (he died when I was eighteen) was an alcoholic who bounced from state to state and dishwashing job to dishwashing job. The relatives were not always glad to see him arrive and always happy to see him leave. He was unemployed much of the time, and "homeless" all of the time, the way the word was used then. Now we would say he was homeless much of the time.

To me and my brother and parents, it was clear why he was homeless and unemployed—he was an alcoholic. That seemed like a perfectly good explanation then because it linked two characteristics that were extraordinary to me about this uncle: none of my other aunts and uncles was an alcoholic, and all of them had homes and jobs and families. When the family gets together now, I still find it a good explanation. But as I've become older, I've acquired some different perspectives. In the broader context of the U.S. population and American history, I've learned that my uncle's alcoholism was not so extraordinary: there have always been many people who were alcoholics, and some of them have always been homeless and unemployed. And so when I tried to explain why homelessness rose in North America in the 1980s—an event clearly out of the ordinary—I could not call alcoholism a cause, since the rate of alcoholism in the U.S. population in the 1980s was clearly very ordinary in this new context. I could of course say, and be truthful when I said it, that if there were much less alcoholism there would be much less homelessness, but this is like saying that if a meteorite had obliterated Europe in 1930, World War II would not have happened. Alcoholism is no more an explanation of homelessness than meteorite failure is an explanation of the war.

Richard Arnott, in a personal communication, pointed out a helpful way to think about this issue. The number of people in any group—alcoholics, say—who are homeless is the product of the size of the group and the proportion of its members who are homeless. If the size of the group goes up and the homeless proportion stays the same, we would probably say that the increased number of alcoholics explains why there are more homeless alcoholics, since the ordinary situation is usually that the proportion stays about the same. Conversely, if the proportion goes up and the size stays the same, we would probably say that the increase in proportion caused the rise, not the failure of size to decrease.

Trying to decompose changes in homelessness into changes in size and changes in proportion is the basic approach I take in considering the popular pathology explanations. The reason I reject these explanations, except the one involving former prisoners, is because changes in proportion and not changes in size explain almost all of the changes in homelessness among these groups.

I start off my book with definitions and a discussion of why homelessness is bad. Almost always, people really don't know what they're talking about when they discuss homelessness, and the resulting confusion is one major reason why data on homelessness are so meager and so poor. My strategy is not to search for an overarching, all-purpose definition but instead to study various well-defined groups of homeless people; adding up the numbers serves no real purpose. Thinking about why homelessness is bad lets us see why we should be concerned with each group—the reasons are different—and forms the basis for the policy recommendations that come later. So far there has been almost no analysis of why homelessness is bad—everybody just assumes it is. But there are many reasons to judge homelessness bad, and each of them implies a different emphasis in choosing groups to study and a different way of evaluating policies.

The second section of the book is primarily descriptive and historical. The goal is to find out what happened, in order to analyze it later. I differ from other writers on homelessness by concentrating on a few cities rather than on a whole country, and by spreading those cities over four nations on two continents. It would have been nice to use more cities and more countries, but as Chapter 2 makes clear, the price would have been high: even with only six cities, sorting out the definitions and institutions was very hard, and I was probably overextended. Better to understand a few places than to misunderstand many.

The six cities are not a representative sample: New York, Newark, Chicago, Toronto, London, and Hamburg. New York was an obvious choice, since the new homelessness is best documented and most discussed there, and that's where I work. Newark is an interesting contrast: it is in the same labor market and media market as New York, but many legal and administrative rules and procedures are significantly different. Getting information about Newark was also relatively easy because I have lived there almost all my life. Chicago and Toronto are both Great Lakes cities, in countries with fairly similar cultures but with very different social safety nets. London is a city the size of New York, one that was also booming in the 1980s, but its housing-market institutions are different—so different, it turned out, that I found comparisons almost impossible. Hamburg rounds out the group: because of World War II, it has a much smaller proportion of old housing than the other cities, and so housing markets might work differently. Unfortunately, I don't have as much information about Hamburg as I do for the others.

Conspicuously absent from this list are cities in developing countries. The differences in institutions are too great, I think, for any meaningful comparisons to be made between homelessness in wealthy countries and the common varieties of housing distress in developing countries. The basic problem is the wooliness of the definition of homelessness in developed countries: if comparing New York and London is difficult—and the next several chapters should convince you of this—comparing New York and Lagos must be nearly impossible.

Thus I trace out the histories of several varieties of official homelessness in six cities. By "official homelessness" I mean a housing condition—places where people sleep. Since the early eighties, government officials and scholars have used the word homeless to refer to some sort of housing condition—though what kind is abundantly unclear—and for most of the book I follow this convention. Yet there is a much older tradition in America of using "homeless" as a synonym for "vagrant" or "bum"; homelessness then has to do with ties to the community, clothing, alcohol consumption, and occupation (or lack of it), not where you sleep at night. This usage still prevails among the American public. Almost nothing is known, however, about the disheveled, apparently destitute people who are visible during the day. I try to fill part of this gap in Chapter 5, with an informal survey of Manhattan's streetpeople.

The third major section of the book is analytical, to figure out why it all happened. We have to know how to think about housing markets, especially those markets in which housing is continuously getting older and more dilapidated. There are quite a few different ways in which homelessness could have risen, and I want to describe for each possible way the other changes that would have accompanied the rise in homelessness if that was really the way in which it rose. We shall look at these linkages in light of much more detailed information about other phenomena: income distribution, a smaller middle class, interest rates, operating costs, gentrification, government regulation, public housing, income-maintenance systems, mental illness, deinstitutionalization, substance abuse, and criminal justice.

The final section of the book is about policy. The basic principle I use here is nondiscrimination; policies (even those aimed at reducing homelessness) should not treat homeless people differently from other people. This is always a counsel of practicality, since homelessness seems impossible to define or verify, but there are also other reasons for adhering to the principle.

The major policy I recommend is a housing allowance—one much closer to systems in use in Europe than to the section 8 program current in the United States. When I first encountered European housing-benefit systems I hated them, since they made it impossible for me to count homeless people as I did in North America. Then I came to realize that, in a well-functioning society, one shouldn't be able to do that kind of counting.

Nondiscrimination has many other implications as well. Shanties, for instance, should be torn down, but their occupants deserve the same sort of notice and appeal rights held by other violators of the building code. Chapter 15 contains recommendations for police activities, building and zoning-code regulation, labor markets, regulation of panhandling, income maintenance, and therapeutic programs. Many of the recommendations appear to be about insignificant details (such as protective payee requirements for drug abusers), and perhaps they are. Still, if I may be allowed to quote William Blake, "He who would do good to another must do it in Minute Particulars. General Good is the plea of the scoundrel, hypocrite and flatterer."

# 2

# What Is Homelessness?

To talk about homelessness, we need a definition. The easy way to get definitions is to go to the dictionary, see how everybody else is using a word, and then use it the same way. With homelessness, the easy way is not available. Different people use the word in substantially different ways, often without realizing that their audience is misunderstanding them. Scholarly and legalistic pressures usually produce definitions that people eventually conform to, but in the case of homelessness it hasn't happened. Instead, the official American definition is so vague and circular that it gives us no meaningful standard to conform to. This muddled state of affairs is probably one reason why the policy debate about homelessness has so often been less than illuminating.

## Etymology

In the United States, homelessness used to refer to a status in society rather than to a condition of housing. At least as early as the 1920s, skid-row residents, people who roamed from place to place, and vagrants were all referred to as homeless (see, for example, Anderson, 1923). In the 1950s and 1960s sociologists studying skid row used "homeless" as a synonym for "disaffiliated." Researchers from Columbia's Bureau of Applied Social Research included the Seamen's Home Institute among its "habitats of homeless men in Manhattan" (Nash, 1964), and Bahr and Caplow (1973) wrote: "Homelessness is a condition of detachment from society characterized by the absence or attenuation of the affiliative bonds that link settled persons to a network of interconnected social structures . . . the man who occupies the same lodging on skid row for forty uninterrupted years is properly considered homeless. The essence of the concept goes beyond residential arrangements" (pp. 5, 7).

This usage appears to have survived at least until the early 1980s. Briefs and orders filed in 1979 in the landmark *Callahan v. Carey* case in New York City treat "homeless" and "derelict" as synonyms. All three homeless plaintiffs in this case were in fact residents of Bowery flophouses. Until 1983, the *New York Times* indexed all stories about homelessness under the heading "vagrants and vagrancy."

Colloquial American usage still reflects this tradition. Discussions about homelessness invariably turn to discussions of panhandling, and most Americans usually refer to shabbily dressed people they notice in public places during the day as homeless. Most Americans feel comfortable about labeling someone homeless without having to know where the person slept last night.

British usage has been quite different. The London *Times* index contains 68 references to "homelessness" in its 1969 index—more than in any year until 1990. But these stories are chiefly about squatters, not vagrants. Homelessness in Britain, then, was considered a housing-market phenomenon. The Homeless Persons Act of 1977 is explicitly about access to housing—only fleeting reference is made to the single adult vagrants who were the only people being called homeless in the United States in 1977.

The two different usages converged in the United States in the political atmosphere of the early Reagan years and produced the massive confusion that continues today. By 1984 an official governmental definition for homelessness had emerged. It reflected the British usage, rather than the American, because it treated homelessness as a housing-market phenomenon: where you slept last night determined whether you were homeless. But the American tradition was not altogether ignored: the sleeping places that qualified you as homeless were those where, it was thought, only vagrants slept. And so since 1984 homelessness, for government officials and specialist scholars in the United States, has meant the number of people sleeping on the streets plus the number of people sleeping in shelters. This ingenious compromise between two disparate traditions has had several unfortunate consequences.

## Miscommunication and Confused Causes

When policymakers in the United States talk about homelessness, they are not discussing the group of people that the general public thinks they are talking about. The daytime streetpeople colloquially referred to as homeless are not the same group as the officially homeless people whom the experts write about. To be sure, the groups overlap to some extent, but not nearly so much as to justify using one term for both. Peter Rossi (1989), for instance, found that only about 20 percent of the people sleeping in Chicago streets or shelters in 1985–86 had income from handouts, including panhandling. Interviewers also rated the appearance of most of the people they saw as "neat and clean" (p. 93).

In the other direction, information is more spotty. Goldstein (1993) did an intensive study of a small group of panhandlers around Yale University in New Haven; eight of his twelve regulars had fairly conventional abodes. Police in London with direct experience estimated that beggars were about evenly split among persons "sleeping rough" (outdoors), squatters, hostel residents, and regularly housed individuals. Similarly experienced police in Newark estimated that the majority of disheveled individuals visible in daytime were "methadonians" (on Methadone) with homes. The Columbia survey of daytime streetpeople in New York, which I discuss in Chapter 5, finds a somewhat higher proportion sleeping on streets (64 percent) but very few sleeping in shelters (8 percent).

This last figure is perhaps the most stark example of miscommunication. In New York, more than most cities, expert discussions of homelessness are about the shelter system; the large municipal expense and sophisticated information systems make this propensity easy to understand. On the other hand, daytime streetpeople are very visible in New York and part of the everyday experience of many, especially those who live or work in Manhattan. (In 1989 a *New York Times* and CBS poll found 82 percent of the registered voters in New York City—91 percent in Manhattan—stating that they personally saw homeless people around their neighborhood or on the way to work.) Thus in New York the group the experts talk about and the group the public thinks they are talking about are worlds apart.

Shelters are set up to give people an alternative to sleeping on the streets. People use shelters to avoid the street, just as people get vaccinated to avoid contracting smallpox. Shelters are measures to combat street homelessness, but they aren't street homelessness; and when you add shelter population to street population, the sum is a number just about as confusing as the sum of people vaccinated and people with smallpox.

Other than forging a compromise between British and American usage, there is no good reason for adding these two numbers. Some say, for instance, that the numbers should be added because people in shelters would be on the street were it not for governmental or charitable action. But even if this statement were true—and many writers such as Main (1982), Ellickson (1990), and Filer (1990) would argue that it is not,—just as it is not true that all of us would have smallpox if we were not vaccinated—it would give no reason for excluding many other people from the ranks of the homeless: a welfare family living in public housing, say, or a park ranger getting both his paycheck and his housing from the government. A priest in a rectory relies on charitable action for his housing, and millionaires can stay in their mansions only because the government's police powers enforce their property rights.

Others argue that shelter users should be added to streetdwellers since they are housed only because of benefits they receive by virtue of having been streetdwellers. The analogy here is to the inclusion of WPA workers among the unemployed during the 1930s depression. But then the many families who received subsidized permanent housing because their homeless status placed them at the head of queues should also be considered homeless. On the other hand, the Goodwill Home and Mission in Newark "will never turn a sober man away" (so it doesn't check on whether its residents are homeless), and its goal is to preach the Gospel. On this argument, the two hundred or so men who sleep at Goodwill every night should not be considered homeless.

Adding the two numbers together obscures whether a rise in the sum called homelessness stems from increased difficulty in finding conventional housing or from increased ease in finding shelters. Increased homelessness could be either a more serious problem or a better-treated one—just as a greater sum of vaccinations and small-pox could indicate either a more virulent disease or a more active inoculation program.

## Shelters, Hostels, and Squatters

Another unfortunate consequence of this compromise is that no-body knows exactly what shelters are. Federal regulations imple-menting the McKinney Act (24CFR576.3b1) define homeless people as people who sleep in shelters, and shelters (575.3) as places where homeless people sleep. (This way of defining shelters is strong evi-dence of how the compromise was reached.) Even in the United States there are many facilities whose classification is ambigu-ous—battered women's shelters, Salvation Army rehabilitation cen-ters, various kinds of missions, roominghouse rooms vouchered from welfare funds, flophouses, various kinds of detoxification facilities.

These differences are not trivial. In late 1989, Martha Burt (1992) and her researchers counted the number of shelter beds in American cities. They relied on local officials to tell them what places were shelters. The U.S. Census did just about the same thing in March 1990, also relying on local people to identify shelters. Outside New York and Los Angeles, the two data sets are wildly discrepant—sometimes one number is higher, sometimes the other[1]—hardly a result to en-gender confidence in either survey.

Two specific examples from my six cities also make this point. In May 1977, Toronto's planning department took a census of skid row. They found 893 men in the traditional hostels, but 430 men in other institutions for public inebriates: treatment facilities, detox centers, lockups. The population in the ambiguous places was 48 percent of the population in the facilities that everyone would call shelters. Similarly in Chicago in 1985, Rossi surveyed what he con-sidered shelters but excluded battered women's shelters, detox facilities, and children in family shelters. He estimated that these exclusions amounted to over half of the shelter population he counted (pp. 224–225, n. 4; p. 65, table 3.3).

The problem is even more serious for international comparisons. Things called shelters don't exist in London, and the places where vagrants traditionally stayed ("hostels") have the same name as places where more respectable people stay. There are many different kinds of hostels—for working people, students, battered women, young people from Norway, ex-offenders, alcoholics, disaster victims—and to compare homelessness in the United States and Britain, we need to decide which hostels are really like American shelters and which are not. Similarly, refugee resettlement centers are important in Hamburg, almost nonexistent in the United States.

But the circular U.S. definition of shelter gives no guidance on how to make these decisions. Nor do the other criteria that come readily to mind. Charging rent, for instance, is not a good way of distinguishing shelters from nonshelters. In Britain, all hostels charge for staying, except for a few of the alcoholic hostels that bill the Department of Health and Social Security directly, and a few that make exceptions for special groups (such as Austrian students) and for people in the process of filing for housing benefit. Often hostels have two rates: one for people receiving housing benefit and a lower "working rate" for people who are not. So a rent criterion would eliminate all hostels—but it would also eliminate many American shelters, since they collect rent too, especially from people who are working or getting public assistance.

Nor is work a usable criterion—many hostel residents are working, but so too are nontrivial numbers of American shelter residents. Many British hostels refuse people who come directly off the street, but so do many American shelters. Cities like New York and Chicago have elaborate hierarchies that allow individuals to graduate from one level to the next, and other shelters accept referrals only from specific agencies. Probably none of the residents at hostels like the Austrian Catholic Centre in London came directly from spending a night on the street; but neither did most of the residents in the New York single-adult shelter system. Probably none of the residents of the Austrian Catholic Centre would end up on the street if it closed; nor would all the residents in the New York shelter system.

Some hostel residents stay for a long time, and so do some residents of U.S. shelters.

Because U.S. classifications are not based on principle, they cannot be extended to novel circumstances. About as many people are squatting in London as are staying in family shelters in New York City. But still the American compromise gives no guidance: squatters are not conventionally housed, but they are not doing the sort of thing derelicts do either. Consider the McKinney Act definition again. Two different paragraphs in this definition might be applied to squatters. A person is homeless if she (a) "lacks a fixed, regular and adequate nighttime residence," or (b.3) if her primary nighttime residence is "a public or private place not designed for, or regularly used as, a regular sleeping accommodation for human beings."

Most squatters would not qualify under (b.3), since most squats were designed as living spaces; neither would inhabitants of derelict residential buildings. Squatters in commercial and industrial buildings would qualify, however, as would inhabitants of derelict commercial and industrial buildings. Such a distinction would not seem to be of great value.

Paragraph (a), on the other hand, is incredibly broad. Perhaps squatters are homeless under the "fixed, regular" requirement; in this case "fixed, regular" is being interpreted as a legal requirement. Nothing in such an interpretation would exclude deadbeat tenants or doubled-up individuals from the ranks of the homeless. If squatters do have regular abodes and are therefore not homeless, how can they be distinguished from people who sleep in the same abandoned building for many years or in the same elaborate shanty? Perhaps the key distinction is physical adequacy: squatters who live in sufficiently nice places are not homeless and those who live in nasty ones are. But under (a), the adequacy test is controlling for legally inhabited buildings too, and so even legal tenants whose residences do not meet some unspecified physical standard (perhaps the relevant municipal building and maintenance codes) should be considered homeless as well. No studies of homelessness have tried to implement any of the tests (original design, legal fixity, or physical adequacy) that study of the McKinney Act would lead us to believe are relevant to squatters.

The implicit U.S. census definition used in counting "persons visible in street locations" is similarly of little help. Enumerators were supposed to wait outside abandoned or boarded-up buildings "identified by local officials prior to the census as likely to be used by homeless persons," and count them as they left. The first problem here is abandoned buildings—clearly abandoned cannot mean physically uninhabited (or else the exercise would be vacuous). So it must have something to do with disinterested ownership (since in major U.S. cities real property has to be owned by someone). Then from all those inhabited buildings with disinterested ownership, persons visible in street locations came out of buildings where homeless people were believed to sleep; regular people came out of the other buildings. The procedure is once again circular: if squatters are homeless people, they will come out of homeless-people buildings and be included in the count of persons visible in street locations; if they are not, they won't be.

The vagueness of the compromise definition makes comparisons of homelessness for the same place at different times just as difficult as those for different places at the same time. When "homeless" means different things at different times, it is difficult to tell whether reported changes in homelessness are real changes or simply relabelings of existing phenomena. In New York City, for instance, families in emergency housing in hotels and shelters did not start being called homeless until late 1982; before that they were referred to simply as families in emergency housing. Almost everyone in New York says that homelessness was a problem exclusively of single adults before 1982, but in fact the population in family emergency shelters was probably at least as large as the population of the single-adult shelters and lodginghouses throughout the 1970s—but then no one called families in emergency shelters homeless. Similarly one should be skeptical of reports of rising shelter homelessness in small American towns during the 1980s; at least part of this growth may be due to the relabeling of such facilities as battered women's shelters and detox centers.

These problems indicate that we need to be very careful with words when talking about homelessness—not tongue-tied, just very careful. We also need to make explicit decisions.

The first decision I have made is to focus on official homelessness, the housing-market definition, rather than colloquial homelessness, the concept prevailing in the minds of most Americans. In one sense the decision was easy—almost no information is available about daytime streetpeople. I will also argue, in Chapter 3, that official homelessness is probably a more serious problem than colloquial homelessness. Nevertheless, colloquial homelessness is still a serious social problem that has received far less attention than it deserves, and so it will be the subject of Chapter 5. Also, because the public will view any policy that makes no dent in colloquial homelessness as a failure, policies must be explicitly directed to streetpeople. Otherwise, for most of this book, homelessness will mean official homelessness: the housing-market phenomenon.

Yet I won't accept the compromise definition hook, line, and sinker—partly because it is too ambiguous to be usable, partly because adding diverse populations together seems only to confuse matters further. Instead I will disaggregate and try to follow several separate groups of people: people sleeping on streets or in parks, transportation terminals, and other unconventional places; squatters; people staying in various kinds of shelters. I see no reason to add all these people together. But in defining groups by what they do in the housing market, not the labor market or the clothing market or the alcohol market, I will be accepting a large part of the compromise definition.

The problem in dealing with a batch of separate numbers, of course, rather than an aggregate, is that comparisons become impossible when one number goes up and another goes down. Fortunately, for North America in the period of greatest concern, we don't run into this problem; for the most part, all the numbers seem to move together. So, for instance, since New York has more people per capita on the streets than Chicago, more single adults in shelters, and more families in shelters, saying that homelessness is greater in New York than in Chicago is a harmless way to save a few words and is not precluded by my insistence on disaggregation. Yet disaggregation makes a simple, one-sentence comparison of New York and London impossible, since London has more squatters and families in hotels while New York has more people on the street. Still I don't consider this inability to generate a one-sentence comparison in every circumstance to be a major drawback to the disaggregation approach. Things that can't be compared in one sentence shouldn't be compared in one sentence.

My final decision is about the time dimension of homelessness. Here again there is a conflict between two traditions. In the American tradition, being homeless was a status, just like being a scholar or a celebrity, and it didn't particularly matter where a person slept last night in determining whether he was homeless. Michael Jordan playing baseball was still a basketball superstar, and a derelict who spent one night at the Waldorf Astoria would still be considered homeless. In the British tradition, on the other hand, with its emphasis on the housing market, being homeless was more ephemeral; like being clean for a child, it was something that had to be renewed every day, not a condition that persisted indefinitely. Homelessness, in this tradition, is a one-night count; in the American tradition it is something like the number of different people who have passed through a shelter or slept on the street in the past year.

Since 1984 or so, the one-night count has been the major way to measure homelessness, and I continue to use it. The alternative American tradition shows up in certain early estimates: attorney Robert Hayes's 1979 estimate of 10,000 homeless people in New York—later amended to 30,000—is based on the number of men showing up at least once at the men's shelter during a year, and a frequently quoted figure of 12,000 homeless in Chicago in the early 1980s was in fact a one-year count from the city's social-service department. But the one-night count seems to be more appropriate for a housing-market definition of homelessness. If you think of homelessness as the difference between the number of people living in conventional housing and the number of people you might want to be living in conventional housing, the one-night count is the natural measure to use.

If you think duration matters, moreover, the case against full-year counts becomes even stronger. Consider Long Town and Short Town, where a thousand people are homeless every night in each town. In Long Town the same thousand people are homeless every night, and so every homeless person is homeless for a full year. In Short Town no one is ever homeless for more than one night, so that 365,000 different people are homeless for a year. A full-year count would call homelessness much more severe in Short Town than in Long Town, although almost anyone would say that Long Town had more hardship. The full-year count gives precisely the wrong answer, but a one-night count, supplemented with an analysis of duration, proves of some use.

# 3

# Why Is It Bad?

Some people eat no broccoli. Others consume no meat, and still others lack sports cars, boats, fax machines, or telephones. Most of us, though, are more upset to learn that some people lack housing than we are to learn of these other deficiencies. Is this reaction justified? If so, on what basis? You wouldn't want to read this book unless the reaction were justified. But more than that, the different reasons why homelessness is worse than broccoli-lessness have distinct implications for what we should study, how we should study it, and what type of policies we should try to enact.

You might think these are easy questions, but they aren't. The glib answer is that "housing is a necessity" or "essential." What these words mean, and why that should cause concern, is unclear. To economists, a necessity is a good to which richer people devote a smaller proportion of their total expenditure. By this definition, toothpaste and Thunderbird wine are also necessities. Since few of the people who say that homelessness is bad because housing is a necessity are upset by the fact that a lot of people don't drink Thunderbird wine, they must have some other definition of necessity in mind.

To physiologists, necessities and essentials mean things without which life is impossible for any sustained period of time. But life without housing is possible for long periods, especially in temperate climates. After all, the subject is homeless people, not homeless corpses. True, homelessness raises the risk of dying, and people have died as a result of being homeless. But many other deficiencies also increase the risk of dying: lack of green vegetables, bicycle helmets, vacations in salubrious climates, sidewalks, bodyguards, home medical kits, smoke detectors, health-club memberships, and lightning rods. Probably more people die in the United States every year from lack of seatbelts than from lack of homes. (In making these comparisons I don't mean to attack the idea that homelessness is a problem, only the glib explanation of why it is a problem.)

So people who talk of necessities and essentials aren't using the economic or the physiological or any common meaning of these terms. Figuring out what sort of meaning is behind this intuition is what we have to do. This is a task that will take us to the fringes of the philosophical world that economists inhabit. Instead of beginning there, however, let's start closer to the center of that world, working with propositions that command widespread assent.

## Effects on Others: Inefficiency

The ethical system of mainstream western economics is built on the proposition that what matters is how well people are achieving their goals and satisfying their desires, no matter what they might be. This, in fact, is the only thing that matters. Far from being cold-hearted, imperious, and numbers-oriented, mainstream economics in its ethics is soft in the extreme: the views of ethical observers have no standing whatsoever, nor can they impose any standards; all that matters is how people themselves, using their own standards, assess their own situations.

Anything that makes someone better off without making anyone else worse off is therefore desirable. Voluntary trade is good, for instance, because all parties end up better off—according to their own perceptions—than they would have been without the trade; otherwise they would not have agreed to participate. Conversely, any situation where it is possible to make someone better off without making anyone else worse off and something prevents that improvement from happening is a bad situation—"inefficient" in economists' parlance. Giving a chocolate-lover vanilla icecream and a vanilla-lover chocolate icecream and forbidding trade between them is inefficient; both would be better off and no one would be worse off if the allocation were reversed.

Since voluntary trades promote efficiency, you would expect to see inefficiency only in places where something prevents those trades from happening. Say that encounters on elevators between smokers and nonsmokers are generally too brief for negotiation and trade to take place. As a result, in a regime where smoking is permitted on elevators, a nonsmoker will often have to inhale tobacco smoke, even though both she and the smoker would be better off if she paid the smoker a little money and the smoker refrained from smoking for a few minutes. (In a regime where smoking is prohibited, inefficiency arises when smokers with a very strong desire to smoke are unable to pay indifferent nonsmokers to ignore their smoking.) In this mode of thinking, homelessness is bad because it is inefficient. Everyone could be made better off, and if this were done there would be less homelessness.

Homelessness is inefficient in several ways. First, because it is unhealthy to be without a home, homeless people are abnormally susceptible to tuberculosis.[1] TB is also highly contagious. The more homeless people someone encounters in her daily activities, the greater the probability she will contract TB. Since people becoming homeless do not consider the effect their doing so will have on people who might catch TB from them, the resulting level of homelessness is too high. People who come into contact with the homeless would be better off if they had a little less money but encountered slightly fewer homeless people. A few homeless people would be better off if they had this money and weren't homeless. Since TB contagion is a public detriment, there is a clear case for government intervention.

The intervention can take the form of either penalizing people who become homeless or rewarding people who don't. The only reasonable penalty is jail (fines would be uncollectible, and corporal punishment is generally unacceptable), and since jails are also breeding grounds for TB, jail doesn't seem to be a good way of reducing this inefficiency. If provisions are made for keeping people off the streets, the TB inefficiency would argue that these provisions must be reasonably attractive—so as to reduce the actual street population—and that they be hygienic. A homeless policy that included unattractive, unsafe shelters, like some of the old New York City armories, or permitted open-air encampments would not be justified on these grounds. Nor would a wholesale relaxation of building codes.

A second kind of inefficiency deals with the use of public space and public facilities. A homeless person using a sidewalk or a terminal as his home deprives other people of the use of some portion of the facilities. Aside from increasing congestion or obstructing passage, a homeless person in one of these venues may also upset others by looking or smelling unpleasant, by acting strangely, or by contributing to the fear of crime.[2] Often the presence of homeless people leads to the removal of such amenities as benches and public toilets. Robert Ellickson (1996) emphasizes the ramifications of this inefficiency—that it keeps people from using the public spaces that make urban life urbane.

Naive economists might suggest that the solution for this problem is for affected passersby to bribe the homeless person to go away, if the homeless person is viewed as having property rights to the sidewalk space; or for the homeless person to compensate the passersby if they are viewed as having property rights to the sidewalk space. If either situation prevailed, everyone would be better off. Neither, of course, is feasible. Pedestrians or nearby propertyowners face a huge free-rider problem in trying to collect enough money to bribe the homeless person to go away: there are many people, and each would rather have the others pay and enjoy the fruits of their paying. Even if they could all gather enough money, the homeless person could not credibly promise to stay away if he received the bribe. Similarly the transaction cost in requiring homeless people to dole out compensation to passersby makes the proposal ridiculous.

The public policy that this sort of inefficiency implies is the provision of offstreet shelter—as an enforceable bribe to leave the street—or the more active police enforcement of laws against loitering, obstructing, and vagrancy.

Closely related to this sort of inefficiency is the problem of fire. Fires started by homeless people often do considerable damage. The Staten Island Ferry terminal fire did much more damage than it would have cost to house the people who started it like kings for the rest of their lives. Again, everyone would have been better off if the homeless people had been paid handsomely to leave the terminal.

Another kind of inefficiency, far less traditional than the others, is that many conventionally housed people feel sorry for homeless people; seeing homeless people makes us unhappy. All efficiency problems connected with such a reaction could usually be resolved with a direct, voluntary monetary transfer, if donors (like mainstream economists) were concerned only with how well the recipient is satisfying his own desires as he sees them. Satisfaction of desire, however, is often not what concerns potential donors; instead they are upset by the begging and shabby clothes. They may have little confidence that their donations will be used for housing or clothing and cannot write contracts with recipients to assure that they would be. Similarly, although potential recipients might prefer donations for housing, clothing, or food to none at all, they find themselves unable to promise not to use the money for drugs and alcohol. Mechanisms tying donations to what the donors consider meritorious use can therefore make everyone better off.

The potential donors' inability to make these transfers sometimes causes another problem: they dislike their own cynicism. A person who avoids Manhattan because she fears her reaction to homeless people will make her cynical is no more irrational than a person who avoids Florida because he fears his reaction to sunlight will make him sunburned. Both bear a cost.

The public policy that this externality implies is once again the provision of decent shelter. Tied voucher schemes, like those in Berkeley and on the upper west side of Manhattan, seem to address the issue, but are in fact quite silly—recipients of food vouchers are perfectly free either to resell them or to reduce their cash expenditures on food and use the cash instead for drugs. Tough policing schemes are not justified by this inefficiency, but neither is the toleration of open encampments. It is still squalor—not unhappiness—that is the source of the inefficiency.

Finally, note that for three of these four inefficiencies (and possibly for the first one as well) what people do during the day is more important than what they do at night, and so daytime streetpeople should matter just as much as officially homeless people. Indeed, since many daytime streetpeople try to encounter as many passersby as possible, and some groups of officially homeless people encounter very few—families in shelters, for instance—daytime people in some cases matter more. Squatters and people who double up matter little, except possibly in the spread of disease.

The relevant temporal dimension is the one-day (not one-night) count. What affects others is the number of homeless people now, not all those who have been homeless in the past.

## Effects from Others: Capability

An alternative approach to ethical evaluation grew out of development economics. It is more paternalistic than the mainstream approach: people's well-being depends not only on how well their desires are being satisfied, but also on how well they are achieving certain "functionings" that an outside observer can judge as well as they can, or better. Amartya Sen (1992) gives the best statement of this position. He argues that homelessness is bad because homeless people lack certain capabilities that contribute to their well-being.

These functionings include being well nourished and reasonably healthy, taking part in the life of the community, and "appearing in public without shame" (Adam Smith's phrase). Judging a person's well-being by her functioning is more reasonable than judging by how well she thinks she is meeting her own goals.

> A thoroughly deprived person, leading a very reduced life, might not appear to be badly off in terms of the mental metric of desire and its fulfilment, if the hardship is accepted with non-grumbling resignation . . . Indeed, in situations which the individuals cannot individually change, prudential reasoning would suggest that the victims should concentrate their desires on those limited things they can possibly achieve, rather than fruitlessly pining for what is unattainable. (p. 55)

Resources are also an inadequate way to judge deprivation because people differ in how well they can use resources to achieve good functioning. The nutritional requirements of a pregnant woman, for instance, are different from those of an elderly man.

In dealing with poverty, Sen emphasizes the capability to function rather than achieved functionings:

> The example . . . of the person who fasts out of choice, as opposed to another who has to starve because of a lack of means, is relevant here. Both may end up starving, and fail to be adequately nourished, but the person without the means—and thus without the capability to be adequately nourished—is poor in a way that the fasting person is not. So the focus of poverty analysis has to be capability as opposed to achievement (even though we may sometimes use information about achievement to try to surmise the capability enjoyed by the person). (pp. 111–112)

This may explain part of the difference between homelessness and broccoli-lessness.

This approach seems to imply that the homeless are in terrible shape. Being sheltered itself is a functioning that Sen cites several times, but being homeless implies deprivations that go beyond not being well sheltered. Homeless people are not secure, in their persons or in their possessions; they are subject to disease and premature death;[3] without refrigerators or stoves they find it more difficult to be well nourished; saving money is nearly impossible; being neat and clean is hard, as is appearing in public without shame; receiving mail takes an effort; and participating in the life of the community is problematic. Homeless children have their educations disrupted, suffer the taunts of other children, and lack routine and predictability in their lives.

Note that the reasons Sen gives for the superiority of the capability approach are peculiarly applicable to the study of homelessness. Consumer sovereignty has little appeal when applied to mentally disturbed individuals, to children, or to confirmed alcoholics. Looking only at resources also seems inapplicable to the fraction of homeless people who are mentally ill or substance abusers, and to the totality of homeless people who have trouble with nutrition, clothing, and security.

A capability approach implies a public policy designed to provide shelter—shelter with security, epidemiological safety, and ways of living with dignity—not necessarily fancy quarters, but more than a bed in an armory. Since the capability approach is paternalistic, it might also be compatible with strong enforcement measures; it is probably not compatible with tolerating shantytowns.

Unlike efficiency arguments, capability arguments view official homelessness, even invisible official homelessness, as a more serious problem than colloquial homelessness. Daytime streetpeople with conventional residences lack some capabilities but not as many as officially homeless people do. The same argument applies for squatters and people who double up.

In the temporal dimension, the capability approach implies something like a one-night count unless being homeless for a week is just as harmful to a person's lifetime well-being as is being homeless for a year. The advantage of the one-night count is that it weights the more severe deprivations of long-term homelessness more heavily than the less severe effects of short-term homelessness.

Thinking about what to count and how to count it, though, points to a deep weakness in the capability approach. There is no principle for deciding which capabilities matter. The mainstream approach has a way of answering this question—they are the capabilities that matter to the person herself—and Sen raises telling objections to this answer. He gives lists of capabilities, but doesn't say why one capability should be on the list and not another. If someone claimed, say, that being able to make telephone calls should be on the list, I don't know how I could decide whether to agree with her, and if I disagreed I don't know how I could argue against inclusion.

In many ways, the capability approach is a philosophically sophisticated attempt to express the intuition behind the glib explanation that focuses on "necessary" and "essential." Because these ideas are widespread, they should be taken seriously. But the attempt is incomplete as long as there is no way of deciding which capabilities belong on the list and which do not.

## Resource Deprivation

Another strand of thought, one much closer to mainstream economics, would argue that homelessness is bad because it shows that homeless people are seriously deprived of resources they might use to satisfy their desires. People would never go without housing unless they had to. Such a lack of resources is bad, and so to help the most seriously resource-deprived people is to help the homeless. This is probably the argument that most American economists would come up with as to why homeless people should be helped. The policy implications are cash transfers and the toleration of open encampments.

The major problem with this argument is that it says nothing about why homelessness per se is bad; it only says that homelessness might indicate something bad. Homelessness is acceptable in this view to the extent that homeless people have unusual tastes for freedom or drugs or delirium and so don't spend money on housing even though they could (or they could earn it and spend it). Similarly, the argument gives no reason to help homeless people who are substance abusers or mentally ill or just unusually free spirits. If homeless people are not the most seriously resource-deprived people around, this argument provides no reason for helping them at all. And there is no evidence that homeless people are the most deprived.

People who want to help the most seriously resource-deprived would do well, then, to use more direct measures of deprivation. (If money were targeted to homeless people, this would be even more true, since it is fairly easy to be homeless for a short time if the payoff is large enough.) The same is true for people who want to estimate the extent of resource deprivation.

## The Obligation to Help

The final approach we come to says that helping homeless people is good for those who help. Several religious traditions emphasize the duty of hospitality (see Murray, 1990, for a brief survey). In these traditions, believers have an obligation to provide shelter, an obligation entirely independent of any consequences their actions might have, and thus entirely independent of any argument for why homelessness is bad.

In North America, the most articulate proponents of this view are the people at Catholic Worker houses. The Catholic Worker philosophy is personalist, anarchist, and pacifist. Catholic Worker houses offer hospitality, no questions asked, to anyone who shows up at the soup kitchen and wants to spend the night. People at the houses do this because of gospel injunctions (Matthew 10:40–42, 25:35–46; Luke 14:12–14, 6:32–35), advice in the epistles (Hebrews 13:2), and the tradition of sheltering the poor as one of the seven corporal acts of mercy. Paul's letter to the Hebrews, for instance, states: "Do not neglect to show hospitality to strangers, for thereby some have entertained angels unawares." The poor are "ambassadors of God," and serving them is serving God. "People who are in need and not afraid to beg give to people not in need the occasion to do good for goodness' sake" (Maurin, 1933).

The question for an economist is what makes housing and food so different from toothpaste, refrigerators, and automobiles. The answer, I think, is that hospitality is something that everyone is capable of, and so providing it is something everyone should do. Worker houses do not establish training programs: "Anyone who is young and reasonably healthy can expect to move rapidly into a position of responsibility in the house" (Murray, p. 221). Some people are better at serving soup than others, but the variance in soup-serving abilities is far less than the variance in mathematical, entrepreneurial, or athletic abilities.

Hospitality, for this reason, can be provided without a hierarchical organization. Poor people need medical care too, but it is impossible to imagine a Catholic Worker house where doctors were treated better than other people and had to be listened to. Personalism means taking individual responsibility because the costs—broadly interpreted—of running organizations more than offset the gains from trade and specialization:

> [Personalism is] the acceptance of a personal responsibility for social justice, for Christian charity, for the Works of Mercy . . . But it's not making a contribution to the Community Chest, and that doesn't mean we shouldn't contribute to the Community Chest. It means we don't satisfy our obligations as Christians by that; we have a personal responsibility to do what we can in addition to contributing money. It's a matter of doing something, of feeding a hungry person, of taking care of someone, visiting the sick, visiting those in jail. (Murray, p. 213)

Delegating responsibility for works of mercy is no more feasible than delegating responsibility for toothbrushing. Even in a technologically advanced society, there are some things you have to do for yourself. Catholic Worker houses set an example of how society should operate—"creating a new society within the shell of the old." The real way and the best way for addressing problems like homelessness and poverty is for people in general to practice works of mercy.

Are there policy implications in the Catholic Worker approach? Probably not, since anarchists don't look for policies. But Catholic Worker writings do contain many opinions about policies. City-run shelters, for instance, are a bad idea: "the hospitality that the Muni [municipal shelter] gives to the down and out is no hospitality at all because what comes from the taxpayer's pocketbook does not come from his heart" (Maurin, 1933).

Perhaps the goal of something like policy should be to make it easier for people to be good. Municipal shelters, by removing individual responsibility, fail this test. So do any police activities that discourage panhandling and shantytowns or reduce the visibility of the homeless. Good policies are those that encourage individual housed people to offer hospitality to individual homeless people. There may be other ways, but the best encouragement is a good example.

Thus for all of these reasons—they are not incompatible, and there may be more—homelessness in its own right deserves study.

# 4

# Homeless Histories

This book is about the rise of the "new homelessness." When did it rise? Where? How much? And, in light of Chapter 2, what kind are we talking about? These are the basic questions that must be answered before we can get to the more difficult issues of why it happened and what should be done.

I don't how many homeless people there are in the United States, and, further, I can't think of any purpose for which it would make much difference whether the number were 100,000 or 3 million. Nor, as I said earlier, is there any sensible definition on which to base such one-number estimates. Instead I will concentrate on my six cities and on several different categories of homelessness (or possible homelessness). For each category I will trace what has happened in each city since about World War II, with emphasis on the period after 1980. (Homelessness was widespread in all these cities during the 1930s, but data for this period are scarce, and it happened so long ago that the trail of historical links has grown quite faint.) This task is difficult, and the story will have many gaps, especially where they probably matter most, in the history of street homelessness. Sometimes I make indirect and circuitous inferences—say, from changes in the arrangement of street furniture (benches and such) to changes in the size or location of street populations.

If my subject were something like unemployment, where definitions are reasonably sharp and measurement is relatively proficient, this chapter would be very short: all we would have to say is, "So-many people used to be, and now this-many people are," and we'd be done. But with homelessness neither definition nor measurement is precise or even consistent, and so this option is closed. We will have to work our way through a thicket of methodological and informational brambles to gain any understanding of what has gone on. But our slow excursion is not just added work: along the way it will give us an opportunity to observe the scenery more closely and carefully.

Two major themes emerge from this excursion. The first is heterogeneity at the level of hard facts: the experiences of the six cities differ widely in the timing and direction of changes, in the size and composition of the homeless population, in the institutions set up to deal with the problem, and in the ways people use and understand the word "homeless." There was no worldwide cataclysm that set off rises in homelessness everywhere simultaneously, no meteorite crashing into Siberia around 1980 and eliminating the old order overnight.

The second theme is recurrence in the history of homelessness: many of the problems, dilemmas, and proposed solutions that seem new in the 1990s were around in the 1960s. The rich heterogeneity of the homeless experience almost guarantees this. Homelessness is nothing new.

## Streetpeople

The one area of agreement among students of homelessness is that people who sleep regularly on sidewalks or heating grates or park benches, in transportation terminals or dumpsters, under bridges or highway overpasses, in cardboard boxes in vacant lots or shanty-towns on piers, in abandoned vehicles and buildings or empty hallways, alleys, subway cars, platforms, or in some other of the myriad nooks and crannies of modern urban and suburban life—these people are homeless. Public images of homelessness are those of the street homeless, as I will call this group, and many other forms of accommodation for the homeless, such as missions, shelters, and housing tickets, are provided by those who want to keep people from sleeping on the street. Monetary economists sometimes refer to Federal Reserve credits (gold in the old days) as "high-powered money" because other forms of money such as checking accounts and credit cards can be authorized only when banks hold enough high-powered money. I sometimes think of people on the street as "high-powered homelessness."

But streetpeople are almost impossible to count. Many take elaborate precautions not to be found; if a census taker can find you, so can a thief or a rapist. Sleeping places often change; Hopper (1991) documents wide night-to-night fluctuations in a single week in 1990 in a major transportation terminal (from 315 one night to 412 three nights later). And public attention to homelessness has not been great enough for long enough to have generated any significant history in most cities.

New York is something of an exception, but even there the record is spotty. People have always slept outdoors and in unconventional places in New York, but the number doing so used to be fairly low, especially in the winter. The colony of tunnel people in Grand Central Terminal, numbering perhaps forty, has a history that may go back as far as World War II (Kleiman, 1977), although some observers consider most of this apocryphal. E. D. Love's book, *Subways Are for Sleeping,* was a bestseller in 1957. Skid-row studies make frequent references to people sleeping on sidewalks and in doorways, and many books include photographs of the practice.

The first serious attempts to estimate street populations in New York were made by Columbia University's Bureau of Applied Social Research (BASR) in 1964. The BASR had a contract with the city government to study the Bowery, New York's skid row, and as part of that project undertook a number of censuses. The first, at 5:00 in the morning of February 29, 1964, found forty-three men sleeping outdoors on the Bowery and in the vicinity (Nash and Nash, p. 2). The number was so small that although the BASR continued regular winter Bowery censuses, they never again looked for men on the street, even though February 28–29, 1964, had been a particularly cold and snowy night (Baker, 1965), and the jail population of derelicts was high (Markel, 1964).

On April 25, 1964, a group of BASR researchers again scoured the Bowery in the early hours of the morning. Although the temperature had risen to 48 degrees Fahrenheit, they still found only seven men sleeping on sidewalks, ten in parked vehicles, and seven in tenement hallways. But there were 145 men walking and standing on the streets and 32 men in bars, many of them asleep; nine women were standing in the street and seven women were in the bars (Nash, 1964a). Later, a warm-weather Bowery expedition found 115 men on the street in July 1964 (Nash, 1964b).

Finally, the BASR researchers looked around the rest of Manhattan in an attempt to find homeless men. They found men on piers, in sewer pipes, on subways, but concluded that the Bowery was "the one place in New York City where there are men lying down on the street asleep" ("Habitats," p. D-6). "The one statement we can make with some assurance after having studied Manhattan's homeless men both by observation and through the records is that there are no shanty towns left in Manhattan . . . Indeed we can say with a feeling of assurance that there are no large organized groups of men camping or squatting free or illegally in any parts of Manhattan" (p. E-2). BASR researchers searched Central, Riverside, Mount Morris (now Marcus Garvey), and High Bridge Parks at night, and found only one homeless man—in Riverside Park.

It seems reasonable to conclude that in 1964 only a few hundred people, maybe a thousand, slept on the streets on a typical night. Almost all of them were men, and most were white.[1] This low street population does not seem to be unique to New York. In 1958, Bogue (1963) conducted a skid-row census in Chicago much like the BASR study of the Bowery. He found a similar number of men sleeping on the street, 110. Kessler (1965) reviewed a great deal of information about Newark's skid row, which led one to believe that some people slept on the streets but not enough to warrant any effort at quantification.

New York's street population began to look different in the mid-1970s. One important change was the presence of women in notice-able numbers for the first time in this century. Newspapers were reporting more women derelicts in 1974 (Moritz, 1974). By 1976 the "shopping-bag woman" was a character in everyday New York parlance (Clines, 1976), and in 1977 designer bag-lady shopping bags were on sale in Soho (Baxter and Hopper, 1981).

The third important change was the spread of vagrancy beyond the Bowery, particularly into more respectable districts. How much of this represented an actual increase or how much was simply relocation is impossible to determine. In 1976 the *New York Times* reported that vagrants, panhandlers, and windshield washers were appearing in midtown: "In a 3-mile walk on the West Side on a summer day, a reporter saw 50 vagrants." The garage attendant at the Coliseum in midtown reported ten to fifteen people sleeping there each winter night (Hess, 1978). By 1978 the *Times* was still noting an increase in "drunks" in the Times Square area, and the morning breadline at St. Francis of Assisi Church on West 31st Street had grown to 300 a day, from 150 a day in 1976 (McNeil, 1978). Also in 1978, two blocks from St. Francis, Madison Square Garden removed the benches on its plazas (Bird, 1980).

It is possible, of course, to assign too much weight to anecdotal newspaper articles. Like Alligators in the Sewers, "derelicts on the loose" seems to be a story particularly liked by journalists; there were similar stories in the 1961 *Journal-American*, for instance (Bahr, 1973). Moreover, the explanations given in these articles are not all that coherent. Often the headlines speak of released mental patients, but the stories generally portray the new midtown homeless as traditional skid-row types—older white alcoholics—pushed out of the Bowery by mental patients, drug addicts, and young black hoodlums. But fear of young black men is a traditional theme in the literature, dating back at least to the 1960s. Still, the hard data on St. Francis of Assisi or the Madison Square Garden benches and the emergence of the term "bag lady" lead one to think that something more than journalistic musing was happening in the later 1970s.

The Madison Square Garden benches are particularly telling. Recall that the BASR described the Bowery as the only place in Manhattan where men slept on the sidewalk. The new Garden had been built in 1968 with benches on the surrounding plaza. The Garden's management had no reason to remove these benches before 1978. So something new and different had to be happening by 1978.

Were the new midtown street homeless merely exiles from the Bowery? The BASR reports would indicate not. Very few people were homeless on Bowery sidewalks in 1964, and I have seen nothing about Bowery street homelessness rising between 1964 and 1978; indeed, most stories of the Bowery in this period are about how the whole place was fading away and becoming more sedate.

In neither Chicago or Newark, however, is there any evidence of rising street homelessness in the late 1970s. By contrast, Toronto's street homelessness in this period was fairly large: a city skid-row census on May 6, 1977, found 200 men in "illegitimate" accommodation ("parks, hallways, etc.") but gives no description of how this figure was obtained (Toronto Commissioner of Planning, 1977).[2]

What happened next in U.S. cities is well known and yet almost entirely undocumented: street homelessness grew. Most of the evidence for this growth is indirect. In Newark, for instance, Sergeant (now Deputy Chief) John Dough was a police officer patrolling the downtown area. During the summer of 1982, he noticed growing numbers of homeless people on the streets and took his concerns to Brenda Beavers of the Salvation Army. This led to the establishment of the Newark Committee on the Homeless. There are also anecdotal reports of increasing numbers of people on the street in Chicago beginning around 1980 (Brown interview, 1991).

The first serious estimates of the street population came around 1985, made by Richard Freeman and Brian Hall in New York and by Peter Rossi in Chicago. The methods and results were very different. Freeman and Hall (1987) interviewed homeless individuals in New York and tried to determine how they divided their time between streets and shelters. Based on these interviews and some mathematical modeling, they estimated that there would be 2.23 people on the street for each person in a shelter.[3] From the summer 1985 shelter population of single adults, this ratio implied about 15,000 people on the street.

Rossi (1989), by contrast, took a random survey of street locations, relying on a group of interviewers (including plainclothes police) and screening questions to establish who fit his definition of homeless. Rossi's population estimates are 1,383 for fall 1985 and 528 for winter 1986. These estimates, though, are subject to wide sampling errors. All that the sample size allows us to say with 95 percent confidence is that the number of streetpeople was between 0 and 2,800 in fall 1985 and between 0 and 1,100 in winter 1986. Even though the differences in methodology were significant, it is clear that more people were on the street in New York than in Chicago, and that many more people were on the street in both places in 1985 than there were twenty years before.

The next set of observations clusters around 1990 and 1991. In the U.S. cities, the census bureau conducted a street count as part of the 1990 population census on the night of March 20–21, 1990, a raw and rainy night in the eastern part of the country. The census didn't count homeless persons but rather "persons visible in street locations"; no screening questions were asked. Between 2:00 and 4:00 in the morning, enumerators counted people who were on the streets and who were not dressed in uniforms or obviously engaged in commerce, and between 5:00 and 7:00 they went to "abandoned buildings that homeless people were believed to use" and counted the people who left. The census count was 10,447 in New York; 1,584 in Chicago; and 842 in Newark.

The census study has three flaws. Lending it an upward bias is the possibility of counting people who weren't really homeless. This may have been mitigated by the reluctance of enumerators to follow their directions to the letter. Biasing it downward was the study's incomplete coverage: clearly the list could not have included all public locations used by the homeless, and it explicitly excluded nonpublic locations such as the stairwells of housing projects and the roofs of tenements. Also biasing the count downward was an incomplete coverage of the sites designated: in New York an assessment study by the Nathan Kline Institute for Psychiatric Research found that only about 56 percent of its "plants" had actually been counted (Hopper, 1991).

In Chicago a similar assessment (Edin, 1991), though largely anecdotal, provided no basis for contradicting the Hopper finding. Chicago observers found many sites with homeless people and no enumerators, many with the reverse, but only one where they saw an enumerator counting a homeless person.

The only separate analysis, to my knowledge, of the characteristics of the street homeless arises out of the census evaluation effort. It was done in New York City by the Kline team headed by Kim Hopper. They conducted 164 interviews with people who were waking up in public places very early in the morning; one person refused to describe himself as homeless. Of the respondents 91 percent were male, 69 percent were African-American, and 12 percent were Hispanic. The proportion of whites among the street homeless, though, was higher than the proportion among the New

York single-adult shelter homeless (17 percent as opposed to 7 percent). (Chicago police estimates of the ethnicity of the street homeless in that city also imply that whites are overrepresented, relative to their share in both the poor population of Chicago and the single-adult shelter population.) Almost half of the New York street homeless were over forty, as opposed to a little over a quarter of the shelter homeless, and 46 percent had been homeless for most of the last five years. Two-thirds had used public shelters in the past, and of those 73 percent cited danger or regimentation as the reason for no longer using shelters.

While street populations were rising in U.S. cities, the street population in Toronto appears to have been stable. In early 1992, the Metropolitan Toronto community-service commissioner's report stated: "We estimate that 200–300 people, mostly single men, continue to live outside. This number almost never includes families with children." This estimate is corroborated by the police—"If a woman and a child were on the street, we wouldn't permit it" (Boothby interview, 1991). Recall that this is the same estimate as for 1977. There seem to be no estimates for street populations at intermediate times, although there are reports of people being turned away from shelters in 1980–1982 (press coverage in this period was minimal, and so it is also conceivable that there was no noticeable increase in the street population). Although there are reports of Native Americans living on the street, there are no reports of blacks. Toronto's climate is not significantly worse than Chicago's: the January mean temperature is 24 degrees Fahrenheit, as opposed to 23 degrees in Chicago, and average snowfall is 55.5 inches, as opposed to 40 inches in Chicago. Yet Chicago has eight times as many homeless people on the street.

London also seems to have had a relatively stable street population since 1960, at least in contrast to the U.S. cities. For the night of April 21–22, 1991, the Office of Population Censuses found 1,275 people sleeping rough in London. This compares with 1,123 people in the category of "campers and persons sleeping rough" in 1981; 745 people in the category of "campers, vagrants, and those enumerated in caravans that were not the usual residences of any of the persons present in them on census night"; and 667 people in the category of "other population (campers, vagrants, etc.)" in 1961.

A surge in 1975 of young people sleeping rough in London received heavy press coverage, but since it didn't take place in a census year, there is no way to gauge its size. Rough sleepers in 1991 received press coverage, in part because of where they were sleeping: Camden and Westminster boroughs contain the editorial offices of many newspapers and magazines, many government offices (including that of the census), the University of London, and the London School of Economics. This census category is approximately comparable to the U.S. census's "persons visible in street locations." The U.S. definition, however, includes two categories absent from the London figures:

(1) People visible in street locations between 2:00 and 4:00 AM who were not sleeping, transacting business, or wearing a uniform. American enumerators were supposed to count everyone they saw, whether they were sleeping or not, while British enumerators had more restrictive instructions.

(2) People leaving abandoned buildings between 4:00 and 8:00 AM. American enumerators were instructed not to enter abandoned buildings but to wait outside and count people as they left. British enumerators had no comparable instructions, as far as I know. London doesn't have a stock of derelict buildings comparable to those in New York, Newark, and Chicago, and inhabitants of such buildings are likely to be called "squatters" rather than "persons sleeping rough." Thus it is likely that this group was not included in the London count.

These two corrections are likely to be minor, however, relative to the administrative difficulties of counting streetpeople. As in Toronto, there are no reports of black people sleeping rough, despite the presence of a large black population in London.

For Hamburg, I have only one estimate of the street population: 400 in 1988 (Oechssler, 1991).

These estimates, rough as they are, imply wide divergences in the proportion of the various cities' populations on the street. Taking the estimates closest to 1990 implies that about one person out of 300 is homeless on the street in Newark; one out of 700 in New York, one out of 1,700 in Chicago; one out of 3,700 in Hamburg, one out of 5,000 in London; and one out of 10,000 in Toronto. The differences are large enough that even these weak estimates are able to show that the street populations of the U.S. cities are proportionately much higher than those elsewhere, and that the difference is a recent phenomenon. Around 1970, for instance, both Toronto and London probably had proportionately more people on the street than New York or Chicago.

## Squatters

Squatting or something like it has been most common in London, New York, and Newark. In London, squatters are people who occupy other people's or public property and live there without paying rent. There are many squatters in London: the London Research Centre estimate for 1988 is 12,500; the Advisory Service for Squatters estimates 30,000; and the University of Surrey–Salvation Army supports the Advisory Service estimate as being more accurate (Surrey, 1989): local authorities reported in their Housing Improvement Programme submissions that 6,178 units in their properties were being squatted in 1987–88; authorities probably underreport; and some private units are also squatted (p. 62). The Surrey samples found an average of 3.75 people per squat. There used to be more squatters in London: at the height of the squatting movement in the early 1970s, some estimate that there were 50,000–60,000 squatters (Widdowson, 1991). To use a cross-Atlantic comparison, the 1988 squatter population of London was of the same order of magnitude as the 1990 shelter population of New York.

Squatting in London has a high-profile, political history. In the 1960s and 1970s it was a major radical activity, and several organizations still exist that advise and assist squatters. It is not unusual for students to be squatters. Many people squat for ideological reasons, but not a majority (Surrey). Most squats have gas, water, and electricity.

New York also has people who call themselves squatters, but there is no large-scale political movement like the one in London. Several hundred "anarchists" on the lower east side live in city-owned properties and call themselves squatters, and a small movement in east New York has also drawn some attention (Hirsch and Wood, 1988). But the phenomenon has not been widespread enough to cause the term to be clearly defined in New York; accounts of fires, for instance, also describe people sleeping in derelict buildings as squatters. The census attempted to include people who slept in derelict buildings in its street count, and most Americans would probably think of such people as homeless, but otherwise little attention has been paid to the lower east side anarchists and others who have accommodations that are reasonably secure physically but tenuous legally. One reason for this is that American law is considerably more hostile to squatting than British law.

Much more relevant than organized political movements in New York has been the actual administration of city-owned properties. In November 1976, the city adopted Local Law 45, which reduced the waiting period for tax foreclosure from three years to one. Overnight the city became the owner of 11,700 residential multiple-family buildings. (The legal action to foreclose was an in-rem action, against property only.) The first vestings under the new law occurred in the spring of 1978 and were surprisingly large. The city also changed its policy for disposing of in-rem properties: it decided to hold them and not sell. Sales stopped in the fall of 1978.

When the management of in-rem residential property was reorganized on September 1, 1978, the city found itself in possession of some 100,000 units—about 5 percent of the total rental housing stock and a much larger proportion of low-rent units. In community district 3 in the Bronx, 40 percent of all housing units were city-owned (NYC Housing Preservation and Development Department, 1979).

The city had little control over or knowledge of the people living in those 100,000 housing units. Some units—about 12,000—had residents who were paying rent. The city's records indicated another 23,000 units occupied by nonpaying tenants, but the records were not accurate. City records also indicated that 65,000 units were vacant, but these records were not accurate either (unit data from Annual Report, October 1979, p. 24; accuracy statements from Eimecke interview, 1992). Over the next few years the city gained a much better handle on its in-rem stock: it learned who was living there, began to provide services, and started gradually to collect rent. Rent collections rose from $19.2 million in fiscal year 1979 to $44.2 million in fiscal 1982, even though the average weekly rent only rose from $154 to $176 and the *recorded* number of occupied units fell.

In the late 1970s, then, there were large numbers of families—most likely tens of thousands—who were living in in-rem property and not paying rent.

Something similar happened in Newark. Newark's inventory of city-owned property began to grow around 1975 because of more aggressive in-rem foreclosure policies by the city and a decided reluctance by landlords to keep their property. The inventory reached around 5,000 parcels (including vacant lots) in 1979, and 6,000 in 1980 (Newark has a total of about 38,000 taxable parcels). Foreclosing on so many properties was chaotic, and the city had difficulty keeping track of what it owned and what was occupied, much less who owed rent. The budget division surveyed city-owned property in late 1978 and early 1979, and found between 500 and 1,000 occupied units that had been unknown to city authorities (Banker interview, 1991). It is unclear what proportion of the tenants of these discovered units were originally tenants of the former landlord, and had merely stayed in the apartment after the city took it, and what proportion had moved in without ever paying rent. (In some cases the date of occupancy is not a good indicator, since some landlords took advantage of the general chaos by continuing to collect rents and admit tenants after the city had assumed title; I am aware also of cases of "squatter landlords" who started collecting rents in derelict buildings after the city had assumed title.)

Moreover, the Newark Housing Authority (NHA) had a severe financial crisis in 1979 and was unable to pay its bills. Part of its response was to reduce population of the high-rise buildings: HUD subsidies, the major source of NHA income, depended on the number of units, not the number of occupied units, and vandalism in the high-rises was an expensive and serious problem. So the number of occupied units fell from 11,121 on May 31, 1979, to 9,070 on March 31, 1982; the 1979 occupancy was about a thousand below the 1972 peak. Vacant apartments attracted squatters, in numbers I have been unable to assess. Squatters concerned the NHA enough that, after a few years of experimentation, it adopted a procedure of welding the door shut whenever an apartment was closed down.

Although the number of unauthorized families and individuals living in city and housing-authority apartments during the late seventies is impossible to estimate with much accuracy, it was almost certainly in the hundreds, possibly as much as a thousand. The number of homeless families in formal shelters and hotels has never been much above five hundred, and so this group is far from trifling in a narrative about homelessness. These activities continued at least until the mid-1980s. In 1985, for instance, it was not unusual for the city division of real property to find a hundred or more people in a single downtown abandoned hotel.

Toronto and Chicago lack the large stocks of publicly owned property that provide the setting for this sort of squatting—Chicago, because its legal structure prevents public entities from holding inventories of structures; Toronto, because it has almost no abandoned structures. Chicago enforces property taxes differently: the city never takes delinquent properties for tax purposes; instead the county sells the property at a "scavenger sale" and distributes the proceeds among the several different layers of government that have claims to the taxes.

As I mentioned in Chapter 2, I don't know whether squatters are really homeless. Even if you think they are not, however, you would want to know about squatting activity in order to understand the housing market that the homeless are part of.

## Missions for Single Adults

Religious organizations have traditionally given poor people places to stay. Sometimes the primary motivations are charity and hospitality; sometimes the primary motivations are uplift, improvement, and conversion; often the motivations are mixed as workers try to minister to both body and soul. People who stay at missions are generally considered homeless.

The category of "mission," however, has fuzzy boundaries. On one side are rehabilitation and treatment facilities; on the other are government-run shelters. When religious organizations concentrate heavily on rehabilitation and treatment to the exclusion of the wayfarers, sinners, and people who just happen to be down on their luck, they have probably crossed the first fuzzy border; when they are exclusively agents of the government under strict contracts, they have probably crossed the second.

Crossing the second border is probably a less serious matter than crossing the first. Government-run shelters are another of the homeless categories we consider, but hospitals and therapeutic communities are not. Yet the first is the border most commonly crossed; indeed, the history of missions over the last thirty years has been dominated by a pull to do more and more for fewer and fewer people.

London is the home of the archetypal mission organization, the Salvation Army, which was founded there in 1883, and maintained several large (many-hundred-bed) hostels there for many years. George Orwell (1933) describes his unpleasant experiences in one of the Salvation Army hostels. As in many missions, residents were required to do some work and were exhorted to improve themselves. In 1972 the Salvation Army provided 2,548 beds in London (Digby, 1976); by 1988 this number was down to 847 (Homeless Handbook, 1988). Similarly the Church Army, an Anglican organization, had 698 beds in 1972 but only 126 in 1988. In the early 1970s, the two armies had many old, cavernous Victorian buildings that were increasingly difficult to maintain; most of them have been shut down and replaced, with the new bed spaces considerably more attractive than the old ones.

In Newark too, mission capacity fell significantly between 1964 and 1988. In 1964, four traditional missions had about 440 bed spaces.[4] By the early 1980s, these four missions had around 300 beds. The philosophy of the missions changed as well: higher demands were made on the men sleeping there, and fewer men directly off the street were welcome. The 140 or so men at the Salvation Army Men's Center are mainly there for treatment, and many knowledgeable people don't think of it as a place where "homeless" people stay, even though in 1964 it was the place to which the welfare division referred transients (Kessler, 1965).

Between 1965 and 1981, these missions were the only source of shelter for single adults in Newark. After 1981, several other shelters for single adults were established in Newark, but most of these were also religiously based. The first of the modern shelters was St.

Rocco's Outreach Center, which began operating in early 1981. It is the earliest indication I have of the beginnings of the new homelessness in Newark. Father John Nickas, pastor of St. Rocco's Church in the Central Ward, was trying to open a daycare center. A bank had closed one of its branches and donated it to St. Rocco's in January 1981. While arranging to renovate the bank, Father Nickas allowed a man to sleep in the building in order to provide security. Soon he was bombarded by requests, and the number of men sleeping there grew. With some small foundation help, the bank was operating as a shelter for 25–30 men by March 1981 (Nickas interview, 1991). (One might object to labeling this incident as the beginning of the new homelessness in Newark because Father Nickas did not have first-hand knowledge of where the men were living before they came to the bank. Perhaps, some may say, this is an instance of supply creating its own demand. But such a criticism is misdirected: even if it is accurate, it cannot explain how soft-hearted priests were able to establish daycare centers in Newark before 1981, if nothing new and different was happening in 1981.)

During the rest of the 1980s several other religiously oriented shelters for single adults came and went, but the major change was a return to traditional philosophy at the venerable Goodwill Home and Rescue Mission. This occurred around 1989. In the 1990s about 90 percent of the 600 or so shelter beds for single adults in Newark are provided by religious organizations (using a wide definition that includes the Salvation Army), some 40 percent by Goodwill alone.

Chicago is similar to Newark in the history and importance of mission beds, but the decrease was not so precipitous, and after 1985 the religious dominance has not been so great. Bogue (1963) found 975 men in Chicago missions in 1958. Putting together a list of shelter resources in a 1982 report of the Interagency Emergency Task force with capacity estimates from the 1990 Comprehensive Homeless Assistance Plan (CHAP) yields a 1982 estimate of about 600 mission beds. This was just about all of the shelter available to single adults in 1982.

Since 1985, many other shelters have been established, but the single largest source of free shelter in Chicago today is the Pacific Garden Mission, just as Goodwill is the largest single source of free

shelter in Newark. Pacific Garden, like Goodwill, accepts no government funds but will take any sober man who walks in, letting him
sleep in a folding chair if need be. Both missions date from the
nineteenth century, are devoutly evangelical, and rely on sophisticated direct mail for fundraising.

In Toronto too, the missions got smaller. They accounted for
about 630 of the 980 beds available for single adults in the 1977
planning-commission survey, but by 1992 the number of beds had
fallen by about half. The Fred Victor Mission, which had 181 beds in
1977, closed as a mission in 1981, and the Salvation Army reduced
its size by about a quarter. Fred Victor didn't close because it ran out
of money or people to serve; rather, its leaders decided that it would
be best to devote their resources to providing permanent housing
for a small number of men.

The same trend is visible in New York, but it differs from the other
cities in the relatively small size of its missions. There is no establishment similar to Goodwill or Pacific Garden. Even in the early
1960s, New York had fewer mission beds than Chicago, and by the
late 1970s it probably had fewer than Newark.

New York missions sheltered about 1,500 men a night in 1949,
about half that in 1964–65, and probably could account for no more
than 200 men and women in the late 1970s. Table 4-1 gives the
details. As in the other cities, most of the reductions came from
changes in philosophy: the Bowery Mission, for instance, sheltered
276 men a night in February 1964 and provided each with little more
than a bed to sleep in; by 1990 it was engaged in a wide variety of
service activities but had a shelter capacity of only fifteen. The
Salvation Army Hotel on the Bowery became a rehabilitation center,
supported in large measure by its guests' Supplemental Security
Income checks (Baxter and Hopper, 1981, p. 68). Table 4-1 reports
1990 capacity, but as far as I can tell all the reductions took place well
before 1980. Interviews with people whose memories of the lower
east side and the Bowery go back to the mid-seventies produced no
recollection of mission closings.[5]

On the other hand, several other kinds of religious efforts in New
York City have grown. First in the middle and late seventies was the
growth and proliferation of what Baxter and Hopper (1981) labeled
"Digger" shelters—small, informal places where lines between staff

*Table 4-1* Traditional Missions in Manhattan, 1949–1990

| Mission | 1949 occupancy | 1964–65 occupancy | 1990 capacity |
|---|---|---|---|
| Bowery | 823 | 140 | 15 |
| Salvation Army | | | |
|   Hotel | 525 | 288 | – |
| Near Bowery | 148 | 131 | 79 |
| Rest of Manhattan | ? | 200 | 68 |
| Total | 1,496+ | 759 | 162 |

Bowery: Bowery Mission and Salvation Army Rehabilitation Center for 1964–65; Bowery Mission for 1990. Salvation Army Hotel: On the Bowery; Nash considers this a lodginghouse rather than a mission, since it charged (slightly above) the market price and accepted ticketmen (93 of the 288 guests); but many churches outside the Bowery had charge accounts (Nash, 1964b). Near Bowery: Volunteers of America, Catholic Worker, Holy Name. Rest of Manhattan: Salvation Army Men's Social Service Center, Emergency Shelter, McAuley Cremorne Mission, McAuley Water Street Mission; Nash includes the Seamen's Institute (700 beds) in this category, but I exclude it.

*Sources.* 1964–65: All figures except Rest of Manhattan from Nash and Nash (1964); Rest of Manhattan from G. Nash (1964b). 1949: Bowery from Nash and Nash (1964). Salvation Army Hotel and Near Bowery are 1964 capacities; Nash and Nash state that in winter 1949 the Bowery area was at capacity. 1990: Coalition for the Homeless.

and clients were minimized, if not nonexistent, and indoctrination was almost absent. Catholic Worker houses are the prototypes for these places, beginning in 1933. Not only did Catholic Worker activities expand during the seventies—Maryhouse, for women, started in 1975 and is perhaps another indication of growing numbers of women on New York streets—but several other new houses sprang up (Baxter and Hopper provide details).

The larger effort, in terms of numbers, came during the 1980s as shelter and street populations were rising rapidly. In December 1981, Mayor Ed Koch asked churches and synagogues to help in the developing crisis (Mayor's Management Report, January 1982, p. 302), but by January 1983 only 160 men and women were reported as staying in church and private shelters (Report, January 1983, p. 374). By mid-March of 1983, however, 46 churches were providing 447 beds (with over 5,000 people sleeping in city shelters), and the city was hoping for 1,000 beds by the winter of 1983–84 (Report, January 1984, p. 325); by 1985 the goal was reached (Report, February 1985, p. 383; September 1985, p. 477). Since then, the program has been fairly stable but marked by wide seasonal fluctuations: about 1,200 beds are available in January, 500–700 in warm months.

Chicago has a similar program of backup sites available for shelter in the cold months.

I have no data on missions in Hamburg; there may be none.

In short, we have seen in every city since 1960 the same trend—fewer missions, fewer mission beds, but more intensive services for the fewer people they did see. I don't know why this change occurred. Perhaps there is a natural human inclination, when doing good, to prefer working noticeable changes in a few people's lives rather than making such minor perturbations to the lives of many that each single encounter seems like a failure. But what released missions to follow this inclination after 1960 is not clear—perhaps it was the declining seriousness of street homelessness or the growing availability of government funding for programs that could be described as therapeutic.

Whatever the cause, shrinking missions made the problem of growing street homelessness in the United States in the 1980s all the more severe. Even at their largest, U.S. missions were small compared with street homelessness in the eighties (although this was not the case in Toronto or London), but still their unavailability was one more problem contributing to the rise of street homelessness.

There could well be a lesson in this history. Current governmental discussions of shelter policy are coming more and more to emphasize intensive therapy for a few rather than minimal accommodation for many. This is the same policy that the missions chose again and again over the last thirty or more years. It is far from clear that anything in the historical record indicates that this choice is one worth repeating.

## Ticketman Systems

After World War II, the primary way that U.S. cities sheltered single adults was through ticketman systems. These continued to operate in Newark until 1965, and in New York and Chicago until the 1980s. Cities outside the United States did not use these systems. In New York and Chicago, tickets are what the city used before shelters were set up. Robert Callahan and his co-plaintiffs in the 1979 case *Callahan v. Carey*, which is usually portrayed as establishing the "right to shelter" in New York, were ticketmen. Social workers generally referred to ticketmen as homeless.

Ticketman systems worked like this. Men came to a central intake point where they had to be determined eligible.[6] In Newark, applicants had to have proof of legal settlement in Newark (loosely interpreted), low income and few resources, and be either employed, registered with the New Jersey State Employment Service, or unable to work (a determination by city doctors). Transients with definite plans to travel elsewhere were referred to the Salvation Army Men's Center for a night's lodging. Able-bodied men were turned away during the summer months, when they were expected to be working. I believe that criteria in the other two cities were similar.

The next determination was more interesting. The normal way these three cities aided needy individuals was "direct relief": they sent them a check, which included money to be used for housing of their choosing. Why were a small number of men singled out to receive a ticket rather than a check? Though a few men got tickets because they were fire victims or temporarily without a place to stay, for the most part the determination was based on whether they were "deemed unable to handle their own funds" (Kessler, 1965, p. 2). If you had pathological symptoms, you were called homeless.

Men who passed both hurdles got several kinds of tickets. One was for housing—it enabled you to stay for a fixed period of time in a hotel or lodginghouse. During the day you were expected to leave the hotel, ostensibly to look for work. The authorized time ranged from a day to several weeks, after which you had to be reauthorized. The ticket enabled the hotel to be reimbursed for your stay. Another ticket was for meals. Meals were served communally in a central place—the Municipal Shelter in New York or the Goodwill mission in Newark. New York occasionally gave men tickets for clothing at second-hand stores on the Bowery, but Newark did not have this kind of ticket: "Referrals for clothing are rarely made, because the clients have been known to sell their clothing" (Kessler, p. 4).

The ticketman system thus was centered on keeping money out of the men's hands. These were the men whom the welfare authorities did not trust with money, and so they established a system that kept the men alive and possibly well without their ever touching cash. The system produced some ironies—for every 1.75 ticketmen in New York lodginghouses in 1964, there was a man living in the same place also supported by the city but receiving cash instead of a ticket. And it also produced problems—since the men could not legitimately acquire enough change to buy a pack of cigarettes or a subway token, much less a beer, they often turned to panhandling and other illegitimate ways of picking up income: "The fact that a local Homeless client [ticketman] is not allowed to touch a penny no doubt encourages some to panhandle or to commit fraud by failing to report earnings from odd jobs" (Kessler, p. 20). But for a long time it kept large numbers of men off the streets at very low financial cost—about a quarter or a third of the operating cost of today's shelters (in real terms).

Figure 4-1 provides a long time series for the number of men receiving tickets on an average night in New York. The winter

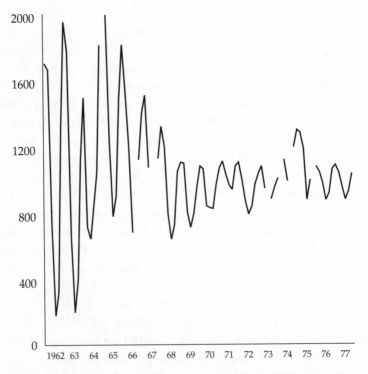

*Figure 4-1* Number of New York ticketmen (average daily census).
*Source.* New York City, Human Resources Administration, monthly reports.

number peaked around 1,900 in 1965, right after most of the Municipal Shelter shut down, and then fell—quickly until 1970 and slowly thereafter until the ticketman system was phased out. Part of the reason why the number of ticketmen stopped falling so fast in the 1970s is that stays grew longer—each average ticket bed was used by about 2.6 different people in November in the sixties and by about 1.8 different people in the seventies. The trend in the July number is quite different—it jumps drastically in 1964, probably reflecting both the phaseout of the Muni and some easing of policies on summer work—and then bounces around without much direction until the phaseout.

For Chicago and Newark, I don't have similar details. In 1959 in Chicago, there was an average of 3,650 tickets per night;[7] in December 1964 in Newark, 183 men received tickets (this is probably slightly more than an average night count). Thus around 1960 about one person out of 800 in Chicago was sleeping on a ticket, one out of 2,000 in Newark, and one out of 4,000 in New York.

Most men used tickets for only a short time, although some stayed put for years. Relative to current stays in shelters in these cities, durations seem short. In 1963 and 1964 in Newark, the average stay was over three months; about 10 percent stayed less than a month. In New York in the late 1970s, the average stay was fifty days, and 65 percent of new clients left on their own within seven days.[8] By contrast, in 1992 the Cuomo Commission found a median ongoing stay of about two years in the New York men's shelters.

Ticketmen were also probably somewhat older than shelter residents today, and somewhat more likely to be white. Kessler (1965) says that "many" of the men were over fifty. The average age of ticketmen in New York was over fifty in 1968 and had fallen to forty-one by 1978 (Hayes trial memorandum, 1981). A majority of Newark ticketmen in the early 1960s were black, but about 40 percent were white.[9] In New York, the proportion of men's shelter clients who were white appears to have fallen from about 51 percent in 1970 to 36 percent in 1980.[10]

The end for all three ticketman systems came quietly. In fact, it came so quietly in Chicago that I have been unable to establish a date or a reason. In New York and Newark, the ostensible reason was a failure of the city and owners to agree on ways to increase the accountability of owners: in New York the dispute was over security, and in Newark the dispute was about verifying whether men were actually using the beds the owners were being paid for. Revelations that the hotels were racially segregated also accompanied the end of ticketmen in Newark in 1965.[11]

The reason that the endings were so quiet is because direct cash relief is a good substitute for tickets. In Newark, since summer was approaching when the Local Homeless program ended, most cases were closed following the usual procedure. The remaining clients "were asked to find their own rooms and are assisted by check as are ordinary Welfare clients" (Kessler, 1966, p. 1). Thereafter, any homeless men who applied received cash assistance. There are no reports I can find of unusual numbers of street homeless in Newark in 1966 or 1967.

In New York, the change was even smaller. The men in the lodginghouses went on regular welfare; the lodginghouses raised their rates to match exactly the welfare shelter allowance; and many men started to receive restricted shelter checks that had to be cashed by the owner.

Just as New York was phasing out the ticketman system in the late 1980s, however, Newark's Division of Public Welfare (DPW) was reviving something very close to it. The single individuals (and a few couples) who make up the DPW homeless caseload get vouchers for lodging in various commercial and noncommercial establishments (like ticketmen) and receive assistance checks during their stay (unlike ticketmen). They must be recertified every month (like ticketmen). All of the "new" shelters for singles have DPW clients (and often refer people to DPW), and most of the people in these shelters are receiving DPW funding. But most DPW clients stay in commercial establishments—some in the Berger chain hotels, the largest number in a network of roominghouses. (Miles Berger, the owner of these hotels, is a close friend and political supporter of Newark's mayor, Sharpe James.) In 1991, DPW supported a proposal by one of the roominghouse operators to establish a commercial shelter with several hundred beds; neighborhood opposition defeated the project.

Since DPW records are not automated, it is difficult to find numbers on these new-style ticketmen (and ticketwomen). Very few vouchers were given in 1985, but by 1990 the number was well over 500—four or five times the size of the ticketman system in the sixties.

## Shelters for Single Adults

In the United States the growth of shelter capacity for single adults has been the best-documented and most conspicuous component of the rise in homelessness. The impression one gets is that shelters expanded steadily and quickly through the 1980s everywhere, or at least everywhere in this country. For the three U.S. cities we are studying, this impression is wrong. Their experiences are quite varied, and none experienced steady large growth throughout the 1980s. Outside the United States the picture is even more mixed.

In Newark, the rise in shelter capacity for single adults was neither large nor steady. Aside from the traditional missions, in 1991 there were only about 170 shelter beds for single adults—fewer than there were in 1985. Table 4-2 gives my estimates of capacity by year. The trend is upward, but it is not steady.

As noted before, St. Rocco's was the first of the new shelters set up in Newark. The Committee on the Homeless started Newark's second new shelter: the Trailer. This was simply a 12 by 60 foot trailer parked outside a downtown church that could accommodate up to 60 individuals. "Accommodate" meant "provide a chair to sleep in." The first (and only) study of the characteristics of Newark's new homeless—Simpson and Kilduff (1984)—is a report on the trailer people.

The trailer people were mostly black (63 percent), which was about the same proportion as Newark's population. Relative to Newark's population, non-Hispanic whites were overrepresented (27 percent as against 22 percent in the 1980 census) and Hispanics were severely underrepresented. Almost all (91 percent) of the trailer people were men, and almost all were local—only 4 percent were living outside the Newark metropolitan area a year before. They had little or no income: most (57 percent) reported no sources of income, and almost all the rest had less than $2,000 a year in income. Some (23 percent) received income-maintenance payments,

*Table 4-2*  Shelter Capacity Estimates for Single Adults in Newark, 1964–1991

| Year | Traditional missions | New shelters | Commercial | Total |
|------|------|------|------|------|
| 1964 | 438 | 0 | 183 | 621 |
| 1980 | 309 | 0 | 0 | 309 |
| 1981 | 309 | 25 | 0 | 334 |
| 1982 | 309 | 100 | 0 | 409 |
| 1983 | 309 | 110 | 0 | 429 |
| 1984 | 309 | 130 | 0 | 439 |
| 1985 | 309 | 210 | 0 | 519 |
| 1986 | 299 | 90 | 310 | 699 |
| 1987 | 280 | 100 | 500 | 880 |
| 1988 | 310 | 130 | 570 | 1,010 |
| 1989 | 345 | 130 | 570 | 1,045 |
| 1990 | 380 | 190 | 600 | 1,170 |
| 1991 | 405 | 170 | 750 | 1,325 |

For traditional missions and commercial facilities, "capacity" is an estimate of average daily population, since the binding constraint on usage is generally either the mission rules or the welfare agency's willingness to pay.

*Sources.* Traditional missions. Goodwill: Kessler (1965); conversation with Rev. Schmookler, generally confirming conversation with Deputy Chief Dough. Salvation Army: conversation with Brenda Beavers for 1986 and 1991; interpolation. Guild: conversation with Michael Hurley; NJ Department of Human Services, "Inventory of Community Services to the Homeless," Dec. 1985; Archdiocese of Newark, Secretariat for Charities and Social Ministry, "Planning Document FY 1991/92." American Rescue Workers: telephone conversation; 1991, Essex County CHAS.

New shelters. St. Rocco's Outreach Center: 1981–83, conversation with Rev. Nickas; *Star-Ledger*, Dec. 4, 1982; 1984, *Star-Ledger*, Feb. 21, 1984; 1990, Archdiocese of Newark, "Planning Document"; 1991, Essex CHAS. Trailer: *StarLedger*, Dec. 4, 1982, March 4, 1984. UCC: *Star-Ledger*, Feb. 21, 1984; 1985, NJ Department of Human Services, "Inventory"; *Star-Ledger*, March 7, 1988; 1991, Essex CHAS. Working Together for the Needy: *Star-Ledger*, Nov. 20 and 21, 1985, Oct. 20, 1986. Lighthouse: conversation with Gloria Parsons, administrator.

Commercial. Based on conversations with Karen Highsmith, director of DPW; her estimates on total homeless caseload of DPW, minus upper bounds on number of these persons in noncommercial shelters.

but most did not. Over half (59 percent) had highschool diplomas. The majority (55 percent) were under thirty-nine years old.

Attachment to the trailer was tenuous. Of the 399 people who registered at the trailer during the 1982–83 winter, only 44 percent stayed more than three nights. The modal stay (36 percent) was one night. What did these men do the rest of the time? Most (71 percent) slept in abandoned buildings or loitered in public buildings; 13 percent visited with friends and relatives. Some 11 percent said they were using the trailer because their homes lacked heat or hot water.

The trailer closed in spring 1984. It had moved from St. John's church downtown to Pennington Street in the 1983–84 winter, and there had met an outcry from the neighborhood—even though it was parked next to the Salvation Army Men's Center, which sheltered twice as many people. A few days before the trailer shut down, the United Community Corporation (UCC), Newark's antipoverty agency, opened a shelter with twenty beds. This has become the only noncommercial shelter that receives direct city funding—about $100,000 a year—and it has grown to a size of about seventy beds.

By the beginning of 1986, there were about 300 shelter beds in Newark, aside from those in the traditional missions. (The 1985 figures in this table include 120 shelter beds for the Working Together for the Needy Shelter. This short-lived shelter never received a certificate of occupancy and never received the county financing it was anticipating. When the courts ordered it closed as a fire hazard in November 1985, an unusually high proportion—for the time—of the occupants, 41 out of 46, were receiving public assistance [*Star-Ledger*, November 21, 1985], and signing their checks over to the shelter.) There were no significant changes in this number after 1986.

Chicago showed steadier and larger growth than Newark, but only after about 1985. In the early eighties, shelters were not permitted under Chicago zoning codes, and some that were set up during this time were forced to close down. Even though new shelters were not being established, people involved with the organization that became the Chicago Coalition for the Homeless saw increasing numbers of people on the streets and rising requests for services, beginning around 1980 (Brown interview).

Mayor Jane Byrne thought that Chicago should not increase services for the homeless. In December 1982, the *Chicago Tribune* was still reporting the number of shelter beds, all of them private, as between 500 and 700. Since this was about the number of mission beds, it appears that very few if any new shelters had been established. Toward the end of the Byrne administration in 1983, city-council initiatives led to the establishment of a small shelter funded by the city but run by Catholic charities and to a building code for shelters.

A report of the city's Task Force on Emergency Shelter dated October 1983 gives a picture of the situation at the end of the Byrne administration and the beginning of the Washington administration. There were about 30 shelters of various kinds (including missions), with 1,078 beds. This includes 168 beds for battered women,

185 seasonal beds, 32 beds in rehabilitation facilities, and 253 "programmatic emergency beds." Only 440 beds were available year round for people who didn't fit into any particular category (this probably undercounts the missions). The report shows activities that might imply rising street homelessness: large numbers of people turned away from shelters in April 1983, 181 people housed by police during July (homeless people have always been permitted to sleep in Chicago police stations), and the number of people receiving tickets rising from 2122 persons in all of 1982 to 3715 in the first three quarters of 1983. (I don't know how to convert the last figure into more conventional units.)

Homelessness was an issue in the 1983 mayoral election, and after Harold Washington took office in mid-1983, the city's involvement grew. The city helped nonprofit organizations set up and run shelters; it ran no shelters itself. By 1984, Chicago had seen the New York shelters and did not want to imitate them, and the nonprofits were strong, both politically and programmatically. Hotels were also rejected as an option. Table 4-3 shows the growth of city and state expenditures on homelessness.

More money created more shelter beds. The big years for expansion were 1985–1987 (Brown interview, 1991; Driscoll interview, 1991). By 1990, the city counted about 3800 shelter beds for single adults (including several hundred mission beds). About 2,000 of these beds were directly funded by the city (Chicago CHAP, 1990). Per capita, this number of shelter beds for single adults is higher

Table 4-3   Government Funding of Emergency Shelters in Chicago, 1982–1990 (in $1,000)

| Year | City | State | Federal | Total |
|------|------|-------|---------|-------|
| 1982 | 257 | 0 | 20 | 277 |
| 1983 | 318 | 0 | 68 | 386 |
| 1984 | 270 | 61 | 171 | 503 |
| 1985 | 2,102 | 381 | 201 | 2,685 |
| 1986 | 4,320 | 689 | 331 | 5,349 |
| 1987 | 4,345 | 2,466 | 287 | 7,098 |
| 1988 | 3,257 | 2,114 | 2,294 | 7,665 |
| 1989 | 4,157 | 2,114 | 1,756 | 8,027 |
| 1990 | 5,130 | 4,107 | 2,689 | 11,926 |

Source. Chicago Department of Human Services (1990).

than Newark's and about the same as New York's. This conclusion, of course, would be different if missions and ticket operations were counted differently. Still it seems that, relative to street population, Chicago has a lot of shelter capacity for single adults.

New York has a much longer continuous history of municipal shelters than either Newark or Chicago, and shelter usage began in New York several years before it began rising in either of the other two cities. But single-shelter usage in New York stopped rising in 1986 and has been declining rather swiftly since 1988.

All three cities had municipal shelters during the depression, but only New York continued to operate its men's shelters after the war, The New York women's shelter closed shortly after World War II, but two different shelters for men continued to operate. One shelter, sometimes called the Municipal Shelter or the Muni, was on East 3rd Street, just off the Bowery, and housed 1,280 men on a typical night in the winter of 1949. Lodging was free, but a little bit of work was required in return. Shelter capacity had fallen to 580 by 1964, probably because of renovations that made sleeping spaces more commodious, but even on a cold, snowy February night that year only 443 men slept there (Nash and Nash, 1964). In 1965 New York decided to close the Muni but was not entirely successful, since between 50 and 250 men continued to sleep each night in the "Big Room" over most of the next two decades. The Big Room was where men used to sleep when there weren't enough tickets to go around.

The other shelter, Camp LaGuardia in upstate Chester, had been established in a former women's prison during the depression. Men were bussed in from the city and could stay as long as they wished, if they remained sober. If they had money, they were required to pay something to the city; otherwise they could stay for free. They were expected to do a little work as well. Emphasis was on older men, and stays of twenty-five years were not unheard of (Bird, 1981).

Camp LaGuardia was originally designed to hold 1,050 people and was operating at close to that capacity in 1966 (Bahr and Caplow, 1973). But capacity apparently fell to the 700 range before the end of the seventies: average population was only 655 for the 1978–79 fiscal year, and 697 for the 1979-80 fiscal year, but the Human Resources Administration described the camp as operating at capacity ("Fiscal Year 1981 Management Plan," pp. 135–136). The reason for the reduction in capacity was probably the elimination of double bunking.

A new women's shelter opened in 1970 with a capacity of 47. Before this, women were housed in the Pioneer Hotel (a real hotel, not a lodginghouse) on the Bowery.

Figure 4-2 shows shelter populations from 1962 through 1979, as well as the total shelter population and the ticket population. From 1962 to 1979 the trend is downward, with a very small exception for the severe 1975 recession. Seasonality also becomes less severe: the January average population (including ticketmen) was 2.5 times the

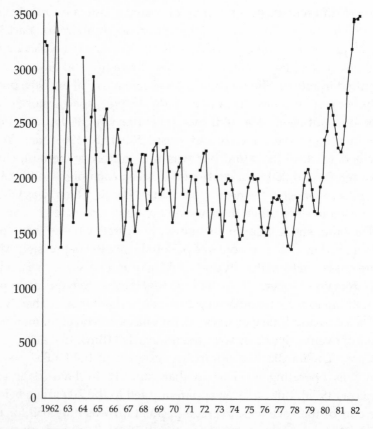

*Figure* 4-2  End-of-month population in New York shelters for single men. Sources. 1962–1977: HRA, monthly reports. After 1977: Hopper and Baxter, "One Year Later: The Homeless Poor in New York City, 1982" (Community Service Society).

July average population in 1963, and only at most 1.5 times as great after 1969.

Apparently conditions in the Big Room deteriorated in the late 1970s, probably because of an increase in the proportion of mentally disturbed men. Ed Koch, then a congressman representing the shelter's neighbors in the east village, wrote to the city human-resources commissioner in June 1977, deploring the violent behavior of men in and around the shelter. By 1979 the state social-service department was threatening to reduce aid to the city because of deplorable conditions in the Big Room, and a task force had developed a "Joint City-State Proposal for the Decentralization of the Shelter Care Center for Men." That proposal described the population as "smaller but more troubled."[12]

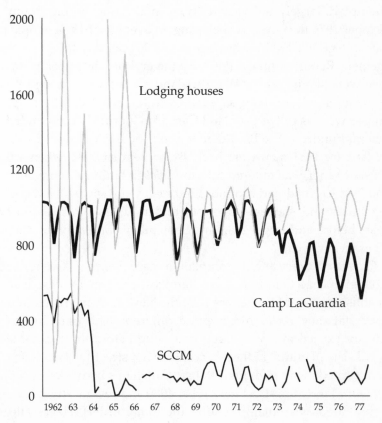

*Figure 4-2 (continued)*

Much more important than these bureaucratic maneuverings, however, was the suit launched in October 1979 by Robert Hayes, an attorney in a large Wall Street firm who was doing pro-bono work with the Legal Aid Society: *Callahan v. Carey*. Hayes represented three ticketmen (Robert Callahan, Clayton W. Fox, and Thomas Damian Roig) who were suing a panoply of local and state officials. They complained about unsafe conditions in the Big Room and in the lodginghouses, and alleged that men who sought shelter were being turned away. They asked that the city shut down the Big Room and establish new shelters with an expanded capacity of at least 750 beds.

In December 1979 Judge Andrew Tyler issued a preliminary order mandating that the city provide more shelter capacity. In response, the city opened a new shelter on Ward's Island in late 1979 and attempted, largely unsuccessfully, to phase out the Big Room. In October 1979 the city was sheltering an average of 1,654 people per day; in October 1980 the average was 2,069 per day (Mayor's Management Report, January 1981). By the end of November 1980, 518 men were staying at the Ward's Island shelter, even though it had been designed less than a year before for only 300; the lodginghouses were as full as ever, and Camp LaGuardia had expanded by several hundred. The Big Room was empty in November 1980, but by January 1981 men were back. By September 1981, when a final consent order was entered into in *Callahan v. Carey*, more shelters had been opened and around 2,500 men were staying in the lodginghouses and shelters—up from under 1,600 at this season two years before and larger than any September population in the previous twenty years.

*Callahan v. Carey* and its companion cases (*Eldred v. Koch* for adult women and *McCain v. Koch* for families) are usually described as establishing a right to shelter under the New York state constitution, but what they really did is quite different. The right to shelter already existed and was recognized long before these cases were heard. The plaintiffs in these cases were not streetdwellers who had been turned away (although Robert Callahan's body was found on a lower Manhattan street in October 1980 and several streetdwellers were added as co-plaintiffs after the initial order). Hayes alleged that men had been turned away from the Muni, but he produced no evidence—not a single affidavit from any man claiming to have been turned away—and the city denied the allegation.

What these cases did, instead, was to establish a principle of judicial oversight on the quality of New York shelters. The legal documents on *Callahan v. Carey* were almost three feet thick, and growing, in 1994. What is in these files, and why are they still growing? We find motion after motion and order after order on the minutiae of shelter life. How many toilets were working in the Bedford Avenue shelter? Was there enough space between cots at Fort Washington? How much soap should there be in the showers? The litigation is not over whether there will be shelters, but about what kind.

It is tempting, then, to attribute some of the growth in the number of single adults in shelters in the early eighties to better shelters, especially since shelters were not expanding in the other cities at this time. Since the litigation probably made the shelters of the 1980s more pleasant than the Big Room or the lodginghouses in the 1970s—fewer work and recertification requirements, less chance of staff brutality, cleaner fixtures and beds, fewer lice, better plumbing and meals—this attribution is probably accurate.

There is room for some skepticism, however. The primary issue for the 1979 ticketmen was safety, and there is no evidence that all the litigation has made shelters safer. Indeed, by placing restrictions on shelter operators the litigation may have made shelters more dangerous. The complaints about unsafe shelters we hear in the 1990s sound like the ticketmen's complaints in 1979 (and the proposed remedies—smaller shelters and more therapy—also sound the same). And even if litigation did succeed in producing what were generally nicer shelters, that cannot explain the concomitant rise in street populations.

Table 4-4 shows that once single-shelter population started to rise in the winter of 1979–80, it continued to increase until the winter of 1986–87. These figures include Camp LaGuardia and the lodginghouses. Then it stabilized and started to decline in the spring of 1989. Since then the shelter population has declined steadily, although not precipitously, until by 1994 it remained below two-thirds of its peak level. At its peak, in the winter of 1988–89, between 10,000 and 11,000 people were sleeping in the city's singles shelters every night, over five times as many as were sheltered in the late 1970s.

*Table 4-4*   New York City Single Shelter Population (averages),
1979–1992 (quarterly)

| Period | Total | Period | Total | Period | Total |
|--------|-------|--------|-------|--------|-------|
| 1979 Oct | 1,654 | 1984–1 | 6,235 | 1988–1 | 10,177 |
| 1980 Oct | 2,069 | 1984–2 | 6,175 | 1988–2 | 9,960[a] |
| 1980–3 | 1,900 | 1984–3 | 5,878 | 1988–3 | 8,993 |
| 1980–4 | 2,400 | 1984–4 | 6,628 | 1988–4 | 9,570[a] |
| 1981–1 | 2,900 | 1985–1 | 7,326 | 1989–1 | 10,555[a] |
| 1981–2 | 2,600 | 1985–2 | 7,128 | 1989–2 | 9,633 |
| 1981–3 | 2,500 | 1985–3 | 6,771 | 1989–3 | 8,534 |
| 1981–4 | 3,300 | 1985–4 | 7,641 | 1989–4 | 8,645 |
| 1982–1 | 3,800 | 1986–1 | 9,057 | 1990–1 | 9,216 |
| 1982–2 | 3,700 | 1986–2 | 8,807 | 1990–2 | 8,612 |
| 1982–3 | 3,400 | 1986–3 | 8,363 | 1990–3 | 8,031 |
| 1982–4 | 4,000 | 1986–4 | 9,333 | 1990–4 | 8,280 |
| 1983–1 | 4,900 | 1987–1 | 10,179 | 1991–1 | 8,708 |
| 1983–2 | 5,000 | 1987–2 | 9,736 | 1991–2 | 7,830 |
| 1983–3 | 4,801 | 1987–3 | 10,060[a] | 1991–3 | 6,975 |
| 1983–4 | 5,638 | 1987–4 | 9,537 | 1991–4 | 7,241 |
|  |  |  |  | 1992–1 | 7,745 |
|  |  |  |  | 1992–2 | 7,182 |

a. Denotes year of greatest shelter population in this quarter.

As Table 4-5 shows, the growth in the female single-shelter population has been much steadier than the growth in the male population, and it has been much larger in proportional terms. The number of women staying at shelters continued to grow through 1990 and then declined slowly; as a result, the proportion of female single-shelter residents rose from 6 percent in city fiscal year 1981, to 13 percent in 1988, to 17 percent in 1992.

Almost all of this growth occurred among minorities, and a large portion resulted from longer shelter stays. If 36 percent of the 1979 shelter population was white, and 7 percent of the 1988–89 population, there were about the same number of white people in the shelters (including the lodginghouses) at both times. (Since the proportion of women increased significantly, there probably were fewer white men in the shelters in 1988 than in 1979.) The average duration of ongoing stays increased from about 50 days to about 500 days, and if average duration of completed stays increased by

*Table 4-5*   Average New York City Single Shelter Population by Gender,
1979–1992

| Fiscal year | Men | Women | Total | % Women |
|:---:|:---:|:---:|:---:|:---:|
| 1979 | – | 57 | – | – |
| 1980 | – | 76 | – | – |
| 1981 | 2,315[a] | 159 | 2,474[a] | 6% |
| 1982 | 2,972[a] | 214 | 3,186[a] | 7 |
| 1983 | 3,154 | 303 | 3,457[a] | 9 |
| 1984 | 5,002 | 711 | 5,712 | 12 |
| 1985 | 5,905 | 836 | 6,740 | 12 |
| 1986 | 7,132 | 937 | 8,069 | 12 |
| 1987 | 8,335 | 1,068 | 9,403 | 11 |
| 1988 | 8,462 | 1,221 | 9,683 | 13 |
| 1989 | 8,372 | 1,316 | 9,688 | 14 |
| 1990 | 7,401 | 1,351 | 8,752 | 15 |
| 1991 | 6,913 | 1,299 | 8,212 | 16 |
| 1992 | 6,043 | 1,243 | 7,286 | 17 |

a. Some temporary shelters omitted.

the same amount, shelter population would have increased to 20,000 instead of 10,000. Clearly the correct measure of average duration didn't increase ten times, but this simple calculation should be sufficient to indicate that longer stays played a major role in expanding the shelter system; it was not simply just an onslaught of new people.

Outside the United States, it is even more difficult to find a sustained increasing trend in the single-adult shelter population. Of these cities Toronto follows U.S. definitions most closely. Like New York, Toronto has long had a municipal shelter for single adult males: Seaton House (and it's called a hostel, not a shelter). Seaton House capacity rose from 380 to 600 between 1977 and 1992 (peak capacity was 748 in 1987). This rise, however, chiefly made up for the decline of the traditional missions.

In Toronto the missions, the newer religiously affiliated shelters, and shelters run by nonprofit groups are all almost entirely funded by the government, and so it is not inappropriate to add the numbers together. Table 4-6 does just that. The picture is surprising by U.S. terms: over a fifteen-year period from 1977 to 1992, the single-male shelter population rose by only about 10 percent. As the table shows, even this slight increase was not uninterrupted. Single-male

*Table 4-6*   Single Men's Shelters in Toronto, 1977–1992

| | Exclusively male | | Coed | |
|---|---|---|---|---|
| Date | Capacity | Occupancy | Capacity | Occupancy |
| May 1977 | 983 | 893 | – | – |
| Avg. 1980 | 1,192 | 1,025 | 17 | 15 |
| Avg. May 81–Apr. 82 | 1,267 | 1,115 | 143 | 184 |
| April 1982 | – | 1,110 | – | – |
| June 1982 | 949 | 913 | 17 | 17 |
| July 87–June 88 | 1,201 | 949 | 19 | 15 |
| Jan. 1992 | 1,074 | – | 85 | – |

*Sources.* May 1977: Toronto City Commissioner of Planning (1977), pp. 8, 10. April 1982: Liss and Motaynes (1982), p. 14; includes 154 persons at All Saints, a church that permitted people to sleep on floor during winter 1982 crisis. Average 1980, Average 1982, and June 1982: Toronto Community Services Department (1983), pp. 49, 5. July 1987–June 1988: Metro Toronto Community Services, Hostel Report, for capacity. Occupancy rate based on 82% estimate from Municipality of Metropolitan Toronto, "Briefing Notes for Members of Council" (1988). January 1992: Metro Toronto Commissioner of Community Services (1992). According to this report, capacity utilization is 90–95%; so occupancy is probably in the 970–1,020 range.

homelessness increased during the 1980–1982 recession, and then subsided gradually. Toronto has distinctly fewer shelter beds per capita for single men than New York or Chicago do now, although it probably had more in 1977.

The growth in shelter population for single people in Toronto has been among women and youth. It began in the early 1970s when battered women's shelters began to be set up. Table 4-7 records the growth in bed capacity for these groups since 1982. Metropolitan Toronto Community Services has continually reported far higher occupancy rates for these shelters than for single men's shelters.

Toronto's shelter population is different from that of the United States in several important respects:

*Table 4-7*   Capacities of Other Nonfamily Shelters in Toronto

| Date | Youth | Battered women | Other women | Total |
|---|---|---|---|---|
| June 1982 | 31 | – | 113 | 144 |
| July 87–June 88 | 185 | 245 | 219 | 649 |
| Jan. 1992 | 261 | 305 | 219 | 785 |

*Source.* See Table 4–6.

*Ethnicity.* In Toronto, hostel users are overwhelmingly white Canadians, despite the presence of large African-Caribbean and Asian communities.

*Migration.* In 1991, 40 percent of the hostel population had addresses outside Metro Toronto a year before they entered the hostel (Commissioner of Community Services, 1992). I don't know how this proportion differs among demographic groups, but some anecdotes suggest it is higher among youth and single males. Toronto attracts large numbers of job and adventure seekers from southern Ontario and the Maritimes; some of them become homeless.

*Duration.* Shelter stays are very short by U.S. standards—an average of 12.7 days per stay in 1989 and 10.9 days per stay in 1990. In fiscal 1988, 62.3 percent of stays were under five days.

In London, the rough translation of shelters is also "hostels." The total number of hostel bed spaces listed in the London Hostel Directory for 1988 is 21,963; the Surrey estimate of bed spaces for that year was 18,281 (p. 30). Occupancy is high, often in excess of 90 percent. Only a few of hostels are like American shelters: there are, for instance, many youth hostels, and the largest category of hostel is that for working people.

The trend of hostel capacity in London, like the trend of mission capacity, is downward. The last thirty years have seen a precipitous decline in the number of beds in large, "direct-access" hostels—the type that most resembles American "tier I" shelters—and an increase in the number of beds in small, more specialized hostels. I don't know whether the increase has offset the decrease—studies at different times use different definitions—or, if it has, whether the new small hostels serve the same sort of individuals that the big ones did. It appears that they don't.

One way to look at the decline is to see what has happened to the largest nonreligious hostels in London in 1981. This is shown in Table 4-8; the number of bed spaces fell from about 4,800 to about 800.

The Rowton Services hostels were privately owned (perhaps they were closer to lodginghouses than shelters). Rowton went out of business in 1982; the Greater London Council took over its three hostels, reduced them in size, and handed them over to the boroughs when it was abolished in 1986.

*Table 4-8*  The Largest Nonreligious Hostels in London, 1981 and 1988

| Name | Beds 1981 | 1988 | Comment |
|---|---|---|---|
| Rowton Services, Arlington Road | 1,066 | 300 | LB Camden now runs |
| Rowton Services, Tower Hamlets | 703 | ? | Closed in 1989? |
| Bruce House, Westminster SS | 700 | 70? | Being refurbished |
| DHSS Centre, Consort Rd., Southwark | 550 | 0 | |
| DHSS Centre, Lewisham | 550 | 150 | Closing threatened |
| St. Mungo's | 500 | 0 | Replaced (new, small) |
| Rowton Services, Lambeth | 431 | 0 | Taken over by GLC |
| Camden Social Services, Parker St. | 285 | 285? | Probably smaller |
| Total | 4,785 | 805? | |

*Source.* The 1988 update is based on the *Homeless Handbook*; some hostels listed without capacity.

Of particular interest are the direct-access hostels—places that accept people from the street without prior reservations or specific qualifications. A number of studies have found large decreases in this class of bed spaces. The GLC-LBA 1981 study estimated 9,751 direct-access beds in London; a 1986 study by SHIL (Single Homeless in London) found 4,885; and the 1988 Surrey study found 4,931. The followup SHIL study for the end of 1989 claimed that the number of direct-access beds had fallen to 2,350 (Watkins, 1990). There is no reason to believe that any two of these studies used the same definition.

The trend in shelter usage and capacity was also downward in Hamburg, at least until late in the 1980s. Except for 1990, I am unable to separate out shelters from hotels or singles from families. Shelter usage, though, fell from 4,177 in 1982 to 2,616 in 1987, before increasing to 3,450 in 1990, with an additional 1,900 people in hotels and pensions. These figures refer only to West Germans; ethnic Germans and refugees were counted separately, as were East Germans until reunification in 1992. Of the 3,450 people in shelters in 1990, about 1,000 were single men and 200 were single women; probably just as many were in hotels and pensions. Per capita shelter beds for single men in Hamburg appear to be about as plentiful in 1990 as they were in New York and Chicago.

Hotels were used to house homeless people beginning in the early eighties, but only in small numbers until 1986 or 1987. Shelter capacity declined along with shelter ocupancy until 1986, and the number of people in hotels was not large or volatile enough to offset this trend. The authorities reduced capacity by renovating shelters instead of closing them. Then they had to rely more and more on hotels when homelessness rose again. Since fall of 1989, Hamburg has been unable to guarantee homeless people their right to shelter.

Family shelters are similar to low-quality subsidized housing units. A family of four in Hamburg typically has an apartment of about 400 square feet, including a small kitchen and a bathroom. Men's shelters typically have double rooms of between 90 and 180 square feet, with central shower and bathroom areas and no kitchens. User fees of about $43 a month (single male) or $117 a month (family of four) are charged and usually paid directly from the welfare office.

People stay in the public shelters for very long periods of time, even by U.S. standards. In men's shelters, the average length of an ongoing stay was 6.2 years. Only 12 percent of the men had spent less than six months, and 21 percent had spent more than ten years. In family shelters, the average stay was also six years. Only 6 percent of families had spent less than six months, 45 percent had been in the shelter more than five years, and 15 percent for more than ten years.

The nonprofit shelters are more designed for short stays. People get help for reintegration, and there is also time-limited financial support. The average ongoing stay is only 131 days. As in the United States, the Hamburg homeless are mainly local—90 percent had their last address in the city. But they are old—in the men's shelters, 75 percent were over forty and 10 percent were over sixty in 1988.[13]

## Shelters and Hotels for Families

With the possible exception of Hamburg, for which I do not have complete data, the number of families with children being housed in shelters and hotels grew substantially in all my cities during the 1980s. The trend is much more uniform and substantial than the trend for single-adult shelters.

Before roughly 1982 in North America, families were not thought of as homeless for two main reasons. The first was linguistic: homelessness meant disaffiliation, and if you were part of a family you couldn't be disaffiliated. The second reason arose from the centrality of street homelessness: since very few families were seen on the street, it was difficult to think of shelters or hotels as keeping their inhabitants off the street. But given the unprincipled way the term "homeless" is applied to single adults, invoking some sort of principle to exclude families doesn't seem warranted.

In North America during the 1960s and 1970s, the families that would come to be called homeless were usually referred to as "families in emergency housing" or "families in disaster centers" or "families of battered women."

In New York, two separate city agencies were created to place families in emergency housing: HRA and the Housing Preservation and Development department (HPD). The HPD's operation was the larger of the two; it concentrated on families who had been victims of fires, had been served notices to vacate premises unfit for human habitation, or who were being moved as part of an urban renewal program. The HRA concentrated on welfare recipients, including those who had been evicted. This department, in particular, had received a large amount of bad press in the early seventies for its use of "welfare hotels," and its program shrank considerably. About two-thirds of the total number of families stayed in hotels, the rest in shelters, but almost all HRA families used shelters. In 1976, the average length of ongoing stays for HRA families was 4.7 months; for HPD public assistance families, 1.7 months (Office of Special Housing Services, 1976). Together the two programs generally housed between 500 and 1,000 families at a time, although there were over 1,300 families in March 1971 at the height of the welfare-hotel scandal and fewer than 300 six months later.

The first rise in family homelessness did not occur until the second half of 1982, two years after single-shelter homelessness started its rise. Precisely when and how is not clear. At the end of June 1982, there were 950 families in hotels and shelters. The

September 1982 mayor's report, reviewing the fiscal year that ended in June, made no mention of emergency housing for families. The January 1983 report noted an increasing demand for shelter in fiscal 1982 (6,000 public-assistance families, as opposed to 4,000 such families in fiscal 1981), but it did not use the term "homeless families." By that month, the family census had risen to 1,922, and thirty hotels and shelters were in use, twice the number available in July 1982. In February 1983, in-rem housing stopped renting apartments to walk-in applicants; henceforth (until 1989) vacant and rehabilitated apartments would be used to move homeless families out of hotels and shelters. By June 1983, a new agency, Crisis Intervention Services, had been formed to deal with homeless families, as they were now called, and formal reporting systems had been established.

Much of the original increase in family homelessness may have been due to longer durations of homelessness. The census slightly more than doubled from June 1982 to June 1983, but "average stay" increased by 90 percent, from 3.0 months to 5.7 months (Mayor's Management Report, September 1983). Similarly, average duration rose from 3.5 months in December 1982 to 4.3 months in February 1983, to 6.3 months in December 1983 (HRA, 1984, app. A). These figures are the average durations of ongoing stays; an influx of new families would at some point have reduced the average duration as measured in this way.

The year 1983 and the first use of the term "homeless families" also coincides with the filing of *McCain v. Koch*, designed to establish judicial oversight over the family-shelter system. The city opposed this suit more vigorously than it opposed the companion suits (*Callahan v. Carey* and *Eldred v. Koch*) for single adults, and the case was not finally decided until 1986, but it may have hastened the linguistic change and may also have been responsible indirectly for some improvement in the quality of shelters. After 1986, *McCain v. Koch* was probably significantly more successful than *Callahan v. Carey* in improving quality—most notably forcing the city to phase out congregate shelters by January 1993.

After 1983 the number of families sheltered rose in almost straight-line fashion to March 1988, when it peaked at 5,226 (see Figure 4-3). Then it plunged to a trough of 3,196 in June 1990 and

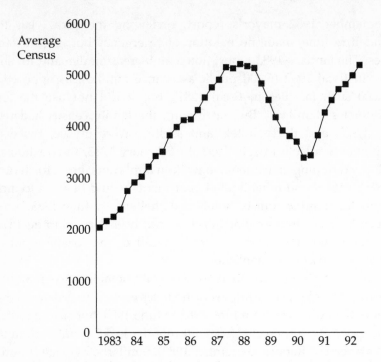

*Figure 4-3* Homeless families in New York. *Source.* Monthly shelter reports.

started back up again. The second peak was reached in July 1993 and was higher than the first—5,709 families. The decline after the second peak has been extremely gradual. Families at the second peak were smaller on average than families at the first (roughly 3.1 versus 3.4 persons), and so the total population in the family-shelter system at the 1988 peak (17,751) was greater than that at the 1993 peak (17,547). (The overall population peak occurred in July 1987 with 18,668 persons, or 3.7 per family.)

This is a very large number of people: two or three times the number in shelters for single adults. Even though most families contain only one adult—generally the mother—there were still almost as many adults in family shelters as there were in single-adult shelters. By 1993 in New York, it seemed that a majority of the shelter population were children and a majority of the adults were female. Homelessness is no longer the exclusive province of single adult men.

As with most other shelter populations, many of the families who enter the New York system leave quickly—about a third during the first month. After the first month, families leave less quickly; the average stay of those who last the first month has probably been in the neighborhood of ten to twelve additional months.[14]

One of the more controversial aspects of New York's family system has been its link to subsidized housing. Subsidized houses are rationed in New York and most other American cities—more people want to get in than can get in. Being placed on top of the list is therefore very desirable. In its efforts to remove families from hotels and shelters, New York put some of them on top of its lists for various kinds of subsidized housing, especially in-rem housing that the city had renovated. Before 1988, such city placements were more talked about than done, but substantial activity began to take place in 1989 and especially in early 1990, when Mayor David Dinkins, having just taken office, tried to move everyone out of hotels. In the peak month, about 15 percent of the shelter population was placed in subsidized housing.

Since getting into subsidized housing is valuable, the prospect of placement may attract families into the shelter system. This argument is made more plausible by the fact that almost no families enter the shelter system from the street; most have been doubling up with friends or relatives or are breaking up in some way. Because the second rise in shelter population followed closely on the Dinkins surge in placements, the conventional wisdom in New York City (for example, Dugger, 1993; Berlin and McAllister, 1992, 1994) has been that these placements made shelters so attractive that new families flooded in; this effect alone could explain the second rise in the shelter population. (For an early dissenting view, however, see White, 1991.)

Michael Cragg and I have been investigating this story: it contains a grain of truth but more than a few grains of falsehood. Better placement prospects do indeed attract people to the shelter system, but the effect is not nearly large enough to offset the reductions in shelter population that come from getting families out. Placement rates had fallen back to 1989 levels by the end of 1990, and so even without a sophisticated analysis it is difficult to see how a temporary condition lasting a few months in early 1990 could keep people flooding into shelters in 1993. Administrative practices matter, but they probably don't matter as much as administrators think they do.

The contrast between Newark and New York lends more credence to the idea that administration matters. Although Newark and New York share much of the same regional economy and much of the same culture (they get the same television stations and newspapers), family homelessness in the two cities was often moving in opposite directions. Yet administrative differences can only explain so much: both cities are marked by heavy family homelessness.

Like New York, Newark (or more specifically the Essex County Welfare Division, which administers federally funded public assistance in Newark) originally had programs for families who needed emergency housing for short periods of time. From the late 1960s to the early 1980s, fire activity was intense, and hotels and the YMWCA were used to house fire victims. These stays were generally quite short. In 1978 Newark Emergency Services for Families (NESF) was formed, primarily to deal with fires and domestic violence. When it opened a family shelter at the YMWCA in July 1982, the average stay was three or four days, "possibly as long as two weeks" (*Star-Ledger*, November 15, 1982).

Several small family shelters started in the early eighties, shortly after NESF, but like NESF they were for specifically labeled groups of families, and the label did not include the word "homeless." Babyland, part of the New Community Corporation, opened a home for battered women, and the Missionaries of Charity—Mother Teresa's order—came from India to open a shelter that has also concentrated on victims of domestic violence. The first family shelters not designed for a special group and describing themselves as for "homeless families" were Apostle's House and (again) St. Rocco's. They opened in 1984 and 1985 respectively, by which time the earlier shelters were also being referred to as homeless shelters. So the first increases in family-shelter usage came several years later in Newark than in New York.

In fact, the major growth did not occur until 1987 and lasted until 1992. During most of this time the shelter-system census in

New York was falling. The expansion involved the use of hotels and roominghouses by welfare agencies, and closely followed several New Jersey court decisions expanding the Emergency Assistance (EA) program (which is 50 percent federally funded). Hotels, we have noted, were used in a small way throughout the seventies and eighties by welfare agencies for clients involved in fires and condemnations, but the numbers involved at any one time were small—27 families, for instance, in June 1986 (*Star-Ledger*, November 9, 1987). In the summer of 1986, New York City created an uproar by placing homeless families in some of the Berger chain hotels in downtown Newark; by winter 1987 all these hotels were filled by the Newark homeless, and the county welfare agency was exporting families to hotels throughout the state.

Since Essex County has twenty-one municipalities other than Newark—including East Orange, Orange, and Irvington, which have significant numbers of welfare recipients—counting "Newark families" in the county group presents problems. Families whose last residence was East Orange may be housed in Newark hotels; families whose last residence was Newark were housed in East Orange hotels; families from either place were housed out of the county altogether in a Jersey City hotel.

Table 4-9 shows where Essex County families were staying in January 1991, close to the peak of the family shelter population. Over 500 families were being sheltered, over 300 of them in New-

*Table 4-9*  Essex County Homeless Families, January 15, 1991

|  |  |
|---|---|
| Commercial hotels | |
| Newark | 216 |
| Other Essex | 87 |
| Outside Essex | 11 |
|  | 314 |
| Nonprofit shelters | |
| Newark | 61 |
| Other Essex | 45 |
|  | 106 |
| Transitional housing | |
| Newark | 132 |
| Total | 552 |

*Source.* Essex County CHAS, p. 25.

ark, mostly in the Berger hotels. Because I don't know where in Essex County these families came from (nor am I exactly sure of how to define the "residence" of a homeless family), I can't tell whether Newark was a net exporter or net importer of homeless families.

Between the late 1980s and 1993 at least, all of the family shelters (with the possible exceptions of Babyland and the Missionaries of Charity) were almost completely populated by AFDC recipients, and the number of AFDC recipients in the hotels exceeded the total number of families in the noncommercial shelters. From about 1989 to about 1993, the majority of sheltered homeless people in Newark were members of AFDC families, and most of those families were staying in Berger hotels.

A September 1990 survey of New Jersey EA recipients conducted by the state Department of Human Services provides some information about family homelessness. However, because Essex County had only a fraction of EA recipients in the state that month (and because Newarkers comprise only about three-fourths of the Essex EA caseload), and because about 38 percent of EA recipients receive only payments of back rent and utilities to prevent homelessness and so are not homeless, these data are far from perfectly informative about homeless AFDC families in Newark. Still it is interesting that the average EA recipient in New Jersey was younger than the average AFDC recipient, had more children (2.31 as against 1.97), was more likely to be black (66 percent as against 51 percent), and less likely to be Hispanic (14 percent as against 27 percent). Indeed, knowledgeable observers of the hotel population in Newark say that it was less than 2 percent Hispanic, although the city itself is around 26 percent Hispanic (1990 census). The report says that the average spell for a recipient who stays in a motel (and receives no other EA service) was 5.4 months; the average stay for a recipient in a noncommercial shelter was 3.4 months.

Newark's family-shelter population began falling in January 1991, right in the middle of the second expansion in New York. From 478, the number of families in hotels and shelters fell to 115 by July 1993 (Walsh, 1993). The reason commonly given for this fall is TRAS: "transitional rental allowances," limited-time rental subsidies for families who leave shelters and move into private housing.[15] In Newark, the agency responsible for homeless families—the county welfare division—was distinct from the agencies responsible for subsidized housing and in-rem housing—the city government and the city housing authority—and so being in a shelter was no advantage in securing housing subsidies when the family-shelter population was rising.[16] Subsidized housing became available on a significant scale only when the shelter population was falling, and conventional wisdom made it responsible for that fall, just as conventional wisdom fifteen miles away, on the other side of the Hudson River, made subsidized housing responsible for the rise in shelter population. Another illustration of the pitfalls of relying on conventional wisdom.

In Chicago, the timing of the growth of family homelessness is probably about the same as it was in Newark. Neither of the 1983 reports has more than a sentence about family homelessness, and neither has any hard information. Most of the increase probably came in the 1985–1988 period, and by 1991 there were about 500 homeless families—a number about the same as Newark's, although Chicago is ten times larger. Chicago families don't stay in hotels or municipal shelters; instead all shelters are run by private nonprofit organizations, although most are funded by the city. Chicago shelters probably give their residents less privacy and freedom than New York hotels or shelters, but they may offer greater security. There is no link to subsidized housing.

Toronto has maintained a family shelter since World War II, at least, and it has operated close to capacity. Starting around 1982, Metro Toronto began to fund additional nonprofit shelters for families, and by 1987 it was also using some motel rooms when the other shelters were full. By 1991 it had purchased a motel and was operating it as another family shelter. In terms of total population, about 210 people were staying in family shelters in June 1982, 240 in 1987 (excluding motels), and 370 in January 1992.[17] This means that slightly over 100 families were being sheltered in 1992—considerably fewer than in Newark, which has only about a tenth of Toronto's population, or than in Chicago, which has about the same population. Toronto has no explicit link between family shelters and subsidized housing.

## Statutory Homelessness

Statutory homelessness in Great Britain bears certain resemblances to family homelessness in cities like New York that link shelters closely to subsidized housing, but there are enough differences to warrant separate notice.

The Homeless Persons Act of 1977 set out duties for local housing councils in dealing with certain homeless people: "In brief, councils have an obligation to rehouse people who apply to them having become homeless through no fault of their own and where the applicant's household contains either a pregnant woman, dependent children or a person regarded as 'vulnerable' due to age, illness, disability, or another 'special reason'" (London Research Centre, 1991, p. 57). Becoming homeless does not mean spending time on the streets; it is enough to have received a notice of eviction or (the most common way) to be told by the people you live with that you're no longer welcome. These obligations were continued under part 3 of the Housing Act of 1985 and have been litigated extensively. There are lawyers who specialize in homelessness.

The council's ultimate obligation is to provide a regular unit to everyone "accepted" as homeless. Council tenancies are at subsidized rents and carry strong rights: council tenants, for instance, can be evicted only by court order; on death they can pass on their leaseholds to people who have lived with them at least a year; they can make improvements and be compensated for them; and they can take in lodgers. But the councils don't have vacancies immediately available for everyone accepted as homeless, and so they must provide temporary accommodations until a regular council dwelling is available. Waiting time is measured in years.

The rate at which London households are accepted as homeless has grown considerably since 1978. This is illustrated in Figure 4-4. During this period the number of vacancies filled through regular waiting lists has fallen drastically, partly because the number of vacancies has fallen as new construction has slowed (the turnover rate hasn't changed much), and partly because the proportion of vacancies going to the homeless queue has risen. In 1981–82, waiting-list applicants got 47 percent of new lettings, and the homeless got 29 percent; by 1989–90, 63 percent of new leases went to home-

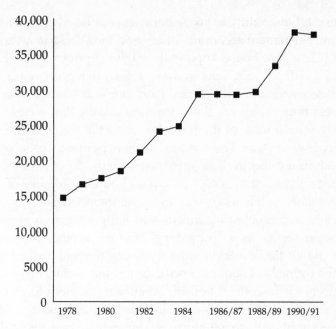

*Figure 4-4* Households accepted as homeless in Greater London. *Source.* London Research Centre, "London Housing Statistics, 1991."

less applicants and 25 percent to waiting-list applicants (LRC, 1991, pp. 93–94). The number of lettings to the waiting list has fallen from about 22,000 a year to about 6,000 a year.

This has probably had an effect on homeless acceptances. As the London Research Centre put it,

> Whilst there is little firm evidence on the subject, it is highly likely that a considerable proportion of households being accepted as homeless are people who were previously registered on their council's waiting list. As a result of greatly reduced chances of being housed off the list, waiting times lengthen and there is an increased likelihood that many of those registered will have become homeless before they rise to the top of the waiting list queue.

There may also be incentive effects. Some observers have characterized the homeless act as merely shaking up the queue for council housing, and the shakeup in terms of demographic characteristics may not have been large.

Councils have a duty to house homeless applicants while they are awaiting permanent accommodation, and they do so in a variety of ways. (They also house apparently eligible applicants during the several months it may take to make a final determination.) Wherever they are temporarily housed (and five-year waits are not rare), homeless households are liable for rent; usually this is close to the housing benefit most of them receive as part of the British income-maintenance system. For the rest of their housing costs, councils generally must use local tax-generated funds. So councils usually have incentives not to accept people as homeless (dislike of queue jumpers adds to this incentive), to house them temporarily as economically as possible (this means that temporary accommodation sometimes serves as a "purgatory" that encourages self-sorting), and to move them from temporary accommodation quickly. The Camden council (a Labour council), for instance, offers up to £20,000 to households in council housing to encourage them to move and free up places for homeless families, and it offers up to £3,000 to homeless applicants to get mortgages on private housing and leave the queue (LB Camden, 1991a). The major modes of temporary accommodation and the numbers of households using them are set out in Table 4-10.

Homeless households in temporary accommodations numbered over 43,000 in 1992, and so constituted by far the largest group of homeless people in London. Most of these households have more than one member (the entry preference for families is compounded

Table 4-10   Number of Homeless Household in Temporary Accommodation, London, 1978–1992

| Date | B&B | Hostel | Own | PSL | Other | Total |
|------|-----|--------|-----|-----|-------|-------|
| 1978 | 940 | 970 | 0 | 0 | 0 | 1,910 |
| 1980 | 990 | 1,330 | 0 | 0 | 0 | 2,320 |
| 1982 | 1,140 | 1,270 | 0 | 0 | 0 | 2,410 |
| 1984 | 3,130 | 1,392 | 752 | 0 | 2,382 | 7,656 |
| 1986 | 6,700 | 1,792 | 2,658 | 425 | 3,385 | 15,228 |
| 1988 | 7,637 | 2,088 | 3,046 | 2,951 | 5,742 | 21,464 |
| 1990 | 7,554 | 3,000 | 4,433 | 12,669 | 5,604 | 33,260 |
| 1992 | 4,406 | 3,623 | 3,342 | 23,510 | 8,285 | 43,166 |

Source. London Research Centre, London Housing Statistics 1992, p. 17. B&B is bed and breakfast; PSL is private sector leasing.

by the relative slowness with which larger council flats become available). Until 1990, bed-and-breakfast hotels were the most heavily used type of temporary accommodation. They are expensive for councils, because the housing benefit doesn't come close to covering the full cost, but have two major advantages: they are flexible, and they are the only type in which households don't develop tenancy rights after a few months (Williams, 1988). As noted in the table, B&B usage peaked in 1987.

Private-sector leasing (PSL) is now the most common form of temporary accommodation after a meteoric rise in recent years. Councils lease regular flats from private owners (the leases can't exceed three years); they move homeless households in and charge rent; the tenants get the rent money from the housing benefit. If councils follow the rules correctly, this operation is almost costless to them—which is one reason why PSL has grown so rapidly. PSL tenants don't have the full tenancy rights that regular council tenants do, but they still have some rights: they can be evicted only after a court hearing, even if the council finds that they don't qualify as statutorily homeless or if they unreasonably refuse the offer of a council flat (since much PSL stock is newer and in better condition than much regular council stock, unreasonable refusals are likely to become an issue in the near future). Eviction can take three or four months.

The final mode of temporary accommodation is now called "own temporary accommodation"; it used to be called "homeless at home." The Camden Council pamphlet "If You Are Homeless" explains the process this way:

> Some people prefer to make their own arrangements to stay with friends or relatives while they are waiting to be rehoused. As long as you let the Council know where you are staying, this does not affect your chances of rehousing. You will not be rehoused any more quickly because you are in a B&B or another type of temporary or short term accommodation. But if these arrangements break down, the Council will arrange temporary accommodation for you.

Are the "homeless at home" homeless? Possibly. These people are receiving the least public assistance of all the groups in temporary accommodations, and their housing quality may in fact be the lowest—after all, they are living under conditions that have been officially judged to be most unsatisfactory.

## Refugees

In Hamburg, refugees are prohibited by law from making their own housing arrangements. Ethnic Germans began coming in large numbers only after the changes in Eastern Europe, beginning in late 1989. In May 1990 the authorities housed 15,838 ethnic Germans in Hamburg, 4,415 of them in hotels. Refugees other than Germans numbered 2,392 in city shelters in February 1991 (these were not the same as the shelters for the West German homeless), and 3,182 were in shelters run by districts. This number is up from only a few hundred in the early 1980s.

Toronto may also house significant numbers of refugees in its shelters, but they are not accounted for separately.

So what happened? The quickest answer is that street homelessness rose drastically in the United States, beginning around 1978 in New York, but nowhere else. Shelter homelessness for women and families rose almost everywhere, but later. Shelter homelessness for men rose in the United States, but probably not elsewhere. Behind these broad trends, however, there are many important caveats and counter-movements.

Excluding London, it is fairly easy to rank the cities in severity of homelessness because cities with large numbers of homeless (or possibly homeless) people in one category usually have large numbers in all categories. As of 1990–91, Newark and New York, in that order, had the most severe problems; Toronto had the least severe; Chicago and Hamburg were somewhere in between. These rankings are fairly robust because the differences are very large; Newark has about ten times more people, per capita, in each category than Toronto. But they are not stable over time: Toronto and Chicago would probably have ranked above New York in 1975. London is hard to classify because though it has few people on the streets, there are large numbers of squatters and statutory homeless families in temporary accommodations.

# 5

# Daytime Streetpeople

People panhandling on your city's streetcorners, rummaging through garbage looking for cans, offering to wash your windshield for a tip, holding the door open at a deli, or just hanging around in a bus station looking destitute—these have become the public symbols of extreme poverty in wealthy industrialized countries.

Most Americans call these people homeless, but it is labor-market activities that bring them to public attention, not housing-market activities. Homelessness, in the official parlance of scholars, bureaucrats, and policy experts, is a condition of housing—it depends on where you sleep at night, not what you do during the day—and so studies of official homelessness do not tell us much about the labor-market symbols of extreme poverty. This group doesn't even have a name. I will use the terms "colloquial homeless"—to acknowledge that these are the people most of the public calls homeless—and "daytime streetpeople"—to emphasize their visibility and the contrast with the nighttime definition of official homelessness.

Not even the most basic facts are known about colloquial homelessness. No one has propounded a formal definition—although we will look at some evidence that in New York at least there is widespread agreement about who comprises this class. There are no estimates of the size of this population at any time in any city—much less a legitimate time series or cross-section. Casual empiricism suggests that the class is bigger today than it was fifteen or twenty years ago, and that it is more apparent in New York than in the rest of the United States and Canada, but this empiricism is very casual indeed. And despite public concern, governments seem to do little about daytime streetpeople: in April 1993, for instance, New York City was financing nighttime shelter for over 20,000 people, but fewer than 1,000 people a day used its daytime drop-in centers.

In this chapter I will attempt to remedy some of these shortcomings, drawing on a survey of daytime streetpeople in New York that David Bloom and I supervised in late March and early April 1993. A number of our students at Columbia interviewed a total of 209 streetpeople over several weekends. The sampling technique was informal (though it covered most of the well-known locations of streetpeople in Manhattan), but the survey represents, as far as we know, the most extensive data-collection effort yet carried out with this population.

The informal sampling protocol makes it more difficult than usual to generalize from the data, but it is not clear what a correct sampling protocol would be. Since part of our goal was to find out about the people the general public sees, acting like the general public was not totally inappropriate. Since the survey was conducted entirely by questionnaire, with no attempt made to verify respondents' answers, there may also be questions about veracity. Yet Bahr and Caplow (1974) in their Bowery surveys found a remarkable degree of truthfulness, and so there is reason to suspect that some answers will be accurate. A third weakness of the survey is that we did not include panhandlers working on subway trains: we simply couldn't figure out a reasonably convenient, nonthreatening way of interviewing them.

In the next section I try to answer the basic question about the most famous symbols of extreme poverty: how well off are New York's daytime streetpeople? Are they in fact destitute? Or are they charlatans or lazy or hopelessly addicted to drugs and alcohol? After that I try to assess the relationship between colloquial and official homelessness. To what extent are colloquially homeless people also officially homeless, and vice versa? More important, to what extent do housing-market and shelter policies aimed at coping with official homelessness affect colloquial homelessness?

## Quality of Life

How good is life on the street? Probably the strongest evidence on this point comes from our survey question about length of time in New York City. If people could make an unusual amount of money with little effort from colloquial homelessness in New York, one would expect to see migration to take advantage of this opportunity. The high density of foot traffic, large numbers of wealthy people who don't have cars, a recycling law that compels supermarkets to accept cans, an extensive network of soup kitchens, relatively generous welfare benefits for the nation, a statutory right to shelter—all of these make New York probably the most inviting place in the United States for colloquial homelessness.

Table 5-1 shows almost no migration; almost everyone has been in New York City for a long time. Over 70 percent of respondents have been there over twenty years; 62 percent have their nearest relatives in the city. Goldstein (1993) finds similar strong local ties for panhandlers in New Haven. It is hard to believe that being homeless in New York is an eagerly sought opportunity. Only one person out of the 209 in our sample both slept in a shelter the previous night and had been in New York less than five years. To

*Table 5-1*  Migration of Daytime Streetpeople to New York

| Years in NYC | Number | Percent |
| --- | --- | --- |
| Less than 6 mos. | 5 | 2.4% |
| 6 mos.–1 yr. | 3 | 1.4 |
| 1–2 yrs. | 3 | 1.4 |
| 2–5 yrs. | 6 | 2.9 |
| 5–10 yrs. | 24 | 11.5 |
| 10–20 yrs. | 21 | 10.1 |
| 20+ yrs. | 146 | 70.2 |
| Blank | 1 | – |
| | | |
| Where nearest relatives are | | |
| NYC | 74 | 61.7% |
| NY (outside NYC), NJ, CT | 14 | 11.7 |
| Other U.S. | 29 | 24.2 |
| Out of U.S. | 3 | 2.5 |
| Blank | 89 | – |

maintain that panhandlers are being attracted to New York by the shelter system is untenable.

One reason for the lack of attraction is that the colloquial homeless generally work hard and long. They are not lazy. Standing in a cold wind, shaking a cup, being scorned by passersby, is not pleasant; nor is scouring the sidewalks for soda cans, digging through garbage cans, carrying big bags, and ultimately being shortchanged by a store manager who doesn't want to see either you or your cans. Table 5-2 shows that hours are long. Most respondents worked seven days a week, and 78 percent worked more than seven hours a day. Some 15 percent worked more than eleven hours a day. Hours per day and days per week are approximately independent. Of those who worked seven days a week, for instance, 15 percent also worked more than eleven hours a day. We didn't receive many responses, however, on the hours-per-day question. (There is some selection bias here. The longer a person works, the more likely we were to encounter them. But then so is a member of the general public. Our data are not rep-

Table 5-2 Working Time of Colloquially Homeless People in New York

| Days worked per week | Number | Percent |
| --- | --- | --- |
| 0 | 9 | 5.3% |
| 1 | 3 | 1.8 |
| 2 | 7 | 4.1 |
| 3 | 9 | 5.3 |
| 4 | 10 | 5.9 |
| 5 | 18 | 10.7 |
| 6 | 12 | 7.1 |
| 7 | 101 | 59.8 |
| Blank | 40 | |
| Hours worked per day | | |
| Under 3 | 3 | 4.1% |
| 3–5 | 6 | 8.1 |
| 5–7 | 15 | 20.3 |
| 7–9 | 31 | 41.9 |
| 9–11 | 8 | 10.8 |
| 11+ | 11 | 14.9 |
| Blank | 135 | |

resentative of the colloquial homeless in general, but of the colloquial homeless the public is likely to encounter.)

The only other reports I am aware of are Goldstein (1993), which details the life of about twelve panhandlers around Yale, and Kreeger (1992). Relying on his own observations rather than the self-declarations of panhandlers, Goldstein finds far shorter hours. This might reflect fewer panhandling opportunities in New Haven than in New York, since pedestrian density is low until mid-afternoon and nights are dangerous. Kreeger's small (about fifteen) sample of *Street News* sellers and collectors in New York reports very long hours of work, longer than our survey.

The other reason for lack of attraction to street occupations in New York, of course, is low earnings. Earnings are difficult to gauge with great precision. They vary randomly from day to day and come in small pieces, and colloquially homeless people don't have accountants or accounting systems to keep track. Many (36 percent in our sample) work in groups, and many (about 20 percent) share income. There also may be some incentives to underreport income, either to engender sympathy or to avoid taxation by welfare authorities. On the other hand, braggadocio may make some people overreport (see Dordick, 1994, for a discussion of exaggerated receipts from panhandling at a New York transportation terminal).

These caveats should be borne in mind in looking at Table 5-3, which reports daily earnings. Although a quarter of the respondents had a day in the last week when they made over $70, for the median respondent last week's best day was only $32.50. The median worst day's earnings were less than $5. A typical day's earnings, therefore, are probably in the $10–$30 range, and a typical week's earnings in the $70–$200 range.

With seven to nine hours of work, it appears that most respondents are working below the minimum wage, with many considerably below.[1] A few, but only a few, appear to be making more than the minimum wage. In a low-wage job they would have to pay FICA, but they might get benefits. People without children did not get earned-income tax credit when we took the survey. Of our respondents 74.3 percent said they would take a low-wage job in order to get off the street, and it appears that they are telling the truth.

*Table 5-3*  Daily Earnings of Daytime Streetpeople in New York

| Dollar amount | Most money in a day last week | Least money in a day last week |
|---|---|---|
| Under $10 | 19.0% | 70.8% |
| $10–$25 | 20.1 | 21.6 |
| $25–$40 | 17.2 | 4.7 |
| $40–$55 | 10.9 | 0.6 |
| $55–$70 | 8.6 | 0.6 |
| Over $70 | 24.1 | 1.8 |
| Median | $32.50 | $2.50 |
| Mean | $40.20 | $9.90 |

| Primary occupation | Most money | | Least money | |
|---|---|---|---|---|
| | Median | Mean | Median | Mean |
| Collect cans | $32.50 | $30.30 | $2.50 | $6.70 |
| Panhandler | 32.50 | 38.20 | 2.50 | 8.90 |
| Peddler | 80.00 | 60.00 | 7.50 | 15.30 |
| Windshield | 47.50 | 46.00 | 2.50 | 10.80 |
| *Street News* | 80.00 | 80.00 | 5.00 | 5.00 |
| Odd jobs | 11.30 | 24.70 | 5.00 | 7.50 |
| Nothing | 5.00 | 5.00 | 2.50 | 2.50 |
| Regular job | – | – | – | – |
| Blank | 32.50 | 40.30 | 2.50 | 9.50 |

The table also breaks down maximum daily earnings by street occupation. As expected, people without jobs don't make much money, but of the major occupational groups, only peddlers stand out. They report earning far more money than those in other street occupations. This may stem partly from confusion between net and gross earnings. In part it may reflect the fact that for much peddling activity, net may be gross, and the ability to acquire goods for free generates a surplus. The approximate equivalence of panhandling and canning is comforting to economic theory: since there are no barriers to keep people from moving back and forth between these occupations, returns should be equalized, at least at the margin. The equivalence is disturbing, though, in another sense: begging is not shameful enough to demand a compensating differential.

The estimates in Table 5-3 correspond fairly well with the earnings that Kreeger found among New York streetpeople, but are somewhat

*Table 5-4* How Daytime Streetpeople Would Spend Extra Money

| Extra money | Number | Percent |
|---|---|---|
| Buy cigarettes, alcohol | 26 | 23.6% |
| Buy drugs | 11 | 10.0 |
| Buy drugs, cigarettes, alcohol | 3 | 2.7 |
| | | 36.3 |
| Buy food | 24 | 21.8% |
| Buy clothes | 12 | 10.9 |
| Share with friends, children | 11 | 10.0 |
| Other | 23 | 20.9 |
| Blank | 99 | – |

lower than the numbers reported by Goldstein for the panhandlers at Yale. But the latter incomes fell considerably during the summer, although the panhandlers worked year-round, and Goldstein's averages appear to be for term time. Dawidoff (1994), a journalistic account of New York subway panhandlers, is spiced with anecdotes about high-earning panhandlers, but provides no systematic data.

So it appears that many colloquially homeless people are quite poorly off—they toil long hours for meager wages and suffer many indignities. Two circumstances, however, should temper this conclusion.

First, a considerable number of our respondents—42 percent—were receiving public assistance, with median payments of around $300 a month. Similarly, most of Goldstein's panhandlers also received public assistance. In our sample, those who slept in missions, shelters, shelter hotels, their own apartments, or their own rooms were twice as likely to be receiving public assistance as those who slept on the street or with friends and relatives.[2] Given the group's poverty, one may be tempted to ask why everyone wasn't receiving public assistance, but a more direct implication is that a substantial minority were engaging in fraud by not reporting their earnings. As might be expected, people not receiving welfare tend to work longer hours than those on welfare, but the difference is not large—about seven hours a week in either median or mean. This could either reflect income effects or some fear of detection. The difference, though, implies that we undersampled people receiving public assistance. The "implicit tax rate" on earnings in New York's general assistance program is 100 percent, which means that welfare payments are reduced by a dollar for every dollar of reported earnings. This is a strong disincentive against taking a regular job for many colloquially homeless people—but probably not for a majority.

The second problem is substance abuse. Our questionnaire, by design, had no questions on substance abuse. One open-ended question, though, gave some indication that substance abuse among the colloquially homeless is of the same order of magnitude as it is among the officially homeless. We asked this question: How would you spend extra money if you had it? The distribution of answers is given in Table 5-4. A substantial minority—36 percent—would spend at least part of the extra money on drugs or alcohol. Celebrating good fortune with a beer does not make a person a substance abuser, but the question we used to elicit this information was open-ended. Goldstein and Dawidoff both find substance abuse pervasive in their narratives. Even substance abusers can hold jobs off the street, but policies for dealing with colloquial homelessness need to account for this population.

## Colloquial and Official

Is there a connection between the colloquial homelessness of the daytime streetpeople and the official housing-market homelessness that gets measured, however imperfectly? You can sleep on the street or in a shelter without panhandling or washing windshields, and large numbers of people do. Similarly you can panhandle or wash windshields even if you don't sleep on the street or in a shelter, and many do. In this sense, to a first approximation at least, the labor-market phenomenon of colloquial homelessness should be independent of the housing-market phenomenon of official homelessness.

On the other hand, one might expect a positive correlation between the two types of homelessness for several reasons. (Here I am basically speculating.) First, both phenomena might have a common cause in the deterioration of conventional labor-market opportunities for low-skilled men or men with certain undesirable work traits, such as alcoholism. Deteriorating work opportunities could both make men too poor to afford conventional housing and simultaneously induce them to turn to street occupations like panhandling and recycling. This story is consistent both with the considerable evidence of a rising skill premium in the U.S. economy and with the contrast so often drawn between skid rows forty years ago and homelessness today (for instance, Rossi, 1989; Hoch and Slayton, 1989; Rio interview, 1991). Traditional skid rows were full of unskilled men who took part in a flourishing market of temporary jobs and thereby managed to get enough money to keep a roof (however flimsy) over their heads; modern homeless people do neither.

But this story is not entirely supported by the data. Later we shall see that official homelessness is not well correlated with poverty, either in the time series or in the cross-section. So it is difficult to accept the idea that official homelessness is caused by the deterioration of conventional labor-market opportunities. Second, on the usual human-capital measures at least, neither the official homeless nor the colloquial homeless are unusually deprived. Table 5-5 shows educational attainments for several different samples of officially homeless people. The numbers are consistent: a majority

*Table 5-5*  Education of Officially Homeless People

| Author | Study date | City | Group | Percent completing highschool |
|---|---|---|---|---|
| HRA | 1982 | New York | Long-term shelter men | 52% |
| Simpson, Kilduff | 1983 | Newark | Trailer people | 59 |
| Crystal, Goldstein | 1984 | New York | Single male shelter | 46 or 49 |
| | | | Single female shelter | 58 |
| Rossi | 1985–86 | Chicago | Shelter, street | 55 |
| Sosin, Colson, Grossman | 1986 | Chicago | Now homeless | c. 53–55 |
| Eldred, Towber | 1986 | New York | Hotel Martinique | 25 |
| | | | Family shelter | 34 |
| Moore | 1988 | New York | Single shelter | 53 |
| Cuomo Comm. | 1991 | New York | Family shelter | 55 |
| | | | Single shelter | 61 |
| Hopper | 1990 | New York | Street homeless | 52 |

have finished highschool. While the proportion of highschool graduates is certainly less than the U.S. average (68.6 percent in 1980), the difference is not huge. Data for the colloquial homeless are more meager. Sosin, Colson, and Grossman (1988) found that about 54 percent of soup-kitchen users who are not currently homeless were highschool graduates—just about the same proportion as were those who were currently homeless. So the idea that colloquial and official homelessness are both manifestations of a deteriorating labor market is not too compelling.

A deteriorating conventional labor market is not, however, the only argument for a positive correlation between colloquial and official homelessness. The common cause, instead, might be income inequality. In Chapter 7 I make a case for how rising inequality can operate in the housing market to increase official homelessness. The same connection can be made for colloquial homelessness. For panhandling and its variants (windshield washing, busking, some types of peddling), the theoretical connection with inequality is direct. Holding your own conventional labor opportunities constant, the greater the wealth you are surrounded with, the more likely you are to panhandle. According to this story, inequality manifests itself in the housing market as homelessness, in the labor market as panhandling.

The weakness of this story is that it accounts for only a portion of colloquial homelessness. Canning, for instance, is tied to inequality only in the sense that soda consumption is probably a normal good; it is probably not a luxury (although poorer people may be more likely to redeem on their own). Population density and laws (canning is inconsequential in New Jersey) may matter much more than wealth. For activities like hanging around, the connection with inequality is entirely absent.

Nor does the evidence about donations to panhandlers support this account. Tomoko Yamahara (1993), reporting on a survey by Columbia and Barnard students, provides the only data I know of on who gives money to panhandlers in America. She found that almost everyone gave occasionally. Income, religious, political, and ideological factors made small differences in plausible ways, but were not statistically significant. What really seemed to matter was whether people had loose change in their hands.

Causation could also run from one form of homelessness to the other. Jobs like those associated with colloquial homelessness may be the best sort for people sleeping in shelters or on the street. They are offhand—no one counts on you to show up, and so if you miss a day or an hour there is no retribution. They require little or no capital and not much skill. And pay is frequent—you don't have to work two weeks before you get paid, and you never get a single large sum of money. For people who don't have good methods for safeguarding money—either from others' predations or their own desires—the latter is a very important job characteristic. Getting stuck in a job like this may also be part of the cost of official homelessness.

Data to support this view are largely missing. Only two studies of officially homeless people, both in Chicago, have information about both regular and irregular employment (see Table 5-6). One of the studies—Rossi's in 1989—contradicts this idea; he found that more officially homeless people had income from regular employment than from begging. The earlier Chicago Coalition study (1983), which used a much less structured definition of official homelessness, found the opposite, but the difference was less than a factor of two. On the other hand, ethnographic studies (such as Hill and Stamey, 1990; Dordick, 1994) of officially homeless street populations generally find that most employment is irregular.

Nor is the evidence compelling that one needs to be officially homeless in order to have these problems. Of the daytime streetpeo-

*Table 5-6*  Types of Employment of Officially Homeless People

| Author | Study date | City | Group |
|---|---|---|---|
| Rossi | 1985–86 | Chicago | Street, shelter<br>31.6% had employment income,<br>　includes newspaper sales 15.9%<br>20.6% had income from handouts |
| Coalition for<br>　Homeless | 1983 | Chicago | People met on street<br>Those with occasional income:<br>　begging 23%<br>　recycling 16%<br>　selling newspapers 6%<br>　day labor 29%<br>　illegal activities 12%<br>　other 14% |

ple we interviewed, 74 percent of those who were officially home-less said they had no way of saving money, but so did 59 percent of those who were not officially homeless. The difference is not statis-tically significant.

It is unclear, moreover, why day labor and odd jobs for conven-tional employers—the sort of jobs skid-row men used to do—could not fill the same function. Even the ethnographic narratives that emphasize irregular employment include enough references to odd jobs to show that they are possible. The question is why they are scarce, if they are.

Finally, causation could run in the opposite direction. This is a political story, and it relies on governmental mistakes. Colloquial homelessness upsets voters, who want governments to do some-thing about it. Mistakenly, governments fund shelters. Shelters cause official homelessness to rise. It is difficult for the available data to test this story.

These speculations can be supplemented by data from our Co-lumbia survey. The first question of interest is whether respondents considered themselves homeless: 86.1 percent did. This question is chiefly of linguistic interest; the response shows that Columbia stu-dents and people on the streets of New York use the word "home-less" about the same way. There is a broad colloquial agreement on how the word should be used.

The next question is where respondents slept the previous night. As shown in Table 5-7, most but by no means all of the streetpeople were in fact homeless on the official definition. This proportion is considerably higher than the proportion estimated by police officials in London and Newark, and higher than Goldstein's small sample of panhandlers.[3] Of those who call themselves homeless, 80 percent are officially homeless. Daytime streetpeople in New York speak colloquial American.

The large percentage of daytime streetpeople who are officially homeless lends support to the idea of a connection between collo-quial and official homelessness. To look further at this connection, Table 5-8 disaggregates the nighttime information by the type of work people primarily do during the day (some people work at several different occupations: say canning most of the time but panhandling occasionally).

*Table 5-7*   Where New York Daytime Streetpeople Slept Last Night

| Officially homeless | | Not officially homeless | |
|---|---|---|---|
| Mission | 2.6% | Friend, relative | 10.3% |
| Shelter | 6.2 | Own apart. | 3.6 |
| Train, station, ferry | 45.9 | Own SRO | 2.1 |
| Park, bench, street | 13.9 | Shelter hotel | 2.6 |
| Aband. building | 3.6 | Other | 8.2 |
| Total | 73.2% | | 26.8% |

Where people who said they were homeless slept last night

| Mission | 2.3% | Friend, relative | 8.1% |
|---|---|---|---|
| Shelter | 7.0 | Own apart. | 0.6 |
| Train, station, ferry | 51.2 | Own SRO | 1.7 |
| Park, bench, street | 15.7 | Shelter hotel | 2.9 |
| Aband. building | 4.1 | Other | 6.4 |
| Total | 80.3% | | 19.7% |

The total number responding was 194 people.

Except for peddlers, most of the occupational groups have about the same proportion of officially homeless people. One reason why peddlers are less likely to be officially homeless might be that having a place to store goods overnight is an advantage in peddling. Another possible reason is that peddlers may have higher incomes (Table 5-3) and so can afford better housing.

Table 5-8, then, does not provide much support for the hypothesis that official homelessness predisposes people to take certain types of jobs. If the hypothesis were true, differences in occupations in the proportion of officially homeless people would be expected to form recognizable patterns. As it is, only peddlers are different, and an alternative explanation for their difference is possible.

One other surprising fact is evident from Tables 5-7 and 5-8: very few streetpeople use New York's shelters. We can examine this in more depth by looking at how many times respondents say they have slept in shelters in the previous two weeks. Only 18.7 percent slept even one night in the last fourteen in a shelter, and only 6.2 percent spent as many as twelve nights. The reason for this low shelter use is not seasonal variation: March is usually the month when New York City single shelters are at their fullest, and for some respondents the two-week period before their interview included a

*Table 5-8*   Where People Slept Last Night by Primary Occupation

| | Officially homeless | | | Not officially homeless | | | | |
|---|---|---|---|---|---|---|---|---|
| | Shelter | Nonshelter[a] | Total | Not own[b] | Own[c] | Total | Total | No. |
| Cans | 12% | 77% | 89% | 7% | 4% | 11% | 100 | 26 |
| Panhandler | 3 | 78 | 81 | 12 | 7 | 19 | 100 | 74 |
| Peddler | 5 | 40 | 45 | 25 | 30 | 55 | 100 | 20 |
| Windshield | 14 | 71 | 85 | 15 | 0 | 15 | 100 | 7 |
| *Street News* | 0 | 67 | 67 | 33 | 0 | 33 | 100 | 3 |
| Odd jobs | 29 | 57 | 86 | 14 | 0 | 14 | 100 | 7 |
| Nothing | 50 | 0 | 50 | 50 | 0 | 50 | 100 | 2 |
| Regular job | 0 | 100 | 100 | 0 | 0 | 0 | 100 | 1 |

a. Mission; train, station, ferry; park, bench, street; abandoned building.
b. Friend or relative; other.
c. Own apartment, own SRO, shelter hotel.

blizzard and several severely cold nights. Nor is it because street-people have no experience with the shelter system: 71.1 percent have slept in a shelter at some point in their lives. Streetpeople know about shelters, and apparently they don't like them.

This fact has an important implication. The shelter homeless—the group whose numbers we can track and whose characteristics, for the most part, are studied—are almost entirely distinct (in New York at least) from the colloquial homeless—the people whom the public sees and talks about. To impute findings from, say, the Cuomo Commission report (1992), which deals entirely with shelters, to an individual one sees on the street is therefore quite pointless.

This doesn't imply that shelter policies and housing policies have no impact on street activity. For instance, one could maintain that many more people would be engaged in street activity if shelters weren't available, and that the people now on the streets are a fringe group with unusual tastes. Better shelters could have an income effect—residents could feel more contented and not look for more money—and a substitution effect—shelter rules could make it difficult to panhandle at clubs or collects cans at night. Both of these effects, though, are rather weak. Moreover, the small proportion of daytime streetpeople who use shelters now indicates that a great improvement in the quality of New York's single shelters would be needed to have any appreciable impact on street activity.

Thus, although the deprivations of colloquially homeless people are probably not so severe as those of the officially homeless, they are still significant, and the efficiency losses may be greater. Colloquial homelessness is a serious problem in itself and warrants separate consideration.

# 6

# How to Think about Housing Markets

Figuring out why homelessness rose in North America in the 1980s requires some thought about how housing markets work. People have advanced many different theories about the rise, and to evaluate each possible cause we have to learn the mechanism by which that cause would have increased homelessness, and what evidence that mechanism would have left behind if it had been operating. Then (in the next few chapters) we can look for the evidence and judge whether the theory is plausible.

Thinking about housing markets means focusing on a few aspects of the situation, studying the interaction among them very carefully, and ignoring the rest. The process is like drawing a subway map of Manhattan—you leave out many important things (New Jersey, most cross-streets, topography), but by concentrating on one aspect of reality you get a tool that is very useful for some purposes (transferring from an Uptown 2 train to a Brooklyn-bound D), but not for others (driving in the Bronx or completing tax forms). You simplify so that you can concentrate on things that are important for the problem at hand (how much money people have, for instance) and not waste time and energy on things that are not (the color of houses or the problem of nuclear proliferation).

 The aspects of housing I want to concentrate on are quality differentiation on the supply side and income differentiation on the demand side. So I will think about an array of houses of differing qualities on one side, an array of households of differing incomes on the other, and ask how they get matched up with each other or fail to. I will think about houses (or housing units, to be precise) as differing only in a single aspect called "quality," with higher-quality houses always being better than lower-quality ones, and households as differing only in income. Life is, of course, far more complicated than this—both houses and people differ in ways that can't be placed along a single dimension—but so too is geography far more complicated than what you see on a Manhattan subway map. Just as the map is useful for certain limited purposes, so too is this way of looking at the housing market.[1]

## How People Become Homeless

Think, for now, of homelessness as a quality of "housing" that is free, but below all other possible qualities of housing. There is also no supply problem with homelessness—as many households that want to can become homeless. This is obviously a far less nuanced view of homelessness than I have been advocating in the last several chapters, but the picture you get of, say, Greenwich Village on a New York subway map is also far less nuanced than the one you would hear from a local tour guide.

Why would someone become homeless? The two reasons that come to mind immediately are "There are more households than houses" and "They can't afford it." Both are unsatisfactory, although they contain kernels of insight. We shall have to dig deeper.

More-households-than-houses is unsatisfactory for two reasons. Most important, it begs the question of why there aren't more houses (or fewer households, since migration is always conceivable). Maybe new houses could be built for homeless households or for other households that would move and free up housing for the homeless. Maybe buildings that are being abandoned could be rehabilitated or just stop being abandoned. Why don't these things happen? To answer this interesting question we need a theory of housing markets; merely counting noses and doors without asking why won't do the trick.

The second problem with a simple nose-and-door count is that it can't explain U.S. homelessness. Vacancy rates in this country run between about 2 percent and about 10 percent, and rates of homelessness run under 1 percent. So the interesting question is why vacant housing units don't get matched with homeless households.

Both sets of interesting questions then point to the second answer, "They can't afford it." This is a much better answer than the first, but still incomplete. Peeling away the layers of quick answers and rhetoric slowly reveals the sort of analysis we need.

The first problem is the ambiguity of the word "afford." Sometimes people use "can't afford" to mean they would rather not purchase something: when I say I can't afford a filet mignon dinner, I don't mean I couldn't somehow raise enough to pay for it; instead I mean that I'd prefer to buy a cheaper dinner and use the difference to buy other things I like. Other times people use "can't afford" to mean that a purchase isn't feasible; I can't afford a yacht because no one would lend me enough to buy one, and if they did I could never make enough money to pay them back. Economists care a lot about separating feasibility from preference, and so a word like "afford" that confuses the two issues is a word we avoid.

The first sense of "can't afford" is the one I want to use here, and so I will use the economist's phrase "don't demand" instead of "can't afford." Of course, one reason why people don't demand something is because purchasing it is infeasible, and so we can talk about people not demanding housing without invoking the more troublesome questions of feasibility (would this person be homeless if he didn't purchase so much food or booze? if he worked harder and longer? if she had finished highschool?)

Saying that people don't demand housing is not saying that they are "homeless by choice" and undeserving of sympathy. It means only that their other options are, in their own estimation, worse than homelessness. The ethical implications of such a situation are a delicate issue—one I will deal with in later chapters, since the facts of individual cases will have different ethical implications. (A person who gives up his wallet to a thief who threatens him with a gun is generally thought to be deserving of more sympathy than a person who uses the same amount of money to buy a service, even though in both cases the giving of money is voluntary.)

Nor does thinking about homeless people as people who don't demand conventional housing imply that all homeless people are superbly competent rational calculators. A lot of homeless people are mentally ill—they don't evaluate alternatives and make decisions the way you or I might. But still they (or their guardians) make decisions. Those decisions might not command the same degree of respect from us that more competent people's decisions do. Nor can mentally ill people or substance abusers be easily accommodated within my assumption here that households differ only in income; that's why we need separate chapters for these issues (just as some road maps have separate insets for particularly congested areas). Yet we can still talk throughout about mentally ill people either demanding or not demanding conventional housing.

The second problem with talk about people being unable to afford it is that conventional housing is not a single good, but an array of different qualities of housing. When we say someone can't afford conventional housing, what quality are we referring to? Thinking about demand, though, lets us clarify this issue.

Each quality of housing comes with a price. Better qualities come with higher prices (shortly we will see why this has to be). The more money a household pays for housing, the less it has left for other things. So households don't choose simply among qualities of housing; they choose among combinations, each of which consists of a quality of housing and an amount of money left over to pay for other things. (This is why every household doesn't choose the highest quality of housing.) Each household demands the quality of housing that offers the combination it finds most attractive. Because people will split extra money between housing and other things, higher-income households will demand better housing. Thus a household will be homeless if homelessness is more attractive than the most attractive combination offered by any quality of conventional housing. Homeless households are the ones with the lowest income; since higher-income households demand higher qualities of housing, no homeless household has income higher than any conventionally housed household.

It is useful, then, to distinguish between two different types of homelessness, depending on whether the most attractive type of conventional housing for homeless people is similar to homelessness. In the first case, if the most attractive quality of conventional housing for homeless people is, price aside, only a tiny bit better than homelessness, then what will matter for determining which people are homeless is the rate at which price is rising as quality improves. If that rate is high, not many people will find such terrible housing more attractive than homelessness and many people will be homeless; if that rate is low, terrible housing will be cheap and only the very lowest-income people will remain homeless. On the other hand, in the second case, the alternative to homelessness is a quality of conventional housing noticeably better than the worst. This would happen if even the worst type of conventional housing had a large price. In this case, the absolute level of prices matters, not just their rate of change at the lowest qualities.

In both cases, the amount of homelessness depends on the interaction between the price schedule for different qualities of housing ("the price-quality schedule") and the distribution of income. The price-quality schedule determines the lowest income a conventionally housed household will have, and the income distribution determines how many households fall below that threshold. This doesn't answer the question, though, of what determines homelessness because it doesn't say what determines the income distribution and what determines the price-quality schedule. The dichotomy is misleading, moreover, because sometimes income distribution affects the price-quality schedule.

But we see now the serious questions that have to be answered in order to understand homelessness. Why is income distributed the way it is? Why is the price-quality schedule the way it is? Fortunately, many people have already tried to answer the question, and I have nothing to add to the many excellent works on this subject (for instance, Levy and Murnane, 1992). So I won't have to explain income distribution; I can just examine what happens when it changes. The price-quality schedule, though, has to be explained. All the analysis of the simple, quick answers has pointed in this direction.

## Availability and Suppliers

Someone could raise an objection to this plan of attack: I have talked about housing prices but not about housing availability. Just because a household is willing to pay the price for housing of a particular quality, how can I be so sure that it will be able to find any? Couldn't there be a shortage of some qualities relative to demand?

Of course there could be, at least for a short time following a change in demand. The job of prices, though, is to keep shortages from persisting. If more households demand a particular kind of housing than landlords and builders want to supply, then the price of that kind of housing will rise, demand will fall, supply will increase, and the price will keep rising until the shortage is gone. Conversely for an excess supply of some quality of housing.

So when we look for a price-quality schedule, we will look for one that does this job—eliminating both excesses and shortages. This in fact is the only job that the schedule has to perform, and performing it determines uniquely what the price-quality schedule looks like.

The behavior of housing suppliers is thus the final link we need in explaining homelessness. By suppliers I mean landlords, builders, and, in the case of owner-occupied houses, the owners themselves. You can think of owner-occupants as renting to themselves; after all, by occupying a house they own, they are giving up the rent they could have received from somebody else. They are suppliers and consumers simultaneously. This way of looking at owner-occupants means that the rental price is the price of housing we want to look at.

Suppliers make two kinds of decisions: building and maintenance. The cost of building a house depends on the quality; higher-quality houses cost more to build. Increments in quality also get more expensive as quality increases: the same difference in quality costs more at higher qualities than at lower qualities. So the relationship between quality and building cost looks something like that shown in Figure 6-1.

Once built, houses deteriorate to lower and lower qualities unless they are maintained. Maintenance costs money, but enough of it can stop deterioration; somewhat less can slow deterioration. So housing of a given quality can be produced in two different ways: it can be built and maintained at that quality, or it can be built at higher quality and allowed to deteriorate until it falls to the quality in question. Which process is used depends on which is cheaper.

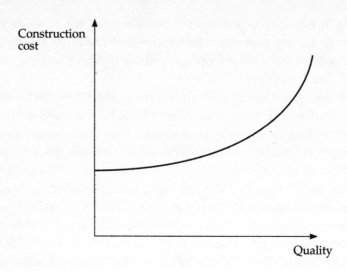

*Figure 6-1*

For higher qualities of housing, construction and maintenance is usually the cheaper process. The money a supplier saves by letting a house deteriorate for a given period of time is about the same no matter what the beginning quality is, but the added cost of building to a higher quality than the one you're interested in is greater for higher-quality houses. This means that for high-quality houses, prices are determined by supply cost. The monthly rent has to pay the mortgage; alternatively, the present value of rents received over the house's lifetime has to equal the cost of construction. If it were less, nobody would build houses of that quality. If it were more, building houses of this quality would be like printing money: everybody would do it, and the only way those houses could be sold would be by lowering rents.

Having prices involved gives us another way to understand why high-quality units are built and maintained. Maintenance is an investment; houses are maintained if and only if the investment is profitable. The return on this investment is the difference between the value of the house with maintenance and the value without. For high-quality houses this difference is great, since big differences in building cost—the steepness of the cost gradient—cause big differences in price—the implied steepness of the price-quality schedule.

This makes the return from investment big, and a big return makes people invest. Since high-quality units are all maintained, the only way they can be supplied in the first place is through construction. So building is done in the higher part of the quality distribution.

Below some quality, maintenance is not profitable, and so neither is building. This is because the construction-cost gradient is flatter for low-quality houses, and a flatter gradient implies that maintenance is less profitable. (In the extreme, suppose that construction cost for two different qualities were the same. Then building the lower-quality house would never make sense: if you built the higher-quality house and let it deteriorate until it reached the lower-quality, you would spend just as much on construction as you would have if you had built the lower quality house directly, but you would have gained the rents you would have collected as the house deteriorated from the higher quality to the lower quality.)

The picture that emerges, then, is that above some quality, houses are both built and maintained; below that quality, they are neither built nor maintained.[2] Since poorer people take lower qualities of housing, this means that poor people get their housing as hand-me-downs from richer people—not the richest people, though, because the highest qualities of housing are maintained and not allowed to deteriorate. The housing that filters down to poorer people must originally have been built at or near the bottom of the building range; otherwise it would have been maintained. In between build-and-maintain and don't-build-and-don't-maintain are one or more qualities that are built and not maintained. Very roughly speaking, housing built for the middle class becomes housing for the poor, and then is abandoned (see Figure 6-2).

Figuring out rents for housing as it slides through the deterioration interval is much more complex than figuring out rents in the construction interval. The big difference is that demand influences rents in the deterioration interval, while it has no influence in the construction interval.

There are five different conditions that the price-quality schedule in the deterioration interval has to satisfy. I call them the operating cost, lowest rent, construction cost, construction price, and equal demand conditions. I use the terms again and again. But first I should explain what they are and why they must be met.

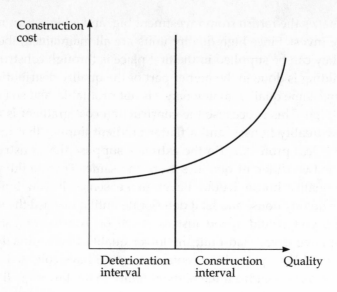

*Figure 6-2*

ᴸ *Operating cost.* At every quality where housing is actually available on the market, rent has to cover all the operating costs—insurance (or the expected loss from being uninsured), property taxes, the cost of collecting rent, minimal utilities, and the opportunity cost of land. These are costs that must be incurred just to keep the house's doors open and to keep rent coming in even if no maintenance is going on; the house can deteriorate even if the insurance bills are being paid.

Notice that the opportunity cost of land is included in operating cost. The house could be demolished at any time and the land turned over to some alternative use (luxury housing or a store, for instance), with proceeds of the sale going into the current owner's bank account and earning interest. So every day that the house is not demolished is a day that those proceeds are not earning interest; this forgone interest is as much an operating cost as an insurance bill.

The operating-cost requirement establishes a floor below which rents cannot go for qualities that are actually supplied. If rent is below operating cost, an owner can do better by abandoning a property or selling it for some other use. This implies that qualities just a little better than homelessness will not be found on the market. If a quality just a little better than homelessness were offered on the market, rent would have to cover at least operating cost, and so nobody would buy it, since he or she could be homeless, which would be only a tiny bit worse but a noticeable amount cheaper. The lowest quality on the market has to be noticeably better than homelessness because the price has to be noticeably higher. Homelessness has to be of the second variety, where the best conventional alternative to homelessness is noticeably better.

2· *Lowest rent.* Price at the lowest available quality of housing cannot exceed operating cost either. If it did, owners could wait a little longer before abandoning and make a little more profit by charging slightly lower rent for a slightly worse quality of housing. For a large enough decrease in rent, they would find customers for these slightly worse qualities of housing, and for a small enough quality difference, the requisite decrease in rent would still keep rent above operating cost. So what we had considered the lowest quality on the market could not be the lowest quality unless its rent precisely equaled operating cost.

3 · *Construction cost.* The present value of the rents net of operating costs that a house generates as it deteriorates from construction quality to demolition quality has to equal construction cost. If it were less, no houses would be built—they wouldn't be able to support their mortgages—and so eventually no low-quality housing would be available because the stock needs continuous replenishing as houses are abandoned. If the present value of rents net of operating costs were greater than construction cost, building houses of this quality would be like printing money, and too many would be built.

I will refer to the present value of rents net of operating costs that a house generates as it deteriorates as its "value." So another way to state the construction-cost requirement is that value at the construction quality has to equal cost at that quality.

4· *Construction price.* This condition establishes the price at the quality at which building takes place at the start of the deterioration process. Developing this condition takes slightly longer than developing the other conditions.

The basic idea is that value must equal construction cost not only at construction quality, but also at qualities slightly above construction quality and slightly below it. If value were rising faster than construction cost as quality increased, then value would be slightly greater than construction cost at qualities slightly higher than construction quality. This would make building houses at that quality like printing money, and everybody in the world would do it; there would be too many houses. Similarly, if value were rising more slowly than construction cost, the value of houses slightly below construction quality would be greater than their construction cost, and building them would be like printing money. So at construction quality, value has to be rising at the same rate as construction cost.

The rate at which value is rising depends on the rental price at the construction quality. Suppose you built a house at a quality slightly higher than construction quality, rather than at construction quality. You would get rent (net of operating costs) at the higher quality for a short period of time, and then after the house had deteriorated to construction quality, you would get the same sequence of rents you would have received if you had built at construction quality. In other words, you get the extra high rent up front, but you have to wait a while before you receive the value at construction quality. Value at the slightly higher quality is greater than value at construction quality by the amount of the extra high rent up front, less the monetary cost of the delay.

Suppose you borrowed the full amount of the value at construction quality when you built the house at slightly higher quality. Then you would have the extra high rent up front, plus the value of construction cost, and the only thing you would ever have to pay is the interest until the house deteriorates to construction quality; after that the principal is perfectly matched with the rent from the house. So the monetary cost of delay is the interest on the loan, and value at the higher quality exceeds value at construction quality by the higher rents up front (net of operating costs), less the interest on the loan.

If the higher quality is only a tiny bit better than construction quality, the extra rent up front is just about the same as rent at construction quality (net of operating cost). From the construction-cost requirement, the amount of the loan (value at construction quality) equals construction quality. Hence the rate at which value is rising is price (net of operating cost) at construction quality, minus the interest rate times construction cost.

This rate has to equal the rate at which construction cost is rising. This equality can hold only if the price (net of operating cost) at construction quality equals the rate at which construction cost is rising, plus the interest rate times construction cost. This is the construction-price requirement.

Together with the lowest-rent requirement, the construction-price requirement fixes prices at both ends of the deterioration phase (see Figure 6-3). Construction cost says something about how high prices have to be between these endpoints. The final requirement says much more about this topic.

$5$ - *Equal demand.* This requirement also needs a lengthy explanation. Houses are continually being built at the construction quality; they deteriorate and are then abandoned or demolished. For the system to be stable over time, the number of houses being abandoned has to be the same as the number being built. But the number of houses being abandoned is the same as the number that were built as many years ago as it takes to deteriorate through the cycle. So system stability requires that the number of houses being built be constant over time.

An alternative way of coming to the same conclusion is to think about what would happen if the rate of construction fluctuated over

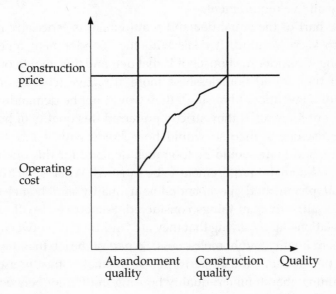

*Figure 6-3*

time. Consider a particular quality in the deterioration interval. The number of houses of that quality will fluctuate in the same way that construction fluctuated, but with a lag of however many years it takes a house to deteriorate to that quality. Then the price for that quality will also fluctuate, as owners and landlords try to fill the fluctuating stock they have inherited. So a stable price system requires a constant rate of construction and an equal rate of abandonment.

Steady construction, though, means that the number of houses at any quality in the deterioration interval has to be the same as the number at any other quality. The quality spectrum at any time reflects building history just as layers of sediment reflect fossil history. If every geological eon's species are the same, every layer of sediment will look the same as every other, and if every time had the same amount of building, every quality will have the same supply as every other.

But if supply is uniform across qualities in the deterioration interval, demand must be uniform too. Making demand the same for every quality in the deterioration interval is the final job that a price-quality schedule must accomplish. This is the equal-demand requirement. Usually only one price-quality schedule will be able to satisfy all five requirements.

One part of the equal-demand requirement is especially important to keep in mind. It deals with the abandonment quality of housing. Consider the households that demand this quality of housing. If they found homelessness more attractive (considering the price of conventional housing), they would not be demanding this quality of housing. If they strictly preferred this quality of housing to homelessness, then so would households with a tiny bit less income, and there would be too much demand for this quality for the equal-demand requirement to be satisfied. What is left? It must be that people find the abandonment quality and homelessness equally attractive, all things considered. Sometimes I will express this relationship by saying that they are "indifferent" between abandonment quality and homelessness. So part of the job that the price-quality schedule must perform is to make the households consuming abandonment-quality housing indifferent between that housing and homelessness.

Notice that the strength of the equal-demand requirement is less than that of the other four requirements. Violation of any of the other four would provoke shortages and vacancies; it is conceivable that equal demand could be violated in a complex system of fluctuating prices that satisfied the other requirements and avoided shortages and vacancies. The appeal to stable systems that gives rise to the equal-demand condition is partly a desire for simplicity (which should not be played down, since it is only because we need simplicity that we turn to maps and models at all), and partly the idea that comparing stable systems is useful.

A good analogy is the effect of a change in air temperature on a person taking a shower. Suppose you are taking a shower with the water at a very comfortable temperature. The system is stable because you are satisfied with the water temperature, and so you don't fiddle with the dials. Then a window opens and the air temperature falls, so you want the water hotter. Now the new stable system—where you aren't fiddling with the dials—is one with hotter water. The best simple analysis of the situation is that colder air implies hotter water; this is a comparison of stable systems.

That doesn't mean that you will go immediately to the new stable system. Your first adjustment may be wrong; so may your second, third, or fourth. It doesn't even mean that you will always be increasing water temperature—you may overshoot, then overcompensate, then overshoot again. Comparing stable systems is just a way to understand in simple terms the general direction in which changes are taking places.

But the shower analogy reminds us to be wary; sometimes intermediate changes—what I call short-run effects—are not in the same direction as the changes in stable systems.

Now in essence we have drawn a map. We have a picture—stylized and abstract, but a picture nonetheless—of how housing markets work. We want to use the map to assess some theories of why homelessness rose—to see the mechanism that each of the theories operates through, and to find out what other ancillary changes had to be operating at the same time if the theory were correct. It's like a detective story—you line up the suspects, find out if they could have committed the crime, and figure out what clues they would have left behind if they had done it. Then you check whether they were in the neighborhood and look for the evidence. The first three steps will be taken in this chapter.

## A Smaller Middle Class

Let me begin with explanations that seem better supported by the evidence.

Consider what happens when the middle class becomes smaller but everything else stays the same. By middle class, I mean households with incomes around the level that buys housing of the lowest construction qualities. Begin by comparing stable systems. Fewer middle-class households means less demand for housing right below the construction quality. So if prices don't change, demand looks as shown in Figure 6-4. This can't be a stable system, since it violates the equal-demand requirement. So prices have to change: either prices for low qualities have to rise to reduce demand there, or prices for high qualities (high in the deterioration interval, that is) have to fall to increase demand there, or both.

Some reflection on the construction-cost requirement leads to the conclusion that both changes have to occur. If prices for low qualities rose and prices for high qualities stayed the same, value would

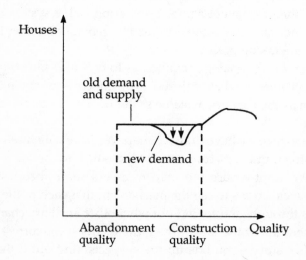

Figure 6-4

rise above construction cost. If the opposite happened, value would fall below construction cost. Only if both changes occur—in such a way that the present value of increases precisely offsets the present value of decreases—can the construction-cost requirement be met.

So the price-quality schedule has to twist as in Figure 6-5. But this shift by itself won't create a stable system. The prices of qualities slightly better than the abandonment quality rise, and so these become less attractive, but the price of the abandonment quality stays the same, and so it loses no attractiveness. Households that were consuming the slightly better qualities therefore switch their demand to the abandonment quality; but this violates the equal-demand requirement.

So the abandonment quality has to fall, and the price-quality schedule twists again, as in Figure 6-6. Notice that reducing abandonment quality and increasing prices go hand in hand: the old abandonment quality's price equaled operating cost under the old price-quality schedule, but is greater than operating cost under the new schedule.[3]

The first noteworthy implication of these changes in the price-quality schedule is that homelessness rises. This is not because more people are poor, but because homelessness reaches higher into the income distribution. To see this, consider the household that was

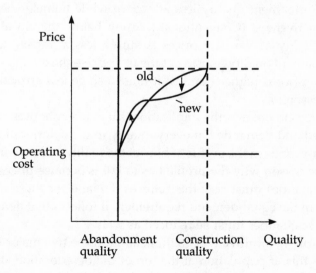

*Figure 6-5*

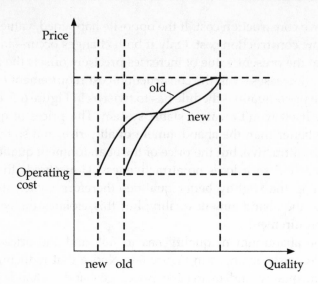

*Figure 6-6*

living in housing of the old abandonment-quality under the old price-quality schedule. This household was indifferent between being homeless and living in abandonment-quality housing at that price. When the abandonment quality falls, this household becomes homeless, because the price rise makes conventional housing at the old abandonment quality less attractive while homelessness loses no attractiveness. (Conventional housing below the old abandonment quality at the new prices is surely less attractive than old abandonment quality housing at the old price—the quality is worse and the price is higher—and so it must also be less attractive than homelessness.)

The second noteworthy implication is that fewer houses are being supplied and demanded at every quality in the deterioration interval. The change in the profile of houses by quality is shown in Figure 6-7. The reason why the profile has to fall is because prices for the lower qualities must rise; this reduces demand for these qualities, and from the equal-demand requirement it follows that demand for the other qualities must be reduced as well.

The rough, intuitive way to think about these two major implications is this: if population at the top of the deterioration slide gets reduced, population everywhere along the slide has to be reduced

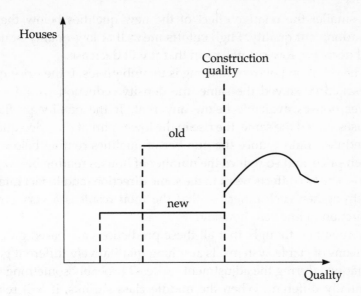

*Figure 6-7*

as well because of the equal-demand condition, and the way this reduction gets accomplished at the bottom is by pushing some people off the slide into homelessness.

These changes in the price-quality schedule and the profile of houses by quality also have implications about somewhat measurable quantities, such as construction, demolition, and the stocks of low-quality and low-rent housing. It is easy to see that the rates of construction and demolition both must fall: fewer units enter the top of the deterioration slide every year, and fewer come out the bottom.

For a stock of something called "low-quality housing" the results are slightly more ambiguous. If abandonment quality stayed the same, the result would be clear and would not depend on what definition of low-quality housing we chose to work with: because there would be fewer houses at each quality, the amount of housing below any quality in the deterioration interval would fall. The fall in abandonment quality, however, works in the opposite direction and makes the definition of low quality matter. At one extreme, suppose we said that low quality means below the original abandonment quality. Then the amount of low-quality housing would rise, from zero to some positive amount. The higher we pick the cutoff we use to define low quality, the greater the effect of density reductions and the smaller the relative effect of the new qualities below the old abandonment quality. High cutoffs mean that low-quality housing will decrease, low cutoffs mean that it will decrease.

The effect on low-rent housing is unambiguous. If the price-quality schedule stayed the same, the density reduction would mean fewer houses available below any rent. If the quality profile of houses stayed the same, the rise in the lower part of the price-quality schedule would reduce the number of qualities renting below any given price, and so reduce the number of houses renting below that price. The two effects work in the same direction (and in fact interact to strengthen each other) so that the total result is a very strong reduction in low-rent housing.

Remember, though, that all these predictions are based on comparisons of stable systems. Is anything qualitatively different going to happen during the adjustment process? Probably something substantially different. When the middle class shrinks, it will release housing it formerly occupied, so that the initial response is a larger amount of housing coming down the deterioration slide and reaching the poor. This transitory surge will cause a temporary reduction in rents for the poor, a temporary fall in homelessness, and a temporary increase in abandonment quality. This temporary adjustment in the other direction will make the movement to the stable system seem all the more severe and battering to the poor.

Finally, notice for this story that it doesn't matter why the middle class leaves the market for housing in the deterioration interval, as long as it leaves. The first reason that comes to mind is the increasing dispersion of incomes in the U.S. economy, a trend that has been well documented. But this is not the only possible reason. Government policies that move some middle-class households to other parts of the market—subsidized apartment buildings in New York, for instance, or federal tax and insurance subsidies that push families well into the construction interval[4]—have the same effect. The same conclusions follow about what they do.

## Gentrification and Operating Cost

The next kind of change to consider is one where operating cost rises but everything else stays the same. An increase in insurance, prop-

erty taxes, or utility costs could be responsible for this rise in operating cost, but a more likely candidate, or at least a more frequently
discussed candidate, is a rise in the price of land. Gentrification or
the revitalization of downtown office markets, in turn, could be
responsible for increasing land costs.

An increase in operating costs affects all qualities, and so the first
reaction might be to raise all rents to make up for it, as in Figure 6-8.
A simple translation like this meets the construction-cost requirement, the operating-cost requirement, and the construction-price
requirement; the problem is with equal demand.

In particular, no one wants to buy any of the lowest qualities of
housing. Consider the old abandonment quality and the household
for which this quality is the most attractive variety of conventional
housing. Because price has increased for every quality in the deterioration interval, the household consuming each quality has to be
richer than the household that was consuming it before, and so the
household at the old abandonment quality must also be richer than
the household there before. The new household at the old abandonment quality must be consuming just about the same amount of
other things as the old household at that quality, since the price of

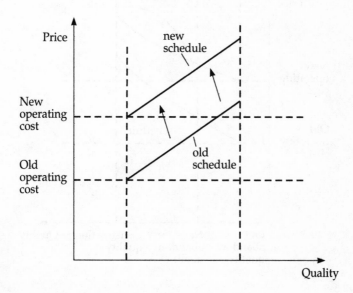

*Figure 6-8*

housing is higher but it has more income. From the equal-demand condition, the old household found this combination just as attractive as being homeless—that is, consuming no housing and spending all its money on other things. But the new household, since it's richer, could buy more of other things if it were homeless, and so, for this household, homelessness is more attractive than the combination of housing quality and other things that the old household consumed. So it will be homeless, and no one will demand the old abandonment quality of housing.

The proposed uniform upward shift of prices won't work. Prices will have to be lower on the bottom, where demand is deficient. But since prices can't fall below operating cost, abandonment quality will have to rise. To meet the construction-cost requirement, though, this loss in revenue at the bottom must be made up for by higher prices at the top of the deterioration interval. Price at construction quality is fixed, and so the price-quality schedule has to twist, rising more steeply at the bottom and becoming flatter at the top (Figure 6-9). This is the price schedule for the new stable situation after operating costs rise.[5]

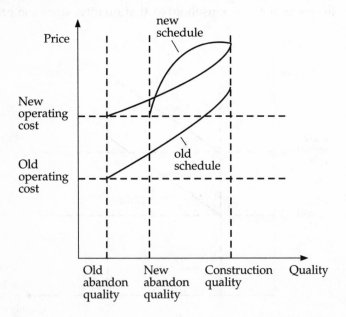

Figure 6-9

The major result of this new price-quality schedule is more home-lessness. Everyone who was consuming housing between the old abandonment quality and the new abandonment quality becomes homeless, plus a few more people. Why more people? Because the household consuming the new abandonment quality would have been consuming a higher quality of housing under the original schedule, since the new price-quality schedule is both higher and steeper. The household that was demanding the new abandonment quality under the old price-quality schedule is now homeless (for-merly it found homelessness just as attractive as the new abandon-ment quality at the old price, but the new price is higher); so are households with slightly higher income.

The second result of the new price-quality schedule is a higher abandonment quality. Some of the lowest-quality houses will disap-pear from the market, and so there will be fewer low-quality units. Whether there will be more or fewer houses of the qualities that remain on the market is impossible to say without specifying the model in more detail; probably the number will stay about the same. This means, in turn, no change in the rates of construction and demolition.

Higher prices for constant qualities and the disappearance of the lowest and cheapest qualities mean that there will be less low-rent housing. This is the final major implication of a rise in operating cost.

Thus rising operating cost—from gentrification, for instance—and a smaller middle class both predict that rising homelessness will be accompanied by a decrease in low-rent and low-quality housing. They differ in their predictions about abandonment quality (up from gentrification, down from a smaller middle class) and about con-struction (at the construction quality) and demolition (down from a smaller middle class, stable from gentrification).

There are also some differences in the way the transition to the stable situation would be made. Higher operating costs would im-mediately trigger a wave of demolition, but this would be accompa-nied by rising rents for low-quality housing, not falling rents. Moreover, if gentrification were the cause of higher operating costs, the demolition sites would soon be rebuilt.

## More Poor People

Another possible cause for increased homelessness is more poor people. If all the added poor households have incomes below that of the richest homeless household, they make no impact on the price-quality schedule. More people are homeless, but rents stay the same. So do stocks of low-rent and low-quality housing.

On the other hand, if some of the additional poor people have incomes high enough to demand some of the lowest qualities of housing originally on the market (even for only a few days a month), the price-quality schedule has to change. If it doesn't, the influx of poor people raises demand at the bottom of the slide, as in Figure 6-10. The equal-demand requirement is violated.

To maintain equal demand, prices have to rise at the bottom of the deterioration interval and fall at the top (both changes are needed because of the construction-cost requirement), just as they did with a smaller middle class. Equal demand, moreover, requires a lower abandonment quality, just as it did with a smaller middle class. So the twist in the price-quality schedule is the same twist we saw with a smaller middle class (Figure 6-11).

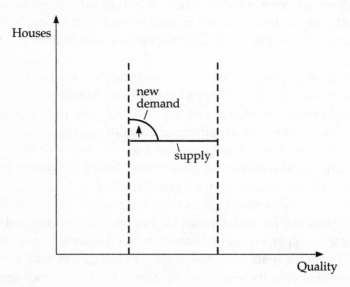

Figure 6-10

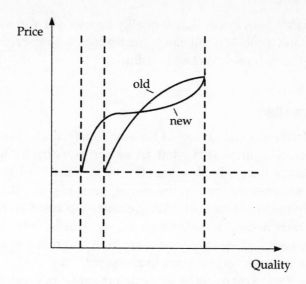

*Figure 6-11*

Homelessness rises for two reasons: because the minimum income needed for avoiding homelessness rises and because more households are below that income. More poor people, however, unambiguously increases the amount of low-quality housing. The inequality between supply and demand was resolved partly by reducing demand (by higher prices at the bottom) and partly by increasing supply (by reducing prices at the top and causing more housing to filter down). The part that was resolved by increasing supply means more houses of every quality in the deterioration interval—in particular, more houses of every low quality. The lower abandonment quality works in the same direction, making some low qualities available on the market.

The increase in low-quality housing implies an increase in the rate of demolition and construction. Although prices of low-quality houses rise, the number of them rises too, and so the overall effect on the stock of low-rent housing is ambiguous. Fewer qualities have rents below any threshold, but each of these qualities is more heavily populated, and some are much more heavily populated.

The transition to the stable situation is also different from the transition caused by a smaller middle class. Instead of a one-time rise in demolition, there will be a one-time cessation, as abandon-

ment quality falls. Prices of low-quality houses will also rise immediately (and probably fall later), instead of falling because of a
surfeit of former middle-class housing.

## Higher Interest Rates

In standard economic stories of housing, interest rates have a very
important role. Interest is what an owner gives up by holding a
house rather than a bank account, and so rents have to be high
enough to offset the interest the owner loses. Higher interest rates
generally mean higher rents. This relationship between rents and
interest rates holds, for instance, in the construction interval in our
model, where high-quality houses are built and maintained. It also
holds for the construction-price requirement.

But for the lowest qualities in the deterioration interval, the qualities most important for studying homelessness, the relationship is
much more indirect and ambiguous. The main effect comes through
the construction-cost requirement. Higher interest rates reduce the
present value of the stream of net rents, and so the value of the old
stream of rents is no longer enough to meet construction cost. To
satisfy the construction-cost requirement prices *somewhere* in the
deterioration interval must rise. The top is the most likely place,
since the construction price forces a rise there anyway, and because
changes early in the life of a house have more impact on its value.
On the other hand, the equal-demand requirement is a force for
bringing the price increase all the way down to the bottom. So prices
may or may not rise at the bottom. Whether homelessness increases
depends on how prices of the lowest-quality houses change.

The only definite prediction about higher interest rates is that they
will cause the number of houses at each quality to fall, along with
construction and demolition levels. Higher prices somewhere mean
less demand somewhere, and by the equal-demand requirement,
less demand somewhere means less demand everywhere.

## Shelters

When governments and concerned citizens find people sleeping on
the streets, they often set up shelters. We need to consider the effects

of shelters for two reasons. First, because their establishment or expansion so often accompanies a rise in homelessness, we should be able to sort out housing-market changes that shelters cause from those caused by whatever was driving the original increase in homelessness. Unless you know the medicine's side effects, you won't be able to tell why the patient got sick. Second, since shelters have been the main policy response to homelessness, understanding shelters is necessary for understanding current policies and devising better ones.

Incorporating shelters into the way we have been looking at housing markets is fairly easy. Suppose shelters are available: they provide free housing of some quality better than street homelessness to anyone who asks for it. (If the quality were not better, no one would use the shelter and nothing more would have to be said.) Although "right to shelter" is far from a universal legal doctrine, the rationing of shelter beds does not seem to be a widespread phenomenon. At various times in various cities, people have been turned away from shelters, but in most cities at most times some shelters have vacancies. Nor are all shelters free. But the analysis of cheap shelters is not altogether different from the analysis of free ones; it just takes more words.

Shelters must cause some low-quality housing to disappear from the market and the former residents of that housing to enter shelters, even if the shelters are of lower quality than any housing on the market when they were introduced. The previous abandonment quality made its consumers indifferent between street homelessness and buying that quality at operating cost. If shelters are available at the same prices as street homelessness but are of higher quality, then the new abandonment quality has a higher hurdle to leap. Just as I argued before that the abandonment quality had to be substantially better than street homelessness because its price was substantially higher, so too must the new abandonment quality be substantially better than shelter quality, since it costs substantially more.

This effect is compounded by the construction-cost requirement. If houses are abandoned after, say, twenty years instead of twenty-five, then they have less time to earn back their construction cost, and so each of the twenty years must contribute more to this end than it did when it was joined by more years. The price-quality schedule must rise over its now more limited interval. Higher prices increase homelessness further; they also reduce the number of houses of each quality. So shelters reduce construction, demolition, and the stocks of both low-rent and low-quality housing.

Thus the first important consequence of shelters is that they make it much more difficult to confront the other explanations for rising homelessness with housing-market evidence. For analysts, they muddy the picture. For instance, the smaller-middle-class explanation and the operating-cost explanation differ sharply on what happens to abandonment quality; smaller-middle-class says it goes down, operating-cost says it goes up, and we need only look at what happened to see which is right. But a combination of smaller middle class with better shelters—also a plausible story—is compatible with a rising or steady abandonment quality. So tests we thought would be decisive may not be; we have to look at the data more carefully.

For policy purposes, the important conclusion is that shelters will always contain people who would not have been homeless if shelters were not there. To the extent that shelters are established for charitable reasons, this result is not necessarily to be decried. If shelter quality is low, the people who enter shelters would have been badly off even if they were conventionally housed. Since everyone who enters a shelter becomes better off by doing so, shelters may still be helping a deserving class. To the extent that shelters are established to keep the streets free of homeless people, however, the extra people are a burden.

These extra people essentially pose a problem of observability. If charitable people or those interested in keeping homeless people off the streets could tell who was poor immediately, without expending any effort or resources, there would be no need for shelters. Households with income below the minimum for conventional housing could be paid the difference between their income and the minimum. Income, however, as we are considering it here, is an abstraction for resources, and resources at the bottom of the social scale (as at the top) are mostly unobservable to outsiders. Good family connections, for instance, are a key resource for the very poor that cannot be easily and verifiably observed by outsiders. Most shelters do not have income-eligibility requirements; they rely on self-selection. A cash-distribution scheme could not rely on self-selection.

The emergence of bigger and better and publicized shelters during the 1980s is therefore one more reason why measured homelessness grew; it seems likely to have contributed especially to the explosive nature of that growth. To say this is not to argue that homelessness exists only because some soft-hearted and weak-minded liberals set up shelters. There are enough other reasons—probably too many other reasons—for homelessness to have risen in North America in the 1980s. A more plausible conclusion is that certain intermediate levels of homelessness are unlikely to persist for long.

Tooth decay is a good analogy. When dentists are around, small cavities do not persist for long. Dentists drill them and make them big in order to put fillings in. They don't cause cavities, but the way they treat cavities makes them bigger. Whether this treatment is the best one is a separate issue from what it does to the size of cavities. Dentists seem to like their method.

## Different Tastes

So far I have assumed that the only way households differ is in income. Of course this assumption isn't true, but it was convenient—it let us concentrate on how income, housing quality, and maintenance fit together, and led us to some reasonably testable, somewhat sophisticated predictions about how various parts of the housing market relate. For some issues in shelter management, however, this assumption is not very useful. For instance, some people sleep on the streets even when shelters have vacancies; if income were the only way people differed, either everybody would prefer streets to shelters or everybody would prefer shelters to streets.

So we should think about the implications of the fact that people differ in tastes as well as income. On one level, this makes observability problems more severe. Even if shelter operators could measure income perfectly and restrict admission to people below some income level (which they can't), they still could not restrict their shelters only to those who would otherwise be on the street. The same is true for cash assistance.

On another level, differing tastes greatly complicate the problem of determining the right quality for shelters to offer, especially for shelter operators who are motivated primarily by a desire to reduce the presence of homeless people on the streets. If everyone had the same tastes, shelter quality could be set just a little better than the quality of life on the streets. Everyone living on the streets would go to the shelter, and only a small number of households that would otherwise be conventionally housed would go to the shelter. The shelter would cause only a slight distortion in the conventional housing market, but would be totally effective in removing people from the streets (although it wouldn't make them much happier).

But because people's tastes differ, this strategy won't work. A shelter only a little better than streetlife will draw only a small fraction of the people who live on the street. Only if shelter quality is pretty good will a substantial number of streetpeople be encouraged to leave the streets, but if shelter quality is good enough to do that, it's good enough to encourage a substantial number of people who would ordinarily be conventionally housed to come to the shelter.

## Hysteresis

Squeezing toothpaste out of the tube is much easier than getting it back in. Simply reversing the conditions that got someone to squeeze toothpaste out won't enable her to put it back in. Economists call such a condition, when history matters as well as current conditions, "hysteresis." Hysteresis matters to the study of homelessness because reducing homelessness is much more difficult than not increasing it. This means that the same current external conditions will be associated with more homelessness in a city where homelessness has been high in the past. Past homelessness is a cause of current homelessness.

On the level of an individual homeless person, hysteresis works in several different ways. There are fixed costs both to entering homelessness and to leaving it. Becoming homeless may involve the loss of possessions, an investment in learning the ropes, and in becoming part of a community. Entry costs alone are enough to cause hysteresis—because there's always a chance that things might get better, a person will hold off incurring these entry costs until things are so bad she is quite certain they won't get better soon. If exit doesn't involve any one-time costs, this waiting means that the conditions required to get someone to enter homelessness are worse than the conditions required to get her to leave.

Exit costs make the problem worse. Because there's always a chance that things might get worse, a person will hold off incurring exit costs until things are so good outside she is quite certain they won't get worse soon. If you buy a new suit for your new job and the job disappears, you still have your investment in the suit. Again this reasoning makes the leaving threshold higher than the entering threshold. And homelessness probably does have a substantial exit cost—searching for housing at the very least, probably putting down a deposit, buying some housewares.

Another source of hysteresis in individuals is medical. Being homeless implies enhanced hazards of physical and mental illness, and both forms of illness make it harder to earn income and secure housing. Everything else being equal, a community with a history of more homelessness in the past is likely to be a community with more disabilities in the present, and so is likely to experience more homelessness in the future.

Finally, Freeman and Hall (1987) point out that being homeless, or having been homeless, labels a person as a higher-risk tenant than other people: "The probability that someone who has been homeless will pay rent regularly may reasonably be viewed as lower than for others. Moreover, while only a minority of the homeless may suffer from serious behavioral problems that may lead them to damage units or engage in behavior that would upset other tenants, the behavior of even a small number can raise the 'expected' cost of renting to any member of the group" (p. 20). Homelessness has a stigma, and people who acquire it have a harder time dealing with the rest of the world.

Individual hysteresis is compounded by hysteresis at the shelter level. Setting up a shelter has several obvious fixed costs—learning about homelessness and shelter operation, searching for and renovating a building, getting licenses. Loss of information is another set-up cost—once you start a shelter, you no longer can tell how

Table 6-1  Summary of Causes and Effects

| Cause | Homelessness | Abandon. quality | Low-quality housing | Low-rent housing | Construction, demolition | Transition |
|---|---|---|---|---|---|---|
| Smaller middle class | up | down | down[a] | down[b] | down | loose markets, much demolition |
| Higher operating cost (gentrification) | up | up | down | down | ? | tight markets, demolish but rebuild |
| More poor people (below income threshold) | up | same | same | same | same | none |
| More poor people (above income threshold) | up | down | up | ? | up | tight markets, no demolition |
| Higher interest rates | up[a] | ? | down[a] | down[a] | down | ? |
| Better shelters | up | up | down | down | down | ? |
| Past homelessness | up | – | – | – | – | – |

a. Probably.
b. Almost certainly.

many people would be on the street if the shelter weren't operating (or how many units of low-quality housing would spring up if the shelter weren't operating). Shelters won't be shut down just because conditions are as good as they were when the shelters were set up.

Because shelters draw people who would not otherwise be on the street, the two levels of hysteresis compound each other. If homelessness has been high, more shelters are open, more people occupy them, and more people stay homeless—which in turn causes more shelters to stay open. Homelessness can of course decrease, but much more slowly than the rate at which underlying conditions improve.

Past homelessness thus is an important determinant of current and future homelessness. In trying to find out the effects of other possible causes, we should not ignore history.

Table 6-1 summarizes the main results of this chapter. For each of the possible causes of increased homelessness, it lists the other changes in housing-market outcomes that would have occurred as well. To return to the detective-story metaphor, these are the clues we will have to look for.

# 7

# Income Distribution

If an explanation of homelessness is to be plausible, two kinds of conditions must be met. First, and most important, there must be changes in the right direction in the right places at the right time. The histories in Chapter 4, for instance, argue pretty convincingly that improvements in the quality or accessibility of shelters were not responsible for the initial rise in measured homelessness in North American cities, although they probably contributed to subsequent rises. Second, the rise in homelessness must be accompanied by the right kinds of changes in rents, housing stocks, construction, and demolition. More poor people and fewer middle-class people, for instance, have different implications for the stock of low-quality housing and the rate of abandonment, and so looking at how these stocks and rates changed can influence the plausibility of our explanations. This is the evidence that would have been left behind, the clues we have to look for.

### Histogram Slopes

In the last chapter we saw that housing for poor people is a byproduct of housing for the middle class, and so what matters is the ratio of the number of middle-class people to the number of poor. A low ratio—few middle-class and many poor—implies high rents for the poor and much homelessness; a high ratio implies the opposite.

The way to find out how this ratio has been changing is to look at what are called income-distribution histograms. These charts show the proportion of households in each income bracket. Since there are usually more middle-class households than either very poor or very rich households, a typical income-distribution histogram would look something like Figure 7-1. A histogram with a low ratio of middle-class to poor people would look like Figure 7-2, and a histogram with a high ratio would look like Figure 7-3.

The graphs suggest that the best way to estimate the ratio is to fit a line to the lower portion of the income distribution. A flat line, as in Figure 7-4, indicates a low ratio, and a steep line, as in Figure 7-5, indicates a high ratio. The way to measure the steepness of a line is to find its slope—how much it rises vertically for every unit of horizontal distance—and so a big slope means a big ratio, and a small slope means a small ratio.

To find out how histogram slopes were changing, first, with the assistance of Seth Weissman I prepared histograms in constant dollars for the four North American cities. I used published census data. For the U.S. cities, the unit of account was 1982–1984 U.S. dollars; for Toronto, 1981 Canadian dollars. The data were for families (to avoid any influence from the growth in the number of

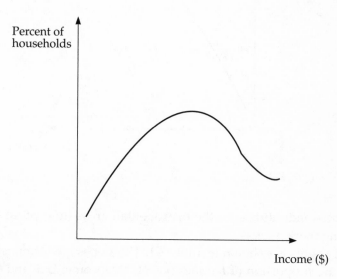

*Figure 7-1*

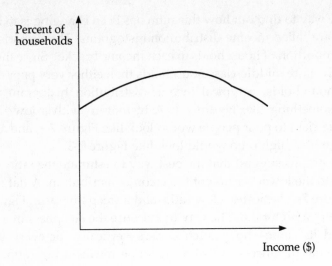

*Figure 7-2*

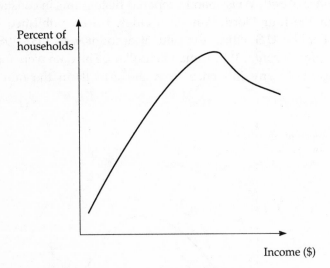

*Figure 7-3*

unrelated individuals) in the metropolitan areas (to capture entire housing markets).[1]

The results are shown in Table 7-1. The slopes are estimated; the units are proportion of families per $1,000 income. U.S. and Canadian slopes are not directly comparable because of the difference between the respective dollars, but this difference is not large.

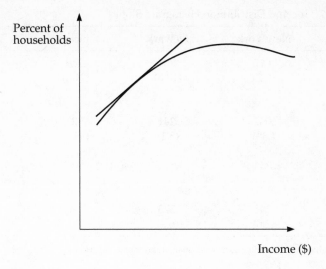

*Figure 7-4*

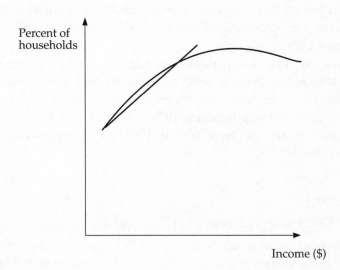

*Figure 7-5*

Table 7-1 supports the idea that change in the shape of income distribution caused the new North American homelessness. The slope falls drastically in all three U.S. cities between 1969 and 1979, but only drifts down slightly in Toronto. Among U.S. cities in 1979, Chicago has the steepest slope and New York the flattest (essentially

*Table 7-1*  Income-Distribution Histogram Slopes

| Year | New York | Newark | Chicago | Toronto |
|------|----------|--------|---------|---------|
| 1969 | .617     | .801   | .749    | –       |
|      | (9.2)    | (18.6) | (21.6)  |         |
| 1970 | –        | –      | –       | .830    |
|      |          |        |         | (3.9)   |
| 1979 | .067     | .241   | .328    | –       |
|      | (.88)    | (5.1)  | (35.5)  |         |
| 1980 | –        | –      | –       | .759    |
|      |          |        |         | (10.4)  |
| 1985 | –        | –      | –       | .656    |
|      |          |        |         | (13.7)  |
| 1989 | .145     | .373   | –       | –       |
|      | (2.0)    | (6.2)  | –       | –       |

The t-values are in parentheses. For explanation and sources, see text.

none), while the slopes for these cities are all considerably flatter than Toronto's. This is the same as the rankings of homelessness in the early and mid-1980s. There is no significant change between 1979 and 1989.

Histogram slopes thus track homelessness very well, both in the cross-section and in the time series (allowing for lags), for our small sample. The only minor anomalies are the insignificant slope increases in U.S. cities between 1979 and 1989 and the difference between Newark and New York in 1989. Did rising poverty cause the flat slopes?

## More Poverty?

Table 7-2 gives the basic trends in poverty for the three U.S. cities. Family poverty went up in all of them between 1970 and 1980, but family homelessness did not. Family poverty went down in the eastern cities between 1980 and 1990, but family homelessness went up; family poverty went up in Chicago between 1980 and 1990, but Chicago had much less family homelessness than the eastern cities did. Homelessness rose among single adults in New York before 1980, but poverty among unrelated individuals in New York fell between 1970 and 1980. Poverty among unrelated individuals in Newark rose between 1970 and 1980, but apparently homelessness did not.

*Table 7-2*   Poverty in Three Cities, 1970–1990

| | Families below poverty level | | | | | |
| | Newark | | NYC | | Chicago | |
| Year | City | SMSA | City | SCA | City | SCA |
|---|---|---|---|---|---|---|
| 1970 | 18.4% | 6.8% | 11.5% | 8.3% | 10.6% | 6.8% |
| 1980 | 29.9 | 8.8 | 17.2 | 11.0 | 16.8 | 8.7 |
| 1990 | 20.1 | 6.7 | 16.3 | 9.1 | 17.8 | 8.7 |

Unrelated individuals below poverty level

| | | | | | | |
|---|---|---|---|---|---|---|
| 1970 | 34.9 | 28.8 | 27.4 | 28.3 | 29.2 | 28.1 |
| 1980 | 39.3 | 21.4 | 24.7 | 22.5 | 26.3 | 20.4 |
| 1990 | 35.1 | 19.4 | 25.0 | 21.1 | 25.8 | 19.8 |

Unrelated individuals under 65 below poverty level

| | | | | | | |
|---|---|---|---|---|---|---|
| 1970 | 27.3 | 22.1 | 20.2 | 20.9 | 22.3 | 21.2 |
| 1980 | 37.5 | 20.1 | 24.2 | 23.0 | 25.5 | 19.6 |
| 1990 | 34.1 | 18.0 | 23.7 | 20.1 | 25.2 | 19.5 |

Unrelated individuals under 65 below 75% of poverty level

| | | | | | | |
|---|---|---|---|---|---|---|
| 1970 | 22.4 | 17.9 | 16.3 | 16.9 | 17.9 | 17.1 |
| 1980 | 29.8 | 15.5 | 16.9 | 16.1 | 19.9 | 15.2 |

*Source.* U.S. Census. SMSA is Standard Metropolitan Statistical Area; SCA is Standard Consolidated Area (bigger).

Looking at severe poverty—the proportion of the population with income below 75 percent of the poverty line—and excluding the elderly gives a picture slightly more sympathetic to the idea of an association between reductions in income and homelessness. The bottom two panels of Table 7-2 show that poverty among nonelderly unrelated individuals rose in all three cities between 1970 and 1980, and so did severe poverty.

The increase in cities, however, was entirely due to intrametropolitan shifts in location. Both poverty and severe poverty decreased in all three metropolitan areas between 1970 and 1980. Since metropolitan areas are economic units, not political units like cities, they seem to be the more relevant unit.

Figure 7-6 gives year-to-year information on severe poverty in New York City, a similarly mixed picture. Family homelessness

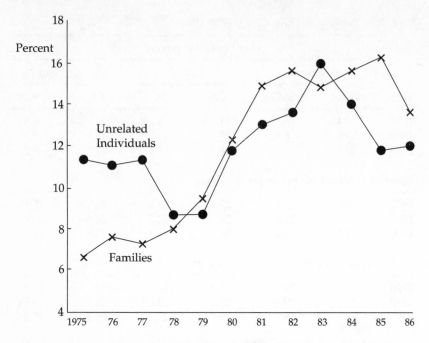

*Figure 7-6* Severely poor New York population, 1975-1986. *Source*: New York City Human Resources Administration, "Dependency," 1986; based on CPS data.

emerged in 1982 when severe poverty among families was at a high point, but increasing single homelessness first became evident in 1978, a historical trough for severe poverty among unrelated individuals. Single homelessness grew rapidly during the 1980s—a time of high and rising severe poverty for unrelated individuals; but the severe poverty peak (1983) preceded the single-shelter population peak (1986–89) by at least three years. Severe poverty among unrelated individuals was just about the same in 1975 as it was at the single-shelter population peak. Severe poverty among families also peaks well before the first peak in the family-shelter population. (Figure 7-6 includes the elderly, but the numbers are small and close to constant as a proportion of the total population.) Blackburn's (1994) finding of almost no rise in the proportion of the U.S. population in households below 75 percent and 50 percent of the poverty line between 1979 and 1986 is consistent with this picture.

Nor is there a strong relationship between poverty and homelessness in Toronto. Hanratty and Blank (1992) show that poverty was rising in Canada between 1980 and 1984, when homelessness was high in Toronto, but it had fallen substantially between 1970 and 1980. For Metro Toronto itself, the low-income proportion of the population was approximately constant between 1970 and 1985, with a very slight downward trend.

I don't have direct poverty data for London and Hamburg. Year-to-year variation in poverty, however, is usually correlated with unemployment. Shelter homelessness in London and Hamburg fell throughout the early 1980s while unemployment rose steadily to unprecedented heights, although the 1990–91 upturn in sleeping rough in London coincided with a severe downturn in the British economy. Similarly, Blackburn shows a noticeable increase in the proportion of the British population with income below 50 percent of the poverty level between 1979 and 1986, and a moderate rise in the German proportion between 1981 and 1984, despite the fall in homelessness.

So changes in poverty do not seem to coincide closely with changes in homelessness over the last two decades. Since the histograms didn't flatten because of more poor households, they must have flattened because of fewer middle-class households. Direct evidence, then, makes a smaller middle class a plausible explanation of rising U.S. homelessness and more poor people an implausible one. But we need not resign ourselves to rely solely on direct evidence; in Chapter 6 we saw that a variety of indirect evidence can also be used to check whether these trends were responsible for the rise in homelessness.

Before looking at the indirect evidence, however, I should note that Peter Rossi and Christopher Jencks come to an opposite conclusion about changes in poverty. Using data from the U.S. Current Population Survey, they find large increases nationally in the number of conventionally housed men (not households or individuals) with extremely low incomes and argue that these increases contributed significantly to homelessness. I will discuss this further at the end of the chapter.

## Low-rent Housing

Different causes of homelessness do not differ strongly in their implications for the number of units with rent below a specific level.

More poor people, higher interest rates, and fewer middle-class people all shift the bottom portion of the price-quality schedule upward, and so reduce the highest quality available at a given rent. More poor people, however, increases the density at each quality, and this offsets (at least partially and maybe completely) the shift in the price schedule. By contrast, fewer middle-class people reduces density and so exacerbates the shift in the schedule.

The data show a very close association between increases in homelessness and large movements in the stock of low-rent housing, and thus are more sympathetic to the smaller-middle-class explanation. Rents rose almost everywhere, possibly because of real interest rates, but only in the places where homelessness grew tremendously were there huge decreases in low-rent housing.

Table 7-3 shows these changes. Newark and New York lost almost half of their low-rent housing between 1970 and 1990, while Chicago lost only about 20 percent. Only New York had evidence of the new homelessness before 1980, and only in New York was there a noticeable decline in low-rent housing before 1980. Most of the pre-1980 loss was among the cheapest units (less than $194 in 1982–1984 dollars), which might be predominantly for singles, and the evidence of rising homelessness before 1980 was confined to singles. After 1980, there were more losses between $200 and $300, and family homelessness started to appear. Even the increase in low-rent housing stock from 1987 to 1990 coincides with a decrease in shelter population (both singles and families) during that time.

For Toronto, the Social Planning Council, a private organization, publishes data on "affordable" rental units in buildings with six or more units. The number of these units fell by about 14 percent between 1981 and 1985, but came back almost to the 1981 level by 1987.

How much of this reduction is due to rising prices for constant quality, and how much is due to loss of density? At least part results from a rising price-quality schedule. Table 7-4 gives some evidence for this by showing rents for some of the lowest qualities of housing in North American cities. Even when flophouses were going out of business, their real prices were rising.

The post-1990 observations for New York reflect two additional events that also raised lodginghouse prices. First was the end of the

*Table 7-3*  Low-Rent Housing in Three Cities, 1970–1990 (1982–1984 dollars, numbers in thousands)

Under $194 ($206 for Chicago) a month

| | 1970 | | 1980 | | 1984 | 1987 | 1990 | |
|---|---|---|---|---|---|---|---|---|
| | no. | % | no. | % | no. | no. | no. | % |
| Newark | 25 | 25.8 | 23 | 26.7 | – | – | 16 | 22.2 |
| NYC | 723 | 33.4 | 526 | 24.7 | 420 | 328 | 389 | 19.6 |
| Chicago | 171 | 23.1 | 141 | 21.2 | – | – | 140 | 23.5 |

Under $244

| | 1970 | | 1980 | | 1984 | 1987 | 1990 | |
|---|---|---|---|---|---|---|---|---|
| Newark | 43 | 45.3 | 37 | 41.9 | – | – | 22 | 31.7 |
| NYC | 1,166 | 53.8 | 915 | 43.0 | 697 | 539 | 562 | 28.4 |
| Chicago | 268 | 36.3 | 219 | 33.0 | – | – | 214 | 35.9 |

Under $304

| | 1970 | | 1980 | | 1984 | 1987 | 1990 | |
|---|---|---|---|---|---|---|---|---|
| Newark | 66 | 68.6 | 60 | 68.4 | – | – | 33 | 46.5 |
| NYC | 1,433 | 66.2 | 1,345 | 63.3 | 1,034 | 858 | 887 | 44.9 |
| Chicago | 416 | 56.3 | 393 | 59.2 | – | – | 333 | 55.8 |

Median rent

| | 1970 | 1980 | 1990 |
|---|---|---|---|
| Newark | $256 | $262 | $319 |
| NYC | $234 | $261 | $323 |
| Chicago | $278 | $280 | $286 |

ticketman system. Ticketman prices in the late eighties were less than the welfare shelter allowance. Ending the system allowed lodginghouses to replace ticketmen with welfare recipients—or to transform ticketmen into welfare recipients—and increase prices. The current lowest price in most lodginghouses—a little over $7—is the daily equivalent of the welfare monthly shelter allowance. The second event was the introduction of rent stabilization in 1992. Rent stabilization gives rights to permanent tenants that make eviction very difficult, even for nonpayment of rent, and so lodginghouse owners don't want permanent tenants. To make sure they don't get any more, owners evict all transient tenants after twenty-one days—so they can't become permanent—and charge them higher

*Table 7-4*  One-Night Prices for Very Cheap Accommodations, 1958–1992 (1982–1984 dollars)

| Year | NY lodginghouse dorm | Toronto | Newark single room | Chicago cage hotel |
|------|----------------------|---------|--------------------|--------------------|
| 1958 | – | – | – | 2.49 |
| 1965 | 2.76 | – | – | – |
| 1973 | – | 2.82 | – | – |
| 1976 | 2.62 | – | – | – |
| 1977 | – | 3.10 | – | – |
| 1978 | 2.95 | – | – | – |
| 1979 | 2.92 | – | – | – |
| 1981 | 3.39 | – | – | – |
| 1982 | – | 4.20 | – | – |
| 1985 | – | – | 4.60 | 3.06 |
| 1988 | – | – | – | 3.64 |
| 1990 | 2.20 | – | – | – |
| 1992 | 4.70 | – | – | – |

*Sources.* New York: 1965: Baker (1965). 1976: Sheppard (1976). 1979: Owen Moritz, "Bum's Rush on Bowery," *Daily News*, Oct. 21, 1979. 1981 and 1990: Drew Fetherston, "A Bowery Institution Hits the Skids," *Newsday*, Nov. 12, 1990. Prices normalized with CPI-U for NY–Northern NJ–Long Island from Bureau of Labor Statistics, "Handbook of Labor Statistics" (August 1989), table 117.

Toronto: Prices for 1973 and 1977 are for flophouses; 1982 price is for "cheapest rented room," since flophouses no longer available. 1973: South of Carlton Working Committee, "Skid Row Report to Toronto Planning Board," Feb. 25, 1974. 1977: City of Toronto, Commissioner of Planning (1977). 1982: Liss and Motaynes (1982). Prices converted to current U.S. dollars using average annual exchange rates from *Canadian World Almanac and Book of Facts* (Global Press, 1991), p. 375. Current U.S. dollars were then converted to 1982–1984 dollars by U.S. city average CPI-U.

Newark: Price for a room at Rio Hotel before it went out of business; interview with Ray Rio, May 1991.

rates. The only permanent tenants established their rights before 1992. Some of them have considerably lower rents than the posted rates—about $4 or $5 a night, according to lodginghouse own-ers—but in real historical terms, even these rents are on the high side.

## Low-quality Housing

The predictions of the smaller-middle-class and more-poor-people explanations of homelessness are starkly different when it comes to low-quality housing. The smaller middle class predicts a smaller stock of low-quality housing, while more poor people predicts more. A good way of measuring low-quality housing stock would resolve this controversy quickly and decisively. Unfortunately, because housing quality has so many dimensions, no really good measures of low quality can be found. What evidence there is, though, points strongly in the direction of less low-quality housing.

The best data come from New York. The Housing and Vacancy Survey there has been assessing the quality of the city's housing stock on a regular basis for the last twenty years. Table 7-5 shows a steady, almost uninterrupted decline in the stock of dilapidated housing. The only disturbing feature is the slight increase between 1978 and 1981.

A second way to find changes in the stock of low-quality housing is to look at the incidence of fires. The idea is that bad housing is more likely to burn. Because the classification of fires differs both between cities and within the same city over time, we can also look at fire deaths, although these include nonresidential fire deaths and introduce considerable noise, since fire deaths are rare events that are often correlated. In North America too, part of the secular decline in fire deaths may stem from the introduction of cheap smoke detectors around 1980.

Table 7-6 presents several different fire series for the six cities. For the North American cities, the New York pattern is typical: a rise until the late 1970s, a trough in the mid-1980s, and a small rise in the late 1980s. Chicago's fire peak was a few years earlier, and Newark's a few years later. Toronto's changes are smaller than those of the other cities. The Hamburg fire series is quite different; it rises up to the early 1980s and then flattens out without any serious decline. There are no discernible trends in the London data; weather apparently matters a lot.

*Table 7-5*  Dilapidated Renter-Occupied Units in New York City, 1970–1987

| Year | Number | Percent of all rented units |
|------|--------|------------------------------|
| 1970 | 106,000 | 5.0% |
| 1975 | 110,000 | 5.7 |
| 1978 | 62,000 | 3.3 |
| 1981 | 79,000 | 4.2 |
| 1984 | 62,000 | 3.4 |
| 1987 | 37,000 | 2.1 |

*Source.* Michael A. Stegman, *Housing in New York: Study of a City* (New York Department of Housing Preservation and Development, Feb. 1984), table 6–1; 1987 data from U.S. Census Bureau and 1987 New York City Housing and Vacancy Survey.

*Table 7-6*   Fire Activity, 1969–1990

| Year | Newark | NYC | Chicago | Toronto | London | Hamburg |
|------|--------|--------|---------|---------|--------|---------|
| 1969 | – | 25,643 | – | – | 43,733 | – |
| 1970 | – | 25,318 | 20,098 | – | 51,835 | – |
| 1971 | – | 26,492 | – | – | 42,593 | – |
| 1972 | – | 31,900 | 18,626 | – | 48,159 | 1,218 |
| 1973 | 694 | 33,197 | – | – | 47,866 | 1,232 |
| 1974 | 493 | 34,735 | 19,092 | – | 46,047 | 1,403 |
| 1975 | 576 | 35,326 | – | – | 51,539 | 1,399 |
| 1976 | – | – | 16,067 | – | 63,524 | 1,673 |
| 1977 | 613 | 34,561 | – | – | 36,851 | 1,800 |
| 1978 | 662 | 32,666 | 14,751 | 1,850 | 43,433 | 1,909 |
| 1979 | 634 | – | 13,900 | 1,850 | 51,676 | 1,604 |
| 1980 | 725 | – | 12,053 | 1,850 | 46,064 | 2,230 |
| 1981 | 635 | 31,156 | 12,733 | 1,500 | 43,793 | 2,161 |
| 1982 | 547 | 29,706 | 11,755 | 1,400 | 44,713 | 1,958 |
| 1983 | 417 | 28,191 | 11,173 | 1,450 | 50,176 | 2,041 |
| 1984 | 487 | 27,433 | 10,697 | 1,375 | 50,860 | 1,899 |
| 1985 | 448 | 27,041 | 9,545 | 1,300 | 50,171 | 1,813 |
| 1986 | 433 | 25,623 | 8,887 | 1,300 | 46,057 | 1,919 |
| 1987 | 376 | 25,880 | 8,179 | 1,600 | 43,235 | 1,762 |
| 1988 | 417 | – | 8,860 | 1,500 | 47,838 | 1,834 |
| 1989 | 296 | 25,143 | 7,781 | 1,400 | 57,861 | 1,912 |
| 1990 | – | – | 7,529 | – | – | 1,872 |

Fire deaths

| Year | NYC | Chicago | Toronto | London |
|------|-----|---------|---------|--------|
| 1969 | 307 | – | – | 167 |
| 1970 | 310 | – | – | 142 |
| 1971 | 292 | – | – | 150 |
| 1972 | 270 | – | – | 138 |
| 1973 | 295 | – | – | 139 |
| 1974 | 273 | 208 | – | 180 |
| 1975 | 245 | 178 | – | 177 |
| 1976 | – | 251 | – | 128 |
| 1977 | 290 | 196 | – | 70 |
| 1978 | 272 | 173 | 26 | 129 |
| 1979 | – | 180 | 10 | 151 |
| 1980 | 289 | 185 | 31 | 195 |
| 1981 | 246 | 171 | 16 | 185 |

*Table 7-6* (continued)

| Fire deaths Year | NYC | Chicago | Toronto | London |
|---|---|---|---|---|
| 1982 | 248 | 130 | 19 | 167 |
| 1983 | 228 | 126 | 9 | 163 |
| 1984 | 206 | 147 | 9 | 125 |
| 1985 | 213 | 104 | 15 | 154 |
| 1986 | 206 | 95 | 12 | 142 |
| 1987 | 245 | 77 | 14 | 194 |
| 1988 | 229 | 156 | 24 | 144 |
| 1989 | 246 | 121 | 27 | 133 |
| 1990 | – | 131 | – | – |

*Definitions of fire activity.* Newark: Sum of "signal 11's" (working fires) and multiple alarm fires. New York: Fires in occupied residential buildings. Chicago: Structural fires. Toronto: Residential fires (approximate). London: Total fires. Hamburg: Fires in housing units.

*Sources.* Newark: Newark Fire Department, annual reports. New York: New York Fire Department, annual reports. Chicago: Chicago Fire Department, annual reports, NFIRS Base Report 18, before 1988; after 1988, Michael Cosgrove, Media Affairs/Public Information, Chicago Fire Department, personal communication, Aug. 2, 1991; before 1980, Fire Data Summary 1983. Toronto: Toronto Fire Department, annual reports, 1988, 1989; covers city of Toronto only. London: London Fire Brigade, Fire Facts. Hamburg: Hamburg Fire Department.

Fire data thus support the idea that low-quality housing decreased in the places where homelessness rose, if fire activity is taken to be proportional to the stock of low-quality housing. Alternatively, of course, fire activity could be interpreted as a way of abandoning buildings. Decreased fire activity is then still supportive of the smaller-middle-class explanation, which implies less abandonment, against the more-poor-people explanation, which implies more.

The third way to assess the low-quality housing stock is to look at particular kinds of low quality—for instance, lodginghouses or roominghouses or SROs (single-room occupancies). The drawback to this approach is that the particular variety of housing being studied is only a fraction of the low-quality housing stock, and other parts of this stock might be moving in a different direction. For instance, the decline of SRO might merely be a shift to roominghouses—a technological change to a less labor-intensive mode of production—and the decline of cheap hotels near the waterfront may reflect only a shift to the on-ship housing of sailors.

Invariably, studies that take this approach show a decline, often drastic, in the particular variety of housing. There is evidence of drastic declines in low quality hotels in Newark, cubicle hotels in Chicago, lodginghouses in New York and London, and flophouses in Toronto. In addition, there are studies of SRO in New York and Chicago, but they suffer from some inconsistency in definitions and, more important, a confusion between low-rent and low-quality housing. In all this work, the most serious gap is the neglect of roominghouses.

Newark offers the most complete picture, because of an extraordinary data set compiled by William Jackson, a firefighter who from 1971 to 1991 was responsible for inspecting all the hotels in Newark. He inspected each one every few months and kept records exceeding the statutory requirements. In particular, he kept all hotel-registration records in two shoeboxes, and he let me review them. He remembered every hotel and, for most, what happened to it, and whenever independent verification was available either in fire-response records (dating from November 1, 1977) or tax-assessment records, it confirmed Jackson's memory.

From these sources I was able to piece together a history of "low-quality hotels" in Newark. I excluded the YMWCA, hotels near the airport (block 5000), hotels with restaurants, "hotels that you might recommend to your relatives if they were visiting from out of town," and two hotels that had reputations as bordellos. After these exclusions, there were 2,331 low-quality hotel rooms in Newark in 1971. At the end of 1991, 69 such hotel rooms were left, on the strictest count. A less strict count of the remaining hotel rooms would include the 251 rooms of the Divine Riviera (which under new secular ownership had converted to apartments with only minor physical changes in summer 1991 and which by 1994 were being used primarily to house homeless welfare clients on a voucher basis), and the 100 rooms of the New Tremont, many of which in 1991 were being used by the county welfare division to house homeless families. The more generous count of 420 rooms in 1991 still implies a loss of 1,911 rooms in twenty years. During this period no new low-quality hotels opened, and no higher-quality establishments became dilapidated (although several went out of business).

When and why were these rooms lost? Table 7-7 tries to answer the question. The greatest losses were in the late 1970s and early 1980s; after 1982 there are only trivial losses. This accords in many ways with the picture of New York lodginghouses in Table 7-8. Notice also that the loss of low-quality hotel rooms falls off when Newark fires fall off.

The most important direct causes were fire, subsidized housing, and city foreclosure for back taxes. City foreclosure generally stopped a hotel's operation, since state laws precluded it. Gentrification and urban renewal were of minor importance; even the conversions to private housing were for low-income family housing or roominghouses. Most of the lots where hotels burned are still vacant or are parking lots. Many of the fires were suspected to be arson. Table 7-7 is thus consistent with the idea that low-quality hotels lost profitability in the late seventies and early eighties and went out of business.

It should be noted that 1971, the beginning year for Table 7-7, has some disadvantage as a starting date. Newark's traditional skid row was on Market Street around Penn Station, and most of the area, including the Comet and the Edison, was torn down as part of the Penn Plaza renewal project between 1967 and 1970. The project's relocation plan does not say how many rooms were involved. But this demolition should have increased the profitability of the remaining low-quality hotels in Newark; that they still closed is evidence of very little profitability.

In the other cities, my good information is confined to what might generically be called "flophouses"—hotels with congregate sleeping arrangements. No such hotels were found in Newark after 1971.

In Toronto, flophouses mean roominghouses where several men sleep in the same room. In 1973 there were about 500 flophouse beds in Toronto's skid row. The number of beds fell to about 300 in 1977, and there have been none, according to most observers, since the early 1980s. (Fire department officials claim a few still exist [Collins interview, 1991].)

In New York, flophouses mean lodginghouses: establishments that include a mix of dormitory rooms with 30–50 beds each, 4 by 6 feet with 7-foot walls and fishnet ceilings, and a few small rooms with complete walls. Almost all lodginghouses were on or very

*Table 7-7*  Loss of Low-Quality Hotel Rooms in Newark, 1971–1991, by Immediate Cause

| Year | Fire | Urban renewal | Subsidized housing | Private housing | City | Waterbed | Other | Total lost | Total left |
|---|---|---|---|---|---|---|---|---|---|
| Unknown | – | – | – | 50 | 60 | – | – | 110 | 1,870 |
| 1971 | – | – | – | 80 | – | – | – | 80 | 1,790 |
| 1972 | – | – | – | – | 30 | – | – | 30 | 1,760 |
| 1973 | – | – | – | – | – | – | 31 | 31 | 1,729 |
| 1974 | – | – | – | – | – | – | – | – | 1,729 |
| 1975 | – | – | 192 | – | – | – | 24 | 216 | 1,513 |
| 1976 | – | – | 83 | – | 118 | – | 19 | 220 | 1,293 |
| 1977 | 88 | – | 113 | – | 190 | – | – | 391 | 902 |
| 1978 | – | – | – | – | 14 | – | – | 14 | 888 |
| 1979 | – | 66 | 34 | – | – | – | – | 100 | 788 |
| 1980 | 120 | – | – | – | – | – | – | 120 | 668 |
| 1981 | 136 | – | – | – | – | – | – | 136 | 532 |
| 1982 | 129 | – | – | – | – | – | 24 | 153 | 379 |
| 1983 | 96 | – | 53 | – | – | – | – | 149 | 230 |
| 1984 | – | 50 | – | – | – | – | – | 50 | 180 |
| 1985 | – | 60 | – | – | – | 51 | – | 111 | 69 |
| 1986–91 | – | – | – | – | – | – | – | – | 69 |
| Total | 569 | 176 | 475 | 130 | 412 | 51 | 98 | 1,911 | 69 |

*Source.* See text. In 1985 the Grant Hotel became a waterbed warehouse. The Christine, the Margaret, and the Savoy were taken by the city in 1976, 1977, and 1977 respectively, but burned down in 1980; I count them in earlier years. The starting number of hotel rooms was 1,980.

close to the Bowery, although city records indicate a few located in Brooklyn, Harlem, and Chelsea. The recent history of Bowery lodginghouses is summarized in Table 7-8. From around 11,200 beds in 39 lodginghouses in 1949, the number declined to around 2,400 beds in 11 or 12 lodginghouses in 1992. As in Newark, almost all of the decline appears to have taken place before 1980.

The loss of lodginghouses in New York, however, is not so clean a story of market forces at work as is the decline of low-quality housing in Newark or Toronto. Many lodginghouse guests were ticketmen, and so demand could have been reduced by city policy decisions to give more men welfare or to send them elsewhere. But the decline in lodginghouse beds between 1960 and 1980 is far greater than the decline in the number of ticketmen, and city decisions that started to allow ticketmen to stay in the summer probably helped the profitability of lodginghouses.

In Chicago, cubicle hotels ("cage hotels" they are sometimes called) are like New York's lodginghouses, except that they generally lack dormitory spaces. The number of cubicle rooms has also fallen drastically. In 1958 Bogue (1963), found 8,038 men in cubicle hotels in the Loop area; vacancies were on the order of 20 percent or 30 percent. Dormitory spaces, which existed in Chicago in the 1920s, had disappeared altogether by that time (Hoch and Slayton, 1989). Hoch and Slayton's 1985 survey gave an implicit estimate of about 600 beds left in cubicle hotels, and this figure was probably still approximately right for 1993. As in New York, though, the city used

*Table 7-8*  Bowery Lodginghouses, 1949–1993

| Year | Number | Beds | Occupancy |
|------|--------|------|-----------|
| 1949 | 47 | 11,219 | 11,219 |
| 1964, Feb. | 39 | 9,797 | 5,423 |
| 1965, Feb. | 39 | 9,797 | 6,055 |
| 1978, March | 12 | 3,000 | ? |
| 1984 | 12 | 3,000 | ? |
| 1993, May | 11 | 2,400 | 1,500 |

*Sources.* 1949, 1964: Nash and Nash (1964); includes Salvation Army Hotel. 1965: Baker (1965); increase from 1964 may reflect closing of Men's Shelter and fewer men in jail. 1978: Goodwin (1978); various 1979 newspaper articles say number of flophouse beds recently dropped from 3,000 to 800. 1984: Jim Metsinger, Bowery Residents Committee, cited in Esther B. Fein, "A Symbol of Despair and Signs of Changes," *New York Times,* Oct. 18, 1984, p. B11. 1993: Kadvan (1993); see also Table 10–1.

these hotels for ticketmen, and so the loss gives no clear clues about market forces.

I have already discussed the decline of direct-access hostels and the Rowton Services hostels in London.

Thus in all five cities, the stock of one particular class of low-quality housing has become much smaller. Has any other type of housing taken its place? Almost certainly the number of SRO rooms of relevant quality has not grown in either New York or Chicago. Studies in both cities have shown large declines. Although the studies do not substantiate the big drops they claim, it seems unlikely that any increase occurred in the number of low-quality SRO rooms.[2]

Roominghouses are the other possible type of low-quality housing. Arguably they are the most relevant for the study of homelessness, but they are the least studied and I don't have a consistent time series on them for any city. Their importance arises from three factors. First, they are abundant. In New York in 1987, the HRA found 21,964 roominghouse units, as opposed to 18,720 low-priced hotel units, and 9,656 "Section 248" SROs (the various categories of SROs in New York are outlined in Chapter 10). Second, historically they have been even more abundant in the African-American community. In the 1940s and 1950s lodginghouses in New York and cage hotels in Chicago were largely inhabited by white men. I have never seen details on where extremely poor black men of that time lived, but the sociological literature (for example, Drake, 1962; and Liebow 1967) makes frequent references to rooms and roominghouses, and never discusses lodginghouses. Finally, roominghouses are cheap. The HRA found median monthly rents in 1985 in roominghouses of $193, as opposed to $220 for Section 248 SROs and $294 for hotels. Lodginghouses were charging about $120 a month in 1985, but 10 percent of roominghouses charged under $100.

Even in 1964, roominghouses were as cheap as Bowery lodginghouses. There were seven roominghouses on the Bowery, and Nash and Nash (1964) reported that the modal weekly roominghouse rate, $6.70, was below the modal lodginghouse rate, although it was above the ticket rate of $5.95. Welfare agencies encouraged the use of roominghouses because they had cooking facilities and could cut meal costs in half. Partly as a result, Bowery roominghouses had an occupancy rate of 83 percent in February 1964, while lodginghouses were only 59 percent full. Of course, part of the low price may be because of different guests—roominghouse guests may have been less transient and less disruptive than lodginghouse guests.

I have found very little information about roominghouse stock. Toronto and Newark both require registration of roominghouses, but in neither city is the registration believed to be close to complete. In Toronto, many respected informants said they thought the number of roominghouses had declined since the 1970s but I could find no consistent time series going back that far, even for registered roominghouses. Registered roominghouses fell from about 750 in the early eighties to about 575 in 1991 (Collins and Breeze interviews, 1991).

In Newark, on the other hand, the number of licensed rooming-houses has been increasing since 1980. It is unclear whether this represents increased compliance or growth in the actual number of houses. The former is quite possible because the census 1980 room-inghouse population is much larger than any plausible number of people who could live in the licensed roominghouses.

To summarize the results of studies of particular kinds of low-quality housing: some kinds have decreased drastically in number, generally before 1980 or shortly thereafter, but not all, and for some important kinds we know basically nothing. The indirect arguments from fires and dilapidation seem more compelling.

The loss of low-quality housing is evidence against the more-poor-people explanation. It is evidence in favor of the smaller-middle-class explanation, but only weakly so, because other explanations—higher operating costs and gentrification, for instance—also predict less low-quality housing. The possible loss of poor housing in Toronto, which experienced a very small decrease in its middle-class population, clearly indicates that other forces were at work too.

## Abandonment Quality

Both the smaller-middle-class and the more-poor-people explanations predict that the lowest quality of housing available on the market will decrease. There is no evidence that this happened. In

Toronto, in fact, the lowest quality rose when flophouses disappeared in the early 1980s, but Toronto is not a city where major income-distribution changes occurred. In the U.S. cities there is, if anything, weak evidence of a small rise in abandonment quality—the virtually complete loss of low-quality hotels in Newark and the reduced occupancy rate of lodginghouses in New York (the fewer people you have to share a bathroom and a shower with, the better the quality of your life). Some Bowery lodginghouses now have air conditioners in their windows, and some owners say that if they were not constrained by city regulations they would increase the price and double the size of cubicles.

Of course, an increase in abandonment quality is consistent with the income-distribution explanations of rising homelessness if the homelessness was accompanied by more and better shelters—which it was. Moreover, the transition period under the smaller-middle-class explanation is a time of loose markets when abandonment quality rises. Since, in addition, abandonment quality is difficult to observe, it does not provide good evidence, one way or the other, about income explanations of homelessness.

## Construction and Demolition

The smaller-middle-class explanation predicts less construction and demolition; the more-poor-people explanation predicts more. Demolition activity is great in U.S. cities, and the demolition record supports the smaller middle class against the more poor people. Figure 7-7 shows the time trend in demolition activity in the U.S. cities. In all three cities there was less demolition in the 1980s than in the 1960s or 1970s. (The erratic pattern of demolition in Newark reflects political considerations and the availability of intergovernmental funding.) In Toronto and London, very few units are demolished.

The construction record also supports the smaller-middle-class explanation. Figure 7-8 shows construction trends. In the United States and in London, cyclical peaks in construction are lower in the 1980s than they were in the 1960s and 1970s. London and, to a large extent, Newark data are dominated by public-sector activity, and so might be discounted.

Toronto is somewhat different. First, demolition is always quite small, but shows a rising trend. Second, there seems to be as much construction in the 1980s as there was in the 1970s, if not more. Part of the reason is because the Toronto metro area was growing, unlike the other five cities. The population of the Toronto consolidated metropolitan area grew from 2.8 million in 1986 to 3.4 million in 1986 (Ontario Ministry of Housing, 1991). But given Toronto's different experience with income distribution and homelessness, it should not be surprising that its housing market also behaves differently.

## Individuals with Very Little Income

The number of working-age people in the U.S. household population who are reported to have very low incomes has increased substantially over the last twenty years. Rossi (1989) places substantial emphasis on this as a factor in the rise of homelessness. Jencks (1994) also attributes some of the growth in homelessness to this phenomenon, but doesn't attach that much importance to it. Jencks gives two reasons for his disagreement with Rossi: first, the number of extremely low-income individuals peaked in 1984 and then fell, but homelessness continued to rise; second, homelessness rose more, in percentage terms, than did the number of extremely low-income individuals.

I too believe that this phenomenon may have had some impact on the growth of homelessness in the United States, but I would be even more restrained than Jencks. My first reason for skepticism is that individuals are not the right units to consider when looking either at well-being or at housing demand; the right unit is households. So I use the Blackburn data, which show no great rise in the proportion of severely poor households. Families share resources and buy or rent housing units. The rise in the number of extremely low-income males without a corresponding rise in the number of extremely poor households shows merely that households are getting better at managing without having all their working-age males making money—either, say, because women are working more or parents are becoming more indulgent toward adult children, or

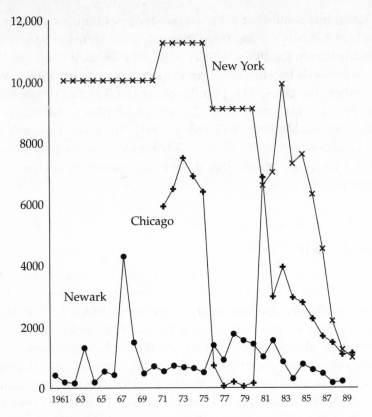

*Figure 7-7a* Demolition series. *Sources:* New York City Council on Economic Education, *1992–93 Fact Book on the New York Metropolitan Region;* City of Chicago, Department of Buildings, special tabulation; Newark: New Jersey Department of Community Affairs, annual building permits.

both. (The growth of the food-stamp program may also play a role here. People with stamps can live in someone's home without imposing a cash drain on their hosts, even if they have no reportable income.)

The second reason for my skepticism is geographical. The number of low-income individuals increased the most in regions where homelessness is least concentrated. Table 7-9 compares the 1989 distribution of low-income unmarried working-age men in the household population with the distribution of "persons visible in street locations"—the census March 1990 street count. (I chose the

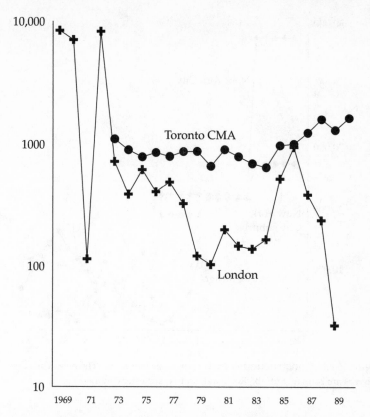

*Figure 7-7b* Demolition series. *Sources:* Toronto Census Metropolitan Area (CMA): Ontario Ministry of Housing, Strategic Planning and Research Branch, "Housing Statistics 1991"; Metro Toronto: Metropolitan Toronto Planning Department, "Housing Trends 1976–86"; London: Department for the Environment, "Housing and Construction Statistics 1969–79" and "Housing and Construction Statistics 1979–89." 1990: London Research Center, "London Housing Statistics 1990."

street count because the shelter count includes varying numbers of children in family shelters, and the census count because its methods were consistent nationwide. Since I was using the census street count, unmarried males seemed to be the best comparison group.) Census streetpeople are concentrated in the Mid-Atlantic and Pacific regions, but low-income unmarried men in the household population are most numerous in the East-North-Central and South Atlantic regions. The regions where the low-income population grew most between 1979 and 1989 were the West-South-Central and

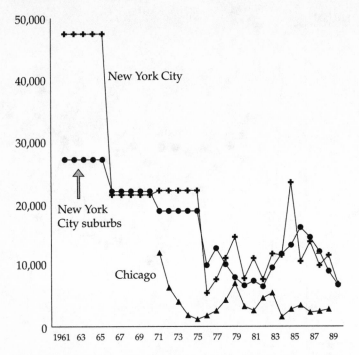

*Figure 7-8a* Construction series. *Source*: See Figure 7-7. The New York City suburbs are Nassau, Suffolk, Rockland, and Westchester counties.

the East-North-Central regions. (Since Rossi did most of his research on Chicago, which is in the East-North-Central region, his emphasis on the growth in number of low-income individuals should not be surprising.)

The ratio between the street count and the low-income male population shows this discrepancy more clearly. In most of the country, there were between 5 and 8 streetpeople for every 1,000 low-income men in the household population, but in the Mid-Atlantic region there were 37 street people for every 1,000 low-income men, and in the Pacific region there were 53 streetpeople for every 1,000. (These are ratios, not probabilities, because only conventionally housed people are included in the household population.)

The six regions with below-average ratios accounted for 64 percent of the 1989 low-income male household population, and 69 percent of the growth between 1979 and 1989. If the three regions with above-average ratios—Mid-Atlantic, Mountain, and Pacific—had the aver-

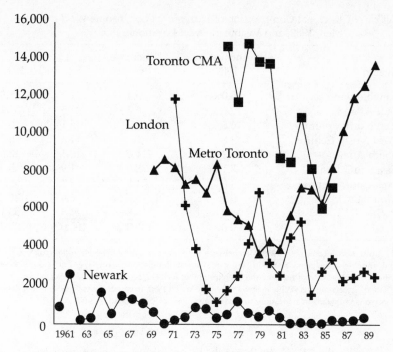

*Figure 7-8b* Construction series. *Sources*: See Figure 7-7.

age ratio of the other six—7.8 per 1,000—the census street count would have been 19,000 instead of 50,000. In other words, whatever it is that made the ratio higher in these three regions is responsible for 62 percent of the census street count. As we will see again and again in this book, it is not the size of the population at risk that matters most and varies most, but the proportion that is homeless.

My last reason for skepticism has to do with changes and errors in measurement. Part of the growth in the low-income household population is merely a change in definition: residents of rooming-houses with between six and ten rooms were not included in the household population in 1979, but were included in 1989 (in 1979 they were considered residents of group quarters). This change, though, probably accounts for less than a tenth of the growth.

More serious are the problems of reporting and finding people. Too many people can end up in this category if they make mistakes in reporting, if they deliberately hide income (maybe because the

*Table 7-9*  Regional Composition of Extremely Low-Income Working-Age Men, 1989, and Visible in Street Locations, 1990

| Region | Low-income men, 1989 | Increase, 1979–89 | Street | Ratio |
|---|---|---|---|---|
| New England | 5.0% | 5.4% | 1.9% | 7.8 |
| Mid-Atlantic | 15.1 | 6.7 | 27.5 | 37.1 |
| East North Central | 16.8 | 18.2 | 5.1 | 6.1 |
| West North Central | 4.8 | 1.4 | 1.6 | 6.7 |
| South Atlantic | 16.3 | 14.0 | 10.1 | 12.6 |
| East South Central | 7.1 | 8.0 | 1.9 | 5.3 |
| West South Central | 14.0 | 21.8 | 4.1 | 5.9 |
| Mountain | 5.1 | 6.7 | 6.6 | 26.2 |
| Pacific | 15.8 | 17.8 | 41.3 | 53.1 |
| Total | 100.0% | 100.0% | 100.0% | 20.3 |

*Sources.* Low-income men, 1989: Men between the ages of 20 and 64 in household population with annual income below $2,500 in 1989; from Current Population Survey tapes. Increase, 1979–89: Difference between latter number and similar number for 1979, but with income corrected for inflation. Street: Persons visible in street locations, March 1990, from U.S. Census, 1992. Ratio: Ratio of persons visible in street locations to low-income men in 1989, divided by 1,000.

source is illegal), if the household members who answer the questions for them don't know what their income is (the interviewers ask one member of the household to report for everybody), or if they work in a family business where the dollars are pooled without any formal accounting of what's whose. Too few can end up here if enumerators miss people (the poorest people have a high probability of being missed), or if family members cover up for people in trouble out of shame. So few people are in this category to begin with that trivial errors for larger groups can seem gigantic here.

The degree of confidence we should have in the accuracy of these numbers, and in particular the accuracy of reported changes, is very low. Since we don't know, for instance, whether the number of people relying on illegal income or the underground economy has been rising, we should be reluctant to base important conclusions on such data.

# 8

## Interest Rates and Operating Costs

In Chapter 6 we saw that higher interest rates and operating costs can also make homelessness rise, although the theoretical implications of higher rates are somewhat ambiguous. In this chapter I want to examine whether changes in these variables contributed to homelessness. The most popular explanation is gentrification, which is a species of rising operating costs.

### Higher Real Interest Rates

Finding out how interest rates changed is not as simple as it sounds. In the simplified discussions of Chapter 6, where inflation was not considered, the role of the interest rate was to weight the value of money at various times so that profit-maximizing housing providers could decide whether to invest their money in houses or to put it in the bank. With inflation, bank accounts pay and hold dollars that are steadily losing value. To account for this loss in the value of dollars, you have to subtract the rate of inflation from the rate of interest actually paid to get the "real interest rate." The real rate is what matters for decisionmaking over time, not the rate actually paid.

Since investment is a forward-looking decision, the ideal way to calculate the real interest rate is to subtract the inflation rate that people anticipate. The ideal way is impossible: economists can't read minds to find out what people expect, and even if they could, they would find that anticipations differ and rarely can be summarized by a single number. The crude method I use to estimate real interest rates is far from ideal. In each year for each country I simply subtracted the contemporaneous inflation rate from the long-term interest rate (long-term is appropriate because housing is a relatively long-lived investment). The results are presented in Figure 8-1.

Real interest rates move in much the same fashion in all four countries. This is not unexpected: enough capital can move fast enough in world financial markets that British real interest rates, for instance, could not long stay far above or far below German rates. Rates in most of the eighties were higher than they were in most of the seventies, and the big increase took place around 1982.

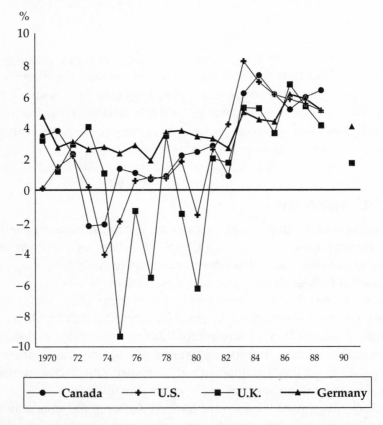

*Figure 8-1* Estimated real long-term interest rates. *Source*: OECD Department of Economics and Statistics, "Main Economic Indicators: Historical Statistics 1969–1988" (Paris, 1990).

It is hard, then, to believe that real interest rates were the major force behind the rise in U.S. homelessness. If they were, homelessness would move in the same direction everywhere, since real interest rates move in the same direction everywhere. But homelessness is frequently going up in one city as it goes down in another. In particular, homelessness was falling in Hamburg and possibly also in London in the early 1980s, when real interest rates were rising.

Even for the United States, moreover, the rise in real interest rates happened too late to have caused the first increases in North American homelessness. Single homelessness, I have argued, started rising in New York around 1978, when U.S. real interest rates were well below historical levels, and probably started rising in the other North American cities in 1980 and 1981. But even the crude calculations of Fig. 8-1 show real interest rates below historical levels until 1982. More sophisticated calculations of real interest rates could only make their rise appear later, and the mechanism by which interest rates influence homelessness implies some additional lags as well.

High real interest rates may have contributed later to the sharp rise of North American homelessness, but they could not have been a definitive factor.

## Higher Operating Costs

There is no evidence of any major increase in operating costs around the time that homelessness began to rise in the United States, although data on operating costs are meager.

My best data are for New York. Figure 8-2 shows an index for real operating costs for rent-stabilized apartment buildings; it was computed by dividing a price index prepared for the Rent Guidelines Board by the New York metropolitan-area consumer price index (CPI-U). Operating costs rose substantially with the first world oil crisis, and have gradually and erratically drifted up since then. Because the weightings used in this (politically very delicate) index may not reflect the shares of actual expenditure for the low-quality buildings we are most interested in, small changes should not be considered important.[1]

No substantial rise in operating costs seems to have taken place when homelessness rose in New York City. This has been confirmed

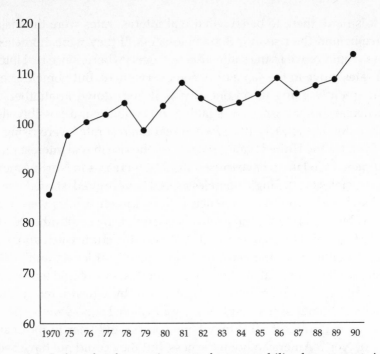

*Figure 8-2* Index of real operating costs for rent-stabilized apartments in New York. *Sources: 1970–1987: Urban Systems Research and Engineering, "1987 Price Index of Operating Costs for Rent Stabilized Apartment Houses in New York City," May 1987 (prepared for Rent Guidelines Board, New York City). 1967 weights are used before 1982, 1982 weights thereafter. Raw price index divided by NY area CPI-U. After 1987: New York City Council on Economic Education, 1992–93 Fact Book on the New York Metropolitan Region.*

in discussions with landlords and landlord representatives in the New York area. In particular, lodginghouse owners recall no major increases in operating costs in the late 1970s and early 1980s. (Insurance costs, they say, rose drastically and now constitute 10–15 percent of operating costs, but the rise occurred in the mid-eighties.)

For the other cities I have no comparable indices, but many components of operating cost are nationally or internationally tradable (such as fuel and insurance) while other components (such as labor) are unlikely to diverge substantially in the short run from the area consumer price index. Probably the most important city-specific component is the property tax. Taxes constitute 18.4 percent of the New York City index, but for low-quality properties a weighting between 20 and 40 percent would be more appropriate.

Because Newark properties have not been reassessed since 1958 and because Newark's property tax system is unitary, the time series of property taxes due from any property is simply the time series of the official tax rate. Figure 8-3 shows that time series: it is downward to the mid-eighties, and then gently upward, with some jumps upward in the early nineties. In Newark, then, homelessness also probably grew at a time of decreasing or steady operating costs.

Chicago properties are reassessed every four years on a rolling cycle. The property tax rate therefore underestimates the increase in a property's taxes over a long period (although usually—75 percent of the time—not over a short period). Because new properties are

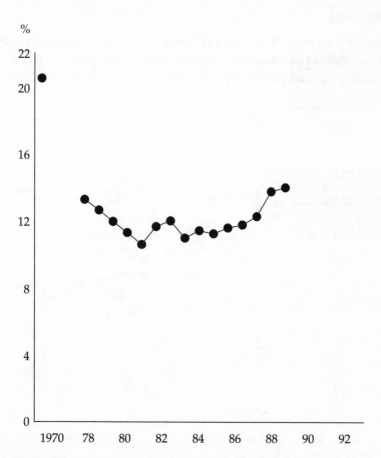

*Figure 8-3* Real property taxes in Newark (nominal property tax rate in 1982–1984 dollars). *Source:* Newark Fair Taxation Committee records.

added to the tax rolls, and because some properties may be appreciating faster than the low-quality properties we are interested in, the change in the property-tax extension (the total amount of taxes levied) probably overstates the increase for individual properties (especially in the short run between reassessments). Therefore in Figure 8-4 I present both the real tax rate time series and the real extension time series. It is clear that real property taxes were falling until 1985; this may have contributed a little to the slowness of the growth of homelessness in the early eighties. After 1985 the trend is ambiguous.

## Gentrification

The data on taxes, fuel, and maintenance miss one important piece of the cost of operating housing: the opportunity cost of land. Gentrification is one reason why the price and hence the opportunity

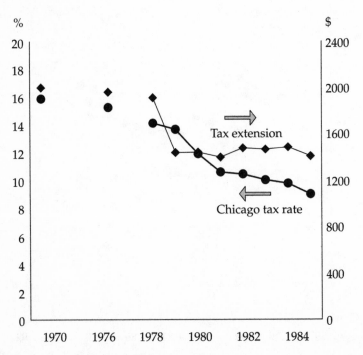

*Figure 8-4* Real property taxes in Chicago. *Source*: Civic Federation, "Chicagoland: A Fiscal Perspective," May 1987 and June 1991.

cost of urban land might have been rising in the 1980s: if wealthier people begin to find living in Cabbagetown or the Lower East Side more attractive, they will bid up the price of land, and so the operating cost of a tenement or a lodginghouse there will increase, since every day you operate the tenement you forgo the interest you could have earned if you had sold the place and put the money in the bank.

Rodda (1992) presents some evidence from a cross-section of U.S. cities that land market forces may have been pushing up rents paid by poor people in the 1980s, and Fallis (1990) puts gentrification at the center of his explanation of why homelessness rose in Toronto.[2] Nor are yuppies necessary for an explanation of this kind: office buildings or immigrants would work just as well at pushing up the price of land.

Anecdotes about gentrification abound. Some former lodginghouses along the Bowery are now artists' lofts, and the southern Bowery is now almost totally engulfed in Chinatown. In Chicago, the main skid row of 1960, along Madison Street, is now office towers, while the Near North Side, where many SROs used to be located, has gentrified, and Uptown, another community that used to include many SROs, has burgeoning Southeast Asian and Chinese populations. In Newark too, the main skid row of 1960, along Market and Mulberry Streets, is now office buildings. Toronto has seen massive gentrification, probably more than any of the other cities, particularly in Cabbagetown, a neighborhood adjacent to the traditional skid row.

Anecdotes of this kind, however, demonstrate only the obvious truth that if less land is used for low-quality housing, and the surface of the earth does not shrink or the oceans expand, more land must be used for something else. In New York, Wall Street now stands where a stockade used to protect New Amsterdam from Indian attack once stood, but that does not mean that the stock market is the reason why New York City no longer builds stockades to protect against Indian attack.

Nor would showing rising land prices in these particular neighborhoods be sufficient by itself to demonstrate gentrification (although it probably is necessary). Activities relocate all the time. The demolition of Ebbets Field and the Polo Grounds did not put an end to major-league baseball; it did not even end the National League presence in New York City. If land prices were going up on the Bowery but down in the South Bronx, low-quality housing could relocate to the Bronx, and operating costs—those that mattered—would go down.

On the other hand, not every neighborhood in New York is a perfect substitute for the Bowery; nor is every neighborhood in Chicago a perfect substitute for Madison Street. Traditional skid rows were located close to the dishwashing jobs of downtown hotels and restaurants (the restaurant-supply business is the other traditional enterprise on the Bowery) and loading and unloading jobs at railroads; they were not located on the cheapest land in the city. But being close to these specific jobs is much less important for today's homeless people than it was for the residents of cage hotels and lodginghouses in the fifties (panhandlers and squeegee men who need to be close to heavy concentrations of pedestrians and stopped automobiles, respectively, are something of an exception, but their numbers appear to be relatively small). Jobs, moreover, have also relocated since the fifties.

So it is hard to believe that land prices in the neighborhoods where derelicts lived forty years ago have any peculiar relevance to homelessness today, any more than the current prices of 1950s baseball cards, collectors' items, have any peculiar relevance to kids who trade baseball cards today. South Bronx land prices are the relevant ones for thinking about homelessness today, not Bowery land prices.

Some facts to support this argument come from a study of families in New York City shelters. In 1986, the HRA looked at the most recent nonshelter addresses and the most recent permanent addresses for a sample of families in its shelters. The distribution of addresses was almost the same as the distribution of all public-assistance families. Most came from the South Bronx and North Brooklyn—areas that were most emphatically not undergoing gentrification.

Land prices are notoriously difficult to observe, particularly in built-up neighborhoods where land is rarely sold on its own, apart from the structures it supports, and so I have no direct knowledge of land prices in the poor neighborhoods that matter most. But recall why land prices rise in accounts of gentrification: because other people (yuppies, immigrants, office buildings) are willing to pay more for the land in order to put it to some other use in which it would earn more (implicitly or explicitly) than it is earning now. For this to work, then, we would have to see new gentrified land uses in these neighborhoods. In the United States—in North Brooklyn, South Bronx, central Newark, Chicago's west side—we don't. We see vacant lots.

The data on low-quality hotels in Newark reinforce this picture. About the closest you get to gentrification is the Hotel Grant, which became a waterbed warehouse. (Borok's, the furniture store next door to the Grant, was as much concerned about a fire in the Grant as it was with expanding its warehouse.) Vacant lots, not condominiums, are the chief "reuse" of the land on which low-quality hotels once stood.

Moreover, even if the price of land did rise in the relevant neighborhoods, the increase would have to be very large to affect operating costs. Take Thomas and Wright's (1990) data on several Chicago south Loop SROs in 1988 as an example. Property taxes were about a quarter of operating costs. The property tax rate for SROs in 1988 was 6.3 percent of value, and assessments were reasonably current. Usually land represents about 10–20 percent of the value of housing (Mills and Hamilton, 1994). Thus land value was around 60 percent of reported operating cost, and if the rate of return was 10 percent, the annual operating cost of land would be around 6 percent of reported operating cost, or 5.7 percent of true operating cost, which is reported operating cost plus the opportunity cost of land. (Chicago property tax data are from an unpublished lakefront SRO study.) So even a doubling of land values would increase operating costs by 5.7 percent; a 20 percent rise in land values would cause only a 1.1 percent rise in operating costs.

A final reason to be skeptical about gentrification lies in some very rough intercity comparisons. Of the six cities, Toronto has the most visible evidence of widespread gentrification and the least homelessness; Newark has the least visible evidence of gentrification and the most homelessness. Even if gentrification were working to increase homelessness, it could not have been very powerful. As a plausible explanation, gentrification is weak.

# 9

# Cross-Section Studies

In the last two chapters I tested the implications of various stories about why homelessness rose against evidence gathered from only five or six cities, sometimes only three. This is a very small sample. A little evidence is better than none, but it would still be better to use information for more cities.

At least five studies have tried to do this: Tucker (1987a, 1987b), Quigley (1990), Elliot and Krivo (1991), Burt (1992), and Honig and Filer (1993). These studies all dealt with large numbers of U.S. cities. They obtained numbers that purported to represent the rate of homelessness in each city, and then used statistical techniques (various types of regressions) to see how the rates of homelessness varied with other characteristics of the cities. For instance, most of the studies tried to find out whether cities with higher rents had higher rates of homelessness, holding other things constant.

Two chief results stand out because the studies all agree on them. The first is that poverty has no discernible effect on the rate of homelessness, everything else being equal. More specifically, the poverty effect was always "statistically insignificant": perhaps poverty was doing something, but the sample was so small and the effect so weak that the statistical tools were not sharp enough to find anything. This result casts more doubt on the more-poor-people explanation.

The second point on which the studies agree is that higher rents are associated with homelessness, everything else being equal. None of the studies asks what high rents are associated with, and so this finding is compatible with a number of different explanations of rising homelessness: smaller middle class, higher interest rates, and gentrification. For most ways of measuring average rents, this finding is probably, though not necessarily, incompatible with a more-poor-people explanation (more poor people implies more low-quality houses, but they are more expensive; it implies more moderate-quality houses, but they are cheaper).

Thus the cross-section results, as far as they go, are similar to the findings of the last two chapters. But don't place too much confidence in the cross-section results: the data used are of very poor quality.

## Rates of Homelessness

The major problem for all the studies is the variable they try to explain, the rate of homelessness. I argued in Chapter 2 that looking for a single rate of homelessness is a hopeless exercise, and the difficulties these studies have in finding that rate illustrate again the problems I pointed out there.

Four studies—all except Burt—use the Department of Housing and Urban Development's 1984 survey results (Tucker added 15 cities on his own with ad hoc methodology). HUD selected a stratified random sample of 60 metropolitan areas and asked experts in each metropolitan area to estimate the number of "homeless people." In usual governmental fashion, HUD defined a homeless person as someone "who at night resides in an emergency shelter or public or private space not designated for shelter." For each metropolitan area, it averaged the estimates.

The U.S. General Accounting Office (1988), in its evaluation of studies of homelessness, found the HUD study to be of "low" quality, next to the bottom category in its survey of estimates (p. 16). GAO argued:

> [Another] major weakness in expert estimate studies of the homeless is subjectivity. Subjective estimates of any phenomenon are suscepti-
> ble to at least two sources of bias. First, experts might have vested

interests in overestimating or underestimating the size of the population, especially if funding or accountability is involved. Second, some experts, such as persons on the front line of service delivery to the homeless, are likely to overestimate the magnitude of the problem, since demand is likely to exceed supply for "free" resources.

A second weakness is that informants may not be clear on what geographic area they are assessing or rating. If, for example, informants are asked to estimate the number of homeless persons in a city and the term "city" is not explicitly defined, estimates might be made for the metropolitan area, the downtown area, or the region bounded by the city limits. An instance of this ambiguity was found in the HUD study. (pp. 19–20)

Even apart from geography, the quantity that experts were asked to estimate was ambiguous because "shelters" is ambiguous. In 1984, moreover, the housing-market orientation of homelessness was considerably weaker among experts than it is today; Freeman and Hall (1987), for instance, use essentially the colloquial definition. So it is also unclear whether, despite HUD's instructions, the experts were reporting on housing-market or colloquial homelessness. Finally, even if the experts somehow understood and followed HUD's instructions completely, the resulting sum of street and shelter popuations is of almost no theoretical interest.

A final difficulty in the use of HUD data is the question of the denominator, since most studies seek to explain per capita homelessness, not total homelessness. Recall that HUD asked experts to estimate homeless populations for Rand-McNally metropolitan areas, not census metropolitan areas. The differences between the two are in many cases significant—for instance, the San Francisco Rand-McNally area is about three times as populous as the census area, while the Detroit Rand-McNally area is slightly smaller than the census area. This problem introduces an unknown bias into the dependent variable when researchers use census area populations to compute homelessness rates (as Honig and Filer did), and introduces other biases when researchers use independent variables for census metropolitan areas. (I am indebted to Kim Hopper for this observation; a more detailed discussion can be found in Hopper, 1987.)

Martha Burt's dependent variable is shelter capacity, not any particular variety of homelessness. (Shelter capacity includes the actual use of commercial facilities.) The obvious problem with this approach, which she acknowledges, is that shelter capacity is a measure proximately of public and private generosity, not of any housing-market condition. Quite apart from housing conditions, for instance, wealthier cities should provide more shelter, since charity is a normal good, and so should cities with more valuable real estate, since removing homeless people from such real estate yields a higher return, and cities where public generosity plays a more important cultural role.

The other serious problem with Burt's data is that "shelter" is an incredibly vague term. Burt did her study in late 1989 and the census was taken in March 1990; if everyone understood the word in the same way, the numbers in Burt's study and the census shelter count should be about the same. They are grotesquely different. Tables 9-1 and 9-2 give some examples of the differences. When applied to homelessness rates for all 177 cities for which both the Burt and census data are available, statistical measures of similarity show little similarity. You would not expect the two sets of numbers to be the same: Burt measured capacity while the census measured occupancy, the census included some cheap hotels, some time passed between the studies, and the weather changed. But the discrepancies seem too large to be explained by these details. The almost inescapable conclusion is that Burt considered some places to be shelters that the census did not, and vice versa. Who was right? Neither used or tried to justify a definition of "shelter." It is not clear what either actually counted.

What are the implications of all these problems for compiling rates of homelessness? For the HUD data, because we haven't found any explicit biases—only reasons to doubt accuracy—the major implication is that very little confidence should be placed in these

*Table 9-1* Comparison of Burt Data with U.S. Census

| City | Burt 1989 shelter capacity | Census 1990 shelter population |
|------|---------------------------|-------------------------------|
| Newark | 462 | 1,974 |
| New York | 29,500 | 23,383 |
| Chicago | 3,040 | 5,180 |

*Source.* Burt (1992), app. A; Census (1991).

*Table 9-2*   Six Highest Homeless Rates (per 10,000 population)

| HUD 1984 | | Burt 1989 | | Census shelter | |
|---|---|---|---|---|---|
| 1. San Francisco | 53.51 | 1. Atlanta | 65.44 | 1. New Haven | 109.3 |
| 2. Los Angeles | 41.20 | 2. Washington | 56.89 | 2. Washington | 74.8 |
| 3. Miami | 34.88 | 3. Boston | 46.69 | 3. Newark | 62.5 |
| 4. New York | 34.62 | 4. Eugene | 46.67 | 4. San Bernardino | 59.6 |
| 5. Chicago | 32.39 | 5. Reno | 43.10 | 5. Atlanta | 57.6 |
| 6. Worcester | 25.99 | 6. New York | 40.62 | 6. San Francisco | 53.4 |

*Sources.* HUD 1984: Honig and Filer, table 1, for 51 cities; rates for SMSAs. Census shelter: Census (1991), divided by Burt's population estimates.

studies. I give no particular reasons why implications drawn from the HUD data should be wrong, but there is little reason to suspect that they might be right.

The Burt data have all of the problems of the HUD data, and one much more severe one. Some of the errors in the Burt data are systematically related to some of the variables Burt uses to explain rates of homelessness. In particular, to the extent that wealthier cities are more generous in establishing shelters than less favored cities are, variables like average income and lack of poverty will appear to be causing homelessness, when in fact they are only causing shelters to be established.

## Explanatory Variables

Most of the studies—Burt once again excepted—also have a problem with the dating of the variables that are supposed to explain homelessness. HUD homeless estimates are for the winter of 1983–84, but many of the independent variables are for 1980. Homelessness grew substantially between 1980 and 1984 in many U.S. cities, and explaining this growth is the primary goal of current discussions of homelessness. Something that changed between 1980 and 1984 explains the growth, and looking at 1980 explanatory variables will not identify what that something is.

A specific problem with the Elliott-Krivo and Filer-Honig studies is their use of data on state and county mental hospitals to represent the entire mental-health system. Even though trends in the population of these hospitals have received a great deal of attention, they represent only a minor part of the institutionalized mentally ill population in this country. In addition, a significant portion of their 1980 population was elderly. (This issue is discussed in more detail in Chapter 12.)

## Results

As far as the individual studies go, William Tucker makes some serious methodological mistakes, and so his results need not be considered. John Quigley's is the first reasonably sophisticated study, but is devoted primarily to showing that Tucker's data do not support his claim that rent control is the primary cause of homelessness. Quigley finds that homelessness is higher in cities with higher temperatures, slower growth, higher average rents, and lower vacancy rates. Holding these other variables constant, poverty does not have a discernible effect on homelessness.

Burt, in a much more elaborate analysis, also finds that higher average rents are associated with greater homelessness and that poverty rates have no discernible effects. She finds too that more homelessness is associated with greater unemployment, more retail employment, more single-person households, the absence of a general-assistance program, and higher general-assistance benefits. The last is one of a number of anomalous results in Burt's analysis that may stem from her peculiar measure of homelessness.

The results of Marta Elliott and Lauren Krivo are largely similar. Once again poverty rates have no discernible effects on homelessness, and once again high rents—this time, the proportion of units renting for more than $150—are associated with greater homelessness. Unlike Burt, Elliott and Krivo find that unemployment is insignificant, but that expenditures on state and county mental hospitals decrease homelessness. It is fairly easy to reconcile these findings. On unemployment, Elliott and Krivo use 1979 unemployment rates to explain 1984 homelessness; Burt uses 1989 unemployment for 1989 homelessness. On mental health, Elliott and Krivo use HUD's estimates, Burt uses objective data. The mentally ill, especially among daytime streetpeople, are often particularly memorable, and researchers thinking about the colloquial definition of homelessness may be strongly influenced by seeing them on the streets.

Marjorie Honig and Randall Filer also used HUD data, and more sophisticated statistical methods than the other studies. They found homelessness positively related to the size of the reduction in AFDC benefits that is triggered by moving in with nonpoor parents, to the African-American proportion of the population, and to absolute population size. Homelessness was negatively related to vacancy rates for low-rent apartments, maximum AFDC benefits, the fraction of births to teenagers, and mental-hospital inpatients per 100,000 population. An anomalous result was that higher SSI benefits were associated with higher homelessness. Filer-Honig was like the other studies in finding higher rents significantly associated with greater homelessness—the variable they used was rents at the tenth percentile of all apartments—and in finding no discernible relation to poverty.

The mental-hospital result is somewhat surprising, given the poor quality of the institutionalization data, but it may well be an artifact of the HUD data, like the Elliott-Krivo result.

In summary, U.S. cross-section studies associate homelessness with changes in the housing market, particularly the decreased availability of low-rent housing, and not with increasing poverty. They don't try to explain the decrease in quantity of low-rent housing.

# 10

# Government and Housing

Among the most popular theories about the rise of the new homelessness in the United States are those that blame the government.
Right-wing theorists say that regulation and rent control are the
culprits; left-wing theorists blame cutbacks in federal housing programs. Neither claim is particularly persuasive, and so I will also
look at some government activities that I think do matter—the European housing-benefit programs and U.S. tenant-rights legislation.

## Regulation

Municipal housing regulation is frequently cited as a cause of homelessness (see, for instance, Honig and Filer, 1990; Filer, 1992; Husock,
1990). The evidence usually used to back up this assertion is the
presence of a complex system of regulations and the absence from
the conventional market of some of the lowest qualities of housing.
Since we have seen that, in an equilibrium without any regulation
at all, some housing qualities may still be absent from the market,
this claim is hard to evaluate. What makes the claim hardest to
evaluate is its lack of specificity: Which regulations matter? Which
cities have them? When were they implemented?

In some ways it might be tempting to dismiss the claim altogether.
Some shantytowns in Manhattan have existed for many years and
show every sign of continuing. They even include rental property,

at rents considerably below flophouse prices (Dordick, 1994). As long as they don't cause trouble, the city leaves them alone (the shantytowns in Tompkins Square Park and Alphabet City that were torn down in 1991 and the shantytown by the Manhattan Bridge torn down in 1993—after standing for a decade—were sources of considerable trouble for the police). One can argue, then, that housing regulations in New York are totally ineffective—as long as you don't cause trouble, you can live in any sort of accommodation, including a cardboard box. Yet New York still includes many homeless, shanty-less people. So how can unenforced regulations cause homelessness?

Ineffective housing regulation is a wrong argument, however. The reason is subtle. Housing regulation in New York has not prevented the construction of shanties, but it has confined their construction to the most primitive technology. City officials won't let you get away with using skilled carpenters, modern equipment, or mass-production techniques to build a shanty. To the extent that city regulations have prevented the lowest-cost techniques from being used to build shanties, they have inflated the cost of shanties and kept people in places like the Port Authority terminal.

Thus the cost of regulation is the difference between the cost of shanty building with the technology that homeless people use and the cost with the best techniques. It is not clear that this difference is positive, or that it is very large if it is positive. The private cost of construction by homeless people is very much less than social cost—they don't pay land rent, for instance—and labor is cheap. Only if the private cost of construction by homeless techniques is much higher than social cost with the best techniques can we say that housing regulation seriously discourages shanty building. I don't know whether it does or not.

Discouraging shanties is not the only way that municipal regulation can affect homelessness. In terms of my categories (Chapter 6), this sort of regulatory function would be setting the minimum quantity that can be constructed conventionally. Another way that regulation can work is to increase an owner's operating costs. For instance, fines for violations that never get corrected are really just increases in operating costs, and so are requirements that smoke detectors be kept in working order and that means of egress be kept clear. With regulations that increase operating costs, though, we have to be careful to remember that what matters is not the out-of-pocket cost of complying with the regulation, but the increase in the minimum cost of providing a given quality of housing. The cost of smoke detectors, for instance, is partially offset by reduced insurance premiums (or fire liability, if the owner is uninsured).

In dealing with regulations, moreover, we should also bear in mind that not all of them exist for totally pernicious reasons (although some do exist for at least partially pernicious reasons). One of the main nonpernicious reasons for regulation is the control of what economists call "externalities"—costs or benefits that someone imposes on someone else without the intermediation of a market. Requiring indoor plumbing, for instance, is costly, but has obvious public health benefits. The regulation of minimum floor space, window size, and ventilation was originally designed in the late nineteenth century to stem the spread of tuberculosis. (Relaxing these requirements in the last decade in homeless shelters may have contributed to TB's resurgence.) Fire codes reduce the resources that the rest of the public has to allot to firefighting to achieve a given level of protection. Even zoning requirements that keep SROS or flophouses or shelters out of single-family neighborhoods are motivated in part by the legitimate fears of homeowners about rowdy and criminal behavior near their houses. Solving the homeless problem by removing these regulations solves nothing; it merely shifts costs to another group of people. Only detailed analysis of specific regulations can determine whether the shifts would be beneficial.

Another nonpernicious reason for regulation is to correct for informational deficiencies. Prospective tenants cannot easily judge the structural integrity of an apartment building or how well it will resist fire, and so regulations and inspectors give consumers some sort of guarantee about matters that would be inordinately difficult for them to observe otherwise. Colwell and Kau (1982) and Colwell and Yavas (1992) have argued that these guarantees could be more efficiently provided by private-market mechanisms. If this claim is correct, then the removal of these codes would have only small effects on the cost of housing—the bargains would still have to be struck, but they would be struck in a more efficient way. If this claim is wrong, then removal of the codes would be detrimental.

A final nonpernicious reason for codes is to offset a bias toward undermaintenance, especially in low-quality housing, and to protect a municipality's implicit equity interest in properties that may be taken for unpaid property taxes. Owners who might forfeit a property sometime in the future will not maintain it at a socially optimal level because its value to them when the city acquires it depends only on the amount of back taxes due, not on what someone would be willing to pay for it.

Any analysis of the effect of regulation on homelessness, then, has to look at specific effects of specific regulations, not just at "regulation" as a single entity. Unfortunately, this is difficult. Regulations for even the most primitive city fill hundreds of pages and deal with such arcane questions as the water pressure in a sprinkler system, the dimensions of J-curves under sinks, and the procedure for counting the number of floors in a building with a sloped roof. Reading the regulations alone is not sufficient: the extent of enforcement also matters. Municipal codes often contain sections that no one knows about, bothers to enforce, or thinks are enforceable; and there are almost always internal contradictions within the code. Finally, for people contemplating capital investments, future regulations matter more than current ones, and so a complete study of the effect on homelessness would also have to account for expectations.

In thinking about codes, one more distinction is important. *Grandfathered* regulations require that only new capital be constructed to new standards; existing capital is exempt. On the other hand, *retrofit* regulations apply to old and new capital equally; they require that old capital be brought up to new standards fairly quickly. In the field of housing regulation, grandfathered regulations are common, especially in the building and zoning codes. The rationale for grandfathered regulations is that housing has a putty-clay technology; installing a certain type of electrical wiring when a building is being built, for instance, is much cheaper than replacing the wiring in a finished building (see Portney, 1990).

These two types of regulation have different economic effects. New binding retrofit regulations decrease the profitability of existing housing, but new binding grandfathered regulations increase profitability. Owners of existing housing are better off because they have something valuable—an exemption from regulation—that is no longer being made (see Maloney and McCormick, 1982; Buchanan and Tullock, 1975). Accordingly, people who anticipate the future tightening of grandfathered regulations are more likely to invest now; people who anticipate the future tightening of retrofit regulations are less likely to invest now. We can also tell whether grandfathered regulations are binding by looking at whether owners of existing capital are earning abnormal profits.

Grandfathered regulations also affect how time-series evidence should be interpreted. They introduce important elements of hysteresis. When demand is low, owners will keep existing capital operating, even at a loss, because of its option value—if demand rises, the regulation exemption attached to the capital will become valuable. When demand is high, expansion will be limited. The effect of new grandfathered regulations, then, will often be seen not when they are implemented, but the next time that high demand follows a period of low demand.

I turn now to actual code regulations in the English-speaking cities.

## New York

New profitmaking low-quality housing has been illegal in New York for over thirty years. This applies to conversion as well as new construction.

Several different provisions apply to different kinds of low-quality housing. The most important is section 27-2077 of the Housing Maintenance Code. Adopted in 1955 "to stem the subdividing and conversion of apartments . . . that had taken place on a large scale during the postwar period," this section bans conversion of any unit to rooming units. "Rooming units" include SROs, roominghouses, boardinghouses, and lodginghouses. By various quirks of definition, conversion includes construction.

Section 27-2077 was amended in 1985 to exempt nonprofits, governments, and even profitmaking firms in alliance with nonprofits, provided they had government backing, but several other code provisions also make it essentially impossible to develop low-quality housing. For instance, zoning room counts are a substantial impediment to converting buildings to "class A SROs" and rooming-houses. Class A SROs (sometimes called "section 248" SROs) are structures where people live independently in single rooms of a converted apartment, and share access to the apartment's cooking and sanitary facilities. The zoning code sets a maximum number of rooms for each particular lot (depending on the lot size and the zoning district), and conversions must respect that maximum.

Suppose someone wants to convert a regular apartment building to an SRO or a roominghouse. Conversion will increase the *zoning* room count, even if the actual number of rooms stays the same. That is because since 1961 the zoning code has counted each rooming unit as two zoning rooms instead of one. "If 3 rooms in a 2-bedroom apartment were converted to rooming units, the total number of zoning rooms would jump from 4.5 to 6" (Mayor's Office, n.d., p. 5). This increase in zoning rooms is likely to be unallowable. In 1961 the zoning code was amended to reduce the number of permitted rooms in most places, but existing buildings were grandfathered. Thus the room-count constraint is likely to be binding. The 1961 zoning amendments were designed explicitly "to encourage developers to build larger apartments for families . . . to discourage subdividing apartments and buildings into small units . . . [and] to slowly decrease the population density in many already built-up areas."

Since lodginghouses are considered commercial rather than residential, room-count requirements don't apply. But the zoning code forbids them in all residential areas. Class A SROs and rooming-houses, by contrast, are permitted in some residential areas and in almost all the commercial areas that permit lodginghouses; lodginghouses are also permitted in some manufacturing districts. Because they are considered transient rather than permanent housing, lodginghouses face more stringent fire-safety requirements than other types of low-quality housing. For instance, lodginghouses (if they are not fireproof) must have sprinkler systems, an interior fire alarm, and two means of egress (these apply to existing lodging-houses as well). In addition, if a lodginghouse were converted from a building that is already a multiple dwelling, it would have to be fireproof (the vast majority of existing structures are not fireproof). But if a lodginghouse were converted from a warehouse or some other building that was not a multiple dwelling, it would not have to be fireproof.

New rooming units also have to meet minimum size requirements. Class A SRO units must have 150 square feet of floor space, rooming-house units 60 or 70 square feet, and lodginghouses 440 cubic feet per bed. Many existing units are considerably smaller than this. Finally, since 1987, all new or converted units have been required to include numerous features designed to facilitate handicapped access.

So it is fairly clear that construction or conversion of new legal rooming units—class A SROs, roominghouses, and lodging-houses—has been nearly impossible in New York since 1955. Because existing rooming units were grandfathered, the effect of this prohibition need not have appeared immediately. Indeed, one can concoct a plausible story that the prohibition should not have been binding until the 1980s, when an increase in demand followed a long decrease in demand.

This plausible story has two serious problems. First, some observers question its legal basis: reestablishing rooming units that were converted after 1955 may be legal. Many former lodging-houses still have lodginghouse certificates of occupancy, and Bowery lodginghouse owners believe that reconversion is legal (though they have no intention of doing any).

Second, whenever the ban on new rooming units is binding, existing grandfathered units should be earning abnormal profits. I have seen little or no evidence of abnormal profits, even in the eighties. Many grandfathered SROs have gone out of business, and more probably would have if New York had not also banned the conversion of room units to other uses in 1983 (Local Law 19). This ban was later thrown out on constitutional grounds, but owners of rooming units still have to get "certificates of non-harassment" before they can close. Lodginghouses, moreover, seem almost always to have been operating with many vacancies. In 1965 Baker found a 62 percent occupancy rate in Bowery lodginghouses and a 70 percent occupancy rate for Bowery roominghouses. In spring 1993 Kadvan found a similar occupancy rate for all New York lodging-houses, including one outside the Bowery (see Table 10-1). Such a

*Table 10-1*  New York City Commercial Lodginghouses, Spring 1993

| Name | Available beds | Occupied | Percent |
|---|---|---|---|
| Union House | 284 | 170 | 60% |
| Hotel Providence | 220 | 160 | 73 |
| World Hotel | 160 | 136 | 85 |
| Grand Hotel | 138 | 124 | 90 |
| Andrews Hotel | 213 | 200 | 94 |
| Mascot Hotel | 42 | 42 | 100 |
| White House | 237 | 200 | 84 |
| Sunshine Hotel | 374 | 322 | 86 |
| | 1,668 | 1,354 | 81 |
| Prince Hotel[a] | 195 | – | – |
| Palace Hotel | 545[b] | 73 | 13 |
| Palma Hotel[c] | 0 | 12 | |
| Vigilant Hotel[d] | 100 | 50 | 50 |
| Total | 2,508 | 1,489 | 64% |

a. Information not available; total occupancy figures exclude the Prince.
b. Correction based on Fuentes (1989) memo.
c. Palma supposedly closed because of 1989 fire, but still some activity.
d. Not on the Bowery.
*Source.* Kadvan (1993).

large vacancy rate makes it hard to believe that the ban on new lodginghouses is binding. Finally, if the conversion constraint were binding, one would expect some surplus of large apartments, of which there is no evidence.

Some objections may be raised to this conclusion. The first is that the vacancy information pertains only to lodginghouses, and the closing information only to lodginghouses and class A SROs. I know very little about roominghouses in New York, and so this is a valid objection.

A second objection is that costs differ in different parts of the city, even though demand might be citywide. The ban on new rooming units might be binding in, say, east New York, where the opportunity cost of land is low, even when SROs on the upper west side, where the opportunity cost of land is high, are trying to go out of business. This objection would be defeated if rooming units were closing throughout the city, not just in areas with valuable land. This may well be the case. Harlem's lodginghouses have all closed, and the one building in Harlem that retains the right to be operated as a lodginghouse (2291 Third Avenue, apparently a bureaucratic error) is partly a furniture showroom, partly vacant. Two grandfathered lodginghouses in Brooklyn have also closed. Only one other lodginghouse, in Chelsea, is outside the Bowery, and city records show no other lodginghouses within modern history. For roominghouses I have no information, nor am I aware of data on SROs.

A third objection is that vacancy rates at lodginghouses might have been lower at other times, perhaps in the late 1970s or early 1980s when the new homelessness was beginning. Some anecdotal reports do suggest that the lodginghouses were "packed to the gills" at this time. But these reports generally also include palpably erroneous data about how many lodginghouses were open, and so are less than credible. Nor are 1980 conditions, whatever they were, relevant for decisionmaking today.

It appears, then, that the ban against new rooming units is not a binding constraint in New York. If regulation made a difference, then, it would do so by raising the operating costs of grandfathered buildings. Innovations in regulations or in their enforcement around 1980 would be needed to explain the rise in homelessness.

Regulation almost certainly affects the operating costs of rooming units in New York. Inspection and "violation"—citing the owner for violating the code—are routine, and fines are a regular part of operating cost. The profit-maximizing mode of operation is almost certainly different from the legal one. Judging from the list of 1989 lodginghouse violations, the most difficult regulations are those requiring operative fire-alarm systems, clean linens and mattresses, adequate numbers of working showers and toilets, unimpeded secondary means of egress, and fusible-link chains at fire-escape windows (Fuentes, 1989). Keeping the plumbing operating is particularly expensive: lodginghouses must have one operative toilet for every fifteen beds, one washbasin for every ten beds, and either one shower for every fifty beds or one tub for every twenty-five beds.

Did any regulatory changes raise operating costs around 1980? A possibility is that enforcement improved following a front-page *New York Times* article on deplorable lodginghouse conditions in 1976 (Sheppard, 1976). But 1976 is several years early for the new homelessness in New York, and it was at the height of the city's fiscal crisis. For city employees to take on new responsibilities or to become more vigorous in pursuit of old ones at such a time is unlikely. Since 1978, the city has been publishing the *Mayor's Management Report* semiannually; every agency tries to write a glowing account of its accomplishments in these volumes. No mayor's report around 1980 contains any news of stepped-up code enforcement.

New York, like most other cities around this time, adopted a smoke-detector requirement, effective January 1, 1982, but though the ordinance affected SROs, it didn't affect lodginghouses. Lodginghouses had been required to be either sprinklered or fireproof since World War II (interview with lodginghouse owners, August 1993). Smoke-detector requirements are at least partially offset by lower insurance costs. The only new regulation affecting lodginghouse operation came in the mid-1980s: Local Law 16, which required hotels to employ fire-safety directors.

One final factor affecting operating costs are the grandfathering regulations themselves. They discourage renovations that might reduce operating costs because this might also eliminate grandfathered status. For instance, the beds at the Sunshine Hotel are old and falling apart; repairing them is costly. Replacing them might maximize profits, but the owner doesn't intend to do that. Beds like those at the Sunshine are no longer manufactured, and so new beds would call for new configurations in the dormitories. This would be construed as a major renovation: the Sunshine would be forced to comply with current codes, and it would be put out of business. Although grandfathering increases operating costs in this fashion, there is still no reason to believe that these costs increased in 1980.

## Newark

Newark's regulatory system is like New York's in many ways—grandfathering is present but not binding, and codes affect operating costs—but it is different in others—there is no housing-maintenance code, and no section 27–2077 banning conversions. Both the building and the zoning codes make it difficult to construct new low-quality units. They date from the early 1950s in their current versions, and both contain grandfather clauses.

The building code is BOCA (Building Officials and Code Adminis-trators), one of three codes established by nationwide organizations that most municipalities adopt by reference. Cubicles and small rooms are impossible under BOCA. Every room (except a kitchen) must be at least 7 feet in every dimension, and every dwelling unit must contain at least one room of 150 square feet or more. But in 1969 the state's Hotel and Multiple Dwelling Law superseded many provisions of the city building code. This law permits rooming units to be as small as 50 square feet for transient purposes (still twice the size of a New York or Chicago cubicle), 80 square feet for permanent purposes. It requires one toilet, one tub or shower, and one wash-basin for every six to eight occupants.

The zoning code permits hotels and roominghouses in certain residential districts and in all commercial and industrial districts (Newark's code is of the traditional apex variety—uses permitted in "higher" districts are also permitted in "lower" ones). The bite in the zoning code comes from the parking requirement: one off-street space for every four rooms.

These grandfathered requirements were and are not binding, since they generated so little profit that almost all of the low-quality hotels in Newark have gone out of business (Table 7-7). Hotels in neighborhoods with very low land prices uniformly went out of business (as did those in neighborhoods with high land prices), and so a story about hotels just being in the wrong place is entirely implausible.

As far as operating costs and retrofit requirements are concerned, the most notable change was the implementation of smoke-detector requirements. City codes first required smoke detectors in 1978. This was a retrofit requirement but did not specify the type of detector. In the early eighties, the code was strengthened to mandate electrical, hard-wired smoke detectors in common areas; individual rooms could still have battery-operated detectors. When New Jersey adopted a uniform fire code in 1985 that superseded the city code, it had a similar provision. The uniform code, like the Newark code, requires two means of egress and, in larger buildings, lighted exit signs and emergency lighting. The 1985 code required fire barriers around interior stairways by 1990, but gave several options that could take the place of this requirement. For instance, sprinklered buildings don't have to construct fire barriers. In general, sprinklers are not required.

## Toronto

Roominghouses are the chief form of low-quality housing in Toronto. (Toronto's definition puts no limit on the number of rooms in a roominghouse; the largest now has 38 rooms. Such an establishment would be called a hotel in Newark or New York.) Most commentators believe that there are as many unlicensed roominghouses in Toronto as licensed ones, and so codes will not matter directly for many establishments. Of course, codes matter indirectly even for illegal roominghouses because they prohibit doing things that can be done only in public. Roominghouse licensing dates from 1974.

Licensed roominghouses are grandfathered; both new construction and conversion of houses under five years old are prohibited. Size requirements are not stringent—only 65 square feet in a room—but one off-street parking space is needed for every six rooms. One water closet and one bathtub are needed for every ten people. Roominghouses are prohibited in the most exclusive residential districts and, since the late 1970s, in industrial districts as well; Toronto has moved significantly away from apex zoning (Brideweiser interview, 1991).

The building code is also grandfathered, and not much different from the BOCA code that Newark uses. It was put in place in 1975; before that Toronto used a property standards by-law dating from 1936. In new construction, bedrooms require at least 118 square feet (11 square meters), and every room has to have windows equal to 10 percent of floor space (Breeze interview, 1991).

Toronto's grandfathered regulations are thus similar to those in U.S. cities, though somewhat less demanding. Where Toronto differs most notably from U.S. cities is in the retrofit provisions of its fire code. These developed rapidly in the 1970s and 1980s, largely in response to a series of fatal roominghouse fires. In 1970 the Toronto fire code was far less stringent than those in U.S. cities; by 1985 it was just about the same.

The major change came in 1983. The retrofit program begun in that year requires electrical, interconnected smoke alarms; two means of egress for rooms on the third floor and above; and walls and doors that can contain and separate fires. Sprinklers are not required. The interconnecting smoke-alarm system is the major expense. In a medium-sized roominghouse of around ten rooms, compliance would cost several thousand dollars. Before 1983, there were no containment provisions, a fire alarm of some sort was required, and the exit requirements were weak. Roominghouses were inspected once a year before 1983; now they are inspected twice a year (Collins interview, 1991).

Despite this major tightening of regulations directly affecting the profitability of roominghouses, homelessness among single adult males in Toronto—the group most likely to use roominghouses—has declined since 1983.

## Chicago

Chicago's regulations are much like those in the other cities, though probably less strict than New York's. SROs (which are not legally defined) and cubicle hotels are grandfathered, largely by zoning rather than building code. Building-code requirements for space are fairly low: 70 square feet per room in general and in roominghouses, with windows being 10 percent of floor area, and 50 square feet per person in men's cubicle hotels. Even these building-code provisions are explicitly grandfathered.

Nor does it appear that the constraints against new SROs and cubicle hotels were binding. Many SROs have closed in the last twenty years, and many of those were in neighborhoods with low land prices (CESO-JCUA, 1985; Lakefront, 1991). A similarly strong statement about cubicle hotels cannot be made because all of them were originally in the Loop, or close to it.

A new SRO, the Harold Washington, opened in the late eighties, but it used a vacant building that had once been a SRO and so could claim grandfathering for zoning purposes (Butzen interview, 1991). Rents in the Harold Washington are heavily subsidized through section 8 vouchers. It is not inconceivable, though, that a new profitmaking SRO, presumably located in a grandfathered building, could open in Chicago.

Regulations affecting operating costs have apparently not changed much, although some requirements for electrical smoke detectors have had an effect. The SRO owners' association defeated an attempt to require sophisticated alarm systems in 1988–89. The major contribution to operating costs, according to the association president, comes not from the letter of the law, but from capricious enforcement. In 1991, for instance, a number of owners had to replace all their sinks, at $400 each, because inspectors found fault with the dimensions of the J-curves in the piping (Rubinstein interview, 1991).

## London

It is hard to compare London with North American cities, partly because each of the thirty-two boroughs has its own building and zoning codes, partly because the private rental sector is minuscule. The fire code is national, however, and considerably less strict than the North American codes. For instance, the Home Office in 1980 stated: "Unless, therefore, significant improvements can be made in the economy and reliability of automatic detection systems, it must be concluded that automatic systems cannot offer a cost-effective means of securing a significant reduction in fire losses in non-industrial buildings" (p. 66). Still even the weak retrofit provisions of the Fire Precautions Act of 1971, which dealt primarily with means of egress, probably contributed to the closing of the Rowton, Salvation Army, and Church Army hostels in the late seventies and early eighties (see GLC-LBA Working Party, 1981; Salvation Army and Church Army, n.d.). Hostel closings, however, don't seem to have been linked to homelessness.

Regulation did not cause the rise of the new homelessness. There is no evidence that grandfathered regulations were binding, and considerable evidence that they were not. Except for the fire code in some places, regulations affecting operating costs didn't change at the right time. Even the fire code changed at the wrong time in

Toronto. Code variations among North American cities are tiny in comparison with variations in homelessness. This doesn't mean that all is well in the world of municipal regulation. Better codes probably could have kept homelessness from rising as much as it did, especially in New York. But constructing better codes is no easy matter.

## Rent Control

The earliest economic writings about homelessness focused on rent control. Tucker (1987a, 1987b) claimed that cities with rent control had much higher rates of homelessness than those without it, but Quigley (1990) showed that Tucker's result vanished when weather, high rents, and a handful of similar variables were considered. Honig and Filer (1993) confirmed Quigley's result.

On theoretical grounds, no clear conclusion can be reached about the effects of rent control on homelessness. Rent control is a limitation on the rate at which rent for a given unit can rise. In the filtering equilibrium of Chapter 6, rents on a particular unit are always falling as quality deteriorates. Unless inflation is very rapid and indexing very poor, rent controls will not be binding in this sort of equilibrium. Moreover, to the extent that rent controls do bind, they will encourage filtering—lowering the quality of units already constructed. This will make more low-quality, low-rent housing available. (The conversions that the infamous section 27-2077 of the New York City housing-maintenance code were designed to discourage were probably inspired by rent control.)

Yet Arnott (1995) has pointed out that rent control can cause an excess demand for housing—too many households seeking too few units—which would allow landlords to be choosy about picking tenants. Mentally ill people and substance abusers are not likely to please landlords. In addition, some rent-control systems (Newark's, for instance) decontrol units that are upgraded; this may provide an incentive that would not otherwise exist for upgrading low-quality units.

The particular details of rent control in the six cities do not support Tucker's contention. All except Chicago now have some form of rent control, but the forms differ substantially. Arnott emphasizes that rent control is not a simple yes-no proposition; systems differ greatly in their degree of "hardness" or "softness."

London's rent control dates to World War I, and is probably the hardest of the systems. Since the private rental stock had probably disappeared by the time homelessness became an issue, rent control can't explain much of the time-series variation in London. Indeed, homelessness rose after a form of vacancy decontrol was introduced in 1988.

Some forms of rent control in New York also date almost from World War I: chapter 136, 1920 N.Y. Laws 228, allowed a defense in legal actions that the rent charged was "unjust and oppressive." Rent control in the normal form of an ex-ante prohibition on certain rent increases began in 1943, when the federal government imposed wartime price controls. After the war, the state and the city continued controls in various forms. At first, rent control applied only to buildings built before 1947, but a modified (soft) form of rent control called rent stabilization was imposed on post-1947 buildings in 1969.

Increases for rent-stabilized apartments are regulated by a board, which sets limits for various classes every year, based on market and cost changes. Generally it permits larger increases for new tenants than for existing ones. In addition, after 1970 rent-controlled apartments have been able to increase their rents by 7.5 percent a year up to a level called "maximum base rent"—enough rent to give the landlord an 8.5 percent return on the equalized assessed value of the building.

In 1971 the state legislature exempted from both rent control and rent stabilization any units that became vacant after June 30, 1971. This action was partially reversed by the Emergency Tenant Protection Act of 1974. After 1974, controlled units that become vacant in large apartment buildings have not been totally decontrolled; instead they have been switched to stabilized. Controlled units in small buildings (fewer than six units) are decontrolled when they become vacant. Thus the number of controlled units has been falling steadily: the number fell from 642,000 in 1975 to 402,000 in 1981 (Stegman, 1985). Apartments built privately after 1974 are exempt.

Thus in 1980 rent regulation was probably less stringent for pre-1947 buildings than it was in 1970 or 1960. Some units were decontrolled, controlled units had large percentage increases, and stabilized units had adjustments for costs. New York's system essentially changed in the 1970s from hard to fairly soft. Legal stringency, of course, would not have mattered if the inflation of the 1970s had made legal rents in 1980 far lower than real legal rents in 1970. There is no evidence that this happened.

The pattern of exemptions also raises serious questions about a link between rent control and homelessness. For tenants who stay at least thirty days, class A SROs and roominghouses have always been covered, but lodginghouses were not covered between 1971 and 1992. Still the stock of lodginghouses declined sharply in the seventies. The new homelessness emerged in 1978, even though the type of housing only a step above shelters and streets was not rent-controlled in any way. Throughout this period, too, and even after lodginghouses were brought under rent stabilization in 1992, transient tenants in roominghouses, hotels, and lodginghouses could be charged market rents. Interviews with lodginghouse owners lead me to believe that, in this segment of the market at least, rent regulations are not binding.

In Hamburg, rents on *all* units were regulated from the end of World War II until 1976. Permitted increases were very limited. Private buildings were first allowed to increase rents in 1976, but only in accordance with a table of comparable rents in the neighborhood *(Mietspiegel)*. In addition, tax changes were made to encourage condominium conversions. Subsidized buildings *(Sozialwuungen)*, which account for over a third of the apartments in Hamburg, were generally not allowed to increase rents. A 1982 law to increase the supply of rental apartments made it even easier to raise rents.

In Newark, rent control started in 1974 but was never too effective. In particular, hotels are exempt, and so rent control could not have caused the spectacular loss of low-quality hotel rooms shown in Table 7-7. Many regular rental units are also exempt because a large proportion (about 27 percent) of Newark's private apartments are in owner-occupied structures of four or fewer units.

Newark has provisions for regular rent increases as well as larger increases for many special reasons. Since mortgage payments are considered a cost for calculating allowable rent increases, a landlord whose rents are below market need only sell his property to receive the present value of market rents. Newark allows rent increases of up to 25 percent on vacant apartments if the landlord spends at least $100 per room for rehabilitation while they are vacant; otherwise vacancy decontrol is not permitted by law.

But de-facto vacancy decontrol exists for most of Newark's rental housing stock. Of the 30–40,000 units that rent control supposedly governs, only about 10–15,000 are registered with the rent-control office. Without registration, a prospective tenant has no way of finding out what the previous rent was, and no incentive to do anything except come to a mutually satisfactory agreement with the landlord.

In Toronto (precisely, in Ontario) rent control is also comparatively recent and fairly soft. It began in 1975. New buildings were exempted from controls for five years after construction. In 1979 the exemption for post-1975 units was extended indefinitely, but in 1986 the exemption was removed entirely and controls were imposed on all post-1975 buildings, including those not yet built. At first, landlords were permitted an annual rent increase that was set by statute; most of the time before 1986 this was 6 percent. Landlords could also ask for additional increases in a variety of special circumstances. After 1986, a formula tied to inflation replaced the statutory increases (Smith, 1988). Even after 1986, Ontario has allowed fairly large rent increases. Automatic increases have been about 5 percent a year, and about 17 percent of properties ask for special increases above that. The average annual increase in the latter group is about 11 percent. Originally, roominghouses were not covered at all. Only in 1986 was rent control extended to roominghouses and post-1976 buildings.

In summary, it is hard to see rent control as a major contributor to homelessness. Rent control was easing most where homelessness was growing most, and tightening most where it was growing least.

## Tenant Rights

Probably more important than rent control has been the evolution since about 1970 of tenant rights, a change in the nature of tenancy contracts. Evicting tenants has become more difficult, and this has increased operating costs, especially for the lowest qualities of housing, where many services are shared and a fair proportion of tenants are likely to be disruptive. In an apartment house where you have your own bathroom and walls that go up to the ceiling, you are less likely to be concerned if your neighbor is a sloppy alcoholic than you are in a lodginghouse. Your neighbor is also less likely to be a sloppy alcoholic in the apartment house. Gradually, though, tenancy contracts designed for apartments have been imposed almost intact on lodginghouses, roominghouses, and SROs.

In New York, for instance, "SRO tenants have substantially the same rights and legal protections as tenants in other multiple dwellings" (Wackstein, 1990). A tenant who has lived in a room or lodginghouse for thirty days or who has asked for a lease (regardless of the length of residency) can be evicted only if the owner demonstrates good cause to a court's satisfaction and obtains a warrant of eviction. Other tenants may be evicted without a court order, but even in these cases an owner cannot breach the peace. "It is illegal for a landlord or his or her employees to lock [a tenant] out of [his] room or to harass or threaten [him] in any way" (West Side SRO Law Project, n.d.). Under Local Law 56 of 1982, a landlord who evicts someone without using the proper procedures is subject to both criminal and civil penalties.

New York lodginghouse owners estimate that it costs about $1,000 to evict a tenant in a simple nonpayment case. Since eviction costs are basically fixed, the lower the rent, the higher the relative cost of eviction. Eviction also takes time; even after a judge has ordered one, it may be several months before the warrant is actually served.

Because the process by which tenant rights evolved was both gradual and subtle—things such as the attitude of municipal judges and the activism of legal-aid attorneys probably matter as much as written documents—I haven't been able to document timing in the various cities, and so I can't really test for an effect on homelessness. Nor does cross-section variation seem to be large. Still the topic comes up repeatedly in conversations with SRO and lodginghouse owners. A former SRO owner in Newark, for instance, gave as his main reason for leaving the business the hassle and liability that had become part of it; he thought that the only person who would buy a cheap hotel now was the "thickest-skinned SOB in the world" (Rio interview, 1991). Similarly, two of the ten legislative objectives of the Chicago SRO Owners' Association are related to tenant rights: speeding up eviction and reinstating criminal penalties for nonpayment of rent in some cases.

The theory in Chapter 6 points in the same direction. Tenant rights affect operating costs which do affect homelessness. In addition, if owners have more difficulty getting rid of people, they will be more reluctant to accept tenants who might cause trouble—people, say, with a history of mental illness, substance abuse, or incarceration—or who can't pay much in advance. The theoretical connection is much closer than that with rent control.

My hunch is that these changes in tenancy laws did contribute to the rise of homelessness, but I don't have enough data to back it up. Still, the role can't be very large, since tenancy rights are also quite strong—probably stronger than in the United States—in Toronto, where homelessness is small and stable, and in Europe. Even if changes in tenancy laws did not contribute directly to homelessness, they probably played an important role in increasing vacancy rates. The more difficult it is to evict someone, the more expensive a mistake it is to accept the wrong tenant, and the longer the time landlords will be willing to wait with a vacant apartment until the right tenant comes along.

Jencks (1994) has argued that since some measures indicate that U.S. rental vacancy rates were higher in the 1980s than they were in the 70s, housing markets were loose and so could not be responsible for the increase in homelessness. But to the extent that higher vacancy rates are due to greater landlord patience in the face of eviction costs, they are not signs of market looseness; instead they should accompany the rise in homelessness. Vacancy rates are discussed in more detail at the end of this chapter.

## Public Housing

In the United States, new public housing was constructed at a fairly low rate during most of the 1980s. This has frequently been cited as a cause of homelessness (for example, Burt, 1992; GAO, 1985; Wright, 1989).

There are two ways to understand this argument: that because the 1980s were unusual in the low rate of construction of public housing, homelessness increased; and that if the rate of construction had been higher, homelessness would not have increased so much. The first way of understanding the argument is muddled, because it confuses stocks and flows. The stock of public housing is what matters to housing-market equilibrium, and so an unchanging stock, all else being equal, can't explain rising homelessness. The second way of understanding the argument is less objectionable: it says that a larger stock of public housing leads to less homelessness.

Since public housing stock matters, Table 10-2 shows estimates for the five English-speaking cities. The cities differ substantially in the proportion that public housing represents of their total housing stock. In London, 31 percent of all units were council (public) housing in 1981; council housing is considerably more numerous than privately owned rental housing. The other cities are quite different from London: social housing represented 6.4 percent of Metro Toronto's housing stock in 1985; and in 1980 public housing was 9.5 percent of Newark's occupied housing stock, 6.1 percent of New York's, and 3.3 percent of Chicago's.

These figures are far from being comparable. Three defining characteristics of public housing are public ownership and control, subsidized rents, and eligibility based on low income. The latter two characteristics are more important in assessing how this housing affects the overall housing market, but most data, like those in Table 10-2, emphasize ownership. This problem is exacerbated because in all three countries disenchantment with traditional public housing, beginning as early as the 1960s, led to the creation of many different subsidy programs, and none of them includes ownership and control.

In the United States, public housing is owned by housing authorities—public agencies that are legally independent of city governments but controlled by them politically. Tenants must have low incomes, and rents are subsidized by the federal government. Tenants pay 30 percent of their income for rent (before 1982 it was 25 percent), while the federal subsidy depends on the number of units the housing authority manages, whether they are occupied or not. The United States also has a large stock of privately managed sub-

*Table 10-2*   Occupied Public Housing Units, 1970–1990

| Year | NYC | Newark Total | Newark Nonelderly | Chicago Total | Chicago Nonelderly |
|------|-----|-------|-----------|-------|------------|
| 1970 | – | 12,165 | 7,222 | 38,685[a] | – |
| 1971 | – | – | – | 39,665[a] | – |
| 1972 | – | 12,221 | 7,304 | 40,128[a] | – |
| 1973 | – | 12,062 | 7,155 | 40,134[a] | – |
| 1974 | – | 11,049 | 6,384 | 39,830[a] | – |
| 1975 | – | 10,390 | 5,730 | 40,523[a] | – |
| 1976 | 166,000 | – | – | 41,140[a] | – |
| 1977 | 168,000 | – | – | 41,953[a] | – |
| 1978 | 168,000 | 11,089 | 6,322 | 43,829[a] | – |
| 1979 | 168,000 | 11,121 | 6,332 | 44,353[a] | – |
| 1980 | 169,000 | – | – | 39,077[a] | – |
| 1981 | 171,000 | – | – | – | – |
| 1982 | 171,000 | 9,088 | 5,154 | 36,224 | 23,525 |
| 1983 | 172,000 | 8,203 | 4,712 | 35,423 | 23,989 |
| 1984 | 172,000 | 7,904 | 4,617 | 35,877 | 24,962 |
| 1985 | 174,000 | 7,671 | 4,357 | 34,728 | 23,299 |
| 1986 | 176,000 | 7,314 | 3,984 | 34,607 | 23,465 |
| 1987 | 178,000 | 7,239 | 4,044 | 33,439 | 22,745 |
| 1988 | 178,000 | 7,275 | 3,367 | 32,225 | 21,732 |
| 1989 | 179,000 | 7,199 | 3,649 | – | – |
| 1990 | 179,000 | 7,197 | – | 32,204 | 20,064 |

| | London[b] | Toronto[c] Total | Toronto[c] Nonelderly |
|------|---------|-------|------------|
| 1971 | 659,340 | – | – |
| 1981 | 769,996 | – | – |
| 1985 | – | 52,464 | 24,859 |
| 1990 | 702,801 | – | – |

a. Includes section 8 vouchers.
b. Council housing.
c. RGI Units.
*Sources.* New York: Mayor's Management Report, various years; figure is units under management; no indication made of any vacancies. Newark: 1979 and before, Newark Housing Authority, annual reports; 1982 and after, HUD, "Report on Occupancy for Public and Indian Housing," form 51234. Chicago: 1980 and before, Chicago Housing Authority, *1980 Statistical Report*; 1982 and after, HUD form 51234. London: 1971, 1981, Census; 1990, London Research Centre, *London Housing Statistics 1990*; total council housing stock (table 2.1) less vacant dwellings (table 2.2). Toronto: Policy Development Division, Metro Toronto Planning Department, "Housing Trends 1976–1986," table A6.

sidized housing built since the 1960s for low-income people, but these units are not included in Table 10-2.

In Toronto, all traditional public housing construction, except that for the elderly, stopped in the early 1970s, and publicly assisted housing built since then has consisted of 75 percent market-rate units that anyone can rent, and 25 percent rent-geared-to-income units with subsidized rents and eligibility restricted to low-income people. The number in Table 10-2 is the sum of traditional public housing units and the rent-geared-to-income units in the more recently constructed projects. If Toronto figures were comparable to U.S. ones, they would show public or social housing amounting to a proportion of total housing stock somewhere between that in New York and that in Chicago.

In our very small North American cross-section, then, the simple correlation between public housing and homelessness is positive—cities with a lot of public housing (Newark and New York) have a lot of homelessness, and cities with less public housing (Toronto and Chicago) have less homelessness.

Council housing in Great Britain differs from North American public housing in two important ways. Council housing has no income-eligibility rules, although rents are subsidized. Each council (a municipality outside London or one of its boroughs) operates independently, but the central government provides some direction. During the first major growth period for council housing, after World War I, most tenants were fairly well-paid artisans; regular workers couldn't pay the rents (Merrett, 1979). From the end of World War II until the 1980s, selection for council housing was based on an individual council's scheme of merit. Households that were displaced by council activities, households that were living in dilapidated quarters, "key workers," and households that were willing to wait for many years were rewarded with council tenancies, if they looked like good tenants. Legislation has placed the statutory homeless at the head of queue in recent years, but statutory homelessness is a question of current living conditions, not income. Income per se has never been a criterion. Even in 1990, for instance, only about half of the Camden council tenants had income low enough to be eligible for the housing benefit (L. B. Camden, 1991a).

Nor are rents related to income. Each council sets its own rents, subject to a breakeven constraint and a fixed subsidy from the central government, and does not take tenant income into consideration. Subsidies decreased substantially during the 1980s, and so average rents in London went up by 260 percent between 1979 and 1990, although inflation was only 188 percent (London Research Centre, 1991).

At first glance, Table 10-2 shows public housing stock declining in London, Newark, and Chicago, and rising only a very little in New York. Can one then plausibly argue that homelessness rose in the 1980s because the stock of public housing fell? Except for Newark, probably not. The decline in London largely reflects a legal transaction—between 1980 and 1990, 177,000 council units were sold to their occupants (London Research Centre, 1991). These sales change the financial positions of the buyers, but they don't change the supply of units at all in the short run, and probably not much in the long run, since council tenants have very strong tenancy rights (for instance, they can will leaseholds to nonfamily members) and low turnover, especially in attractive estates (lettings to new tenants amounted to about 3 percent of council housing stock in London in fiscal year 1989–90). Physical additions to both council and housing-association stock were positive, as shown in Table 10-3. The table also shows noticeable additions to public and quasi-public housing stock in New York.

In Chicago, the decline is small, largely confined to two high-rise projects, Cabrini-Green and Robert Taylor Homes. Since public housing is such a small proportion of Chicago's housing stock, a small decline is likely to have little effect.

The situation in Newark is quite different. Three large housing projects were pretty much depopulated, as Table 10-4 shows, and population was reduced at other projects as well. The reduction in public housing shown in Table 10-3 amounts to roughly 3 percent of Newark's housing stock—roughly equivalent to the complete elimination of public housing in Chicago.

I have noted that the effect of public housing on homelessness depends on the incomes of the people who live in it. Public housing for the middle class increases homelessness; public housing for the very poor reduces it. Although no good data are available, it appears that

*Table 10-3*  Construction of New Public Housing, 1977–1990

| | New York | | London | | Toronto |
|------|------|------|------|------|------|
| | NYCHA | HPD | Local authorities | Housing assoc. | |
| 1977 | 689 | – | – | – | – |
| 1978 | 300 | – | – | – | – |
| 1979 | 160 | – | – | – | – |
| 1980 | 1,112 | 7,780 | 16,249 | 2,287 | 2,430 |
| 1981 | 385 | 8,805 | 13,406 | 1,934 | 2,519 |
| 1982 | 505 | 6,228 | 7,254 | 1,535 | 5,324 |
| 1983 | 640 | 7,852 | 5,149 | 1,565 | 3,430 |
| 1984 | 540 | 6,757 | 3,504 | 1,560 | 2,388 |
| 1985 | 477 | 7,367 | 2,713 | 1,061 | 2,679 |
| 1986 | 824 | 15,546 | 2,153 | 644 | 1,035 |
| 1987 | 1,033 | 17,216 | 1,384 | 1,177 | 2,357 |
| 1988 | 643 | 21,298 | 1,390 | 806 | 2,322 |
| 1989 | 76 | 28,352 | 922 | 1,467 | 2,293 |
| 1990 | 0 | 17,992 | 1,904 | 1,737 | 1,590 |

*Sources.* New York: NYCHA is unit completions by New York City Housing Authority; HPD is new housing starts assisted by municipal Housing and Preservation Department (excludes rehabilitation starts, which are approximately as numerous); from Mayor's Management Reports. London: Data are completions; London Research Centre, *London Housing Statistics 1990*, p. 132. Toronto: Data are "socially assisted housing starts"; from Strategic Planning and Research Branch, Ontario Ministry of Housing, "Housing Statistics," April 1991, table X-1.

the housing authorities with the poorest population were the ones that lost population. In Chicago in 1980, about 55 percent of families in CHA housing were receiving public assistance (CHA Facts). In Newark, the proportion of families receiving assistance varied erratically between 35 percent and 40 percent during the 1970s (NHA Annual Reports). In contrast, only 11.7 percent of New York City Housing Authority tenants included assistance recipients in 1962, and the proportion had risen only to 28 percent by 1990 (Annual Reports, 1962, 1990). As late as 1975, housing-authority interviewers were directed, in writing, not to offer apartments in certain projects to assistance recipients (New York State Office of the Comptroller, 1976).

In fact, the North American practice of gearing rent to income may contribute to the correlation between poor populations and less public housing. Suppose public housing in a city is unattractive—either,

*Table 10-4*   Troubled Housing Projects in Newark and Chicago

| Year | Newark | Chicago |
|---|---|---|
| Original no. of units | 4,442 | 7,821 |
| Occupied units | | |
| 1978 | 2,945 | – |
| 1980 | – | 7,440 |
| 1982 | 2,286 | 6,816 |
| 1984 | 1,936 | 6,475 |
| 1986 | 1,526 | 6,108 |
| 1988 | 1,452 | 5,765 |
| 1990 | 950 | 5,472 |

Newark: Columbus Homes, Scudder Homes, and Stella Wright. Chicago: Cabrini-Green and Robert Taylor Homes.
*Source.* See Table 10–2.

say, because of poor design or a weak private market. Public housing will be most attractive to the poorest and largest families, because these will be the ones to receive the most subsidy. The more unattractive public housing is, the higher the proportion of poor and large families in the applicant pool.

Poor and large families are also the most costly for a housing authority to accept when rent is geared to income. The poorer a family is, the less rent the housing authority receives, and the larger a family is, the greater the demands it places on the authority for water, elevator service, repairs, and so on. In Illinois and New Jersey in 1993, a housing authority would receive between $3 and $4 a day for a family of three receiving AFDC—about half the price for a night for one in a flophouse dormitory. Since federal subsidies depend on the number of units, whether occupied or not, a large proportion of poor and large families means that a housing authority has less money to operate its projects well enough to make them attractive. The process feeds on itself. Around 35 percent of the homeless women living in family shelters in Chicago said they would never consider living in a CHA project; lack of safety is the chief reason they cited (McCourt and Nyden, 1990).

This process ends with vacancies and abandonment. Once a project becomes unattractive enough, the only families willing to live there are those who are likely to pay less rent than the marginal costs they cause. An authority interested in serving its existing tenants (or in serving itself) has no incentive to fill such a project. Abandonment becomes the reasonable course.

In summary, the diminished public housing stock of Newark probably contributed to homelessness in that city; possibly the same is true on a much smaller scale in Chicago. A much larger housing program, unless it were focused more tightly on poor people, would not have made much difference, and, with existing North American subsidy systems, projects focused on poor people do not last long.

## Housing Benefits

Public housing is sometimes called a supply-side housing program—it is designed to help poor people by constructing housing for them directly. All of the governments we are looking at also operate demand-side housing programs—which give people the resources to buy housing, not the housing itself. Over the last twenty years, demand-side programs have been more popular than supply-side, and they have grown much more quickly.

Germany and Britain both have formal housing-benefit programs that are longstanding components of the welfare state. Thus they are both entitlement programs—in Britain, for instance, you get the forms to apply for housing benefits at the postoffice. The two programs differ significantly, however.

The system called *Wohngeld* was introduced in West Germany in 1965; by 1986 about 12 percent of tenants and a handful of low-income homeowners were receiving benefits. Every household must pay a minimum rent that varies by income and family size; lower incomes and larger households imply lower minimum rents. Subsidies are determined by tables rather than formulas. *Wohngeld* generally pays 85–90 percent of every deutschemark increase in rent for low-income households; the marginal rent subsidy is around 30 percent for high-income eligible households. There is a ceiling rent, however, that varies by location and building age. The tenant is solely responsible for rents above the ceiling. In 1986, 31 percent of recipients had rents above the ceiling. Finally the "taper," the rate at which benefits fall as income rises, is fairly shallow: additional income reduces Wohngeld by about 30–40 percent as much.

For very low-income people, *Sozialhilfe* is like a welfare grant with a shelter allowance. It pays a stipend plus actual heating and rent costs, up to a maximum, just like AFDC and General Assistance in New York. Thus the marginal rate of subsidy to rent is 100 percent up to the ceiling, and nothing above the ceiling. (See Kemp, 1989.)

The current British housing benefit is more like Sozialhilfe than Wohngeld. The marginal rate of subsidy to rent is 100 percent and the taper is so steep (65 percent) that few people not qualifying for income support (welfare) receive the benefit. A network of rent officers and implicit understandings has established a system of local rent ceilings for recipients; they cannot live in apartments where the rent is too high. This system was instituted in 1989; before that the taper was much shallower and so eligibility extended to higher income levels. (See Hills, 1989).

Because they are entitlement programs, Sozialhilfe, Wohngeld, and the British housing benefit make shelter operation and hence homelessness quite different in Europe than it is in North America. Shelters can charge rent, and their financial problems involve attracting residents, qualifying them for benefits, and negotiating ceilings. Shelter residents, since they carry their rent with them, have some opportunity to choose their own accommodations.

In the United States, "section 8" is the most familiar demand-side housing program. The major difference from the European programs is that section 8 is not an entitlement program; only a fixed number of households, far fewer than those eligible, get to participate.

Section 8 actually consists of two different programs: certificates and vouchers. (A third section 8 program, new housing, was a supply-side program terminated in 1983.) In both section 8 programs, a participating household must live in housing that the government finds to be well maintained and of high enough quality, and must pay 30 percent of its income for rent. Thus the income taper is 30 percent, and only families of moderate income or below can participate.

In the certificate program, the government pays the difference between the actual rent and what the tenant pays, provided that the actual rent is less than an amount the government calls "fair market rent" (FMR). No supplementation is allowed, and so except in special circumstances households can't live in apartments renting for more than FMR. As long as they deal with apartments renting for less than FMR, however, tenants pay nothing for improving the quality of their housing; the marginal rent subsidy is 100 percent. Because moving is expensive, some families stay where they are, even though rent is far less than FMR. But one study found that of those who move, 48 percent had rents between 95 percent and 100 percent of FMR (*Housing and Development Reporter*, 1990).

In the voucher program, by contrast, the government pays the difference between FMR and what the tenant pays, no matter what the actual rent is. The tenant pockets the difference if the actual rent is less than FMR and pays the difference herself if it is more than FMR. So the marginal rent subsidy is zero; in fact, a section 8 voucher is just about the same as a straight cash grant, except that the household must live in an apartment that meets the maintenance and quality standards in order to receive it. It is a lump-sum cash bonus for living in a nice apartment.

Both section 8 subsidies averaged about $300 a month in the late 1980s. By 1988, section 8 had become a fairly large program: nationally, about 780,000 households received certificates and 156,000 received vouchers. By comparison, 1.3 million households lived in traditional public housing.

The United States also has several other housing-benefit schemes, although they are usually not recognized as such. The largest of these is food stamps. For a substantial number of households, food-stamp benefits go up by 30 cents for every dollar increase in rent. The formula is complicated, with both ceilings and floors. Figure 10-1 shows for a single nondisabled individual in 1992 the combinations of rent and monthly income where this rent subsidy was operative. Figure 10-2 shows the same for a disabled or elderly individual. In 1992 the subsidy was not operative for very poor people or people receiving public assistance (except possibly in high-grant states like New York). Instead it was operative for people slightly better off—making $5,000 or $6,000 a year, paying $200 to $400 a month in rent. It was also operative for almost all disabled people receiving SSI and for many elderly people.

What are the indirect effects of these large housing-benefit programs? Because applying for section 8 takes skill and patience and

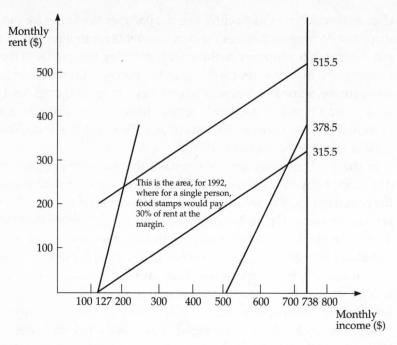

*Figure 10-1*

the income guidelines are fairly generous, few of the poorest people manage to participate. Section 8 grew rapidly in the late seventies and early eighties (the certificate program started in 1975, the voucher program in 1983); food stamps and SSI grew rapidly in the late seventies. In the long run, rent subsidies to people slightly richer than they are should help people at the bottom of the income distribution; a subsidy to consumers of mutton helps consumers of wool. In the short run, though, the effect is probably the opposite: with a fixed stock of housing, if one group consumes more, the other group has to consume less. William Apgar (1988) has been particularly strong in arguing that the expansion of section 8 has pushed up rents for poor people who don't get certificates or vouchers. Section 8 encourages maintenance and slows filtering, while SSI and food stamps encourage household formation. Thus the growth of section 8, food stamps, and SSI may have contributed to the emergence of the new homelessness in this country.

The other forms of housing benefit in the United States emerged as responses to homelessness, not as contributors to it. In all four

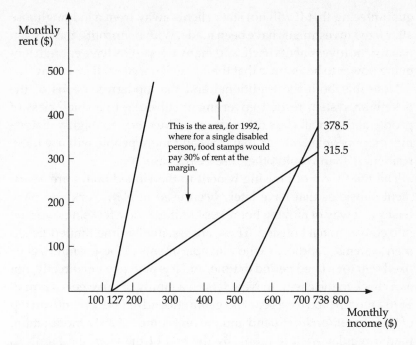

Monthly
rent ($)

500

400

This is the area, for 1992,
where for a single disabled
person, food stamps would
pay 30% of rent at the
margin.

378.5

315.5

300

200

100

100 127 200    300    400   500      600   700 738 800

Monthly
income ($)

*Figure 10-2*

North American cities, the way that private nonprofit shelters are
funded is a modified version of the ticketman system, except that
client involvement with anything remotely fungible is entirely
eliminated. People are free to choose among a limited number of
nonprofit shelters; each shelter documents to the city or county the
number of people who stay each night; and the city pays the shelter
at a fixed per-diem (actually, per-noctem) rate times the number of
people who stay there. The per-diem rate is usually much higher
than the ticket price; when both systems were operating in New
York, the nonprofit per-diem rate was generally about six times
greater than the ticket price.

From the city's point of view, the advantage of the nonprofit system is that it mitigates two other problems: nonprofits have less incentive to reduce standards because they are not residual claimants;
and clients can't sell a ticket on the street because they don't have one
to sell. Of course competition among lodginghouses might resolve
the quality issue in a ticketman system, but quality often depends on
fixed investments, and in a ticketman system the city has no way of

guaranteeing that it will not steer clients away from a lodginghouse after fixed investments have been made. With nonprofits, the city can pay for the investments itself, and many nonprofits have enough lobbying power to be assured that the city will not steer clients away.

Note that both the traditional and the modern versions of the ticketman system restrict government subsidies to a small class of people and a small class of residences. Thus they are highly distorting: more people will join that class and more people will use those residences than would otherwise be the case.

The final form of housing benefit in the United States are apartment subsidies that have lately been used in New York and New Jersey as a way of moving homeless families (and a few single adults) into conventional housing. These are essentially time-limited ticketman systems. Landlords who rent apartments to these families get a fixed rent for a fixed period of time, and it is paid to them directly, not as a check to the client. In New Jersey, a family of three gets a rent of $526 a month paid for a year and gets a stipend of $149 a month on top of this. Together the stipend and the rent come to $250 a month more than a regular welfare grant. By the end of the year, the family is expected to have figured out a way of managing without the extra $250. Recipients can't supplement these allowances, and it is not clear how much discretion they have in deciding where to use them; many of the allowances are dedicated to major contracts between the welfare agency and landlords. The New York program is similar. These programs are much like a time-limited section 8 and can be expected to have the same effects on nonrecipients.

In summary, American housing-benefit programs differ from European programs chiefly by being confined to special groups. Often this confinement has deleterious effects in the short run.

## Rental Vacancy Rates

The apparent rise in rental vacancy rates, even for low-rent units, is one of the chief arguments of those who deny that homelessness is a housing-market problem. Christopher Jencks writes:

> These facts [higher rent burdens for low-income renters] convinced many people that low-income tenants faced a growing shortage of

affordable housing. But if low-quality, low-rent housing had really been in short supply, the cheapest rental units should have had long waiting lists and low vacancy rates. Table 8 shows no such trend. Vacancy rates were slightly higher in unsubsidized low-rent units than in more expensive units throughout the late 1980s. This pattern recurs when we focus on the East and West Coasts, where homelessness was most common. It also recurs when we look at metropolitan areas with more than a million residents. (1994, pp. 83–84)

The relevant portion of Jencks's Table 8 is my Table 10-5.

How should we understand this objection to a housing-market account of homelessness? Note first that it is not an objection to the story I propose. I don't claim that there is a "shortage of affordable housing"; I don't even know what that phrase means. I claim instead that the prices for given quality rose and that the stock of low-quality and low-rent housing diminished. This, we have seen, did happen. The model I use in Chapter 6 to explain why it happened says nothing about vacancy rates. You can't say that a New York City subway map is wrong or useless because Totowa in northern New Jersey is really west of Paterson; New York City subway maps aren't designed to make any statement about the relative longitudes of Totowa and Paterson. The model in Chapter 6 is not designed to say anything about vacancy rates, and it doesn't.

Many economists have developed models to explain rental vacancy rates (just as there are New Jersey maps that show both Totowa and Paterson). Perhaps the best-known are those of Kenneth Rosen and Lawrence Smith (1983) and Richard Arnott (1989). These are the models we should use to interpret the vacancy data that Jencks presents.

The models contain a few basic common ideas. The first is that vacancies arise from the rational calculations of landlords and prospective tenants, even though those calculations often are made

Table 10-5 Percent of Unsubsidized Rental Units Vacant, 1973–1989

| Rent | 1973 | 1979 | 1989 | Change |
|------|------|------|------|--------|
| $250 a month or less | 7.7% | 7.4% | 9.0% | 17% |
| Above $250 a month | 8.3 | 6.1 | 8.7 | 5 |

Source. Jencks (1994), p. 83.

without knowing important pieces of information. Landlords decide, for instance, how much rent to ask for. If they ask too much, they may have to wait a long time with a vacant apartment until a tenant who agrees to that rent comes along; if they ask too little, they won't lose money from vacancies, but they may lose money because they could have received a higher rent if they had been a little more patient. Prospective tenants have to decide whether to accept a landlord's offer or to search more: if they settle for too little, they may be passing up a much nicer and cheaper apartment; if they are too demanding, they may end up with nothing and have to keep searching. Landlords also have to make decisions about advertising (too much is a waste of money, but too little can create persistent vacancies) and tenant standards (too low creates maintenance and crime problems, or worse, but too high also creates persistent vacancies). Tenants have to make decisions about where and how much to search, and how hard to try to act in a manner that will give them credentials as desirable tenants.

The interaction of landlords' and tenants' decisions about these matters produces the vacancy rate we actually observe. It won't be zero—if it were, landlords would start holding out for higher rents and tenants would start agreeing to them. The vacancy rate won't be 100 percent either—if it were, landlords would start lowering the rents they are looking for and tenants would start holding out for them. In between there is some vacancy rate that keeps rents from either rising or falling. Economists call this the "natural vacancy rate"—the rate that is observed when neither landlords nor tenants feel pressure to revise their strategies.

By definition, rents are rising when the actual vacancy rate is below the natural rate and falling when the actual is above the natural. Changes in vacancy rates tell landlords and tenants how and when market conditions have changed and how they should adjust. The natural vacancy rate changes too—higher search costs, for instance, or more variety in the types of apartments offered will make the natural rate higher. Natural rates should differ as well for different types of housing—hotels have higher natural rates than retirement communities.

Actual vacancy rates are like the actual temperature in a house with a thermostat, and the natural rate is like the setting on the thermostat: actual temperatures are always approaching the setting—going up if they are below it, down if they are above—but the setting itself can change too. Understanding the actual course of temperatures requires sorting out which changes reflect new settings and which changes merely reflect convergence to old settings.

The rise in vacancy rates between 1979 and 1987, then, should hardly be surprising. Rents rose after 1979; so 1979 vacancy rates were likely below the natural rate. The 1987 rates are probably closer to the natural rate, or even above it, because rents stopped rising quickly around then. That vacancies should be rising along with homelessness, then, is hardly surprising—both represent the housing market's convergence to a new equilibrium with higher rents. (The fall in vacancy rates between 1973 and 1979 is also consistent with adjustment. Since real rents did not rise after 1973, the 1973 vacancy rate was at or below the natural rate; to get below the natural rate by 1979, it would have had to go down.)

Is it plausible that the natural vacancy rate is above 7.4 percent? Rosen and Smith (1983) estimated the natural vacancy rate for seventeen U.S. cities between 1969 and 1980. Their median estimate was 9.8 percent, but their unconventional way of measuring vacancies biased their estimates upward. Gabriel and Nothaft (1988) used a more conventional measure and looked at sixteen cities between 1981 and 1985. They used two methods of estimation; one gave a median estimate of 7.2 percent, the other a median estimate of 9.5 percent. Thus the adjustment story is plausible; even 1987 vacancy rates might be below the natural rate.

So neither the level nor the gross pattern of vacancy rates argues against a housing-market explanation of homelessness. U.S. rental housing markets do not work with vacancy rates below 7 percent. Similarly, even the best hitters in baseball fail more than 60 percent of the time to get on base. These failure rates don't imply that the players are lazy or drug-crazed or that managers who worry about their pitching staffs are being silly (games can be lost because of bad pitching, even against .250 hitters). They just reflect the nature of the game. Vacancy rates between 7 percent and 10 percent don't mean that prospective tenants are lazy or drug-crazed or that analysts who worry about housing markets are being silly. They just reflect the nature of the housing market.

Still, there is something vaguely disturbing about the details of the Jencks table. If we think of the 1973 and 1987 vacancy rates as both being close to the natural rate, then the natural rate went up, and it went up most for low-rent units. What can explain this? I can think of five different candidates.

*Eviction costs.* Higher eviction costs make it more expensive for a landlord to make a mistake in screening tenants. So landlords will raise their selection standards and take more time screening tenants, even though they lose money from the vacancies incurred as a result. They may also advertise less extensively and rely more on word of mouth, lest they attract the wrong sort of tenants. Since many of the costs of having bad tenants are independent of rent—hiring lawyers, say, or repairing elevators—while the cost of vacancies varies directly with rent, landlords with lower-rent apartments will be more likely to absorb vacancies in order to avoid bad tenants. So eviction costs would raise the natural vacancy rate for low-rent units more than for higher-rent units.

*Composition.* When the price-quality schedule moves upward, the composition of the units renting for under $250 changes: the highest quality is lower and a larger proportion are of lower quality. This change has several ramifications. The average size of a unit becomes smaller, and Guasch and Marshall (1985) have shown that smaller units have higher vacancy rates. The proportion of units like SRO rooms that attract a lot of transients might also increase. So would the proportion of units in smaller metropolitan areas, and smaller metropolitan areas have higher vacancy rates (Arnott, 1989). These composition changes would increase the average vacancy rate for units renting for under $250 without changing the probability that any given unit will be vacant.

*Atypicality.* Jud and Frew (1990) found that the more atypical a unit is, the more likely it is to be vacant. This result is consistent with the models of costly search I alluded to earlier. If low-quality housing became less common—and hence more atypical—vacancy rates would have risen for this reason.

*Measurement changes.* The American Housing Survey, the source for Jencks's data, was revamped between 1983 and 1985 (and its name was changed from the Annual Housing Survey). Jencks writes in a note: "The trend in vacancy rates shown in Table 8 [Table 10-5] should be treated with caution because of methodological changes between 1983 and 1985. The vacancy rate for low-rent units shows no clear trend from 1973 to 1983. Nor is there a clear trend between 1985 and 1989" (pp. 157–158).

Aside from the usual problems of sampling and sample design (the pre-1983 sample was drawn from the 1970 census and updated, the post-1985 sample from the 1980 census), two changes in definition may have affected the vacancy rate for low-rent units. First, vacant mobile homes were counted in the housing stock beginning in 1985. Before that they were ignored, although occupied mobile homes were counted. This inclusion obviously increased the vacancy rate, and since mobile homes are not expensive, it probably increased the vacancy rate for low-rent units more than it increased the rate for higher-rent units.

The second change was the inclusion in the housing stock of rooming houses with between six and ten residents. Before 1983 these were considered "group quarters," like college dormitories and prisons, and so were excluded from the AHS sample (rooming-houses with more than ten rooms are still excluded). Rooming-houses have a considerable transient clientele, and so probably have higher vacancy rates than leased housing. Since they also tend to have low rents, this inclusion would also have increased the relative vacancy rate for low-rent housing.

*Measurement error.* Abandoning a building, especially a multiunit apartment building, is a messy process. Only rarely is it possible to attach a single date such as "June 15, 1989" to the actual abandonment. Abandonment consists of a multitude of acts of omission or commission often spread out over months or years—letting the hallway lightbulbs burn out, going into tax arrears, stopping utility payments, no longer seeking new tenants, stopping rent collection, permitting squatters, and so on. Many decisions in the process are reversible, and they often are reversed when new information becomes available.

At any moment, many units are within this penumbra of abandonment. A survey like the AHS has the impossible task of deciding which are really abandoned and which are not. Since this task is impossible, it can't be done well or consistently, and so there is always the possibility that subtle changes are taking place in how units within the penumbra are treated. Abandonment presents a more definite composition problem as well. Units within the penumbra have low rents and are often vacant. As the price-quality schedule shifts up and the highest quality that rents for under $250 falls, they represent a greater and greater proportion of all the units renting for under $250. This composition change increases the vacancy rate for units renting for under $250.

These five candidates do not exhaust all the possible reasons for the increase in the natural vacancy rate for low-rent units. Assessing the quantitative significance of these reasons and finding better reasons is an important task for economists because we ought to have a better understanding of how low-rent and low-quality housing markets work.

The real weakness of the vacancy-based argument can be seen in the following thought experiment. Try to find a reason for the rise in the natural vacancy rate that excludes housing-market phenomena as a cause of homelessness. It can't be done. Homelessness rose because the price-quality schedule swung upward. That vacancy rates rose at the same time is an interesting phenomenon and one we should try to understand, but in no way is it incompatible with a rising price-quality schedule.

What the vacancy-based arguments do show is that naive "housing shortage" arguments are untenable. If people were to argue that housing is supplied by irrational governments or an inscrutable God or that the Air Force unleashed a secret bombing mission against the South Bronx housing stock, then the fact of positive and rising vacancy rates would be sufficient to show that using them to explain homelessness is wrong. Since silly models have been implicit in quite a bit of writing about homelessness, Jencks has performed a service in pointing out their weaknesses. But an objection to one housing-market explanation of homelessness is not a valid objection to all of them.

# 11

# Income Maintenance

People aren't supposed to be homeless in rich democratic countries. Some sort of safety net is supposed to be in place to keep people from becoming so destitute that they have nowhere to live. Rising homelessness, therefore, might come from failures in the income-maintenance system, just as rising crime might come from failures in the justice system.

Income-maintenance failures, though, should show up in statistics on income before they show up in statistics on homelessness. Only, it would seem, by raising the number of households in poverty or severe poverty could income-maintenance problems contribute to homelessness. Since we have seen, in Chapter 7, that increases in poverty are an implausible explanation for the rise in homelessness in the United States, income-maintenance failures seem to be implausible too, a fortiori.

But welfare money is not like other money. It carries different rules, creates different incentives, comes at different times. To the extent that welfare money is different, income-maintenance failures could have contributed to homelessness. So we should look at these different incentives and rules.

## Grant Levels

Grants matter through their effects on the distribution of income, and through the incentives they set up for staying in shelters or on

*Table 11-1a*  Monthly Benefits for Family of Three

| Benefit | Newark | NYC | Chicago | Toronto[a] |
|---|---|---|---|---|
| Conventionally housed | | | | |
| Year | 1992 | 1992 | 1992 | 1993 |
| AFDC | $424 | $577 | $367 | 0 |
| FBA[b] | 0 | 0 | 0 | 1,066 |
| Child tax credit | 0 | 0 | 0 | 77[c] |
| Child tax benefit | 0 | 0 | 0 | 131 |
| Winter clothing | 0 | 0 | 0 | 13 |
| Back to school | 0 | 0 | 0 | 17 |
| GST tax credit | 0 | 0 | 0 | 26 |
| Ontario tax credit | 0 | 0 | 0 | 13 |
| Food stamps[d] | 248 | 217 | 280 | 0 |
| | $672 | $794 | $657 | $1,343 |
| In shelter | | | | |
| AFDC | 424[e] | 291[f] | 367[g] | 0 |
| FBA | 0 | 0 | 0 | 684 |
| Child tax credit | 0 | 0 | 0 | 77[c] |
| Child tax benefit | 0 | 0 | 0 | 131 |
| Winter clothing | 0 | 0 | 0 | 13 |
| Back to school | 0 | 0 | 0 | 17 |
| GST tax credit | 0 | 0 | 0 | 26 |
| Ontario tax credit | 0 | 0 | 0 | 13 |
| Transportation | 0 | variable | 0 | 0 |
| Food stamps[h] | 248 | 217 | 280 | 0 |
| | $672 | $508 | $657 | $961 |
| In hotel or motel | | | | |
| AFDC | 424[e] | 291 | – | – |
| Transportation | – | variable | 0 | 0 |
| Restaurant | 0[i] | 270[j] | 0 | 0 |
| Food stamps[h] | 248 | 217 | 0 | 0 |
| | $672 | $778 | NA | NA |

a. Canadian dollars were translated into U.S. dollars by taking Blank and Hanratty's 1986 purchasing-power parity estimate of 1.25/1 and updating by using the relative change between 1986 and 1992 third quarter in consumer price indices. This yields an estimate of 1.30/1. The exchange rate in 1992 third quarter was 1.2617/1. Source: *Economic Report of the President*, January 1993.

b. Short-term and immediate benefits in Toronto would be covered by general welfare assistance (GWA) instead of FBA; for a family of three, these grants are basically the same.

c. 1992 amounts.

d. Food-stamp payments were calculated according to the procedures in FRAC (1988), with FY93 parameters for maximum payments from 1993 Green Book. Maximum excess-shelter cost deductions were used because it appeared they would apply with any reasonable amount of rent.

e. This was the rule in early 1991 and before. After mid-1991 the grant was $424 for the first two months, $276 for the next two months, and $148 after that.

f. In some tier II shelters where several meals are served, this amount is further reduced.

g. Most family shelters in Chicago ask families to give them 80–90% of their grant each month. When families leave, this money is returned. See McCourt and Nyden (1990, pp. 16–26).

h. I assume no change in food stamps, though strict adherence to the guidelines indicates they should be reduced in these cases; but they are not.

i. The Newark restaurant allowance was a vendor payment made to the motel proprietor, not to the homeless family; eliminated around 1990.

j. A 1987 figure from Filer (1990).

Sources. For U.S. conventionally housed: Lav, Gold, Lazere, and Greenstein (1993). For Toronto: Ontario Ministry of Community and Social Services, Social Assistance and Employment Opportunities Division, "Social Assistance and Pension Rate Table," rev. July 1, 1993.

the street. Most of the first effect is seen in income statistics, but it is useful to see how welfare contributes to the patterns we see in those statistics.

We would expect, of course, that higher grant levels would reduce homelessness. Time-series data provide some weak confirmation: real U.S. welfare benefits fell substantially, both between 1970 and 1980 and between 1980 and 1990. The national average value of AFDC grants decreased by 23 percent in the 1970s, even when the value of food stamps is included (Sosin, Colson, and Grossman, 1988) and by 43 percent between 1970 and 1992, without counting food stamps (Lav et al., 1993). In the cross-section too there is some weak confirmation: Honig and Filer (1993) find that cities with higher AFDC benefits have significantly less homelessness. Looking at benefit levels, then, is a useful starting point.

Table 11-1 (a–c) sets out grant levels for nonelderly families, single individuals, and disabled individuals for the four North American cities. The outstanding feature of the table is the high grant level in Toronto—roughly twice Chicago's and Newark's, more than 60 percent larger than New York's. Part of this difference is an administrative mirage. The two cities with the lowest grant levels, Newark and Chicago, have flat grants: everyone gets the same amount without any consideration of expenses. New York has a flat grant with a shelter allowance—up to a maximum, the shelter allowance equals rent. Table 11-1 uses the maximum (which is usually binding).[1] Administrators have no discretion in setting grant levels. In Toronto, by contrast, administrators have wide discretion: "Discretionary benefits are almost inconceivable in the United States, where watchdog groups demand that publicly known, uniform regulations be applied to all applicants. In Canada, there appears to be greater trust in the decisions and competence of government em-

*Table 11-1b*  Monthly Benefits for Single Individual

| Benefit | Newark | NYC | Chicago | Toronto |
|---|---|---|---|---|
| **Conventionally housed** | | | | |
| Year | 1992 | 1992 | 1991 | 1993 |
| GA | $210, $140[a] | $352 | $165 | 0 |
| GWA | 0 | 0 | 0 | $510 |
| GST tax credit | 0 | 0 | 0 | 13 |
| Ontario tax credit | 0 | 0 | 0 | 6 |
| Food stamps | 111 | 104 | 105 | 0 |
| Restaurant[b] | 0 | 0 | 0 | 0 |
| | $321 or $251[a] | $456 | $270 | $529 |
| **In shelter** | | | | |
| GA | $210, $140[a] | $45 | $165 | 0 |
| GWA | 0 | 0 | 0 | $369 |
| GST tax credit | 0 | 0 | 0 | 13 |
| Ontario tax credit | 0 | 0 | 0 | 6 |
| Food stamps | 111 | 104 | 105 | 0 |
| Discretionary[c] | 0 | 0 | 0 | 86 |
| | $321, $251[a] | $149 | $270 | $474 |
| **On street** | | | | |
| GA | $210, $140[a] | $137 | $165 | 0 |
| GWA | 0 | 0 | 0 | $369 |
| GST tax credit | 0 | 0 | 0 | 13 |
| Ontario tax credit | 0 | 0 | 0 | 6 |
| Food stamps | 111 | 104 | 105 | 0 |
| Restaurant | 0 | 64 | 0 | 0 |
| | $321, $251[a] | $305 | $270 | $388 |

a. Larger figure for an unemployable person; smaller for employable.

b. Restaurant allowance for individuals without access to cooking facilities; some SROs and lodginghouses might also collect it. Homeless people in Newark placed in hotels are eligible for restaurant allowance of $7.50 per day, but made as vendor payment to hotel.

c. Allowance distributed daily at discretion of hostel supervisor.

*Sources.* For U.S. general assistance, except Chicago, conventionally housed: Lav, Lazere, Greenstein, and Gold (1993, p. 40). For Toronto general welfare assistance: McFarlane (1991, 1993), and Ontario Ministry of Community and Social Services (1993). For New York: Legal Action Center for the Homeless (1993) and New York Code of Rules and Regulations 352.8(f). For Chicago: Public Welfare Coalition.

ployees, and a willingness to grant decision-making authority to government case workers" (Blank and Hanratty 1991, p. 10). The maxima in the table are therefore not often binding. Still the differences are large enough to be striking. Toronto's generous grants probably contribute to its more equal distribution of income and its lower level of homelessness.

*Table 11-1c*  Monthly Benefits for Single, Disabled Individual

| Benefit | Newark | NYC | Chicago | Toronto |
|---|---|---|---|---|
| Not homeless | | | | |
| Year | 1992 | 1992 | 1992 | 1993 |
| SSI | $453 | $508 | $422 | 0 |
| Food stamps | 69 | 44 | 83 | 0 |
| FBA | 0 | 0 | 0 | $715 |
| GST tax credit | 0 | 0 | 0 | 13 |
| Ontario tax credit | 0 | 0 | 0 | 6 |
| | $522 | $552 | $505 | $734 |
| In shelter or street | | | | |
| SSI | $453 | $508 | $452 | 0 |
| Food stamps | 69 | 44 | 83 | 0 |
| FBA | 0 | 0 | 0 | $489 |
| GST tax credit | 0 | 0 | 0 | 13 |
| Ontario tax credit | 0 | 0 | 0 | 6 |
| Discretionary | 0 | 0 | 0 | 86 |
| | $522 | $552 | $505 | $594 |

Maximum excess shelter deductions for food stamps not used; instead monthly rent of $347.50 used for U.S. cities; gives maximum excess shelter deduction for Illinois.

Welfare grants also have incentive effects. The more it costs (in reduced benefits) to enter a shelter or to live on the street, the more reluctant will people be to do so. The most interesting effects are for New York singles: entering a shelter is very expensive, especially compared to living on the street. General Assistance recipients in New York get $305 a month if they live on the street, $149 a month if they live in a shelter. This incentive may be partly responsible for the high proportion of New York's single homeless population that lives on the street. Yet the shelter allowance also means that New York gives GA recipients less incentive than other U.S. cities to become homeless in any form. Newark and Chicago, with flat grants, do not vary the GA grant with housing status. But many single shelters in these cities expect recipients to contribute something.

In Toronto, people in shelters or on the street get only the minimum shelter allowance—a "down payment to secure accommodation" (McFarlane, 1993)—and so they get considerably less than most people in conventional housing. In addition, though, hostel supervisors have up to $86 (U.S.) a month to give to residents for personal needs. "This is given as cash on a per day basis, and is up to the discretion of the supervisor." Toronto also provides another incentive to leave shelters: a "community start-up benefit" of $615 "to set up a new permanent residence" (Ontario Ministry of Community and Social Services, 1992).

For families, New York also provides significant incentives for one form of homelessness over another, but this time hotels are the form favored over shelters. Since the welfare bureaucracy has some control over the use of hotels, though, in contrast to none over the streets, the consequences of subsidizing the less socially desirable form of homelessness may not be as severe. Although New York looks, in Table 11-1, like the only U.S. city using the AFDC grant to discourage homelessness, in fact Newark and Chicago both do so, probably more effectively, in more subtle ways. In Newark, the AFDC grant starts going down after two months in a hotel or shelter, and after five months is only 35 percent of its former level. Chicago family shelters generally require residents to turn over 80 percent or 90 percent of their AFDC grants, and encourage them to save their food stamps. The money is returned when they leave the shelter. SSI also discourages shelter use in a way not directly apparent from Table 11-1: recipients lose their benefits if they stay in a shelter more than six months in any nine-month period.

It should be noted that Chicago differs in another way: it is the only city in which nominal benefits for GA recipients have been cut in recent years. The maximum grant was around $198 a month in 1981. Then a flat grant of around $150 a month was instituted. It increased a little between then and 1992 (Sosin, Colson, and Grossman). In 1992, Illinois eliminated benefits entirely for people deemed employable (Lav et al.).

## Access

Benefit levels can't matter to people who don't get benefits, and so we also have to consider how easy it is to get them. Indeed, the idea of "falling through the safety net" implies that access is the major problem: people are homeless because somehow they are not receiving the benefits due them. Appendix Table 1 shows that very few homeless single adults get public assistance, but most homeless families do.[2] In the United States the picture presented is one of hostile, impenetrable welfare bureaucracies that homeless people can't navigate, leaving them without money for shelter.

Such a view might have some rough empirical support if hostile impenetrability did increase in the United States around 1980, and if it were greater there than in Canada. It seems undeniable that the Canadian system is the more friendly of the two. Administrators in the rule-driven U.S. system, for instance, seem obsessed with minimizing the errors their employees make; their reputations and their federal funding depend on error rates. Administrators in the discretion-driven Canadian system, by contrast, have great difficulty even understanding what an error rate is. Time-series evidence is also weakly supportive. On the U.S. federal level, the Omnibus Budget Reconciliation Act of 1982 and the Tax Equity and Fiscal Responsibility Act of 1982 included many measures designed to tighten the administration of AFDC, food stamps, and SSI. In New York, the changes probably began earlier, soon after the fiscal crisis of 1975–76, but homelessness rose earlier in New York too.

The strongest evidence of difficulty in access comes from New York's Legal Action Center for the Homeless (LACH). These clients are single adults, mainly men, who use certain soup kitchens in Manhattan; LACH often refers clients to receive public assistance. Its 1993 study is based on comparing its own list of referrals between March and December 1990 with records of the city's Human Resources Administration (HRA).

Access involves two steps: getting on welfare initially and staying on. The LACH study showed that for homeless single adults both steps were hard, with the second considerably harder than the first. Of the LACH homeless referrals, only 47.1 percent were active cases on HRA's rolls three months later. Some referrals, of course, may not have been legally eligible, but LACH workers are fairly skilled lawyers who are familiar with eligibility criteria. HRA reported "no activity" for 31.9 percent of the referrals; these people either didn't make it to the intake center or didn't wait long enough to be interviewed. Of the referrals 21.0 percent were recorded as closed cases three months later; almost all of these people were probably denied benefits, although a fraction (less than a quarter) may have received a check or two.

Staying on welfare was harder. Only 25.0 percent of the homeless LACH clients whose cases were active before July 1, 1990, were still active at the end of the year (the same was true of only 23.1 percent of LACH clients who were not homeless). Putting the two steps together, a LACH client appeared to have only one chance in eight of opening a case and maintaining it for a year. GA receipt among the homeless populations in Appendix Table 1 is higher than would be implied by this process (the most comparable population is probably that of the Columbia study, where the GA receipt rate was three times higher).[3] LACH clients are probably not typical, but still their extraordinary difficulties highlight the fact that access is not easy.

Why? For New York's GA program, LACH's authors point (without detailed evidence) to the problems of scheduling appointments. GA clients are frequently mandated to attend conferences with caseworkers, to make sure they are maintaining eligibility. Missing several of these appointments is grounds for termination. Notices for appointments are sent through regular mail and, as might be expected, homeless clients often don't get them or, if they do, fail to attend the meetings. But doesn't explain why LACH clients who are not homeless seem to have the same difficulties in staying on welfare.

Sosin, Colson, and Grossman (SCG) provide a more elaborate discussion of access problems in Chicago. Of the currently homeless people in their 1988 sample, 39 percent had either been cut off an income-maintenance program (excluding food stamps) in the previous six months or had filed an unsuccessful application. Not everyone who was cut off remained off; the vast majority of AFDC cutoffs in particular were reinstated within six months, although they remained in shelters.

Table 11-2 gives the reasons why homeless people in this sample were cut off or denied benefits, according to them. The outstanding feature of this table is the large proportion of GA cutoffs arising from missed appointments, just as in the LACH story. SCG write: "the GA program includes a strong work program in which regular meetings about job search, or regular classes, are required. It is likely that a large number of these dropped individuals have had particular problems in making all of the required meetings. Particularly with the renewed interest in work programs this problem bears a close

*Table 11-2*  Stated Reasons for Unsuccessful Applications and Cutoffs
from Income-Maintenance Programs by Homeless People
in Chicago, 1986

| | Percent stating reason | | |
|---|---|---|---|
| Unsuccessful application | AFDC | GA | Others |
| Financially ineligible | 0.0% | 0.0% | 0.0% |
| Ineligible, other rules | 0.0 | 25.4 | 42.6 |
| Can't prove eligibility | 35.1 | 7.9 | 0.0 |
| No address | 14.9 | 17.5 | 57.4 |
| Uncooperative, missed app't | 14.9 | 21.6 | 0.0 |
| Changed circumstance | 0.0 | 5.8 | 0.0 |
| Pending | 20.1 | 15.8 | 0.0 |
| Other | 14.9 | 11.7 | 0.0 |
| (Number | 5 | 14 | 2) |

| | Percent stating reason | | |
|---|---|---|---|
| Cutoffs | AFDC | GA | Others |
| Missed app't, rule violation | 18.4% | 66.6% | 0.0% |
| Admin. or other mixup | 14.9 | 7.2 | 8.3 |
| No address | 5.0 | 1.9 | 0.0 |
| Moved | 21.6 | 5.3 | 8.3 |
| Changed circumstance | 18.4 | 9.7 | 61.2 |
| Other | 21.6 | 9.2 | 9.3 |
| (Number | 16 | 56 | 10) |

*Source.* Sosin, Colson, and Grossman, (1988), tables 4.5, 4.8; excludes food stamps.

watch" (p. 217). The reasons for the denial of GA benefits have no
such definite pattern, but don't include financial ineligibility.

The reasons for unsuccessful applications and cutoffs in SCG can
be contrasted with reasons for not receiving assistance given by
long-term shelter residents in Crystal and Goldstein (1984), as
shown in Table 11-3. They seem quite different: the Crystal and
Goldstein data stress characteristics of the homeless—seeking independence, wanting to avoid hassle—rather than characteristics of
the income-maintenance system. The two data sets, though, are
complementary. If a hurdle is high, some people won't be able to
jump it; the ones who fail will be the bad jumpers. SCG data are about
why the hurdle is high; Crystal and Goldstein data are about how
to identify the bad jumpers.

*Table 11-3*   Stated Reasons for Not Receiving Public Assistance, Long-Term
New York Shelter Residents, 1982

| | |
|---|---|
| Don't want welfare | 20% |
| Can't deal with hassle | 19 |
| Keep getting rejected | 10 |
| Not eligible | 9 |
| Not ready | 9 |
| Can't live on grant | 8 |
| No ID | 8 |
| No address | 8 |
| Applic. pending | 8 |
| Vague | 2 |

*Source.* Crystal and Goldstein (1984).

The SCG study also documents substantial access problems with
AFDC. The major reason why otherwise eligible families were rejected for AFDC was the inability to produce a birth certificate for
someone in the family. Federal regulations require birth certificates,
and recipient families that don't provide them become part of state's
error rate. AFDC cutoffs in the SCG data show no decisive element,
only "general rigidity" (p. 217). After the SCG study, however, Illinois began to require mothers to provide a great deal of information
about children's fathers, with threats of grant reductions and terminations for failure to do so. McCourt and Nyden (1990), found that
by 1990 child-support enforcement sanctions and terminations
figured prominently in the difficulties of homeless families.

The emphasis on AFDC access problems, however, seems unique
to Chicago. In Newark and New York, so many homeless families
are AFDC recipients that the issue hardly arises. Nor are similar
problems raised often in Toronto or London. Since Chicago has less
family homelessness than the U.S. cities where AFDC access is no
issue, AFDC access difficulties (as distinct from GA difficulties) probably do not contribute much to homelessness at this time. To the
extent that welfare reform makes staying on AFDC harder by adding
work and child-support requirements, this situation could change.

Supplemental Security Income is the final large U.S. income-
maintenance program, and the one where access figures most
prominently and universally. As shown in Table 11-1, SSI grant
levels are much higher than other U.S. grant levels—high enough

that almost all SSI recipients purchase conventional housing. This is why so few homeless people receive SSI.[4] The grant, moreover, was designed to give aid to poor people who are aged, blind, or disabled. Substantial fractions of homeless people are debilitated by mental illness and substance abuse (probably a substantial number suffer from standard physical disabilities as well, but data on this question are sparse; Drapkin, 1990), and so it would seem that SSI should be able to end a substantial fraction of nonfamily homelessness in the United States. Why hasn't it?

Becoming eligible for SSI is complex and time-consuming. According to SCG:

> Some legal aid workers go so far as to imply that denials for the first visit are routine, and that it is "unusual" for someone to be accepted without an attorney. There is a general view that the "squeaky wheel gets the grease" in the SSI system.
>
> The issue of time may also be important. Legal aid workers believe that the cases they deal with generally take about nine months to resolve. In addition, many of those with mental impairments may make mistakes in the process that result in even longer delays. (pp. 193–194)

These access difficulties seem to persist despite almost a decade of federal efforts to reduce them. Between 1981 and 1983, the Reagan administration tried to slow the growth of the SSI disability caseload by bringing pressure on the number of applications and conducting administrative reviews that removed several hundred thousand people. By 1984, however, congressional and legal action had stopped these processes and in many cases reversed them. Since then, eligibility standards for mental illness have been broadened to include anxiety, affective disorders, somatoform disorders, and personality disorders; extensive outreach efforts have been mandated; special procedures have been instituted to speed eligibility determinations for homeless applicants; and persons with AIDS (1988) and HIV (1991) have been declared presumptively eligible so that they can receive almost immediate payments (Green Book, 1993, pp. 855–856). Cities, especially New York and Newark, have tried very hard to get shelter residents declared eligible, usually with unspectacular results.

These efforts have probably gone about as far as could be expected in a rule-driven system like ours, especially for the mentally ill. The number of adults between eighteen and sixty-four who were receiving SSI payments because of disability grew from 1.6 million in September 1983 to 2.8 million in September 1992 (Green Book, p. 842). About 700,000 of this group have a primary diagnosis of mental illness. The number of mentally ill homeless people in the United States is plausibly in the range 50,000 to 200,000. If no homeless people receive SSI (a reasonable assumption), and all SSI-eligible, conventionally housed mentally ill people are receiving it, the takeup rate for SSI among the mentally ill is between 78 percent and 93 percent. Blank and Hanratty (1991), estimate U.S. takeup rates at between 46.1 percent for food stamps and 74.5 percent for AFDC. Even if around 500,000 conventionally housed SSI-eligible mentally ill people were not receiving benefits, SSI would still have a takeup rate in the range experienced by other U.S. income-maintenance programs. So nothing appears extraordinarily difficult about SSI for the mentally ill.

Here again the contrast with Canada is instructive. Disability in Canada is a simple judgment by any physician. Authority figures have more discretion, and more authority, than they do in the United States. I don't know if this results in higher takeup rates.

In the United States SSI treats substance abusers differently from the mentally ill; for them, access is deliberately more complicated. Substance abuse or addiction by itself is not a sufficient condition to qualify for SSI. Substance abusers are medically eligible only if their addiction causes a disabling condition such as tremors, psychosis, AIDS, or cirrhosis. Substance abusers also have to participate in treatment programs "when available and appropriate," and SSI will not send them checks directly. Their checks go to a representative payee. Only about 20,000 persons diagnosed as disabled drug addicts or alcoholics were receiving SSI benefits in 1991 (Green Book, p. 856).

In Toronto, by contrast, substance abusers "are considered permanently unemployed"—and therefore eligible for the higher Family Benefit Allowances—"if a doctor states that it is a chronic and unrecoverable problem" (McFarlane, 1993).

Finally, note that in none of these programs did we see "not having an address" as a reason for the denial of benefits. Such a disqualification had disappeared from regulations in both the United States and Canada by the mid-eighties if it ever appeared at all. A smattering of the homeless people that SCG interviewed in 1986 cited this difficulty; they probably either encountered an incompetent caseworker or made up a story. The 1982 responses from 8 percent of Crystal and Goldstein's sample may have been more representative of that time, but no address, even then, was a minor reason.

## Emergencies

Newark and New York have large and elaborate programs to aid poor people facing emergencies. Chicago has a tiny program, and Toronto has none at all. In Newark and New York, among the emergencies treated are imminent eviction and homelessness, and both have extensive "prevention programs" to forestall evictions. Emergency assistance funds many shelters and hotels in these cities as well. In Chicago, emergency assistance is limited essentially to natural disasters. Emergency assistance is a foreign concept in Toronto, since discretion obviates any need for a formal policy. The small cross-section provides no support for the hypothesis that formal emergency-assistance programs reduce homelessness.

## Incentives to Share Housing

Different income-maintenance programs give recipients different incentives to share housing. Economic theory implies that incentives to share housing should affect homelessness in two ways: first, by encouraging people to double up rather than be homeless; second, by shifting the demand for housing because some households that would not otherwise be homeless will not be purchasing their own housing either. Honig and Filer (1993) found a positive relationship in the 1984 cross-section between homelessness and the reduction in AFDC grant caused by moving in with nonpoor parents, but the relationship was not quite statistically significant at conventional levels.

The U.S. national programs, food stamps and SSI, have strong disincentives for sharing housing. SSI reduces benefits by one-third to recipients who are "living in another person's household and receiving support and maintenance in-kind from such person" (Green Book, p. 823). Food-stamp maxima increase by less for larger households—the maximum allotment for a household of two is only 82 percent more than the allotment for a family of one—and the standard deduction is the same for all households regardless of size, as is the excess shelter-cost deduction. Thus, for instance, an individual with $210 a month in income (the Newark unemployable GA grant) and $150 a month in rent would get $90 a month in food stamps. If two such individuals shared a bigger room with $300 a month in rent, together they would get only $161 a month in food stamps, instead of the $180 a month they got living separately. And if by living together they were able to reduce rent below $300, their food-stamp allotment would be reduced by 30 cents for every dollar of rent reduction they managed.

To mitigate this disincentive, the food-stamp program often allows people who are living together to apply as separate units, but separate applications are forbidden in some of the most popular doubling-up combinations. Brothers and sisters living together must apply as a single unit and suffer the reduction that this brings; so must children over eighteen living in the same household with their nonelderly parents unless minor children are present; so must nonelderly parents living in the same household as their children, unless minor children are present; so must children under eighteen "under parental control" of someone in the household; and so must husbands and wives living together (FRAC, 1988).

In contrast with the federal programs, the strictly local GA programs in the United States don't discourage doubling up. As classic flat grants, GA grants in New Jersey and Illinois are completely unchanged if a recipient doubles up. In New York, however, prorating applies—doubling up generally reduces the shelter allowance.

Incentives under AFDC are more mixed. New Jersey again uses classic flat grants and so does not adjust payments for doubled-up households. The same is true for Illinois, but if a parent on AFDC under twenty-one were still living in the home of her parents, those parents as legally responsible relatives would be ordered to reimburse a portion of the welfare agency's payments. No such requirement would apply for parents over twenty-one. New York, by contrast, has a shelter allowance as part of its AFDC grant. Regulations that took effect in October 1982 reduced benefits to doubled-up families by about $50 a month because of requirements to prorate shelter and utility costs; about 40,000 families were affected (Mayor's Management Report, September 1982). The timing of these regulations, just as family homelessness was starting to rise, is intriguing.[5]

In Canada, doubling up generally causes grant reductions, but the magnitude is hard to compute: "Generally, those who share a house, apartment, or room receive assistance to cover only their part of the cost of accommodation" (Ontario Ministry of Community and Social Services, 1992, p. 30). Discretionary administration may reduce some, but not all, of the incentive effects.

Finally note that in the United States the income-maintenance programs with the largest doubling-up disincentives, food stamps and SSI, were the programs whose relative size and importance were growing most rapidly in the 1970s. They are both inflation-indexed, in contrast to the programs without strong doubling-up disincentives, and both were also expanding in real terms, especially among the nonelderly. State, local, and federal expenditures on conventional assistance programs were twenty-four times larger than expenditures on food stamps and SSI in 1970, four times larger in 1974, and three times larger in 1979 (*Statistical Abstract*, 1981).

## Work Incentives

Work incentives in family assistance programs have been studied extensively, both in the United States. (see Moffitt, 1992, for a detailed survey) and in Canada (for example, Blank and Hanratty, 1991). The conclusions are generally that incentive effects are present but are not large. More interesting for the study of homelessness, though, particularly colloquial homelessness, are work incentives for single adults, which economists have studied very little. Generally, single adults are probably more responsive to the labor market than lone mothers are, and so the incentive effects are probably bigger. But this is mainly speculation.

Differences among cities here are significant. The Illinois GA program of the mid-1980s did not discourage working. Essentially all earned income was disregarded so that earned income almost never reduced the grant; specifically, between $210 and $225 a month in earnings were disregarded. New Jersey disregards $60 a month and one-third of the remaining income. Toronto disregards $58 (U.S.) and a quarter of the remainder. New York, though, has substantial disincentives to work: the grant is reduced dollar for dollar for any earned income. Everywhere in the United States, SSI recipients get to retain the first $65 of earned income plus one-half of the remainder.

All of these programs interact with food stamps. A one-dollar increase in income causes a 24-cent reduction in food stamps for a household where the excess-shelter deduction limits are binding, a 36-cent reduction for a household where the limits are not binding. Thus Newark GA recipients, for whom the deduction limits are usually binding, face an implicit tax rate of 74.7 percent, and SSI recipients face a tax rate of 62 percent if the deduction limits are binding, 68 percent if they are not.

In addition, all of these programs except SSI have work requirements—recipients must show up either at appointments to discuss getting a job or at specific public work assignments for a few hours a month (workfare). These requirements may also make it hard to hold a regular job.

Finally, note that work disincentives are not really disincentives to working; they are disincentives to working at jobs where you get paid on the books and have to work regular hours. They don't discourage panhandling and canning. New York City's high GA grant and 100 percent implicit tax rate on earnings are thus quite consistent with the heavy concentration of panhandlers on its streets.

Changing patterns in income-maintenance programs probably contributed something to the rise in U.S. homelessness in the 1980s. Especially important was the large growth in incentives to form small households rather than doubling up. These incentives arose largely from the tremendous relative growth of food stamps and SSI, but revisions to more traditional AFDC and GA programs also contributed.

Growing access problems in GA and possibly also in AFDC may also have contributed to the rise in homelessness. To the extent that access problems concentrate the most severe poverty among the most disorganized people and the people least able to cope with rules and bureaucracies, access difficulties can increase homelessness without changing the reported income distribution. (And they can make it appear that pathologies are responsible for the rise in homelessness.)

Work incentives in GA programs also declined in the 1980s—another consequence of the spread of food stamps. Although this change may have raised colloquial homelessness, the effect on official homelessness was probably small.

In all, I suspect that the effect of income-maintenance changes on the rise of U.S. homelessness was small. The significant changes—including the reduction in grant levels—were everywhere about the same in the United States (the most important being the rise in relative importance of food stamps and SSI), but rates of homelessness differ greatly.

# 12

# Mental Health

One popular explanation for the rise of homelessness is that mentally ill people used to be in psychiatric hospitals, and now they're on the streets. I don't think this argument is persuasive; at most, deinstitutionalization accounts for only a very small part of the growth of homelessness in the United States.

Of course mental illness does help to explain why certain homeless individuals are homeless; effective treatment of their mental illnesses would probably enable many of these individuals to become conventionally housed. But stories of this sort about individuals cannot explain historical trends. Many soldiers who failed to duck got killed between 1861 and 1865, and if you were my friend I'd make sure you knew how to duck, but it would be ridiculous to suggest that an atrophy of the ducking reflex was the reason for the increase in deaths by gunshot wound between 1854 and 1864.

Mental illness doesn't doom you to be homeless: even today in the United States the vast majority of severely mentally ill people—even the vast majority of severely mentally ill people who are not institutionalized—are housed. Mental illness does increase the probability that you will be homeless, and if that probability had stayed constant, we would have to attribute the rising number of mentally ill homeless people to a rise in the number of mentally ill people—or, more precisely, to a rise in the number of severely mentally ill people who are not institutionalized. But if most of the rise in the number of mentally ill homeless people stems from an increase in the probability that you are homeless, given that you are mentally ill and not institutionalized, then we have to look to causes other than deinstitutionalization—to the housing market, say—to explain why there are now more mentally ill homeless people.

By analogy, if the probability you would be killed if you didn't duck had stayed about the same between 1854 and 1864, we could attribute the rise in gunshot deaths to atrophy of the ducking reflex. But if the rise in gunshot deaths was due to an increase in the probability that you would be killed if you didn't duck, we would have to look to some other cause—to the Civil War, for instance. (But "Be sure to duck" would still be good advice.)

In this chapter I will argue that the reason more mentally ill people are homeless is because the probability of being homeless, given that you are mentally ill and not institutionalized, has risen substantially. The rise in the number of people who are both mentally ill and not institutionalized accounts for almost nothing.


## How Many Homeless People Are Mentally Ill?

Appendix Table 2 summarizes the results from several studies of various kinds of homeless people in five of my six cities. I know of no studies of mental illness among homeless people in Newark. Severe mental illness can be measured either by previous treatment history or by current diagnostic tests, and I include studies that use each method. To the extent that treatment works or illness is episodic, treatment histories overstate current mental illness. Diagnostic studies are expensive and time-consuming; they may also miss episodic mental illnesses (such as schizophrenia) that are currently in remission. Calibration is also a problem: "conventional instruments of assessment have proven ill suited for use with an often fugitive population, practicing what may be highly irregular modes of subsistence, whose 'baseline' levels of functioning are but poorly defined" (Hopper, 1988, p. 158).

Despite these difficulties, a clear picture emerges from the studies. Almost all of them find the proportion of mentally ill between 10

percent and 30 percent. This holds over a variety of times, populations, and locations. These numbers are consistent with the sort of
numbers that Eagle and Caton (1990) found in a more extensive
survey of U.S. mental-health studies and with the various studies of
unidentified British populations cited by Cohen (1992).

One difficulty in interpreting the studies is that the measures
of mental illness do not necessarily include the conditions that pre-
dated an individual's becoming homeless. The direction of causality is unclear: homelessness may create the symptoms of mental
illness rather than the other way around. Snow et al. (1986), for
instance, argue that many of the behavioral patterns alleged to be
symptoms of mental illness may be consequences of the homeless
way of life, or even adaptations to it. The General Accounting
Office (1988) points out two particularly salient paths for such a
process. The first deals with questions on psychological tests that
are designed to measure depression: homeless people may find
life bleak and their prospects grim, even without any mispercep-
tion of their environment. Second, women who live on the street
may become dirty and disheveled and act strangely in order to
discourage would-be attackers. Behavior that would be pathological for a woman with a place to live may be reasonable for a homeless woman.

Still, total skepticism is not warranted. *Severe* mental illness is
unlikely to be caused by homelessness, and severe mental illness is
present in considerable numbers of homeless adults. Hopper (1988)
reports on research that tried very hard to mitigate causality problems; careful controls reduced the estimated incidence of mental
illness by about a third.

What are we to make of these figures? First, mentally ill people
are more likely to be homeless than people who are not mentally ill.
Jencks's estimate (1994) is that about 1 percent of the U.S. adult
population is severely mentally ill—enough to preclude working—and less stringent definitions do not produce estimates of more
than 5 percent (for example, Barker et al., 1992; Locke and Regier,
1985). Second, aside from methods, the estimates do not vary much
by time or place. If patterns of institutionalization vary greatly by
time and place, that would raise questions about how much such
patterns can matter.

## How Many Mentally Ill People Are Institutionalized?

In all three English-speaking countries, many fewer people are in psychiatric hospitals now than forty years ago. For Britain and the United States as a whole, 1955 was the peak year for numbers in psychiatric hospitals, while 1958–1960 was the peak for Ontario (Liss and Montaynes, 1982), The decline is greatest for state and county mental hospitals in the United States: from 559,000 inpatients in 1955 to 90,000 in 1990. These hospitals were once the centerpiece of the U.S. mental health system, but now they are only a small piece of it.

Several factors contributed to this decline in institutional population. Throughout the world, the perception that mental institutions were horrible places (and that making them pleasant would be incredibly expensive) and the introduction of psychotropic medicines in 1955 were probably the most important. Other advances in medicine also mattered: the number of patients in state and county mental hospitals suffering from "organic brain syndromes associated with syphilis," for instance, fell from 29,000 in 1955 to 4,000 in 1973 (Kramer, 1977).

In the United States, the hope at the start of deinstitutionalization was that community facilities would be developed; in Britain and Canada, the plan was for care to be shifted to general hospitals (Goering, Wasylenki, and Grisonich [GWG], 1990). In Canada the 1964 Royal Commission on Health Services recommended that "henceforth all discrimination in the distinction between physical and mental illness in the organization and provision of services for their treatment be disavowed for all time as unworthy and unscientific" (cited in GWG, p. 2). In the United States few of the planned community facilities were developed: only about half of the centers planned under the Community Mental Health Centers Act of 1963 were actually built (U.S. Department of Health and Human Services, 1992). Similarly in Ontario the bed capacity of general-hospital psychiatric units increased from 431 in 1960 to 2,201 in 1987, but this increase is less than a fifth of the decrease in psychiatric hospital beds. Moreover, according to GWG: "Unfortunately, the new general hospital psychiatric units did not provide care for patients suffering from severe, major mental disorders. Rather these units

*Table 12-1*   People in Public Mental Hospitals, 1953–1991

| Year | NY state Total | NY state Under 65 | NJ | IL | ONT | England |
|------|------|----------|--------|--------|--------|---------|
| 1953 | – | – | – | – | – | 193,097 |
| 1955 | 93,314 | – | – | – | – | – |
| 1960 | 88,768 | – | – | – | – | – |
| 1961 | – | – | – | – | 14,158 | – |
| 1965 | 84,859 | – | – | – | – | – |
| 1966 | 82,765 | – | 11,449 | 39,857 | 11,456 | – |
| 1967 | 80,321 | – | 10,812 | 36,585 | 11,051 | – |
| 1968 | 77,984 | – | 9,709 | 33,520 | 7,829 | – |
| 1969 | 70,765 | – | 8,687 | 30,069 | 7,278 | 175,839 |
| 1970 | 64,364 | – | 7,943 | 27,055 | 7,278 | 171,990 |
| 1971 | 57,625 | – | 7,240 | 22,936 | 7,348 | – |
| 1972 | 49,590 | – | – | 19,638 | 7,096 | – |
| 1973 | 44,081 | 23,773 | – | 16,778 | 6,896 | – |
| 1974 | 39,237 | – | – | 14,653 | 5,027 | 148,129 |
| 1975 | 35,222 | – | 5,349 | 13,140 | 4,457 | 145,238 |
| 1976 | 31,972 | – | 4,792 | 12,058 | 4,128 | – |
| 1977 | 29,076 | 15,727 | 4,304 | 11,253 | 3,912 | – |
| 1978 | 27,376 | 14,863 | 4,134 | 10,813 | 3,911 | – |
| 1979 | 26,278 | 14,285 | 4,515 | 10,186 | 3,911 | 127,497 |
| 1980 | 25,000 | 13,670 | 4,545 | 9,942 | 3,840 | 124,607 |
| 1981 | 24,269 | 13,649 | 3,578 | 9,604 | 3,984 | 119,507 |
| 1982 | 23,942 | 13,712 | 3,552 | 8,934 | 3,919 | 116,749 |
| 1983 | 22,947 | 13,382 | 3,608 | 8,627 | – | 113,241 |
| 1984 | 22,864 | 13,614 | 3,439 | 8,417 | – | 108,473 |
| 1985 | 22,419 | 13,609 | 3,261 | 8,161 | – | 102,855 |
| 1986 | 21,836 | 13,442 | 3,019 | 7,947 | – | 97,064 |
| 1987 | 21,649 | 13,767 | 2,977 | 7,902 | – | – |
| 1988 | 20,502 | 13,442 | 2,909 | 7,968 | – | 85,321 |
| 1989 | 18,428 | 12,257 | 2,842 | – | – | 77,628 |
| 1990 | 16,483 | 11,266 | 2,751 | – | – | 70,627 |
| 1991 | – | – | 2,783 | – | – | – |

Average annual loss

|  | NY | NJ | IL | ONT | England |
|------|------|------|-------|------|---------|
| 1966–75 | 5,283 | 678 | 2,969 | 778 | 2,991[a] |
| 1975–81 | 1,826 | 295 | 589 | 79 | 4,289 |
| 1981–88 | 538 | 96 | 234 | – | 5,982 |

a. 1959–1975.

Sources. New York: Before 1977, except 1973: Rockefeller Institute of Government, *1983–84 New York State Statistical Yearbook* (Albany, 1983), table B-7. 1977–1987, New York Office of Mental Health, annual reports. 1973 and 1978: "Five Year Comprehensive Plan for Services to Mentally Ill Persons in New York State" (1979), p. 98. 1988: *1989–90 Yearbook*, table K-6. 1989: *1991 Yearbook*, table K-6.

New Jersey: State Budget, various years; figure is average daily population. 1991: Department of Human Services, "Legislator's Briefing Book" (1992).

Illinois: Department of Mental Health and Developmental Disabilities, "Illinois Mental Health Statistics FY 1988" (Springfield, 1989), p. 54; figure is average daily population of residents at inpatient facilities.

Ontario: Ontario Ministry of Health, annual reports; figures are for provincial psychiatric hospitals. For 1966 and 1967, average daily population is given; for 1975 and 1976, figure is Dec. 31 population; otherwise population on March 31 is given. Source for 1982 is Liss and Motaynes (1982, p. 19). For 1961, figure is bed capacity from GWG, p. 3.

England: Figure is average capacity, not occupancy, of psychiatric hospitals for fiscal years ending Dec. 31 through 1986; thereafter fiscal years end March 31. For 1983 and before, Department of Health, Office of Health Economics, "Compendium of Health Statistics" (1987), table 3.9. Thereafter "Health and Personal Social Service Statistics for England" (1991), table 4.2. Psychiatric hospitals include both mental illness and mental handicap.

discovered a new patient population which was less seriously ill and which previously had not received inpatient psychiatric care" (p. 5).

In the United States, federal policies on income maintenance also mattered. After 1965 states had a big incentive to move patients, especially elderly ones, to private nursing homes, since under Medicare and Medicaid the federal government would pay for 50 percent of their care there, but not in a state hospital.

Similarly, when SSI started in 1974, states found it easier to move nonelderly patients to board and care homes and into the community. Before this, it was hard for a moderate-income family to feed and clothe a mentally ill adult relative who was so ill that he couldn't work, and it was almost impossible (absent grant assistance) for such adults to live on their own. For many mentally ill people who lacked well-off relatives, SSI made it possible to live in the community.

Table 12-1 shows the same general trend in five English-speaking jurisdictions: the number of people in public psychiatric hospitals fell. The perception that deinstitutionalization was responsible for homelessness is rooted in these general trends: fewer people are in mental hospitals and more are on the streets, and so there must be a connection. But when we begin to look closer, the connection disappears.

First take England. Deinstitutionalization didn't really get underway until the 1980s. But when hospital population was declining most rapidly in England, in the early eighties, single homelessness was declining or, at worst, was constant. The high proportions of mentally ill people in the 1973 British hostel survey and the 1970 Camberwell study—proportions higher than those found in most 1980s U.S. studies—cast more doubt on the connection. If a third of homeless people were mentally ill before deinstitutionalization and a third are mentally ill after it, what effect did deinstitutionalization have?

Next look at Toronto. Ontario followed the same pattern of deinstitutionalization as Illinois and New Jersey did, and the province is about halfway between them in population. But metropolitan Toronto, we have seen, has had almost no increase in homelessness among single adults. Timing in North America raises similar questions. It is clear that the fastest decline in North American institutional population occurred well before homelessness rose: almost all of the decline happened before 1975. The New York data show this to be even more true for the nonelderly population.

In the United States, moreover, a number of empirical studies undertaken when deinstitutionalization was proceeding most quickly showed that nearly all released mental patients found a place to live, often with their families (Freeman and Smith, 1963; Michaux et al., 1969; Davis, Dinitz, and Pasaminick, 1974; Schooler et al., 1967). Even in New York City, two-thirds of the discharged patients returned to their families in the mid-sixties, but by 1975 only 23 percent were doing so; 38 percent went to hotels, 11 percent to nursing homes, and 28 percent "to places unknown" (Minkoff, 1978).

The pattern of mental illness among homeless populations also supports the notion that deinstitutionalization was, for the most part, over and done with before homelessness started to rise. One study stands out in showing an unusually high prevalence of mental illness: a 1975 study of the New York men's shelter. This study came at the end of the rapid period of deinstitutionalization, and it shows the effect at its strongest. New York's single-male shelter population went up about fivefold in the first part of the 1980s, but as we saw in Chapter 4 this population was steady or falling when deinstitutionalization should have been affecting it most strongly.

From Table 12-1 we can see that deinstitutionalization in North America happened too early to explain the rise in homelessness. Between 1955 and 1975, vast numbers of people left state and county mental hospitals and went somewhere, but not to the streets or shelters.

The more refined data available on a nationwide level reinforce this conclusion. Looking at the total population of U.S. state and county mental hospitals is too narrow in some ways and too broad in others. The approach is too narrow on one hand in that it excludes many other institutions that house mentally ill people—in particular, other types of psychiatric hospitals, nursing homes, and correctional institutions. I'm not arguing that prisons and nursing homes resemble the mental hospitals (although many think they do), only that people now in them run the same risk—zero—of being currently homeless as do the people now in state and county mental hospitals.

On the other hand, looking at the total population of state and county mental hospitals is too broad because it includes a large number of elderly patients: 28.3 percent in 1955. Almost no elderly people are homeless, and so changes in the number of elderly people in psychiatric hospitals should have had at most a vanishingly small effect on the number of homeless people. The elderly population of state and county mental hospitals decreased faster than the nonelderly population did, particularly after the mid-1970s; for instance, the reduction in elderly population in New York State's mental hospitals accounted for 54.7 percent of the total reduction between 1973 and 1990, even though the elderly accounted for only 46.0 percent of 1973 population.[1] As we shall see, such large population movements among the elderly mask the movement that might have relevance for homelessness.

Table 12-2, therefore, shows my estimates of how many severely mentally ill working-age people—between eighteen and sixty-four years old, inclusive—were institutionalized in 1960, 1975, 1983, and 1990. Most of the estimates were either taken directly from government reports or derived from them in a fairly conventional fashion (I have shifted the table's long notes to the Appendix).

The exception is the number of severely mentally ill people in correctional institutions, a subject we know little about. Jemelka,

*Table 12-2*  Estimated Number of Institutionalized Mentally Ill People in the
United States, 1960–1990 (ages 18–64, standardized to 1990
working-age population, in thousands)

| Institution | 1960 | 1975 | 1983 | 1990 |
|---|---|---|---|---|
| State and county mental hospital | – | 156.5 | 145.4 | 72.8 |
| VA medical center | – | 33.4 | 17.2 | 15.2 |
| Private psych. hospital | – | 12.0 | 13.5 | 17.7 |
| Nonfederal hospital with separate psych. service | – | 19.5 | 28.8 | 31.5 |
| Subtotal, hospitals | 681.8 | 221.4 | 204.9 | 137.2 |
| Nursing home | 52.5 | 86.6 | 130.8 | 155.9 |
| Prison or jail | 49.9 | 45.5 | 68.0 | 113.2 |
| Total | 784.2 | 353.6 | 403.7 | 406.3 |

*Sources.* See Appendix, p. 306.

Turpin, and Chiles (1989), in a review of several major studies of
mental illness in prisons, conclude that 10 percent to 15 percent of
prisoners had "major DSM-II-R thought disorders or mood disorders and need services usually associated with severe or chronic
mental illness." A lot more—between 29 percent and 56 percent—probably needed outpatient services. They also thought that
since the late sixties there had been a mild trend upward in the
prevalence of mental illness in prisons; Steadman, Monahan, and
Duffie (1984), for instance, found that between 1968 and 1978 the
proportion of men entering state prisons with prior histories of
psychiatric hospitalizations rose from 7.9 percent to 10.4 percent.
Only a few studies have been done of mental illness in jails, and their
results are so disparate that Teplin (1983), in a review of the literature, could draw no conclusion. In compiling Table 12-2, I have
assumed that 10 percent of both prison and jail populations are
severely mentally ill; this seems to be the most conservative possible
assumption.

I have standardized Table 12-2 for population growth, taking 1990
population as the standard. For instance, the U.S. working-age
population was 22 percent bigger in 1990 than in 1975, and so I
increased the 1975 numbers by 22 percent to show how large they
would have been if the working-age population in 1975 had been the
same as it was in 1990.

Table 12-2 shows that the deinstitutionalization of mentally ill working-age people was over by 1975. In both 1983 and 1990, more severely mentally ill working-age people were institutionalized than in 1975, even after accounting for population growth. There were fewer state, county, and VA hospitals, but this loss was more than offset by the growth in nursing homes, correctional institutions, and other kinds of mental hospitals. By 1990, more mentally ill people under sixty-five were in nursing homes than in all forms of mental hospital combined, and at least 50 percent more were in prison or jail than in state and county mental hospitals. Deinstitutionalization on a massive scale did occur between 1960 and 1975, but then it stopped.

All the evidence thus points in the direction of one story, which I believe is essentially correct. Deinstitutionalization occurred between 1960 and 1975, and during that period mentally ill people found housing because the housing market permitted them to do so. After 1975, the movement out of state and county mental hospitals was more than offset by the movement into nursing homes and correctional institutions, and after 1980 homelessness rose among the mentally ill because housing conditions got worse.

Not everyone accepts this account. Two objections are particularly important and need to be discussed.

## Objection: Quality Change

The first objection comes from Jencks (1994), who argues that the reductions in state and county mental hospital population after 1975 were qualitatively different from those before. Pre-1975 reductions, according to Jencks, were accomplished by discharging or refusing to admit the least troubled of the mentally ill and those who had other places to go. After 1975, budget cutbacks and legal restrictions on involuntary commitment forced hospital authorities to relegate to the streets a group of people who would have been hospitalized under the old rules and who were particularly susceptible to homelessness. By comparing 1975 and 1990 hospitalization rates for state and county mental hospitals—but including the elderly in his calculations—Jencks estimates this group's population at 142,000.[2] Most of today's mentally ill homeless people, he contends, are drawn from this group.

Table 12-2 was compiled, in part, to respond to Jencks. Note first that when the elderly are excluded, the loss of standardized population in state and county mental hospitals is about 84,000 (156.5 down to 72.8 in the first line), not 142,000. But the strongest response to the Jencks argument is shown in the table's last line: there was no deinstitutionalization after 1975.

The argument should not be dismissed so easily, though. Perhaps the group of people Jencks is concerned about didn't get back into any other institution when the number of state and county mental hospitals dwindled; perhaps the composition of the institutionalized population changed, with the "worried well" replacing the people who were at serious risk of homelessness. This is precisely the sort of shift, for instance, that GWG describes in Canada.

But that account has a chance to be convincing only when applied to the growth of private psychiatric hospitals and separate psychiatric units in nonfederal general hospitals—for instance, a much larger proportion of their patients have a diagnosis of affective disorders and a much smaller proportion have a diagnosis of schizophrenia (*Mental Health, U.S. 1990*, table 2.6)—and so it is not impossible that a large portion of the 18,000 inpatients that these hospitals added between 1975 and 1990 were people who would not have been hospitalized under 1975 procedures.[3] Most of the increase after 1975, however, comes not in state and county mental hospitals but in nursing homes (69,000) and correctional institutions (68,000). It seems extremely difficult to characterize these people as the "worried well" or to contend that none of them would have been hospitalized elsewhere under 1975 procedures. Indeed, contending that almost all of the 84,000 people who would have been in state and county mental hospitals were included among the 137,000 added to nursing homes and correctional institutions seems more reasonable than contending that almost no one was.

Even if some people who would have been in mental hospitals in 1975 were not in any institution in 1990, Jencks still needs to show that these people are inherently more susceptible to homelessness than people deinstitutionalized before 1975. Jencks advances two arguments to support this contention. The first is what I call the "bad apples at the bottom of the barrel" argument: hospitals first released those patients who were most stable and had the best home environments, and by 1975 all of these easy-to-place patients had been released; the patients who were released after 1975 were the ones who had the least going for them. The second is what I call the "bad motives make bad policies" argument: before 1975, population reductions were motivated by scientific and organizational advances, such as psychotropic drugs, nursing homes, and new psychological insights about community care; after 1975, the reductions were motivated by budget-cutting state legislatures and civil libertarians intent on abolishing involuntary commitment.

Both arguments have serious weaknesses. "Bad apples" implies that the proportion of patients in state and county mental hospitals whom clinicians believe are appropriately placed there should be rising over time, and that after 1975 clinicians should think that almost everyone in such a hospital belongs there. Faden and Goldman (1979) compiled a series of studies in which psychologists and nurses reviewed the records of patients in various state mental hospitals. Studies done before 1975 showed a higher proportion of appropriate placements—a mean and a median both of 40 percent—than the studies done in 1975 and after—a mean of 30 percent and a median of 31 percent. Apparently there were still plenty of good apples at the bottom of the barrel—even more, proportionately, than at the top. (But since by the early seventies state hospital populations were turning over about twice a year, likening the container to a barrel is probably inappropriate anyway.)

Table 12-2 also challenges "bad motives." VA medical centers are much more like state and county mental hospitals in their fee structure and the diagnoses of their patients than private psychiatric hospitals and general hospitals are, but they didn't face the same severity of bad-motive problems that state and county hospitals did. The federal government was not so strapped for cash as state governments were, VA medical centers were a very small part of its budget, and the Veterans Administration was not the most popular target for congressional budget cutters. Nor did involuntary commitments figure heavily in VA admissions. So if bad motives were important in contributing to the decline of the state and county hospital population, that population should have declined more swiftly than VA population did. But it didn't. Uncorrected for general population growth, the working-age population of state and county mental hospitals went down by 43.3 percent between 1975 and 1990; the working-age population of VA medical centers went down by 44.5 percent.

Finally, implicit in both arguments is the idea that if the proportion of the working-age population in state and county hospitals had stayed at or above its 1975 level, homelessness among the mentally ill would not have risen much. In the United States, about 101 working-age people out of every 100,000 were inpatients of state and county mental hospitals in 1975. If the argument is correct, places where hospitalization was at or above this level should not experience much homelessness among the mentally ill. But in New York state in 1986, 115 working-age people out of every 100,000 were inpatients.[4] Keeping the state and county hospital population at or above its 1975 level seems quite incapable of guaranteeing, in the housing market of the 1980s and 1990s, that only a few mentally ill people will be homeless.

## Objection: Baby-Boom Schizophrenics

Another objection focuses on the "young adult chronics" whose numbers are alleged to have increased in the late 1970s and early 1980s (Johnson, 1990; Hopper, Baxter, and Cox, 1982). People develop schizophrenia most commonly in young adulthood, and so the baby-boom cohort was reaching the age of greatest susceptibility to the disease at this time. The people who appeared on the streets in the late seventies and early eighties, then, were people who never got into institutions but should have, not people who were turned out. By using total working-age population, rather than a finer grid that would allow the interaction between the baby boom and schizophrenia to be clear, we have understated how large the 1990 state and county hospital population would have been if 1975 practices had continued, according to this view.

This is a fair objection. The only question is how large an effect the baby boom had. My conclusion is that it wasn't very large. Several different (imperfect) experiments point in the same direction. One is to consider schizophrenia alone. In 1970 psychologists performed a detailed study of the incidence of mental illness in Monroe County,

New York. Kramer (1977) provides a table of age-specific rates of treated schizophrenia based on that study. "Treated" includes both those hospitalized and those not. If these age-specific rates held constant between 1970 and 1990, treated schizophrenia would have been rising faster than the population, but not much faster. The U.S. population between fifteen and sixty-four rose by 19.5 percent between 1970 and 1980, but the population of treated schizophrenics in the age group, if age-specific rates had stayed the same, would have risen 20.5 percent. Population rose by 30.9 percent from 1970 to 1990, but the number of treated schizophrenics would have risen 39.3 percent.

Since schizophrenia is the primary diagnosis of about half of the in-patients in state and county mental hospitals (a fraction that has been relatively stable since World War II), this result implies that the state and county hospital populations should have been rising a few per-centage points faster than the general population between 1970 and 1990, everything else being equal. This is not a big difference: for in-stance, it raises the estimate of the population decrease in state and county hospitals between 1975 and 1990 from 84,000 to almost 90,000.

But everything else was not equal: changes in age structure were slightly increasing the incidence of schizophrenia, but they were decreasing the incidence of other mental illnesses. When we look at age-specific rates of mental hospitalization, the conclusion is the opposite: the changing age structure made mental hospital popula-tions grow slower than the general population, not faster. Kramer gives 1970 census age-specific rates of mental hospitalization (these rates pertain to all types of mental hospitals, not just state and county). If these rates had held constant, mental hospital population between twenty and sixty-four would have risen by 18.0 percent between 1970 and 1980, as opposed to a 20.3 percent growth in the total population, and 32.5 percent percent between 1970 and 1990, as opposed to 36.3 percent for the total population.

Thus the baby boom does not substantially change our picture of deinstitutionalization, if it changes it at all.

## How Many Mentally Ill People Are Not Institutionalized?

To complete the task of figuring out what proportion of the increase in homelessness among the mentally ill is due to population changes and deinstitutionalization, we need to figure out how many mentally ill people of working age are not in institutions. Table 12-3 presents my estimates for 1990 and 1975: about 2.6 million in 1990 and about 2.2 million in 1975. These numbers are well within the range of other estimates, but they are still very imprecise. The year 1990 is higher than 1975 because total working-age population grew, even though more people were in institutions.

## Why Are There More Homeless Mentally Ill People?

Now we have all the pieces we need to assess the extent to which changes in the size and composition of the noninstitutionalized mentally ill population were responsible for the growing number of mentally ill homeless people in the United States. At least since 1975, deinstitutionalization was not responsible for any of the growth of this population, though it may have been responsible for some of the change in composition.

Table 12-3   Estimated Number of Mentally Ill People Not in Institutions, 1975 and 1990 (in thousands)

| | |
|---|---|
| In 1990 | |
| SSI and SSDI | 1,012 |
| Homeless | 100 |
| VA benefits | 30 |
| Conventionally housed, no benefits | 1,484 |
| Total, not in institutions | 2,626 |
| Institutionalized | 406 |
| Total | 3,032 |
| 1975 estimated total | 2,485 |
| Less 1975 institutionalized | 299 |
| Total, not in institutions | 2,186 |

*Sources.* Supplemental Security Income and Social Security Disability Insurance for Mental Disorders: Kennedy and Manderscheid (1992, table 5.5). I subtracted 23,600 children under 18 receiving SSI from unduplicated count in this table; similar to estimate in Jencks (1994). Homeless: Jencks (1994, p. 150n22). VA benefits: Estimate based on recipiency rates in Barker et al. (1992); rates don't correct for multiple receipt of benefits or elderly population. Conventionally housed: Derived from Barker et al. (1992). Specifically I took population between 18 and 64 limited by SMI (table 7.1)—2,141,000—and subtracted an estimate of nonelderly population receiving government disability benefits. This is much higher than Jencks's estimate (300–500,000). Figure includes small group homes and halfway houses. The Barker definition of SMI excludes drug and alcohol abuse and is more restrictive than standard criteria for admission to mental hospitals. Institutionalized: See Table 12–2. 1975 estimated total: I assumed mentally ill population grew at same rate as total working-age population between 1975 and 1990.

Start with 1975. A good guess is that there were around 30,000 mentally ill homeless people then, but this is only a guess.[5] Between 1975 and 1990, the number of mentally ill working-age people who were not institutionalized rose by around 20 percent, solely because of population growth. So if the probability that a mentally ill person was homeless stayed the same, the number of homeless mentally ill people would have risen by 20 percent as well, to 36,000. But the number of mentally ill homeless people was much higher than 36,000 in 1990: Jencks (p. 150, n. 22) estimates 100,000 (this is distinct from his estimate of 142,000 mentally ill people—both homeless and not—who would have been in state and county mental hospitals in 1990 if 1975 practices had continued); the National Institute for Mental Health estimates 200,000 (Manderscheid and Rosenstein, 1992). The Jencks estimate is probably better. The growth of the mentally ill population accounts for only about 6,000 of the 70,000 growth with the Jencks estimate (9 percent) or 6,000 of the 170,000 growth with the NIMH estimate (less than 4 percent). The interesting changes are those that affected the probability that a mentally ill person would be homeless, not the number of mentally ill people.[6]

Jencks presumably would object to this calculation. People who would have been in state and county mental hospitals but weren't, he would say, were different and should be treated differently. There are two groups—the Jencks group and everybody else—and so it is the composition, not just the size, of the noninstitutionalized population that matters.

How big is the Jencks group? Possibly it is empty, as I argued with Table 12-2, and surely it is no larger than 84,000. I will use what I think is a very generous estimate of its size: 50,000. Then the distribution of noninstitutionalized mentally ill people in the two years (in thousands) looks like this (the total is from Table 12-3):

|      | Jencks | Non-Jencks | Total |
|------|--------|------------|-------|
| 1975 | 0      | 2,186      | 2,186 |
| 1990 | 50     | 2,576      | 2,626 |

If the probability of being homeless had stayed at its 1975 level for non-Jencks people (1.5 percent) and if all the Jencks people were

homeless in 1990, the distribution of homeless mentally ill people
would look like this:

|  | Jencks | Non-Jencks | Total |
|---|---|---|---|
| 1975 | 0 | 30 | 30 |
| 1990 | 50 | 35 | 85 |

So even if we assume that all of the Jencks mentally ill are always
homeless, we still can't account for all of the growth in homelessness
among the mentally ill. If the Jencks estimate of 100,000 homeless
mentally ill people in 1990 is correct, this calculation accounts for 79
percent of the growth (55,000 out of 70,000), but only 32 percent if
the NIMH estimate is correct (55,000 out of 170,000).

But how can it make sense to think that the Jencks group is 100
percent homeless all of the time, while the rest of the severely
mentally people in the community are homeless only 1.5 percent of
the time? In the first place, the Jencks group is quite old—probably
a majority of its members are between forty-five and sixty-four.[7]
Many people over forty-five are homeless, but homelessness seems
less prevalent among this age group than for people between
twenty-five and forty-four.[8] It is hard to believe that group this old
would be so much more likely to be homeless than the normal
mentally ill, a group somewhat younger.

Indeed, the greatest implausibility in the Jencks argument is that
it requires the clinicians of 1975 and before to be so acute in their
knowledge of human behavior and homelessness that they would
be able to sort the mentally ill flawlessly into two groups, one that
is almost never homeless and the other that is almost always homeless. And not only must they have learned how to predict flawlessly,
they had to act unerringly in deciding whom to admit and whom
not to admit, whom to discharge and whom not to discharge, even
though they had little personal stake in the outcome.

For the Jencks story to work, moreover, these clinicians must have
acquired their clairvoyant powers almost entirely without the assistance of empirical testing, and then somehow they must have forgotten almost everything they learned, because no one today has the
kind of predictive ability that the Jencks argument requires.

To make some comparison with the best predictive performances
today, the Jencks story implies that pre-1975 clinicians were able to

sort the mentally ill population into two groups, one of which—the Jencks group—was over sixty times more likely to be homeless on any given day than the other (the probability of a member of the Jencks group being homeless was 100 percent; the probability of a member of the non-Jencks group was around 1.5 percent; and the ratio of 100 to 1.5 is about 60). Let me call this ratio between the likelihood of being homeless in the two groups the "discernment ratio." The best predictive system I am aware of today—that of Knickman and Weitzman (1989) for AFDC families in New York City—has a discernment ratio of about 14. Berlin and McAllister (1994) point out that this system partly takes advantage of specific incentives in the New York family-shelter system and uses much detailed information that is not readily available. The more practical Towber and Flemming (1989) system has a discernment ratio of about 5.

The pre-1975 clinicians would also have had a more difficult job than either of these two research teams. They had to distinguish among a population that was almost all severely mentally ill, and so they couldn't use the information that a person was severely mentally ill to improve their discernment ratios. They didn't have complete financial information because they didn't control the subject's pursestrings, as the welfare officials who commissioned the recent studies did. And in many cases they had very little reliable information at all, since the most important changes in state and county mental hospitals in the 1970s were in admission policies, not discharge policies. A discernment ratio five times greater than that of Knickman and Weitzman is simply not plausible.

Even if the discernment ratio was as high as 15, composition effects can't explain much of the rise in homelessness. Suppose the probability of being homeless stayed at its 1975 level of 1.5 percent for the non-Jencks people. Then Jencks people would have been 15 times more likely to be homeless, and so their probability of being homeless would be 22 percent. These probabilities imply the following numbers of homeless mentally ill people:

|      | Jencks | Non-Jencks | Total |
|------|--------|------------|-------|
| 1975 | 0      | 30         | 30    |
| 1990 | 11     | 35         | 46    |

(11,000 is 22 percent of the presumed 50,000 Jencks people.) Size and composition account for only 16,000 of the 70,000 rise in homelessness (23 percent) on the low estimate of the mentally ill homeless population in 1990; or only 9 percent of the 170,000 rise in homelessness on the high estimate. If the discernment ratio is 10—still an implausibly high value—size and composition effects account for only 17 percent of the growth in the mentally ill homeless population on the low estimate, 7 percent on the high.

I conclude that changes in population and composition were responsible for little of the rise in homelessness among the mentally ill. Most of it is due to a rise in the probability of being homeless that is independent of composition. To reach this conclusion I have made a number of assumptions—the size of the Jencks group and the discernment ratio, for instance—but for the most part these results are robust. The number to which the results are most sensitive, and the number about which we know least, is the size of the mentally ill homeless population in the early 1970s. If it were considerably higher (say 60,000) there would be much less growth to explain—40,000 instead of 70,000; population growth would account for more—10,000 instead of 5,000; and the higher base probability would make homelessness in the Jencks group higher even with the same discernment ratio—15,000 instead of 7,500 with a discernment ratio of 10. But even with an extremely high estimate of the size of the Jencks group, and an extremely high discernment ratio, changes in population and composition can just barely account for a majority of the growth in homelessness among the mentally ill. Only if you believe that homelessness has not increased much among the mentally ill since the early seventies can you believe that population growth and composition are reasonably important.

## Other Effects

Although deinstitutionalization probably contributed little or nothing directly to the rise of homelessness, it may have operated indirectly through the housing market. In congregate housing arrangements, interpersonal externalities are extremely important, and so a significant minority of even moderately disturbed individuals can make everyone in a flophouse miserable. Such people can also raise the operator's cost for repairs and liability insurance. So deinstitutionalization may have driven some flophouses and cage hotels out of business both by reducing demand and by increasing costs. Missions would have had similar problems.

Of course, a profit-maximizing flophouse owner would not let men he knew to be disruptive come into his establishment. But often there is no way of telling who will be disruptive until after admission, when the damage is already done. So the greater the proportion of disturbed men among its potential clientele, the less profitable a flophouse will be. There may even be tipping phenomena: a small increase in disturbed men may make a flophouse or mission unatttractive to men who are not disturbed, and this in turn will increase the proportion of disturbed men.

Some shreds of evidence can be marshaled to support this argument. Large numbers of people were deinstitutionalized in the seventies, and they had to live somewhere. The SCCM survey and newspaper accounts document the presence of many mentally ill individuals on the Bowery during this period. In 1976 Arbittier and Winnick discovered that "a man receiving service from the Shelter . . . was just as likely to have psychiatric problems as alcoholic problems" (1976, p. 3); and Hopper (1987, table 6) details several other studies at about the same time showing a growing awareness of a population of mentally disturbed people on the Bowery. Some of the newspaper accounts of rising homelessness in midtown Manhattan cite the presence of a large mentally ill population as a reason for the Bowery's unattractiveness (for example, Goodman, 1978; Hess, 1976; McNeil, 1978).

The closing of flophouses (in both New York and Toronto), cage hotels, and even direct-access hostels in London comes at about the right time. Even the emergence of single homelessness later in Chicago and Newark than in New York fits well with the story: New York's flophouses would have had larger interpersonal externalities than either Chicago's cage hotels or Newark's cheap hotels. The failure of London's single homelessness to rise in any dimension in the early eighties shows that the story is incomplete, but it still has some explanatory power. Deinstitutionalization probably did contribute to single homelessness by making flophouses and missions more difficult to run.

Finally, it could be argued—though not persuasively—that deinstitutionalization had a demonstration effect. Perhaps street homelessness was low in the 1960s because people couldn't imagine sleeping on the streets or, if they could imagine it, thought it too terrible to try. Deinstitutionalized mental patients suffered from no such inhibitions, slept on the streets, and, when others saw what was happening, set an example for the rest of society to follow. It is always difficult to disprove demonstration effects, but this one is weak in several respects. If looking at the world differently gives the mentally ill certain advantages in making inventions, then deinstitutionalization should have brought about a wave of different inventions, not just homelessness. The story is also implausible in that it has higher-status people—the mentally well—imitating lower-status people rather than the other way around.

Nor is it clear that homelessness had to be invented. Tramps and hoboes have long existed in the traditions of all four countries, and in North America and Britain large numbers of people slept on the streets during the depression. Orwell's *Down and Out in Paris and London* was published in 1933, and Love's *Subways Are for Sleeping* dates from 1957. Large numbers of men in military service have slept outdoors, and so have Boy Scouts. The skid-row literature surveyed in Chapter 4 shows that even in the 1950s and 1960s the technology had not disappeared.

The rate of homelessness among noninstitutionalized mentally ill people grew at about the same time and pace as the rate of homelessness among mentally well (or just not mentally ill) people. This is why the proportion of mentally ill people among the homeless stayed more or less the same. (This constancy is especially noticeable between 1983 and 1990, when studies were most frequent and careful but when, as seen in Table 12-2, the size of the Jencks group was rising most rapidly.)

When two things happen in the same way at the same time, you should first try to find out whether both were happening for the same reason. This is the counsel of Occam's razor—that you should never explain in a complicated way what can be explained simply

*(Frustra fit per plura quod potest fieri per pauciora.)* To say that the same forces caused homelessness to rise for both the mentally ill and the mentally well is more effective than to come up with separate stories for each group. And we have seen in this chapter that special stories about the mentally ill don't explain much either.

To argue that deinstitutionalization was not responsible for the rise in homelessness, however, is not to endorse deinstitutionalization.[9] I don't think the war in Bosnia caused American homelessness, but I don't endorse that war. Deinstitutionalization should be judged primarily on psychiatric grounds—whether the current network of nursing homes, prisons, community care, and shelters does a better job of caring for people than the old state and county hospitals did or better than some alternative, untried system could do. About this question I know little, except that the answer will probably change as technology and relative costs change.

The designers of deinstitutionalization were no doubt surprised when housing markets changed in the 1980s and many mentally ill people became homeless (just as I am sometimes surprised when it rains after I leave home without an umbrella), and so their calculations about the benefits of deinstitutionalization turned out to be wrong. But since I don't know the rest of the calculations, I can't tell whether this surprise makes a difference (nor do I seriously believe that my leaving home without an umbrella was responsible for the rain). Massive increases in the mental-hospital population would surely decrease homelessness, but even today there is no reason to think that the decrease in homelessness would be more than 10 percent or 20 percent of the increase in the hospital population—probably a lot less for increases of 100,000 or more. Hospitals are expensive, and these modest decreases in homelessness can be only one among many factors in deciding how they should operate.

# 13

# Substance Abuse

Next to mental illness, substance abuse is the most popular explanation for the new homelessness that emphasizes the frailties and faults of homeless people themselves. Many homeless individuals are substance abusers, and many of them wouldn't be homeless if they didn't abuse substances. This is an important fact for social workers and the friends of homeless people to remember. But it doesn't answer our question of why the number of homeless people grew—unless the number of substance abusers grew sharply at the right times and places and unless the probability that a substance abuser would be homeless stayed about the same. Even then, such an explanation could not account for the rise in homelessness among people who were not substance abusers.

This sounds like what I just said in the last chapter, but there is an important difference. Unlike mental illness, substance abuse is a pattern of consumption, not a disease. Although addiction is treated as a disease in some ways, becoming a substance abuser involves elements of volition that becoming mentally ill—or becoming a foster child or a noninstitutionalized mentally ill person—does not. Volition means economics. We can't think of an army of substance abusers parachuting down from the sky (the way we thought of deinstitutionalization); we have to ask why consumption changed and what these changed patterns imply for housing demand.

The story of substance abuse is also different from the story of mental illness because the time when homelessness was rising appears to be, with one possible exception, a time of declining substance abuse in the United States Alcohol abuse was steady or declining between 1970 and 1990, and so was the use of heroin and marijuana between 1976 and 1990. All measures of drug abuse were declining between 1979 and 1985. So it is almost impossible to think of any argument that would link increasing substance abuse to the first large rise in homelessness that took place before 1985.

After 1985, though, some measures of drug abuse did increase because of the introduction of crack-cocaine, and Jencks (1994) argues that crack was responsible for some or all of the rise in homelessness among single adults after this time. We will have to examine this claim. On an empirical and conceptual level, the claim is hard to think about because so few people in the general population are serious users of crack that its arrival hardly makes a dent in the downward trend of drug abuse, except in a few targeted areas and by a few select measures. The claim is hard to think about from an economic standpoint because crack use rose not because of some change in people's tastes but because its price went down.

This sort of fall in price has several consequences. First, it is likely to have decreased the consumption of close substitutes for crack, such as amphetamines and alcohol.[1] This would not be unprecedented: pharmacologists believe that cocaine is a close substitute for amphetamines in particular, and that cocaine's popularity during the early part of the twentieth century came to an end in the 1930s when cheaper amphetamines went on the market (Rouse, 1991). This substitution would change what homeless people do, but it wouldn't change who or how many are homeless. The fact that a lot of people in the New York single-adult shelter system use crack does not imply that they would be conventionally housed if cocaine had stayed expensive and crack had never been invented. In the absence of crack, many of them might be using alcohol, amphetamines, or another cheap illegal drug instead.

The second consequence of the drop in crack price is that it changed the demand for housing. Logic alone is unable to show how the demand for housing changed. On one hand, to the extent that crack is a substitute for housing—say, if oblivion is a substitute for comfort—cheaper crack might mean less demand for housing. When housing became relatively more expensive, demand should have gone down. On the other hand, cheaper crack might mean that the same degree of intoxication could be achieved with more money left over for housing. This would have increased the demand for housing. Which effect actually prevailed is something we will try to find out in this chapter.

## How Much among Homeless People?

Historically, substance abuse has often been associated with homelessness. Bahr and Caplow (1974) entitled their Bowery study *Old Men, Drunk and Sober*, and throughout the skid-row literature, almost all variables of interest are cross-tabulated with drinking behavior. But only about 30–40 percent of the men who lived on skid row were heavy drinkers (Bahr and Caplow, p. 249, summarize the results of five studies). Among ticketmen, though, the proportion of alcoholics was probably higher; after all, you became a ticketman only if the welfare authorities thought you were too much of a drunk to be trusted with cash.

Today, still, many homeless people are substance abusers. The drug of choice varies city to city: crack appears to predominate in New York and Newark, alcohol in London, Toronto, and probably Chicago. Appendix Table 3 summarizes the results of some studies for New York, Chicago, London, and Hamburg. I am unaware of any studies of substance abuse among homeless people in Newark or Toronto.

Most of these studies find that between 20 percent and 40 percent of homeless singles abuse substances, results remarkably consistent with the skid-row studies. These studies are also in line with those surveyed by Shlay and Rossi (1992): twenty-two U.S. studies found that an average of 29 percent of whatever group was studied had some detox experience, and twenty-seven studies found an average of 27 percent with alcohol addiction.

Few of these studies enable us to find the proportion of homeless people who are *either* substance abusers or mentally ill; so in a sense

they underestimate the extent of pathology among homeless populations. Yet few of these studies deal with homeless families, among
whom pathology rates may be lower.

The Cuomo Commission (1992) in New York conducted what
probably is the most extensive survey of substance abuse among
shelter users in modern times. They used both questionnaires and
urinalysis. Their results, summarized in Table 13-1, are out of line
with the results from other cities (and earlier New York results)
in several respects. First is the extraordinarily large proportion of
single-shelter residents *using* drugs. The proportion *reporting* drug
use is also large, by comparison with other studies, and the gap
between use and reporting is large too. Less noticeable is the
extremely small use of alcohol for both families and singles. The

*Table 13-1*  Cuomo Commission Results on Substance Abuse by NYC Shelter
Residents

| Questionnaire result | Adults in family shelters | Single shelters |
|---|---|---|
| Drinks alcohol every day | 3% | 11% |
| Used drugs in past year | 18 | 48 |
| Uses drugs at least once a month | 10 | 32 |
| Ever in rehab program | 23 | 38 |

| Urinalysis results: testing positive | |
|---|---|
| Family shelter | 29% |
| Single shelter | |
|   Specialized | 39 |
|   Assessment | 63 |
|   General | 80 |
| Total, single shelter | 65 |

| Specific drugs: singles testing positive | | |
|---|---|---|
| | | *Of all those tested* |
| Cocaine | 83% | 53% |
| THC[a] | 30 | 20 |
| Alcohol | 11 | 7 |
| Opiates | 4 | 3 |
| Amphetamines | 1 | 1 |
| PCP | 0 | 0 |

a. Tetrahydrocannabinol is the active ingredient in marijuana.

contrast with earlier New York studies, especially the Welte and Barnes (1992) findings for 1986, suggests that crack has become a substitute for alcohol. Drug use among adults in families seems to be in line with that found in other studies of shelter populations.

In thinking about the single-shelter results, it should be kept in mind that in New York City the majority of single homeless people live on the street and that the population of single shelters has been shrinking since 1989. Among homeless streetpeople, shelters are considered dangerous (Hopper, 1991), and the Cuomo Commission findings support these beliefs. Tipping can happen in any congregate housing arrangement—in a shelter as well as a mission or lodginghouse. These results may be a specifically New York phenomenon of the 1990s. (There may also be some reasons to doubt the accuracy of the findings. Hopper [1992, p. 21] writes that "it was based on a single urine test . . . [and] quality control procedures in the testing were badly wanting.")

The results of Welte and Barnes for 1986 are about the same as those of Bahr and Caplow for 1964. If an increase in substance abuse were fueling the rise in homelessness, this is not what you would see—instead you would see a rise in the proportion of substance abusers among the homeless. So before 1986 there is no evidence that a rise in substance abuse was responsible in any way for the rise in homelessness.

After 1986 the results are more mixed. In New York, the Cuomo Commission shows a vast increase in substance abuse over anything reported before 1992, but it is the only post-1986 New York survey. In Chicago, by contrast, there is no trend or maybe even a downward one: the O'Hare Airport survey of 1990 asks a question similar to Rossi's in 1985–86, and finds fewer people with detox experience; Sosin, Colson, and Grossman in 1986 ask a question similar to the Chicago Coalition's in 1983, and find less use of intoxicants, especially marijuana.

Outside the six cities in 1987, the Urban Institute took a survey of shelter residents and service users who said they were homeless in a probability sample of cities across the United States. The substance-abuse question was like Rossi's—have you ever been in an outpatient chemical-dependency center?—and the proportion answering affirmatively was the same, 33 percent (Burt, 1992).

## How Much in the Nation?

Increasing substance abuse cannot explain the rise in homelessness because substance abuse has not increased.

When homelessness first began to rise, and at least until the mid-1980s, alcohol was the drug of choice among the homeless. In the general U.S. population, alcohol consumption was on the decline in this same period. The decline in alcohol use is apparent from a household survey that the federal Substance Abuse and Mental Health Services Administration (SAMHSA) has been taking for almost twenty years.[2] This study reports a decrease in the proportion of adults who report having consumed any alcohol in the past month, as shown in Figure 13-1.

General use, however, tells little about heavy use. Unfortunately, the SAMHSA survey started asking about "heavier" alcohol use only in 1985. "Heavier" means averaging two or more drinks a day over the past two weeks. On this standard, 7.7 percent of the adult

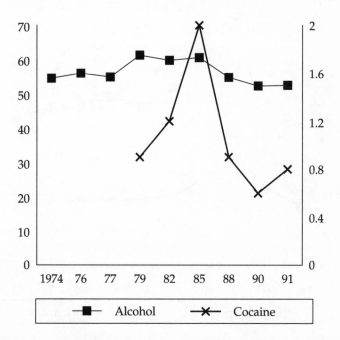

*Figure 13-1* Proportion of U.S. adults, 26 or older, who used alcohol or cocaine in past month. *Source*: U.S. Dept. of Health and Human Services, "National Household Survey on Drug Abuse, Highlights 1991."

(eighteen and over) population nationwide were heavier drinkers in 1985, 5.5 percent in 1990.

The best place to look for a longer time series on heavy use is the death rate from cirrhosis. Because most liver damage is caused by alcohol, cirrhosis has long been an accepted measure of heavy drinking (Cook and Tauchen, 1982). How likely you are to get cirrhosis depends on how much alcohol you have consumed in your lifetime. If the weight of the alcohol you have consumed is less than four times your body weight, you are pretty sure not to get cirrhosis; if the weight of the alcohol is over forty times body weight, you are almost sure to get it (Lelbach, 1974).

Figure 13-2 shows that cirrhosis deaths have been falling since 1970, both for the total population and for black men, the group with the highest rate.[3] This is strong evidence that alcohol abuse was also falling, at least from the early 1960s to the early 1980s. The time lag

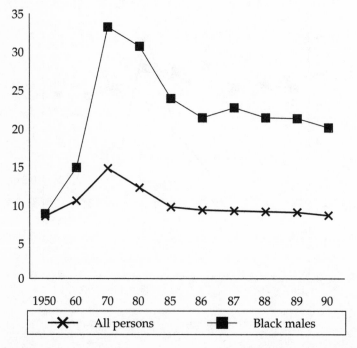

*Figure 13-2* Age-adjusted death rate in U.S. from cirrhosis (deaths per 100,000 population). *Source*: National Center for Health Statistics, "Health, United States, 1992."

*Table 13-2*  Surveys of Cocaine Use in U.S. Household Population

| Year | Use in last 2 weeks by those 18–25 | | Use in past month, HS grads 1–12 years after school | Use in past month by those over 25 |
|---|---|---|---|---|
| | All | Blacks | All | All |
| 1974 | 3.1% | – | – | – |
| 1976 | 2.0 | – | – | – |
| 1977 | 3.7 | – | – | – |
| 1979 | 9.3 | – | – | 0.9 |
| 1982 | 6.8 | – | – | 1.2 |
| 1985 | 7.6 | 6.4 | – | 2.0 |
| 1986 | – | – | 8.2 | – |
| 1987 | – | – | 6.0 | – |
| 1988 | 4.5 | 4.3 | 5.7 | 0.9 |
| 1989 | – | – | 3.8 | – |
| 1990 | 2.2 | 3.6 | 2.4 | 0.6 |
| 1991 | 2.0 | 3.1 | 2.0 | 0.8 |

*Sources.* Columns 1 and 2: "Health, United States, 1992," p. 104. Column 3: Johnston, O'Malley, and Bachman, "National Survey Results on Drug Use from Monitoring the Future Study," US DHSS, NIDA (1993). Column 4: "National Household Survey on Drug Abuse, Highlights, 1991," p. 80.

between alcohol consumption and death from cirrhosis means that the data in Figure 13-2 have little to show about what happened later, but the SAMHSA household survey does cover that period and shows that the decline continued.

The same sort of picture holds for most forms and measures of drug abuse. SAMHSA reports the proportion of the U.S. household population using illegal drugs in the previous month from 1976 through 1991. The trend is clearly downward, especially for heroin and marijuana. Stories about homelessness, though, aren't about those drugs—they're about cocaine. Table 13-2 sets out several different survey results about the use of cocaine. All the indicators are down after 1986, and use by people between eighteen and twenty-five starts down in 1979. The only increase after 1980 is for adults twenty-six and over in 1979–1985—a period when cocaine use was unimportant in the homeless population. The number of "current cocaine users" in the country decreased from 5.8 million in 1985 to 1.6 million in 1990 (Miller, 1991, p. v).

Only by concentrating on a particular way of ingesting cocaine (by crack) and on heavy use is it possible to discern an upward trend after 1935 from the survey data. The number of people who used cocaine at least weekly rose from 647,000 in 1985 to 662,000 in 1990—an insignificant difference—and the number reporting daily use rose from 246,000 to 336,000, though this increase too may be attributable to chance in how the sample was drawn.

Crack—"cocaine sold in smokable form" (Kleiman, 1992)—was unknown before the mid-eighties, and so no household surveys contain much historical information. The first *New York Times* story about crack appeared in November 1985, and in that year smoking (including free-basing) was the method used in only 10.0 percent of hospital cases in Chicago; in New York, only 3.3 percent (SAMHSA, 1987). Table 13-3 shows crack use within the last thirty days among highschool graduates one to twelve years out of school. The peak is in 1988, when 1.2 percent of this population reported crack use in the last thirty days; by 1990 this proportion had fallen to 0.4 percent. Notice that these numbers are only about 15–20 percent larger than comparable figures for cocaine use. Crack use was more than offset by the decreased use of other forms of cocaine.

In 1990, about half a million people reported using crack in the previous month (NIDA, 1991). Fewer than this number, obviously, were regular weekly or daily users. This is about the same as the number of current heroin addicts, and probably fewer than the number who were addicts at the peak of heroin epidemic in the early seventies (Kleiman, 1992).

*Table 13-3*   Crack Use among Highschool Graduates (1–12 years after school, use in past month)

| Year | Percent |
|------|---------|
| 1987 | 1.0% |
| 1988 | 1.2 |
| 1989 | 0.7 |
| 1990 | 0.4 |
| 1991 | 0.4 |
| 1992 | 0.4 |

*Source.* Johnston, O'Malley, and Bachman (1993).

Even though the number of crack users is small and the number of cocaine users is declining, the arrival of crack coincided with a series of important changes in the cocaine market. In the 1980s cocaine went down in status: associated with "rock stars and yuppie greed-heads" in 1980, it came to be the drug of "unwed teenage mothers" in 1990 (Kleiman, p. 301). Part of the reason is that prices plummeted: from about $103,000 (1987 dollars) per kilogram in the late 1970s, the price of wholesale cocaine in the United States fell to $34,000 (1987 dollars) by 1983 and as low as $10,000 in the late 1980s.[4]

Part of the reason is crack's marketing properties. Before crack, the smallest practicable dose in which cocaine could be retailed was a gram of powder; although this amount was almost invisible, it cost $100. Crack allowed cocaine to be packaged in much smaller dosages, about a twentieth of a gram, and so opened up new, cheaper markets. Crack also had desirable pharmacological properties: "Because smoking any drug delivers its molecules to the brain very quickly—within a few seconds—its effects are more immediate and more dramatic than if the same quantity of drug had been snorted. The very rapid increase in drug concentration in the brain can generate the same sort of euphoric 'rush' produced by injection (but rarely by snorting or swallowing)" (Kleiman, p. 296).

With crack and lower prices, cocaine changed from a drug used a little by many fairly affluent people to a drug used intensively by a lot of poorer people. In the seventies, cocaine was like marijuana; in the nineties it is like heroin. Where this change shows up most clearly is in the statistics on emergency-room episodes. Even though cocaine users were less numerous, they used the drug more intensively and so were more likely to get into medical trouble. They were poorer and so more likely to use emergency rooms rather than conventional medical services when they got into trouble. As time passed, crack users also became older and more feeble, and so even more likely to visit emergency rooms.

Figure 13-3 shows data that SAMHSA collected on emergency-room admissions in a sample of hospitals for problems stemming from the use of illegal drugs. Note that these are numbers of visits, not numbers of people—one person who makes ten emergency-room visits in a half-year is counted ten times. The series goes back to 1976, but 1986 and 1987 are missing because the series was being revamped.[5] Data from 1985 and before, moreover, are not strictly comparable with data from 1988 and after, since the hospitals in the pre-1985 data are not a representative sample.

For the New York and Chicago metropolitan areas, we have all of the remaining years. Before 1985, the emergency-room data agree with the household data: drug abuse was declining. The case for substance abuse as a cause of the initial rise in homelessness becomes weaker still. After 1985, though emergency-room data tell a different story: fewer people were using drugs, but they were visiting emergency rooms more often. Figure 13-3 also shows why—cocaine. Noncocaine drug episodes are approximately stable, after an initial decline from 1976 to about 1982–1984. (This series slightly understates noncocaine emergency-room episodes because I simply subtracted cocaine mentions from total drug episodes. Some cocaine mentions are part of drug episodes involving several drugs. One should also be wary of comparisons between the pre-1985 and post-1988 series.)

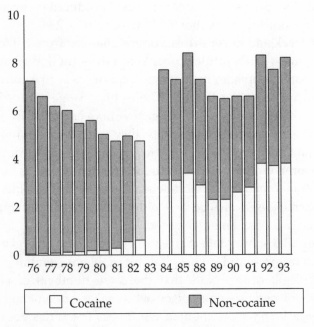

*Figure 13-3a* Emergency-room mentions, Chicago

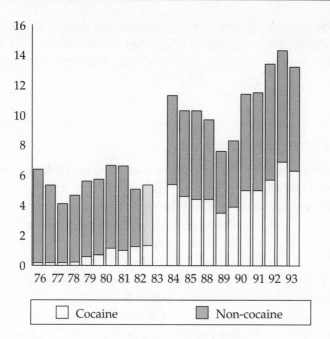

*Figure 13-3b* Emergency-room mentions, New York

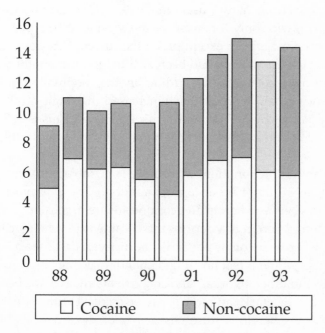

*Figure 13-3c* Emergency-room mentions, Newark

So the number of people using and abusing drugs has been steadily declining since the mid 1970s. That trend cannot have caused homelessness to rise. Still, a small group of people now use crack intensively, and no one did that before 1985.

## Did Crack Increase Homelessness?

A good way to start thinking about the effect of crack on homelessness is to think about heroin. The number of hard-core serious heroin users is probably about the same as the number of hard-core crack users, and it has been slowly declining for quite some time; so it was once higher. Like crack users, heroin users are drawn primarily—though not exclusively—from the poorest groups around. For both groups, the desire to buy drugs is very strong and could conceivably displace the desire to buy housing.

The studies in Appendix Table 4 generally show that about 5–7 percent of single-shelter populations say they are "occasional" heroin users. Allowing for shadings of truth, I would take this to be the number of serious heroin users in shelters. (The Cuomo Commission report, with only 3 percent of the sample testing positive for heroin, is once again an exception.) If the current U.S. population of serious crack users, then, had been airlifted in from another planet, it would have been just like adding another population of heroin users. Such an airlift would have increased the single-adult homeless population by 5–7 percent of its 1985 level. This is a first approximation to the effect of crack on homelessness, and I think it is a good one.

Like any approximation, of course, it is subject to error. (If it weren't, it wouldn't be an approximation.) The pharmacological differences between heroin and cocaine are great: cocaine is a stimulant, whereas heroin is a depressant; cocaine is psychologically addictive, whereas heroin is physically addictive. I don't see how these differences would affect housing demand. Injecting heroin requires a needle and other "works," and so a private room is the best place to store things; crack can more easily be enjoyed without paraphernalia. But the heroin culture has plenty of shooting galleries and sharing of works, and so especially before the spread of AIDS, a room was hardly a necessity. Indeed, since possessing paraphernalia is a crime, it could be a burden.

But a much stronger case can be made that the first-cut approximation is too high because crack users didn't arrive in an interplanetary airlift. They were here already, but they became crack users because a cocaine high became better and cheaper. This caused three sorts of effects: some people stayed just about as intoxicated as before, but had more money left over to spend on housing and other things; some people spent their money on crack instead of alcohol, marijuana, or heroin, and had just as much money left over to spend on housing; and some people spent more money on crack and less money on housing. The latter two categories would show up in shelter counts, but only the third kind represents gross additions to homelessness. The first effect reduces homelessness and cannot be seen in studies of the characteristics of homeless people.

If the first effect outweighs the third, then the 5–7 percent approximation is a huge overestimate—crack, in fact, decreased homelessness. What evidence is there on the size of the three effects? None for crack, but economists have done a number of studies of how the demand for various intoxicants responds to their price. The question these studies seek to answer is whether a 10 percent fall in the price of a substance raises the demand for it by 10 percent or less. If demand goes up by less than 10 percent, then the first effect is dominant: the total amount spent on the substance goes down, and so more money is left over to spend on housing and other things. If demand goes up by more than 10 percent, more money is spent on the substance, but some of it may be coming from other intoxicants rather than from housing. Obviously these studies are difficult to do and individually not definitive.

Silverman and Sprull (1977) found that the demand for heroin was quite unresponsive to price: a 10 percent fall in price increased demand by only 2.7 percent. If crack were like heroin, it would be contributing to the reduction in homelessness. Osterberg (1982) cites a number of studies of beer demand in Finland, Ireland, and the United States, which found demand as unresponsive as Silverman and Sprull did. Similarly, Becker, Grossman, and Murphy (1994) found that a 10 percent decrease in the price of cigarettes would increase consumption by 4 percent in the short run, 7.5 percent in the long run. Even stronger are Chaloupka's (1991) results for a 10 percent decrease in cigarette price: 2 percent in the short run, 4.5 percent in the long run.[6]

Nisbet and Vakil (1972), on the other hand, find that a 10 percent decrease in marijuana price increased the demand among UCLA students by about 10 percent. Johnson and Oksanen (1977) find a similar result for alcohol demand in Canada. Since some of this increased demand is at the expense of other intoxicants, these findings too, if applied to crack, would indicate that crack did not contribute to the rise of homelessness.

Finally, Cook and Tauchen (1982) estimate that a 10 percent decrease in the price of distilled spirits would cause an 18 percent increase in demand. But since distilled spirits are a small part of the intoxicant market, it is still possible that a price cut there could reduce overall spending for intoxicants; surely it would not increase it much.

Thus at least as good an argument can be made that crack reduced homelessness as that it increased homelessness. The empirical information from my six cities is too sparse to resolve the question: in Chicago, the single-adult shelter population increased after crack was introduced, but not the proportion of substance abusers; in New York, the proportion of substance abusers probably increased (though with a great deal of substitution), but not the single-adult shelter population. After 1990, cocaine emergency-room episodes increased in all three U.S. cities, but not homelessness among single adults.

In summary, substance abuse was declining in the United States when homelessness was rising. Crack is something of an exception to this trend after 1985, but if it increased homelessness at all, the effect was small.

# 14

# Criminal Justice

The way that laws are enforced matters to the study of homelessness in two distinct ways. First, prison and jail experience may make people more likely to be homeless. Second, police action may affect the number and visibility of homeless people on the street. Let's see how much, if any, changes in the criminal justice system have contributed to the rise in homelessness.

## Incarceration

Many homeless people, especially single individuals living in shelters, used to be prison inmates. Appendix Table 4 provides some details from representative studies. These are consistent with Shlay and Rossi's (1992) average of several U.S. studies: 18 percent with prison experience, 32 percent with jail experience, 41 percent with either. Even though popular discussions link homelessness primarily to mental illness and substance abuse, the association with incarceration is almost as strong, especially for single males in shelters.

Note that many of the data in the appendix deal with prison as opposed to jail experience. People are sentenced to prison for felonies. Disorderly-person offenses, which one is more likely to be arrested for simply by virtue of homelessness, are not felonies; they might result in jail time but not in prison time. Prison experience doesn't result from homelessness.

The prison population has risen dramatically throughout the United States since the 1970s; this has been one of the outstanding trends of the last two decades. The prison population has also risen in Ontario and Great Britain, but far less drastically. Table 14-1 gives population time series for the areas we are interested in. Taken by itself, an increase in the stock of prisoners is an increase in the number of people, most of them poor, who are housed at government expense. As such, it should reduce the demand for housing and reduce homelessness.

*Table 14-1*   Prison Population, 1974–1991

| Year | NYC | NY state | NJ | IL | ONT | England, Wales |
|------|------|----------|------|--------|-------|----------------|
| 1974 | – | 12,532 | 3,576 | – | – | – |
| 1975 | – | 13,832 | 3,546 | – | – | – |
| 1976 | 6,527 | 14,959 | 3,681 | – | – | – |
| 1977 | 6,960 | 16,595 | 4,135 | – | – | – |
| 1978 | 6,286 | 17,961 | 4,241 | 10,944 | – | 35,561 |
| 1979 | 6,673 | 19,755 | 3,906 | 11,263 | – | 35,591 |
| 1980 | 7,890 | 20,563 | 3,875 | 12,102 | 2,219 | 35,981 |
| 1981 | 8,780 | 20,926 | 3,951 | 13,141 | 2,188 | 36,022 |
| 1982 | 9,669 | 22,271 | 5,605 | 13,967 | 2,410 | 35,928 |
| 1983 | 8,867 | 26,386 | 6,797 | 13,735 | 2,699 | 35,486 |
| 1984 | 9,852 | 28,992 | 7,468 | 16,549 | 3,031 | 34,321 |
| 1985 | 11,499 | 31,195 | 8,896 | 17,649 | 3,165 | 36,305 |
| 1986 | 13,201 | 34,165 | 9,575 | 19,184 | 3,246 | 36,571 |
| 1987 | 14,187 | 35,276 | 10,945 | 19,928 | 3,270 | 37,531 |
| 1988 | 16,348 | 39,107 | 12,396 | 20,554 | 3,342 | 38,188 |
| 1989 | 19,072 | 41,766 | 13,434 | 21,721 | 3,469 | 37,885 |
| 1990 | 20,283 | 45,556 | 15,346 | – | 3,642 | – |
| 1991 | – | 53,345 | – | – | 3,827 | – |

*Sources.* NYC: Inmates under custody as of Dec. 31; *1992 New York State Yearbook,* table H-18; primarily jails rather than prisons. NY state: Inmates under custody as of April 1; *NY State Yearbook,* various years. New Jersey: 1974–75, adult population in prisons as of June 30; 1976–90, average daily prison population for June; NJ Department of Corrections, annual reports. Illinois: End of FY adult population, including contractual facilities; Department of Corrections, *Human Services Plan* (1990), vol. 3, p. 66. Ontario: Number of offenders sentenced in Ontario who were on register of federal correctional institution as of Dec. 31 (for 1991, Aug. 22); in Canada, felons are incarcerated in federal rather than provincial prisons (personal communication from Audrey McConnell, Information Officer, Research and Statistics, Correctional Service of Canada, Aug. 23, 1991).

*Table 14-2*  Releases from Prison, 1974–1991

| Year | NY state | New Jersey | Illinois |
|------|----------|------------|----------|
| 1974 | 6,840  | 1,536 | –      |
| 1975 | 7,369  | 1,470 | –      |
| 1976 | 7,596  | 1,194 | –      |
| 1977 | 8,723  | 1,256 | –      |
| 1978 | 8,102  | 1,684 | 7,219  |
| 1979 | 8,063  | 1,611 | 7,948  |
| 1980 | 9,128  | 2,144 | 8,482  |
| 1981 | 9,316  | 1,863 | 8,372  |
| 1982 | 9,115  | 1,569 | 9,050  |
| 1983 | 10,458 | 2,078 | 11,715 |
| 1984 | 12,668 | 2,069 | 7,270  |
| 1985 | 12,215 | 2,322 | 8,828  |
| 1986 | 14,461 | 2,969 | 9,224  |
| 1987 | 15,770 | 3,141 | 10,887 |
| 1988 | 18,859 | 3,565 | 10,119 |
| 1989 | 19,902 | 4,582 | 10,115 |
| 1990 | 23,313 | 4,727 | –      |
| 1991 | 26,700 | –     | –      |

*Sources.* New York: *State Yearbook,* various years; includes some deaths. New Jersey: Department of Corrections, annual reports. Illinois: Department of Corrections, *Human Services Plan,* 1990; includes some deaths.

Another effect, though, may be more important. Prison population in the United States rose partly because of the increased incidence of imprisonment and partly because of increased duration (longer sentences). Increased incidence implies that a few years after prison populations start rising, the flow of releases will start rising too. Table 14-2 shows that this is just what happened. There is an immediate increase in the stock of newly released ex-offenders and, over time, an increase in the total stock of ex-offenders.

Freeman (1992) has shown that ex-offenders face serious problems in the labor market, even after age, education, and job experience are held constant through statistical techniques. The same might be the case in the housing market. Some landlords might be reluctant to rent to people with records, and people who have been in prison for a long time are likely to be cut off from families and friends. Even a short prison spell can lead to a cutoff from family and friends if they now think you can't be trusted.

Taste may also matter. Many large government shelters operate just like prisons, complete with gangs and hierarchies. To quote one man from the shelter at the Fort Washington Armory: "This is like an outside jail . . . In a jail you got homo's. Same thing they do in jail they do here. This is just like jail. The people in here take it as jail. They put that image in their mind that they're locked up again. Sometimes it really gets to them because sometimes they do things like they are in jail" (Dordick, 1994, p. 194). For these reasons, increases in the flow out of prisons might imply increases in the flow into shelters.

Table 14-1 and 14-2 are surprisingly friendly to this interpretation. The United States has had a huge increase in flows out of prison and a huge increase in single-male homelessness; in Canada and Britain, both increases have been much more modest. Even within this country, Chicago's relatively low homelessness is associated with Illinois' relatively modest increase in prison releases. The state's big jump in releases in 1983 was followed by Chicago's first big expansion of shelters, and New Jersey's 1980 rise coincided with the first new-generation shelters in Newark. No such coincidences, however, stand out in the time series for New York, and releases kept rising in the late 1980s, even when the single-shelter population was going down.

The proportion of ex-prisoners in the homeless population doesn't seem to be increasing over time, and so it is probably not appropriate to say that the rising stock of ex-prisoners was driving the rise in homeless population. But it wasn't holding back the rise either. During the 1980s the number of ex-offenders was probably rising just about as fast as the single-male homeless population, and so the conditional probability that an ex-offender would be homeless was not changing much. This is a far stronger statement than what could be said about mentally ill people or substance abusers. So although former prisoners account for a somewhat smaller share of the homeless population than do the mentally ill or substance abusers, the growth of the population of released prisoners contributed at least as much to the growth of homelessness as did the growth of those two other populations, and probably more.

## The Police

How much of the variation in street homelessness can be attributed to different laws and different policing strategies? In our sample of cities, not much. This is because police practices are quite similar in the five English-speaking cities, despite substantially different laws. Both the laws and the practices have changed over the last thirty years, but the change took place well before the new homelessness. (In New York City, in fact, the law against public drunkenness has not been enforced since 1935.[1])

The important point to remember in thinking about laws and police is that as far as homelessness is concerned, the police see their job as keeping the peace and the laws as tools to be used for this purpose. Referring to laws as tools is quite a common practice among U.S. police departments; enforcing the law is not an end in itself. This point was first made by Egon Bittner in his study of skid-row policing in midwestern cities in the 1960s:

> But it is the rare exception that the law is invoked merely because the specifications of the law are met. That is, compliance with the law is merely the outward appearance of an intervention that is actually based on altogether different considerations. Thus it could be said that patrolmen do not really enforce the law, but merely use it as a resource to solve certain pressing problems in keeping the peace. (1967, p. 710)

The laws on obstructing sidewalks, loitering, vagrancy, begging, public drinking and drunkenness, and involuntary commitment to mental hospitals are the important ones when considering street homelessness.

Laws against loitering and vagrancy were declared unconstitutional in the early 1970s and are no longer on the books in Newark and New York. They remain on the books in Chicago, but since they are "incredibly broad" and almost certainly unconstitutional, departmental policy since the mid-seventies is not to enforce them (Kelly interview, 1991). The Newark police, however, have a law against obstructing sidewalks or public places. Similarly, Chicago has a disorderly-person charge that can be used to move people on. These laws could also be interpreted to prohibit aggressive begging. Even in New York, the Port Authority police have loitering laws for specific buildings, such as the Port Authority Bus Terminal (Deitch, 1993).

Canada and Britain never had loitering laws and don't have them now, but both had vagrancy laws. Canada's vagrancy law included provisions that allowed the police to arrest persons found in a public place who couldn't give an account of themselves (vagrancy A) or who were begging (vagrancy B). These sections were enforced until they were repealed in 1971. Nothing has taken their place. Laws that effectively prohibit aggressive begging, however, remain in place (Boothby interview, 1991).

In London, by contrast, section 4 of the Vagrancy Act of 1824 is still in effect. It "provides a power of arrest if persons 'wandering abroad or lodging in the open air' fail or refuse to go to reasonably accessible places after being so directed" (Green, 1991). Begging is generally not legal, and panhandlers who claimed to be homeless have been charged with fraud when under questioning they gave addresses.

Public drinking as a disorderly-person offense was decriminalized in New York in 1976, but both drinking in public places and being intoxicated "to the annoyance of any other person" are unlawful in Newark. Toronto and London also prohibit public drinking.

Laws on involuntary commitment for mental illness are about the same. An officer can initiate an involuntary commitment only if a person poses an imminent danger to himself or others; the officer can't rely on hearsay for this decision; and psychiatric personnel have to make the final determination. Acting strangely is not grounds for commitment. The phrasing of the danger standard, however, differs from place to place. In Newark, as in North America generally, the standard is whether "there is a substantial likelihood the person will inflict serious bodily harm upon another [or himself] or cause serious property damage within the reasonably foreseeable future" (New Jersey P.L. 1987, chap. 116). In London, by contrast, the standard in section 136 of the Mental Health Act is that the person should appear in immediate need of care and control.

In practice, though, where the laws are different they are administered similarly, and where they are the same they are administered differently. For instance, despite the similarity between commitment standards in New York and London, a New York officer might go through his or her entire career without ever making an involuntary commitment, especially if the officer didn't work in midtown (Ryan interview, 1991); but commitment procedures in London are "frequently used" (Baggott interview, 1991). The Toronto police make around 3,000 arrests a year on alcohol-related charges; the Newark police make almost none.

On the question of police attitudes toward street homelessness, however, all five cities are the same. Tolerance, perhaps even sympathy, is the dominant theme. (John Donahue, director of the Chicago Coalition for the Homeless, told me in an interview in August 1991 that the average Chicago police officer is basically sympathetic to homeless people. Several months before, Donahue himself had been arrested, for allegedly punching an officer, when Mayor Daley ordered the homeless out of O'Hare Airport.) A homeless person sleeping or sitting in a public place will generally not be disturbed if he is not committing a crime or is in no imminent danger of becoming the victim of a crime. He may act bizarrely, offend propertyowners, or render the space unusable by others, but the police will not intervene. Homelessness is not a crime.[2]

The most cogent arguments for this policy are set forth in an "informal note" by the commander of the Holborn police district in London, Chief Superintendent Paul A. Green. The immediate issue (in 1991) was how to deal with the homeless people in Lincoln's Inn Fields, but the note has much wider applicability. Green describes the advantages of the tolerant approach as being "relatively low cost in policing terms, public support (particularly from the local authority and many others who are concerned with the problems of the homeless as opposed to seeing the homeless as a problem), and continued job satisfaction for those officers currently employed." And a more aggressive policy that involved frequent invocation of the Vagrancy Act would have considerable disadvantages:

> If police action was seen as oppressive, then support and cooperation from other agencies would be quickly withdrawn. Increased police activity would do nothing to resolve the problems in the "Fields." Police resources would be tied up with processing people through the Criminal Justice system, placing vagrants before the courts, whose only option is a fine, or return back to the Fields. Neither police nor the courts have powers of referral to other accommodation. The arrest of

a vagrant is at least as time-consuming as the arrest of a person for a criminal offense, with the possibility of much increased time if delousing is necessary of both vehicles, officers and police premises.

A major operation to clear the Fields would have further disadvantages: "It would not necessarily do anything to resolve the problem of the homeless; at best it would displace them. That displacement would be uncontrolled and may create immediate problems at new locations. There is also the chance of substantial public backlash if such an action took place with demonstrations and opposition to police action . . . The cost of mounting the operation would be high, bearing in mind that it would need to be repeated on more than one occasion."

In short, enforcement efforts aimed at removing homeless people from public places are extremely costly and likely to accomplish little. Fining homeless people makes no sense, and a stay in a warm jail is not much of a deterrent. To quote Bittner:

> officers point out that sending someone to jail from skid-row does not upset his relatives or his family life, does not cause him to miss work or lose a job, does not lead to his being reproached by friends and associates, does not lead to failure to meet commitments or protect commitments, and does not conflict with any but the most passing intentions of the arrested person. (p. 714)

In London, accordingly, the police have decided that the "reasonably accessible" accommodation the Vagrancy Act refers to is not available, and so only twelve arrests were made under it in 1990, none in Holborn. Police in the other four cities have come to the same conclusion. Even the Port Authority police, when they invoked loitering laws to reduce the 42nd Street bus terminal's population in 1992, relied chiefly on aggressive referrals to shelters.

Some sort of hands-off policy like this, moreover, seems to have been in force even in the United States in the 1960s, when almost all of the old laws were in effect (at least for white derelicts). In Bittner's midwestern cities,

> [The reduced relevance of culpability] becomes partly visible when one views the treatment of persons who are not arrested even though

all legal grounds for an arrest are present. Whenever such persons are encountered and can be induced to leave, or taken to some shelter, or remanded to someone's care, then patrolmen feel, or at least maintain, that an arrest would serve no useful purpose. That is, whenever there exist means for controlling the troublesome aspects of some person's presence in some way alternative to an arrest, such means are preferentially employed, provided, of course, that the case at hand involves only a minor offense. (p. 710)

Similarly, Richard Kopperdahl (1994) writes of his time on the Bowery in the late sixties: "The best thing about the Bowery was that no cop ever told you to move on: if you were a bum, it was your place."

This attitude was also apparent in New York courts in the 1960s. In 1963, 91 percent of the sentences delivered in the Social Court, which handled Bowery cases almost exclusively, were suspended (Markel, 1964). But this day-to-day policy doesn't preclude occasional one-shot operations that clear particular high-visibility locations: in New York, Tompkins Square Park and the Colisseum: in Chicago, O'Hare Airport; in London, the "Bull Ring." This was true even in the sixties: an effort to clean up New York streets in preparation for the 1964 world's fair resulted in placing an additional 1,600 men in jail on an average night, largely because of stricter sentencing.[3] To the extent that certain of the best locations for street living are eliminated by these sweeps, they may reduce the total amount of street homelessness, not merely rearrange it. But this is no viable mode for everyday operation.

Where cities differ in practice is the unwritten code on structures. The London police tolerate "bashes"—generally cardboard shanties, but sometimes more elaborate structures with tarpaulins and wood—and so did the New York police for most places until recently. The Newark police do not—but with the abundance of empty buildings in Newark, this is probably irrelevant. I don't know the Chicago or Toronto policies, but I didn't see shanties in either city. Policies against structures are fairly easy to enforce, since the removal of a structure is a fairly large penalty to its builder.

Police departments also differ in the extent to which they render positive assistance to homeless people. The homeless are, after all, citizens who have a right to call on the police for help. The major form of assistance that homeless people look for is probably protection from criminals, and all departments acknowledge their responsibility to provide it. Beyond this, Toronto, London, and Newark have no formal assistance policies, although Deputy Chief Dough's role in Newark has been noted in Chapter 4. New York police officers (and within New York and Newark, Port Authority police) will transport homeless people to shelters in cold weather, if they agree to go, and so will the Chicago police. Chicago is alone in maintaining the old tradition that the precincts are housing of last resort for the homeless.

Cities differ too in how they treat daytime streetpeople, particularly panhandlers in transportation systems. There are even differences within cities. Until recently, for instance, the New York City subway system and the PATH (Port Authority Trans-Hudson) system had radically different panhandler densities and radically different police policies toward panhandling, although both operated in Manhattan with fairly similar physical setups (and both had about the same written rules). Schwartz (1988) provides an overview of transportation system polices on panhandling and homelessness. Outside skid row, laws against begging were probably reasonably effective until the early 1970s.[4]

Most of the evidence thus points to the conclusion that changes in *laws* had no impact on the rise of homelessness in the United States in the eighties, and that changes in police practice had only minor, cosmetic effects.[5] Kopperdahl even argues that life on the streets is harder now than it was in the sixties: "To me, the saddest thing about some poor drunk's being a member of the new homeless class of the 90s is that there is no place where he 'belongs.' Instead of a 10-block-long skid row, we now have dozens of mini-Boweries where drunks are constantly hassled by local merchants, residents, and the police." Police officers in the 1950s and 1960s, moreover, grew up during the depression; they may have had more first-hand experience with poverty and alcoholism than later police cohorts and so may have been more sympathetic toward homeless people.

Yet I have one serious reservation about this conclusion. It concerns race. We know how the police treated white derelicts in the fifties and sixties; we don't know how they treated black derelicts.[6] More important, we don't know how black men believed they would be treated by officers who found them sleeping or drunk on the street.

We do know that in the United States almost all the men on the street in the sixties were white, and that is still the case in London and Toronto, even though both cities have substantial and growing black populations that are overrepresented in, say, family shelters. In Chicago and New York too, even today, black people are less heavily represented on the street than they are in shelters.

It may be, then, that the fear of maltreatment by police forces and white civilians was an important reason why so few blacks were on the streets in the sixties, especially in white neighborhoods, and that this fear had diminished by the eighties. Black men in American cities in the sixties were neither prosperous nor free from pathologies, and so their absence from streets and underrepresentation on skid rows is a puzzle. The well-grounded fear of white police and civilians is a plausible answer to this puzzle. It might also explain the continuing absence of black people from the streets in cities like London and Toronto, where they are a minority group with little political power.

In U.S. cities, the growth of street homelessness in the 1980s (and maybe the late 1970s too) was much more rapid among blacks than among whites. Reduced fear may be a big part of the reason. In this case, what almost everyone would say were better police practices—less brutality, more even-handedness, less overt racism, more willingness to protect blacks from whites—may have contributed to the rise in homelessness. (Conversely, the failure of police in Toronto and London to instill a similar degree of trust may be keeping street populations down in those cities.)

I don't argue that all of the growth in black street homelessness is due to a greater trust in the police. Trust building is too gradual a process to explain the sharp rise of the late seventies and early eighties (though we don't have real data on how sharply street populations rose), and white street populations probably increased at the same time. But a plausible story can be made that a growth in trust made a noticeable contribution, and that the rise in black street homelessness would have been impossible without it. This is no doubt the most important way that policing has contributed to the growth of homelessness.

In 1940 or 1960, a black man would have been risking serious bodily harm or even death if he tried to sleep all night in Grand Central Terminal or on Park Avenue. That hundreds of African Americans were doing so in 1990 is something of a tribute to the NYPD. Anatole France said that the rich and the poor had an equal right to sleep under the bridges of Paris, but I doubt that blacks and whites had such equal rights in America before the civil-rights movement. Black people now have a de facto right to be homeless on the streets of most American cities, and this represents progress of a sort. The bad part is that so many have to exercise this new-found "right."

# 15

# What We Should Do

The puzzle of why North American homelessness rose in the 1980s may never be solved. Measurements of homelessness, particularly street homelessness, are so poor and so sparse that doing a definitive study is probably impossible. After all, in over a century there is still no basic agreement about what caused the Civil War.

Still, I think I have shown that certain explanations are more plausible than others. Income distribution changed; this changed housing prices; changes in housing prices caused homelessness; homelessness caused shelters; and shelters caused more homelessness. In the background, exerting some sort of force I can't begin to quantify, are increasing tenant rights, more former prisoners, and possibly a growing trust among African Americans in the safety of streets in white neighborhoods.

Surely there would have been less homelessness if in the 1980s severe poverty had decreased or if large numbers of mentally ill people had been reinstitutionalized or if building codes were eviscerated or if huge amounts of cheap public housing had been constructed—but none of this happened. What stories can I then tell about the six cities? Something like this.

*New York.* The drastic shrinkage of the middle class is the major force here. This happened in the 1970s; the result was extreme looseness in the low-quality housing market for a while—fires and rapid abandonment in the mid-seventies—followed by much higher rents and homelessness. This problem was exacerbated by the difficulties that Bowery flophouses faced in dealing with mentally ill people, by strict housing-maintenance and zoning regulations, by severe difficulties in evicting tenants, and by a large flow of ex-prisoners back to the streets. City shelter policies became more generous, and the adjustment to these new policies kept homelessness rising throughout most of the 1980s. After 1987, the housing market eased and homelessness fell for several years (reduced intoxicant prices as a result of the crack invasion may also have helped). Probably the rise in unemployment associated with the early 1990s recession caused family homelessness to increase.

*Newark.* Newark's story is much like New York's, but it lagged behind by a few years. In particular, the adjustment to greater shelter generosity was still going on when the housing market eased, so that for most of the 1980s and 1990s homelessness was moving in opposite directions in the two nearby cities. The loss of public housing stock probably also contributed to homelessness in Newark.

*Chicago.* Chicago did not experience the drastic change in income distribution that the two eastern cities did, and so the rise in homelessness was much smaller and somewhat later. The flow of former prisoners was also smaller than it was in the eastern cities. The rise in shelter provision was also late.

*Toronto.* Toronto escaped the U.S. increase in homelessness for several different reasons. There was no loss in middle-class population, but the near absence of abandonment leads one to suspect that an income-distribution change wouldn't have mattered anyway, since Toronto's housing market may be in a cheap maintenance equilibrium rather than in a cheap construction equilibrium. The low rate of severe poverty, the generous welfare benefits for families, and the small flow of released prisoners also play a role.

*London.* Definitional problems make it difficult to say what happened here. The housing-benefit system was probably sufficient to keep "shelter" and street homelessness from rising. London is also like Toronto in having very little demolition; perhaps maintenance is cheap relative to construction so that the models of Chapter 6 don't apply. Tougher laws reduced squatting, but statutory homelessness probably responded mostly to the laws shaking up the queue for public housing.

*Hamburg.* Here, too, cheap maintenance and the housing-benefit system probably kept homelessness from rising for most of the 1980s. I don't understand why it was falling at the beginning of the decade.

Policies, however, are not uniquely determined by causes. The lesson of the Garden of Eden is not that we should renounce apples. Understanding the causes of homelessness is a good first step in devising policies to deal with it, but still only a first step.

The large trends that have been driving the rise in homelessness—growing income inequality, larger prison population, more liberal tenancy laws—are not likely to be reversed soon. A greater confidence in police behavior among African Americans may also have contributed to growing homelessness, but that is a trend we should not want to see reversed.

Since policies that reverse the trends leading to more homelessness are for the most part either impossible or undesirable, the question becomes how to cope with an environment where substantial numbers of people have a hard time keeping a conventional roof over their heads.

There is, I think, one underlying principle for designing good policies in such an environment: homeless people should be treated in the same way as everyone else; they should not get special treatment. The principle applies no matter what your motivation is in wanting to alleviate homelessness—whether it is concern over how well homeless people satisfy their desires, or their objective circumstances, or the well-being of other people, or even your own felt obligations. The principle doesn't rule out designing policies to relieve homelessness; what it rules out is policies that say to someone, "Because you're homeless, you will be treated in such-and-such a manner; if you weren't homeless, you would be treated otherwise."

This principle represents a natural continuation of the general elimination of status crimes (or class crimes, some would say). Fifty years ago, when vagrancy laws were in force, you could be arrested simply because you couldn't give a good account of where you lived or what you did. You could also be denied regular cash welfare payments and be given tickets and chits instead. Bums, simply because they were bums, were treated differently. Some of these status differences are gone now, but all sorts of activities are still restricted to homeless people. The last vestiges of these status distinctions should be eliminated.

The main reason for adopting the nondiscrimination principle is practicality. (Even if you believe that the tide of history is running in this direction, you still need an independent argument about why this is the right direction.) People can't agree on a definition of homelessness, and even if they could, the definition is unlikely to be useful for determining eligibility. Useful eligibility criteria are easy for program operators to observe, but hard (or impossible) for potential participants to acquire on their own. Wearing a green shirt meets the first criterion but not the second; having an unresolved oedipal complex meets the second criterion but not the first. Short-term homelessness meets the first criterion but not the second; long-term homelessness, the second (sometimes) but not the first.

The appeal of the nondiscrimination principle is that it works. Using it gives consistently good answers to knotty policy problems, answers that stand up well by the usual criteria used to judge policies. So now I will apply the nondiscrimination principle over and over to actual problems, and you can judge for yourself the strength of my claim.

I will begin by asking how police forces should deal with homeless people. This topic is important in itself, but I take it first because of the specially clear illustration it gives of the power of the nondiscrimination principle. Next I turn to issues of housing policy: shelters, public housing, and regulation. Then I look at labor-market policies and income-maintenance policies, or how people get money to buy housing. Finally, I consider the role of therapy of various kinds. Although quite popular now, therapy is, in my view, a misguided approach.

I am writing this chapter as an outsider, trying to make people in government listen to me. I have no illusions that they will. Some of my recommendations are fairly radical, and some go strongly against the grain of current discussion. But I won't say: "X should be done but only Y is politically palatable, so let's do Y." Compromise is the job of insiders, not outsiders. Outsiders who act like insiders are insipid and ineffectual (just as insiders who act like outsiders are bombastic, untrustworthy, and ineffectual). Adam

Smith, Karl Marx, and John Maynard Keynes—the economists who have had the most influence over the world we live in—all worried first and foremost about whether their preaching was right, not whether anyone would follow them. Theirs is a good example to keep in mind.[1]

## The Police

The nondiscrimination principle implies that thinking about homeless people as citizens is the best way to devise policies for the police to follow. What does this mean?

The main responsibility of police departments is to protect citizens—including homeless people—from crime. Protection may increase street homelessness and the associated costs it imposes on others, because it encourages people to live outdoors. But a police department that abdicated its responsibility to protect people from crime for the reason that they were engaging in antisocial activity would be a police department that had renounced the claim to a monopoly of force that is its raison d'etre. Pollution and congestion don't imply that the police, even in Manhattan, should condone automobile theft; nor should muggers be entitled to a free hand with jaywalkers or people who sneeze in public without covering their mouths.

The responsibility of protection, however, does imply that the police should encourage homeless people to get off the streets, especially dangerous places, whenever possible. This is like warning tourists not to keep wallets in their back pockets, and it is very much in keeping with the job police officers see themselves as performing. Tourists who keep wallets in their back pockets are not arrested, of course, nor is crime against them condoned (hospital emergency rooms don't refuse treatment even to injured motorists who were not wearing seatbelts). Similarly, homeless people who remain on the streets don't waive their right to protection.

I argued in Chapter 14 that asking the police to be more aggressive—arresting panhandlers and people sleeping unobtrusively in public places—is futile. Police officers—as a routine matter, which is what counts—won't do it, and homeless people, since jail is warm, wouldn't be deterred much if they did.

I'm not arguing that the police should do nothing. Aggressive but nonpunitive referral is a positive strategy; it has a record of reducing street homelessness and the attendant costs it imposes on other people. The Port Authority bus terminal in New York is the clearest example of success for such a policy, and the experience of Grand Central train terminal is somewhat similar. (Some may object that the Port Authority and Grand Central have merely displaced the street homeless, but even if this is true, the displacement has some positive social benefit because of the enormous flow of pedestrian traffic in the two terminals.) Probably part of the difference in street activity between New York and Chicago is attributable to the Chicago police department's more aggressive attitude in making referrals.

Police must also act decisively against homeless criminals. Both the nonhomeless public and homeless people benefit directly from this effort—homeless people probably more than anyone else. Note that both of these desirable activities are in step with the primary mission of police departments—protecting the public from crime. Police don't need a homeless policy; they need only an anticrime policy that recognizes that some people are homeless.

The most knotted question is the policy toward structures, and here again nondiscrimination points the way. Should homeless people be allowed to build shanties? I think the answer is no. The reason is simple: shanties violate the building code. Many portions of standard building codes are meritorious—the indoor-plumbing requirement, for instance. The same citizenship that entitles homeless people to protection from crime obligates them to obey the same laws as everyone else. We don't allow quadriplegics to be swindlers or innocent shooting victims to violate the gun laws.

Homeless people, then, are not entitled to violate building codes. Shanties that violate the codes should be treated just like other structures that violate the codes. Upgrading to meet code—hooking into sewers, say—is not feasible (in part because it would constitute a crime, the expropriation of public land), and so shanties should be removed in the same way that other violating structures are removed. This argument does not countenance midnight forays; homeless people are entitled to the same protections (notice, appeal, and so forth) that belong to other alleged building-code violators.

## Shelter Policies

All the efficiency and capability arguments for why homelessness is bad imply that getting many people, if not everyone, off the street is desirable, and both practicality and some of the arguments themselves require that this be accomplished by providing some decent offstreet shelter. It is not surprising that most discussions of homeless policy are about how shelters should be run.

Shelter provision entails some unavoidable dilemmas, as noted in Chapter 6. Free shelters that are hygienic, safe, and dignified enough to accomplish some of the goals they should accomplish are also attractive enough to bring in many people who would not otherwise be on the street. By itself, that need not be a problem. Shelters, though, eliminate the market provision of housing, even at qualities substantially higher than the quality the shelter itself provides (market housing must at least meet operating costs and so must charge a finite positive rent, but for qualities of housing only a little better than a free shelter, consumers are willing to pay only a little rent).

This gap causes several problems. For shelter residents, it is a disincentive to work and an incentive to abuse substances, since increasing their housing expenditures by a small amount doesn't increase the quality of their surroundings. The gap is also a housing-market distortion, since lower qualities of housing offered for free are replacing higher qualities of housing. Some shelter residents would be better off, and no one would be worse off, if they could use all the money that is spent on shelter operating costs, and some of their own, on slightly better housing.

The nondiscrimination principle points to a way of avoiding these problems: using a shelter allowance rather than shelters. In its simplest form a shelter allowance of, say, $10 or $15 a night would be paid to anyone who housed anyone else. The housing consumer, if she wished, could supplement this amount by any private agreement she could make with the housing provider. Public shelters would operate only during natural disasters. The allowance would have to be high enough to get most people off the streets.

Many features of the shelter-allowance system are already in place. The closest analogy is probably the British housing benefit, the system that makes it impossible to find American-style shelters in London. The main differences would be that the shelter allowance would probably be a bit smaller (this would eliminate the problem Hills [1989] cites with the housing benefit—for many recipients, housing quality has zero marginal cost), that it would be payable to relatives and informal housing providers as well as formal landlords, and that it would be less carefully means-tested. The shelter allowance would also be like the system of per-diem allowances that finances most nonprofit shelters in North America (and even some governmental ones like Seaton House in Toronto). The difference is that commercial and familial housing providers would be treated just as nonprofit organizations are.

In treating family members like nonprofit organizations, a shelter allowance is somewhat like Rossi's (1989) suggestion of "Aid to Families with Dependent Adults." In letting housing consumers supplement the basic accommodations covered by the stipend, the shelter allowance implements Filer's (1992) recommendation of gradations in shelters.

The shelter allowance wouldn't have to be explicitly means-tested and should be available to anyone who shows valid identification. Receipt of a shelter allowance should be recorded and can be taxed ex post, possibly at high rates, in both income-maintenance programs and the regular income tax. Anyone who maintains several IDs is able to commit fraud, but dual-ID people can also defraud the means-tested programs we have now.

Most shelter-allowance payments should probably be two-name checks. Putting the recipient's name on the check makes it harder for a landlord to invent fictitious tenants. Putting the landlord's name on the check makes it less fungible for the recipient and establishes the landlord's responsibility to provide housing. Since the shelter allowance will usually cover only a portion of the rent, the tenant will retain the ability to negotiate with the landlord and to withhold some rent.

Units covered by the shelter allowance will have to meet building, zoning, and fire codes, but so do all other units, even now. No new inspecting would be required.

Humanitarian efforts to shelter the homeless could continue, and they would be assured a steady stream of income, no matter what their political or religious orientation was, provided they were sufficiently attractive to homeless people. Donations could be used for food, social services, indoctrination, training, or whatever the humanitarian group wanted to use them for. These services are not housing, and decisions—both by homeless people and by people helping out—about housing and about these services should be kept separate.

No changes in public-order laws would have to be made. The police would have an easier job of encouraging people to leave public places because many different facilities would take people with little or no money. There would also be a new crime to prosecute: landlords would be criminally liable if they did not maintain accommodations for the tenants they were being paid for. If the police found a person sleeping on the street, they could investigate whether a shelter allowance was being paid for him. If it was, and no bed was available, the landlord would be in trouble—criminal trouble.

Shelter allowances have several important advantages. First, they concentrate resources on minimum accommodations—getting people off the street—because that is the major problem we have identified. Homelessness, on almost all grounds, is worse than living in low-quality housing; yet most housing programs concentrate their funds and efforts on moving households from bad housing to better housing, and not from homelessness to any quality of housing. Shelter allowances don't make this mistake.

Second, shelter allowances make money useful again in the housing market for very poor people. Because side deals are permitted, a little more money can buy you a little nicer place to live, and so you have one more reason to earn a little more money, and one more reason not to spend it on alcohol or drugs.

Third, allowances level the playing field among nonprofit shelters, commercial establishments, and families. If a family or a roominghouse is willing to house someone at $10 a night and a nonprofit shelter spends $20 a night, but the person prefers to stay with the family or in the roominghouse, then it is clearly wasteful to encourage him to go to the shelter by restricting government funding. Shelter allowances remove this waste. And they make it much easier for people to do good—the goal that figures so prominently in Catholic Worker philosophy and many other traditions.

Fourth, allowances improve the incentives of U.S. public housing authorities by making the poorest people generate as much income as better-off people. With a shelter allowance in place, U.S. housing authorities, like British agencies, could charge everyone the same rent, and so they wouldn't be rewarded for having higher-income tenants. They would become just like the operators of section 8 buildings: they would be running housing programs and not income-transfer programs.

Fifth, and probably most important, shelter allowances give a large number of agents a reason to compete among themselves and try to design the most attractive accommodations to lure homeless people in. Generosity is a resource in short supply in modern capitalist societies, never enough to house decently a large number of homeless people, and legal compulsion has proved inadequate—fifteen years of intense litigation and many court victories for homeless advocates in New York have failed to produce a shelter system sufficiently attractive to house as many single adults as the streets do. Greed is a strong and reliable source of motivation. It is instructive that when a group of homeless people in Toronto were asked to design a shelter for themselves, what they came up with—StreetCity—was a couple of roominghouses.

There are, of course, objections to this proposal. Some of them have merit; others don't. The least meritorious objection is that shelter allowances will make it impossible to count the shelter homeless or to design programs for them. But even now, without a definition of shelter, it is impossible to count the shelter homeless, and designing programs with shelter homelessness as an eligibility criterion violates the nondiscrimination principle. In fact, another advantage of shelter allowances is that they eliminate some temptation to violate the nondiscrimination principle.

Another unmeritorious objection to shelter allowances is that they create one more entitlement program, and entitlement programs are bad. The evil of entitlement programs is a superstition believed most fervently in Washington and environs, where many hold that the growth of spending on medicare and social security has contributed the most to the federal deficit. Of course, poorly designed entitlement programs are bad, but so are poorly designed programs of any type. I know of no argument why entitlement programs in themselves are bad. The alternative is, I would guess, discretionary programs—spigots that can be turned on and off at the whim of whoever is in power, or distributed to some lucky or well-connected people and denied to others. People in power almost always want discretion, at least in the short run, and entitlement programs tie their hands. The Bill of Rights also is about tying the government's hands.

Even intelligent people in power often want their own hands tied, just as Ulysses wanted himself tied to the mast to keep him from the Sirens.[2] Some governmental objectives can be achieved only by making commitments—aggressor nations must know that aggression will be resisted, and people who build on high ground in northern climates must know that the snow will be plowed. Defense and snowplowing are entitlement programs too. Discretion isn't a good way of dealing with military aggression or snow-filled streets, and it isn't a good way of dealing with homelessness either.

An objection that might have more merit is that shelter allowances would be too costly. I haven't done the calculations needed to answer this objection definitively. Shelter allowances, though, are not as expensive as they may seem because they would allow spending reductions in other areas. Shelters themselves, are an obvious area, but shelter allowances might also be accompanied by reductions in welfare expenditures and housing-authority subsidies unrelated to occupancy. (Some intergovernmental shifting of responsibilities might occur, since general assistance in this country is a state and local program and shelter allowances might be federal, but general assistance is an area where a strong case can be made for shifting more responsibility to the federal level [Rivlin, 1992].) Existing section 8 certificates and vouchers probably should not be reduced, since they represent government commitments, but they could be retired naturally, and shelter allowances are an obvious substitute for the expansion of section 8 programs.

Still I wouldn't dare claim that shelter allowances would be free. I have argued, though, that homelessness is a bad thing, a legitimate governmental concern, and I don't think many people would disagree with that conclusion. So it is appropriate to devote resources to reducing homelessness.

A final objection, and probably the most meritorious of the lot, is that shelter allowances make no provision for people who are so disruptive that no one wants to house them. Raising the shelter allowance could reduce or eliminate this problem, but it would be very expensive to do so for both disruptive and nondisruptive alike. The solution, I think, is to have a higher shelter allowance for people with a history of being disruptive. But the use of this higher allowance would have to be restricted to special providers, so that people won't act strangely in order to generate a higher allowance to be paid to their family and friends. This scheme won't work perfectly—some disruptive people will end up on the street, and others will feign disruption to collect the extra money—but I can think of no scheme that would work better.

Note that disruptive people are an even bigger problem for free shelters—they must either be accepted, in which case the shelter becomes less attractive for everyone else and so more nondisruptive people sleep on the street, or rejected, in which case they sleep on the streets. There is no middle ground. Even where shelter allowances perform least well, they do better than shelters.

## Public Housing

I have already noted how shelter allowances improve the incentives of U.S. housing authorities. Without such incentives, it is doubtful whether building more public housing—which is frequently advocated—would do much to reduce homelessness, since current funding rules essentially give authorities a choice between running empty buildings and running buildings full of fairly well-off people.

With shelter allowances in place, however, expanding the public housing supply could be helpful—not necessarily because otherwise homeless people would be housed in newly built projects, but because more public supply would probably reduce demand and hence prices for some of the lowest qualities of housing on the market. "Probably" is here because building public housing often requires demolishing low-quality private housing—the New York City projects of the 1940s and 1950s, for instance, were built by an entity called the Mayor's Slum Clearance Commission.

Money devoted to building public housing, though, would almost certainly be better spent on increasing shelter allowances. Largely because low qualities of housing are more cheaply supplied by filtering from better qualities than by new construction, economists have estimated that every two dollars spent on public housing provides tenants with benefits for which they would be willing to pay only one dollar.[3] And shelter allowances are much more egalitarian: they help everyone who has trouble paying for housing, not just a few lucky or well-connected households.

In the absence of shelter allowances, should homeless families go to the head of the queue for public housing? The nondiscrimination principle says no, and again I think this is the right answer. Although journalistic accounts of the incentive effects of queue jumping are exaggerated, at least for New York, such effects do exist, and they make homelessness questionable as a criterion for rationing apartments. Putting people who are homeless at the moment at the top of the waiting list doesn't make it likely that the most deserving households get the apartments and the subsidies.

Neither, however, does giving apartments to households that jump through the right hoops and wait the longest—the main criteria used in New York and London before homelessness rattled the queue. Preference for homeless households may have opened public housing somewhat to groups these criteria had shut out—minorities in London, disorganized households in New York—and so it may have made the distribution of apartments more equitable. But if this happened, it was an accident. If the traditional criteria don't distribute apartments equitably, they should be fixed—replaced by explicitly equitable criteria. If deserving households are not getting apartments under the traditional criteria, they shouldn't have to become homeless to get those apartments.

Rewriting the traditional criteria more equitably, though, requires some clear decisions about what "equity" and "deserving" mean in the distribution of a small number of good things among a large number of poor people. I don't have much to say about this, except that I think it's impossible.[4] Shelter allowances, because they don't treat one household better than another, eliminate this problem—another argument for shelter allowances.

## Regulations

Changing regulations is a way of alleviating homelessness that is in full accord with the nondiscrimination principle. But regulations, we have seen, even the most egregiously misguided ones, probably did not contribute much to the rise of the new homelessness. Nor does it seem that changes in regulations would cause major differences in the volume of homelessness today. There are many good reasons to change many different regulations, but homelessness isn't one of them.

A good example is the prohibition against women in New York City lodginghouses. Anytime a woman enters a lodginghouse, she must be preceded by one man and followed by another, and the men must continually yell out, "Woman on the floor!" This regulation has real costs—owners can't hire female employees and so can't use newspapers or mainstream employment agencies to search for help. These higher operating costs probably contribute something—a very small bit—to the volume of homelessness in New York. The costs can't be too great, though, since the lobbying effort needed to remove the regulation wouldn't be very large. And since the city now employs female lodginghouse inspectors, it is doubtful that the law is enforced.

There are, however, four exceptions to this rule—four areas where regulatory changes could probably reduce homelessness, at least over time. The first is New York City's prohibition on new rooming units. This is embodied in section 27-2077 of the housing-maintenance code and in the zoning-code rules for room counting. These provisions should be repealed. In the short run, repeal will have little effect, but it could make a difference over time, especially if some sort of shelter allowance is instituted. The same applies to the zoning prohibition on new roominghouses in Toronto, and some of the more draconian parts of Chicago's zoning code.

The second area where changes could usefully be made is in the logic of zoning codes. New York and Toronto have moved away from traditional apex zoning and prohibited almost all residential uses in industrial districts. Moving back to apex zoning, at least for industrial districts, might encourage some conversions to low-cost, low-quality housing. Toronto's showpiece shelter, StreetCity, is in an industrial zone and would not normally have been permitted.

Tenancy laws are the area for the most important policy changes. Because what they do affects other people, tenants who share many facilities should not have the same protections against eviction as tenants who share few. Easing evictions for this class of tenants—say by removing the good-cause requirement—would make operating SROs and lodginghouses considerably more attractive. (Indeed, one part of the easing might be to give other tenants some sort of direct voice in eviction procedures.)

Another reason for relaxing tenancy laws in these low-quality establishments is the difficulty that owners would otherwise have in collecting rents. Under common law, when a guest doesn't pay, the owner has a lien on the guest's property. For guests who are essentially without property, the lien is meaningless. When eviction is difficult, propertyless people have no mechanism for making credible promises to be good tenants.

What happens to people who are evicted? Here the shelter allowances for disruptive people come in again. It is important, though, that people who are repeatedly evicted for being disruptive do not benefit as a result. A commitment to zero homelessness is unworkable.

Finally, as Filer (1992) has suggested, liability standards for the operators of lodginghouses and SROs should be revised. Currently owners of these establishments have "innkeeper's liability," which is a higher standard than applies, say, to apartmenthouse operators. In particular:

> An innkeeper has an obligation to reasonably protect guests from injury while at the inn. This duty of reasonable care mandates vigilance in the protection of guests from injury at the hands of other guests and from assaults and negligent acts of his or her own employees. The obligation to protect guests is not met merely by warning

them, but must be coupled with a policing of the premises. (*Guide to American Law*, 1984, vol. 6, p. 180)

Innkeeper liability represents an efficient response to the problem of transient guests with little knowledge of the locality, which is why it doesn't apply to apartmenthouses. With more or less permanent guests who know about other establishments, the efficiency argument for innkeeper liability more or less disappears. This is especially true if tenancy laws continue to give owners such difficulty in evicting guests who might harm others.

## Work

What people do during the day matters as much as what they do at night. Policies that operate only in the housing market and not in the labor market are clearly inadequate for addressing the problems of homelessness. The daytime street population should be as much a concern as the nighttime population of officially homeless people, and we have no strong reason to believe that housing policies can have much effect on daytime activities. Eliminating official homelessness would probably not make much of a dent in panhandling (and if homelessness as most of the public defines it—colloquial homelessness—continued, the policies that ended official homelessness would be failures in the tribunal of public opinion).

Labor-market policies, moreover, can be complementary to housing policies in at least two ways. The first is obvious: more income alleviates many problems. The second way is more subtle. A former owner noted that an SRO with working guests was much easier to operate than one with a welfare clientele. Working guests were gone during the day, cleaning was easier, and the hotel's exposure to damage and liability was reduced.

What then should be done about daytime streetpeople? Law enforcement is unlikely to achieve much—police are reluctant to be aggressive for long, and constitutional issues are involved. Police action would also exacerbate the housing problems that the SRO owner cited. So policies need to provide options that are more attractive than panhandling, peddling, canning, and windshield washing. Recreation is one alternative, but not a good one. The public won't finance a recreation program for single adults.

The remaining alternative is some sort of work program. Two circumstances make it easy to design such a program. First, most daytime streetpeople are working already—under awful conditions for paltry compensation. Inculcating a work ethic is unnecessary, and making jobs more attractive in wages and working conditions should not be too hard. (A work ethic implies a willingness to do what a boss tells you to do or to show up at a regular time even when you're feeling bad, but a readiness to endure harsh weather and social ostracism and to expend large amounts of energy just to get a handful of money is surely one version of the work ethic. Daytime streetpeople aren't lazy—undisciplined probably, but not lazy.)

Second, streetpeople are fairly easy to communicate with. Their own networks are strong: canners exchange news, for instance, as they wait to redeem cans (Conley, 1993), and almost all visit soup kitchens regularly. In the Columbia survey, 47 percent had eaten at a soup kitchen in the previous twenty-four hours, and another 20 percent had done so in the previous week.

But these two circumstances don't remove all obstacles; otherwise existing programs like workfare for GA recipients and the New York City shelter/work program would already have taken everyone off the streets. A good work program would have six characteristics.

1. It would encourage productive work, work that people actually want done. Whether this work is on behalf of the public sector or the private seems immaterial. The nondiscrimination principle has real bite here. A good work program would attract many people not currently working on the streets, and so real efficiency losses would occur if the work were not reasonably productive.

2. Payment would be in cash rather than in kind. If the idea is to entice people to give up wasteful and degrading activities, the most powerful enticements should be used. No doubt a good portion of wages will be used for alcohol and drugs, but people who earn wages doing productive work are generally entitled to spend them as they wish. No one seriously advocates having a recession and reducing national income in order to reduce drug and alcohol consumption in the general population; similarly, no one should try to

maintain streetpeople as beggars for fear that some of them will drink and drug more.

3. It would make working worthwhile. Implicit tax rates from other programs would not wipe out incentives. For the majority of daytime streetpeople who receive no public assistance, this would present no problem, but for those receiving SSI and GA, especially in New York, disincentives can be a serious problem.

4. Payment would come rapidly, in small amounts, since street-people have few opportunities to save and often have urgent needs. Devising ways for homeless people to save would relieve some of this problem, but not all.

5. Wages would be paid on a piecework basis. Even in an uncontrived setting, many streetpeople find unappealing the discipline and regularity that time-rate jobs demand. In a setting where the goal is to keep people off the street, work discipline would be almost impossible. If people were fired for infractions of work rules, many would be fired quite quickly and return to the streets; the program's goals would be thwarted. If people were not fired for infractions, chaos would prevail and no productive work would get done. Piecework removes this dilemma: like the work that streetpeople now do, it allows them to work at their own pace and make their own hours, and this avoids incentive problems. (Cash and piecework are serious departures from the work scheme that Jencks [1994] proposes: four hours of work in exchange for a bed for the night. I don't think this scheme is attractive enough to get many people off the street. More seriously, it doesn't specify what happens to people who work for three and a half hours or who don't work hard enough. If it did lure people off the street, it might also lure many away from regular jobs, becoming a mecca for malingerers.)

6. Hiring would be informal, and eligibility criteria would not be used. The people who should be reached have great trouble dealing with bureaucracies, their income can't be verified (and they probably don't know it with any degree of precision), and eligibility based on status would violate the nondiscrimination principle.

Is it possible to design programs that meet all six of these criteria? I'm not sure. The fact that many existing programs come close is encouraging. About the best is what goes on in Chicago: newspapers pay streetpeople to sell papers to commuters as they leave the expressway. This activity satisfies all the criteria, but is limited in scope. Homeless people in New York sometimes get paid for standing in police lineups. This also satisfies all the criteria, but again is limited in scope.

*Street News* in New York also came close, but in its first incarnation failed the first desideratum, productivity—the newspaper was awful, and people bought it only out of sympathy. (The paper's history of questionable management and finances wouldn't have been a problem if the enterprise had put out a product that people were willing to buy on its own merits, and indeed, in its second incarnation as a profitmaking journal, many of these problems were remedied—and the quality improved. Still its readership was not big enough.) Other cities, Dublin for instance, have similar newspapers, but they may be worth reading and may be more prosperous.

So, too, canning in New York fails only productivity. If outputs were better defined, this would be an excellent activity. The Times Square business-improvement district has tried to improve on canning by defining outputs better—paying for bags of trash rather than cans—and apparently has met the productivity desideratum by doing so. But Times Square pays in kind rather than in cash.

Unfortunately, all of these exemplary activities skirt the problems raised by criterion 3, incentives, by not keeping records. So they are probably condoning fraud by some of their workers—a proportion that would be higher if assistance programs were more accessible. This is probably the best that can be done in current circumstances. A large program to encourage work, however, could not condone welfare fraud. So labor-market incentives have to be coupled with changes in income-maintenance programs.

Finally, more direct policies to reduce panhandling are also needed. Prohibition is inefficient because many panhandling transactions leave both parties better off—the donor feels better for having given, and the recipient feels better for having received. One way to retain this feature but to reduce the costs for people not directly involved in the transaction would be to encourage recognized charities, such as the Salvation Army, to solicit on the street more aggressively. Donors could still act charitably, but panhandling would be less profitable because many people would give to the recognized charity instead. The result would be fewer street nuisances and possibly more money for charities.

The problem with implementing this activity is that the revealed preference of recognized charities is overwhelmingly not to solicit in this manner (the Salvation Army at Christmas is a minor exception). Governmental policies would have to be devised to subsidize this sort of solicitation—perhaps even encouraging charities to hire people through the work programs mentioned here. Because soliciting is a cash business for which recordkeeping is almost impossible, though, the actual design of these subsidies would be difficult.

### Welfare

Like regulatory changes, changes in income maintenance can alleviate homelessness without running afoul of the nondiscrimination principle. Reforming welfare in certain ways would probably be a good way to reduce homelessness, but the important reforms are not the obvious ones. The basic question about welfare is how much. No doubt Toronto's generous assistance grants contribute a good deal to its low rate of homelessness. Is this lesson transferable? I think not. There are many fair reasons for raising U.S. welfare grants, but homelessness isn't one of them. The answer of neoclassical economics—"money, money, money"—doesn't work.

The reason is because homeless people are only a very small fraction of the welfare caseload. Almost all of the money involved in raising welfare grants would go to people who would not otherwise be homeless. It is on the basis of what it does for these people that raising grants must be judged. Welfare reforms that reduce homelessness can best be made in the areas of incentives and eligibility.

The curiously backward structure of New York's GA program is a good example of an area where incentives can be improved. With single adults, a welfare system should discourage two types of activity: sleeping on the street and engaging in panhandling or other unproductive street trades. New York encourages both: it encourages sleeping on the street by paying $156 a month more to people who forgo shelters, and it encourages panhandling by taxing earned income at a 100 percent rate. New York could go a long way in reducing the problems of streetlife simply by imitating good practices that already exist in other North American cities: Toronto's adjustments for living in shelters and Newark's or Chicago's disregard for earned income.

The disincentives against doubling up—in the SSI program, the food-stamps program, and the Toronto and New York welfare systems—are a more troubling issue. Efficiency clearly dictates that public assistance should be neutral with regard to living arrangements, and the efficiency losses caused by the current systems are probably reason enough to end them. The short-run effect would be to reduce homelessness, but this effect would probably be small.

If a shelter allowance is not in place, the way to do this is simply to adopt a flat grant, like the ones in New Jersey and Illinois. With a shelter allowance, household-size neutrality is somewhat more complex. Economies of scale in housing dictate that shelter allowances should not be directly proportional to household size; larger households should get smaller per-person shelter allowances. To preserve neutrality, then, larger households should get larger per-person welfare grants on top of their shelter allowances. Similarly, households not on welfare should have their income taxed back in the same way—higher per-person taxes for smaller households.

The most difficult issue is how to include work incentives in general welfare programs. Even the best public assistance programs in this regard—New Jersey's and the old one in Illinois—had marginal tax rates on reported earned income in excess of two-thirds. Reducing these tax rates is important for reducing panhandling and other daytime street activities, both with and without additional work programs. Work incentives in welfare programs have been studied extensively in the past thirty years, and I have little to add. Most studies, however, have dealt with family heads rather than single adults. Because of the social costs of panhandling, increasing conventional work for single adults has a greater social payoff than increasing conventional work for family heads. The precarious political position of general assistance programs—the Illinois program was effectively ended in 1992 and the New Jersey program almost was—makes generous funding most unlikely. Both considerations argue for programs with low guarantees and fairly low tax rates.

With eligibility, the problem is that many of the people who could avoid homelessness if they received public assistance don't receive it. Most alcoholics and drug abusers are now ineligible for SSI, but easing the strictures that keep them ineligible would be a good idea. Many substance abusers really can't work, and there is good reason to keep them off the streets and reduce the burden to their families. Probably the way to ease eligibility is to soften the requirements for participation in treatment programs but to keep or even strengthen the protective payee requirement, and to allow many other categories of people to receive the check. Treatment programs are scarce and expensive, and there is little hard evidence that they work well. By contrast, concerned relatives, friends, and caseworkers are both easier to find and cheaper. Mastering the technology of ending addictions is a lot harder than mastering the technology of keeping someone from spending all of his or her money on crack or alcohol. Easing SSI eligibility has the added advantage that by removing people who really can't work from GA rolls, it becomes easier to implement a welfare system with strong work incentives.

An intermediate type of SSI might also be helpful for substance abusers and other people who might be able to work a little. Currently, disability for SSI purposes is a yes-or-no proposition: either you are disabled and are not expected to work, or you are not disabled and are expected to support yourself fully. But disability comes in degrees, and most pension systems—veterans' benefits, for instance—recognize that. Intermediate SSI, for people who can work but not much, would have a low guarantee and a low marginal tax rate, and so it would have strong work incentives, though probably not as strong as those in general assistance. Substance abusers are not comatose, and they shouldn't be treated as if they were; nor are they completely well.

Finally, steps to make U.S. assistance agencies more friendly and accessible have merit both for families and for single adults. Patience, cunning, and the ability to deal with bureaucrats are not good bases on which to ration welfare benefits—indeed, they may be counterproductive, since people who have these traits probably have better employment prospects than those who don't. Nor does making welfare receipt a lottery encourage people to make long-term investments in conventional accommodations. Thus including appointment notices with welfare checks and employing client advocates are probably good policies for reducing homelessness.

U.S. agencies should also explore ways to import some of Canada's administrative skill. Why error rates should be the focal point of relations between states and the federal government is unclear. States, since a lot of their own money is involved, have significant incentives not to be sloppy even without federal penalties. Canada's provinces seem to manage in a fairly responsible fashion without any such incentives. It seems odd that U.S. welfare agencies are lagging behind U.S. factories in the discretion they allow their workers.

## Therapy

With the issuance of the Cuomo Commission report in 1992, the cry of "therapy, therapy, therapy" replaced "housing, housing, housing" as the buzzword response in the United States to the problems of homelessness.[5] This runs directly counter to the non-discrimination principle, and it should be resisted. People who need and can benefit from therapy are the ones who should get therapy. Being homeless and being able to benefit from therapy are different states: many homeless people would not benefit from therapy, and many people who could benefit from therapy are not homeless. The problems of a therapeutic system affect both kinds of people.

For those who need therapy, earmarking therapy for homeless people has all the problems that earmarking subsidized apartments does. It means that some people who could benefit from therapy will not get it because they are not homeless, and that people who think they could benefit from therapy have some incentive to become homeless. (This discussion presumes, of course, that therapy is worthwhile and something that people want. If it isn't, the therapeutic movement is all the more misguided.)

The problems involving homeless people who don't need or wouldn't benefit from therapy are also substantial. Gwendolyn Dordick (1994) describes the sad spectacle of men in a private New York shelter who can't get jobs because they spend too much time at Alcoholic Anonymous meetings, even though some of them are not alcoholics. A therapeutic system encourages people who don't need therapy to seek it, just to get a roof over their heads.

These problems are standard with any policy that violates the nondiscrimination principle. A therapeutic system, however, has even more problems because it distorts the incentives of service providers: in therapy, "success" matters, and success means something grander than keeping someone warm on a cold night. Just keeping people warm loses importance.

We have already seen in the history of skid-row missions how this process works. In the 1950s and 1960s many missions decided to concentrate their efforts on the cadre of skid-row men who seemed capable of being improved by their efforts, rather than waste time with incorrigibles. They sacrificed quantity for quality and thus became too small (with a few notable exceptions, mainly in Chicago) to make much of a dent in the sufferings brought about by the new homelessness. "Therapy, therapy, therapy" is a call to repeat the mistakes of the missions.

George Orwell concluded his book about being down and out on a bitter note:

> Still I can point to one or two things I have definitely learned by being hard up. I shall never again think all tramps are drunken scoundrels, nor expect a beggar to be grateful when I give him a penny, nor be surprised if men out of work lack energy, nor subscribe to the Salvation Army, nor pawn my clothes, nor refuse a handbill, nor enjoy a meal at a smart restaurant. That is the beginning. (1993, p. 155)

Sixty-odd years later, these words still have bite. Fifteen years of experience with the new homelessness in North America has produced confusion, controversy, and more than a little knavery, but there is still no consensus about what is wrong and how it can be fixed. People have made enormous sacrifices and performed heroic deeds, but more often than not these heroes have not been rewarded with the results they sought. Excessive homelessness is continuing without much abatement in North America, and it may be increasing in Europe.

It is easy to understand how this sorry state of affairs came about. The causes of the new homelessness are subtle and hard to reverse. Data are meager, and terminology is astoundingly imprecise—we don't even have a definition of homelessness. Studying homelessness draws on a variety of disciplines and requires careful attention to some of the most arcane details of administrative procedure. Policies to deal with homelessness must be designed around gnarly incentive and information problems. Generalized niceness won't work. And compounding all these intrinsic difficulties has been the eagerness with which demagogues of both right and left have seized on homelessness as a symbol of what's wrong with the other side.

Homeless people see themselves as people, not as symbols of somebody else's failed policies, and in this book I have tried to do the same. I wanted to be bold, in both analysis and prescription, not so much because I have overwhelming confidence in what I say, but because only bold statements are worth defending or attacking. That's how you take a subject seriously. Just as much as exchange rates or corporate capital structure or investment tax credits, homelessness has to be taken seriously.

# Appendix: Homeless Studies

## 1. Studies of Public Assistance

Location: Newark
Author: Simpson and Kilduff (1984)
Date : February 1983
Population: Trailer people
Proportion found: 23% get GA, SSI, or VA benefits; 7% get food stamps.

Location: New York
Author: Crystal and Goldstein, Human Resources Administration, Family
   and Adult Services, "Chronic and Situational Dependency"
Date: 1982
Population: Residents of Keener Men's Shelter there at least 2 months
Proportion found: "Current resources" included GA and AFDC for 12.4%;
   SSI for 16.0%; VA benefits for 3.6%.

Location: New York
Author: Freeman and Hall (1987)
Date: 1985
Population: Weighted sample of street homeless, single adults in shelters,
   adults in family shelters
Method: Interview
Proportion found: 12% get public assistance, SSI, or government transfer
   payments.

Location: New York
Author: Eldred and Towber, Human Resources Administration, "Characteristics of Homeless Families, December 1985"
Date: December 1985
Population: Families requesting shelter in the Bronx
Proportion found: 83.1% get public assistance; 72.7%, food stamps.

Location: New York
Author: Eldred and Towber, "A One-Day 'Snapshot' of Homeless Families at the Forbell Street Shelter and Martinique Hotel"
Date: February 1986
Population: Homeless families at shelter and hotel
Proportion found: Public assistance (AFDC or GA) was "usual source of income" for 81.6% of families at hotel and 79.7% at shelter. SSI was usual source for 7.9% at hotel and 1.7% at shelter.

Location: New York
Author: Cuomo Commission
Date: 1991
Population: Municipal shelters
Proportion found: 92% of families in family shelters and 48% in single shelters get public assistance.

Location: Chicago
Author: Chicago Coalition for the Homeless (1983)
Date: 1983
Population: People approached on street who said they had hard time finding places to stay and who stayed at mission, shelter, or on street in past 6 months
Proportion found: GA, 13%; SSI, 5%; VA disability, 3%; AFDC, 3%

Location: Chicago
Author: Rossi (1989)
Date: 1985, 1986
Population: Some shelters and streets
Proportion found: GA, 21.8%; SSI, 5.8%; AFDC, 6.3%; disability, 2.2%.

Location: Chicago
Authors: Sosin, Colson, and Grossman (1988)
Date: 1986
Population: Users of meal programs, treatment programs, and shelters who said they had no normal place to live and meet other criteria

Proportion found: 20.6% of currently homeless get AFDC; 17.6%, GA; 2.7%, SSI.

Location: Chicago
Author: McCourt and Nyden (1990)
Date: June-August 1989
Population: Women in transitional family shelters
Proportion found: 64%, AFDC; 64%, food stamps.

## 2. Studies of Mental Health

Location: New York
Author: Arbittier and Winnick (1976)
Date: 1976
Population: Clientele of Shelter Care Center for Men on the Bowery (primarily ticketmen)
Method: Diverse
Proportion found: 31% had history of state mental hospitalization, and another 22% "(1) said they had been hospitalized, (2) were diagnosed as mentally disabled at the shelter, or (3) 'acted strange.'"

Location: New York
Author: Human Resources Administration, Family and Adult Services, "Chronic and Situational Dependency"
Date: October 1981
Population: Residents of Keener Men's Shelter there at least 2 months
Proportion found: 18.3% acknowledged prior psychiatric hospitalization.

Location: New York
Author: Crystal and Goldstein (1984)
Date: June 19, 1984
Population: All residents that day at Fort Washington and Greenpoint Men's Shelters and at Women's Shelter Annex
Proportion found:

|  | Fort Wash. | Greenpoint | Annex |
|---|---|---|---|
| Psych. hosp. ever | 13.1% | 11.7% | 26.7% |
| Problem observed by shelter | 19.6 | 17.4 | 46.6 |
| Psych. outpatient | 7.1 | 8.9 | 16.0 |
| Any of above | 22.0 | 21.1 | 47.3 |

Location: New York
Author: Freeman and Hall (1987)
Date: 1985
Population: Weighted sample of street homeless, single adults in shelters, adults in family shelters
Method: Interview
Proportion found: 33%.

Location: New York
Author: Elmer Struening
Date: 1986
Population: Single shelters
Method: Interview and assessment
Proportion found: 9% of men and 19% of women had been hospitalized for psychiatric reasons; 18% of men and 25% of women rated moderately to severely impaired by mental disorder.

Location: New York
Author: R. Moore, "Characteristics of Male and Female Residents of the New York City Adult Shelter System," cited in Hopper (1991)
Date: July 1988
Population: Single shelters
Method: Questionnaire
Proportion found: 17% had ever been hospitalized for psychiatric condition; 28% had ever seen psychiatric professional.

Location: New York
Author: Hopper ( 1991)
Date: March 1990
Population: Streetdwellers
Method: Questionnaire
Proportion found: 25% had ever been hospitalized for psychiatric condition; 41% had ever seen psychiatric professional.

Location: New York
Author: Cuomo Commission
Date: 1991
Population: Municipal shelters
Method: Response to questions of ever treated at clinic or hospital or took prescription medication
Proportion found: 19% of adults in family shelters, 22% in single shelters.

Location: Chicago
Author: Chicago Coalition for the Homeless

Date: 1983

Population: People approached on street who said they had hard time finding places to stay and who stayed at mission, shelter, or on street in past 6 months.

Method: Response to question on ever hospitalized

Proportion found: 23%.

Location: Chicago

Author: Rossi (1989)

Date: 1985, 1986

Population: Some shelters and streets

Method: Nonprofessional interviewer impression

Proportion found: 13–20% appeared confused; 25–30% not lucid; 2–10% incoherent. Categories not mutually exclusive.

Location: Chicago

Authors: Sosin, Colson, and Grossman (1988)

Date: 1986

Population: Users of meal programs, treatment programs, and shelters who said they had no normal place to live and meet other criteria

Method #1: Response to question on ever hospitalized

Proportion found: 20%.

Method #2: Psychological tests

Proportion found: 16%–22%, depending on extent of homelessness; proportion with greatest depression among those ever homeless.

Location: Chicago

Authors: City Department of Human Services

Date: March 1990

Population: People at O'Hare Airport, interviewed at various times of day. Most (72 of 110) were neat and clean; most (96 of 110) considered themselves homeless. Not clear how interviewees were selected

Method: Response to question on ever hospitalized

Proportion found: 10% had been in psychiatric or mental hospital.

Location: Toronto

Author: Liss and Motaynes (1982)

Date: April 6, 1982

Population: Adult residents of 18 major hostels

Method: Survey of residents and operators

Proportion found: 10% had psychiatric history, and another 7% had "probable psychiatric problems."

Location: Toronto
Author: Metro Community Services Department
Date: July 1, 1987—June 30, 1988
Population: People admitted to hostels in fiscal year
Method: Coming from psychiatric facility
Proportion found: 0.6%.

Location: London
Authors: J. Nelson, A. Sternberg and E. Brindley, "Avoiding Institutions,"
    1982, cited in Watkins (1990)
Date: 1970
Population: Men at Camberwell Reception Centre
Method: Unclear
Proportion found: 30% suffered mental illness.

Location: Great Britain
Author: Digby (1976).
Date: 1972
Population: Hostels and lodging houses
Method: Combined NHS records and interviews
Proportion found: About 38% experienced some mental illness, 8% seri-
    ously enough to need hospitalization.

Location: Hamburg
Author: Plum
Date: 1988
Population: Residents of men's shelters
Method: Unknown
Proportion: 2% had ever been in psychiatric facility.

## Sources for Table 12-2. Estimated Number of Institutionalized Mentally Ill People in the United States, 1960–1990 (see p. 234).

Population aged 18–64. All years except 1990: *Economic Report of the President* (1994), table B-34; linear interpolation for 15–19 age groups. 1990: U.S. Census, *1990 General Population Characteristics*.

State and county mental hospitals. 1975: Laura Milazzo-Sayre, "State Trends in Resident Patients—State and County Mental Hospital Inpatient Services, 1971–1975," *Mental Health Statistical Note 150* (National Institute of Mental Health, 1978), table 1b, for inpatients of all ages at end of year. 1983: NIMH, *Mental Health 1986*, table 1.7 for inpatients at end of year, times 1986 proportion between 18 and 64 (80.75%) from NIMH, *Mental Health 1990,* table 2.4. 1990: U.S. Census, *Statistical Abstract 1993*, table 195, for inpatients of all ages at end of year, times 1986 proportion between 18 and 64.

Veteran's Administration medical center. 1975: NIMH, *Mental Health 1983,* table 1.7, for inpatients at end of year. I estimated 86% were between 18 and 64 because 7.8% of admissions were over 65 in 1971 (Taube, 1973); in 1986 the proportion of inpatients over 65 was 1.82 times greater than proportion of admissions over 65 (*Mental Health 1990,* tables 2.4, 2.5). 1983: *Mental Health 1983,* table 1.7, for inpatients of all ages at end of year, times 1986 proportion between 18 and 64, from J. Sunshine et al., "Mental Health Services of the Veterans Administration, United States, 1986," *Mental Health Statistical Note 197,* (NIMH, 1991). 1990: *Statistical Abstract 1993,* table 195, for 1990 total population, times 1986 proportion under 65 from *Mental Health 1990,* table 2.4.

Private psychiatric hospital. 1975: NIMH, *Mental Health 1983,* table 2.7, for all inpatients at end of year. I estimated 85% of these inpatients were between 18 and 64 in keeping with Taube's (1973) data on 1971 admissions, and approximate similarity in Taube's data between age distribution of admissions and inpatients. 1983: *Mental Health 1986,* table 1.7, for inpatients at end of year. I estimated 78% of these inpatients were between 18 and 64 because figure matches that for 1980 (*Mental Health 1982,* table 2.10b). 1990: *Statistical Abstract 1993,* table 195, gives 1990 population of 61,800 in private psychiatric hospitals and residential treatment centers for emotionally disturbed children. These are treated as two separate categories of about the same size, and growing very rapidly, in *Mental Health 1990:* 52% of inpatients in private psychiatric hospitals were 18–64 (table 2.4). J. Sunshine et al., "Residential Treatment Centers and Other Organized Mental Health Care for Children and Youth: United States, 1988," *Mental Health Statistical Note 198,* shows that 5.2% of inpatients in residential treatment centers at end of 1988 were 18 or over. I use an unweighted average of 52% and 5.2% as proportion of *Statistical Abstract*'s 61,800 inpatients between 18 and 64.

Nonfederal hospital with separate psychiatric facilities. 1975: *Mental Health 1983,* table 2.7, for all inpatients at end of year. I estimated 85% of inpatients were between 18 and 64 in keeping with Taube's (1973) data on 1991 admissions, and approximate similarity to figures for 1986 (*Mental Health 1990,* tables 2.4, 2.5). 1983: *Mental Health 1986,* table 1.7, for all inpatients at end of year, and 1986 proportion of inpatients 18–64 from *Mental Health 1990,* table 2.4. 1990: *Statistical Abstract, 1993,* table 195, for inpatients of all ages, times 1986 proportion 18–64.

Mental institutions. 1960: Kramer (1977, app. table 2). This table gives 19,169 inpatients 20 and under but no further detail. I assumed 10,000 were under 18. Other years: Sum of specific components.

Nursing homes. 1960: Kramer (1977, app. table 7). Figure is for 1963, includes all persons under 65. 1975: Unweighted average of figures from 1973–74 and 1977 national nursing-home surveys. 1973–74 data from National Center for Health Statistics, 1977, "Characteristics, Social Contacts, and Activities of Nursing Home Residents (1973–74)," *Vital and Health Statistics*, series 13, no. 27. 1977 data from NCHS, 1979, "National Nursing Home Survey, 1977 Summary," no. 43. 1983: I used 1982 total nursing home population from *Statistical Abstract, 1993*, table 192, times an estimated proportion of mentally ill residents under 65. I used 8.2%, a time-weighted average of the 1977 proportion, 6.2%, from 1977 survey, and 8.8% for 1985 from 1985 survey. Source for 1985 survey is NCHS, 1989, "National Nursing Home Survey, 1985 Summary," no. 97. 1990: Total population from *1990 General Population Characteristics*, times 8.8% from 1985.

Prison or jail. For all years I assumed 10% of prisoners between 18 and 64 were severely mentally ill (see text for discussion). 1960: Kramer (1977, app. table 2). Prisoners over 65 are explicitly given, and I assumed all prisoners under 20 were 18 or over. 1975: Jail population is unweighted average of 1972 population (*Statistical Abstract 1979*, table 338) and 1978 population (*Statistical Abstract 1993*, table 342). Prison population from *Statistical Abstract 1993*, table 343. Proportion between 18 and 64 for 1970 from U.S. Census, 1973, *Persons in Institutions and Other Group Quarters*, PC(2)-4E. 1983: Total population from *Statistical Abstract 1992* (table 328 for jails, 329 for prisons). I assumed 99% of inmates were between 18 and 64, which is consistent with 1986 and 1991 proportions for state prison inmates (*Statistical Abstract 1993*, table 344) and roughly consistent with 1983 and 1989 proportions of jail inmates (Department of Justice, *1992 Sourcebook of Criminal Justice Statistics*, tables 6.36, 6.37). 1990: Total population from *Statistical Abstract 1993* (table 342 for jails, 343 for prisons). I assumed 99% of inmates were between 18 and 64.

## 3. Studies of Substance Abuse

Location: New York
Author: Bahr and Caplow (1973)
Date: 1966
Population: Men on the Bowery

Method: Interview
Proportion found: 36% were heavy drinkers (drinking alcohol equivalent
of 8 quarts of beer daily, or 12 quarts several times a week, or 16 quarts
on heavy days).

Location: New York
Author: Human Resources Administration, "Chronic and Situational Dependency"
Date: October 1981
Population: Residents of Keener Men's Shelter there at least 2 months
Method: Questionnaire
Proportion found: Alcohol: 45.1% were occasional users; 21.4% regular
users now; 14.0% regular users in past. Hard drugs: 6.1% occasional
users; 3.4% regular users now; 23.5% regular users in past. Cocaine:
15.6% occasional users; 0.9% regular users now; 10.1% regular users in
past.

Location: New York
Author: Human Resources Administration,"The Homeless in New York
City Shelters"
Date: November 1982–December 1983
Population: Men entering shelters
Method: All regular intake interviews
Proportion found: 17% either current or past regular users of hard drugs.

Location: New York
Author: Crystal and Goldstein (1984)
Date: June 19, 1984
Population: All residents that day at Fort Washington and Greenpoint
Men's Shelters and at Women's Shelter Annex
Method: Questionnaire
Proportion found:

| Alcohol | Fort Wash. | Greenpoint | Annex |
|---|---|---|---|
| Occasional | 29.4% | 44.8% | 24.4% |
| Regular now | 13.2 | 8.5 | 6.1 |
| Regular past | 8.9 | 12.6 | 4.6 |

| Hard drugs | Fort Wash. | Greenpoint | Annex |
|---|---|---|---|
| Occasional | 7.4% | 7.7% | 3.1% |
| Regular now | 4.0 | 7.7 | 4.6 |
| Regular past | 10.1 | 17.2 | 6.9 |

Location: New York
Author: Elmer Struening
Date: 1986
Population: Single adult shelters
Method: Interview
Proportion found: 12% of men and 6% of women had been hospitalized for alcoholism. 11% of men and 6% of women had been hospitalized for drug abuse.

Location: New York State
Author: Welte and Barnes (1992)
Date: 1986
Population: SRO and shelter residents
Method: Telephone interview
Proportion found: 33.3% heavy drinkers (more than two drinks a day); 34% showed signs of dependence in past year.

Location: Newark
Author: Kessler (1966)
Date: 1963
Population: Ticketmen
Method: Unknown
Proportion found: 50% had alcohol problems.

Location: Chicago
Author: Chicago Coalition for the Homeless (1983)
Date: 1983
Population: People approached on street who said they had hard time finding places to stay and who stayed at mission, shelter, or on street in past 6 months
Method: Questionnaire
Proportion found: 26% used intoxicants every day; no mention of cocaine; 22% used marijuana with some frequency.

Location: Chicago
Author: Rossi (1989)
Date: 1985, 1986
Population: Some shelters and streets
Method: Questionnaire
Proportion found: 33.2% had been in detox unit for alcohol or drug abuse; 10.1% unable to work because of alcoholism.

Location: Chicago
Author: Sosin, Colson, and Grossman (1988)

Date: 1986
Population: Ever homeless users of meal programs, treatment programs, shelters
Method: Questionnaire
Proportion found: 23.4% with symptoms of alcoholism; 21.6% binged; 15.8% used drugs, with marijuana (56%), cocaine (46.4% of these), and heroin (33.9%) the major ones.


Location: Chicago
Author: City Department of Human Services
Date: March 1990
Population: People at O'Hare Airport, interviewed at various times of day. Most (72 of 110) were neat and clean; most (96 of 110) considered themselves homeless. Unclear how interviewees were selected
Method: Questionnaire
Proportion found: 25% had been in detox for alcohol or drug abuse.


Location: London
Author: Geoffrey Randall, "No Way Home" (London: Centrepoint Soho, June 1988).
Date: September–November 1987
Population: Young people at Centrepoint Soho night shelter
Method: Questionnaire
Proportion found: 16% drank more than three pints of beer a week; 64% had used drugs, chiefly marijuana; no reported cocaine; no reported heroin in last year.


## 4. Studies of Incarceration History

Location: New York
Author: Human Resources Administration, Family and Adult Services, "Chronic and Situational Dependency: Long Term Residents in a Shelter for Men," May 1982
Date: October 1981
Population: Residents of Keener Men's Shelter there at least 2 months
Method: Questionnaire
Proportion found: 49.1% had been in prison.


Location: New York
Author: Human Resources Administration, Family and Adult Services, "The Homeless in New York City Shelters"

Date: November 1982-December 1983
Population: Men entering shelters
Method: All regular intake interviews
Proportion found: 15% had been incarcerated on felony charge.

Location: New York
Author: Crystal and Goldstein, "Correlates of Shelter Utilization: A One-Day Study," Human Resources Administration, Family and Adult Services, August 1984
Date: June 19, 1984
Population: All residents that day at Fort Washington and Greenport Men's Shelters and at Women's Shelter Annex
Method: Questionnaire
Proportion found: Fort Washington: 15.1% had ever been incarcerated for felony; 48.7% had ever been incarcerated for any reason. Greenport: 15.3% for felony; 49.5% ever. Annex: 8.9% for a felony; 21.8% ever.

Location: New York
Author: Freeman and Hall (1987)
Date: 1985
Population: Weighted sample of street homeless, single adults in shelters, adults in family shelters
Method: Interview
Proportion found: 39% had spent time in jail (or prison), with average jail time 2 years; 61% of time spent in jail occurred before first becoming homeless.

Location: New York
Author: Elmer Struening
Date: 1986
Population: Single adult shelters
Method: Interview
Proportion found: 16% of men and 6% of women had spent 1–6 months in jail or prison; 6% of men and 3% of women had spent 7–36 months in jail or prison.

Location: New York
Author: Cuomo Commission
Date: 1991
Population: Municipal shelters
Method: Interview
Proportion found: 51% of single shelter residents and 15% of adults in family shelters had ever been in jail or prison; 26% of single shelter

residents and 7% of adults in family shelters had been in jail or prison in year before entering shelter.

Location: Chicago
Author: Chicago Coalition for the Homeless
Date: 1983
Population: People approached on street who said they had hard time finding places to stay and who stayed at mission, shelter, or on street in past 6 months
Method: Questionnaire
Proportion found: 16% had been in prison; 50% in jail.

Location: Chicago
Author: Rossi (1989)
Date: 1985, 1986
Population: Some shelters and streets
Method: Questionnaire
Proportion found: 16.5% had been in prison; 40.6% in jail: 28.3% on probation.

Location: Chicago
Author: Sosin, Colson, and Grossman (1988)
Date: 1986
Population: Users of meal programs, treatment programs, and shelters who said they had no normal place to live and meet other criteria
Method: Questionnaire
Proportion found: 14.0% of ever homeless and 11.2% of currently homeless had prison experience; 65.0% of ever homeless and 53.1% of currently homeless had jail experience.

Location: Chicago
Author: Chicago Department of Human Services
Date: March 1990
Population: People at O'Hare Airport, interviewed at various times of day. Most (72 of 110) were neat and clean; most (96 of 110) considered themselves homeless. Not clear how interviewees were selected
Method: Questionnaire
Proportion found: 10% had been in prison; 55% in jail; 6% on probation.

Location: Toronto
Author: Metro Toronto Community Services Department
Date: July 1, 1987–June 30, 1988
Population: Shelter admissions in fiscal year

Method: Questionnaire
Proportion found: 4% gave reason for admission as from correctional facility.

Location: London
Author: Digby (1976).
Date: 1972
Population: Hostels and lodging houses
Method: Questionnaire and check of national insurance records
Proportion found: 36% said they had been in prison, but national insurance records showed 45%.

Location: London
Author: Geoffrey Randall, "No Way Home" (London: Centrepoint Soho, June 1988)
Date: September–November 1987
Population: Young people at Centrepoint Soho night shelter
Method: Questionnaire
Proportion found: 16% had lived in detention or youth custody center; 7% in probation or bail hostel.

Location: London
Author: Randall
Date: 1989
Population: Young people at Centrepoint Soho night shelter
Method: Questionnaire
Proportion found: 27% had lived in detention or in youth custody center; 12% in probation or bail hostel.

Location: Hamburg
Author: W. Plum
Date: 1988
Population: Residents of men's shelters
Method: Unknown
Proportion found: 54% had spent time in prison.

# Notes

## 2. What Is Homelessness?

1. After correcting for population size, the simple correlation ($r$) between the two data sets is 0.55.

## 3. Why Is It Bad?

1. Drapkin (1990, p. 95) reports that assessments of selected homeless populations (unspecified) found clinically active tuberculosis rates of 1.6 to 6.8 percent, which was 150 to 300 times the national rate. Between 22 and 51 percent of homeless populations have been found to have asymptomatic tuberculosis infection.

2. Some inefficiencies should not be the subject of government action, and perhaps this is one of them. The classic example is free speech or free thought: some people may be upset because I reject creationism or speak in favor of Kurdish independence, or put my left sock on before my right sock, but in liberal polities such upsets are deliberately ignored. Does the upset over seeing homeless people fall into the same category—some of us just dislike how they dress and wouldn't be upset about panhandlers in suits and ties with briefcases? Perhaps. This view is strengthened by several court decisions holding that panhandling is protected by the First Amendment—that it makes a political statement about poverty and inequality. But many kinds of purely psychological upset are recognized in liberal polities—there are restrictions on erecting billboards, on hunting endangered species, on appearing in public without clothes, on tearing down historical buildings—and I don't see why the upset that comes from encountering homeless people is any more illiberally meddlesome than the upset that engenders those restrictions. Ellickson argues this point in much

more detail. The existence of these other restrictions, nevertheless, does not prove that they are just or wise, although Ellickson argues that they are.
3. Drapkin provides a review of some of the medical problems faced by homeless people: accidents, tuberculosis, untreated diabetes, arterial and venous disease in arms and legs, hypertension, malnutrition, frostbite, hypothermia.

## 4. Homeless Histories

1. Where were all the poor black men in the 1960s? Since only about a third of the population on the Bowery was black even at the end of the sixties, the question naturally arises of whether there was some hidden pool of black derelicts, deep within Harlem, say, that the white world was unaware of. (Blumberg, 1978, is the only one of the classic skid-row sociology books that asks where the blacks were, and his answer is that he doesn't know.) Since the majority of homeless people in New York today are African Americans, the existence of such a pool would alter the story of homelessness there: the story would be about white society's increasing awareness of black homelessness, not about the increase of homelessness. I am dubious, though, about a hidden pool of black derelicts. First, between the 1930s and the 1960s, several excellent detailed studies of northern ghettos were written (for example, Drake, 1962; Liebow, 1967) and none of them mentions any such pool; it is hard to believe that so many perspicacious writers could miss it. Second, the BASR found that only about 15 percent of Manhattan's potter's-field burials in 1964 were of men from central Harlem, which had 11 percent of Manhattan's population (Nash, 1964b); by contrast, about 20 percent of all burials were from the Bowery. The apparent paucity of black homeless people in the 1960s means that the increase in black homelessness was even faster than the increase in total homelessness.
2. The scrupulous care taken with the other parts of the study suggests that this estimate is probably not guesswork.
3. The interviews gave Freeman and Hall transition probabilities for moving between the street and shelters, and from these transition probabilities they calculated the ergodic distribution of homeless individuals between street and shelter. (The ergodic is the stable distribution that would prevail if the transitions kept happening for a very long time.) The ergodic distribution implied the 2.23 street-to-shelter ratio.
4. Goodwill Home and Rescue Mission, founded in 1896, was and is the largest of the traditional missions. According to Kessler (1965), all of its 169 beds were occupied in 1964. He doesn't mention the other three traditional missions explicitly, except to note that transients were referred to the Salvation Army Men's Center. That shelter probably had a capacity of 130–140, its current capacity, in 1964 (Beavers interview, 1991). The Guild, a Catholic shelter started in 1949, had 110–120 beds in the mid-1960s (Hurley interview, 1991), and American Rescue Workers, a small shelter also dating from the 1940s, had about 30 beds.

5. Varn Hargen, Temple, and Baseda interviews.

6. Very few women were involved with these systems, and they were treated differently. Before New York established a women's shelter in April 1970, women were sent to the Pioneer Hotel, which, though it was on the Bowery, was a real hotel—the rooms had doors and walls up to the ceiling. Newark sent women to a small Salvation Army family shelter. During the winter in New York, when the men's program was not turning people away, the number of men being assisted on an average night was about forty times the number of women. Expenditure records indicate the same kind of ratio in Newark.

7. Bogue (1963, p. 411) reports that public authorities provided 109,560 man-nights of free shelter during a typical month in 1959. Since tickets were the only form in which free shelter was provided, I divide this figure by 30 to get the number in the text.

8. These figures are from an affidavit by Cecil Reid, head of the Shelter Care Center for Men, which was filed in October 1979 in connection with the *Callahan v. Carey* litigation.

9. I derive this conclusion from welfare accounting records that show monthly payments to the Comet Hotel about 50 percent larger than payments to the Edison. White men stayed at the Edison, black men at the Comet.

10. There are reasons to question this figure. First, it is not clear whether men who slept in Camp LaGuardia and the Big Room are included with ticketmen. Second, the classification of Hispanics is inconsistent over the decade. Third, these are not one-night counts like the others. The source is New York City Human Resources Administration (1982, p. 7).

11. The idea that the ticketman system ended in New York because the lodginghouses closed in the late 1970s is a myth. Although 19 lodginghouses accepted ticketmen in 1964 and only 6 did in 1979, all of the decrease in the number of lodginghouses accepting tickets took place by 1976. In 1976 Sheppard reports 6 lodginghouses accepting tickets: the Palace, the Kenton, the Delavan, the Sunshine, the Mascot, and the Newport. By 1979 the Mascot and Newport were replaced by the Union House and the Stevenson (formerly the Comet); these had been the houses with the fourth and sixth heaviest usage in 1976. Only the Newport closed between 1976 and 1979; the Mascot was still open as of 1993 (Kadvan, 1993). Since 1979 the Palace and the Kenton—the two most heavily used lodginghouses—have been purchased by the city as publicly run (and much more expensive) shelters; the Sunshine, the Union House, and the Delavan (now called the Grand) remained open in 1993; and only the Stevenson was closed (it was empty, indicating recent closure).

12. Most of the information in this paragraph is based on documents in the *Callahan v. Carey* files.

13. This section draws heavily on Oechssler (1991).

14. HRA published statistics on the average length of ongoing shelter spells; since 1988 these have generally been between six and eight months. This

measure, though, is sensitive to the rate at which families are entering the system.

15. I discuss TRAs in more detail in Chapter 10.

16. The county welfare division and the Newark Housing Authority staffs negotiated a contract in 1992, but it fueled a great deal of controversy—the housing authority's executive director was fired—and almost none of it was implemented.

17. All three numbers are from documents published by the Metro Toronto Community Services Department in 1983, 1988, and 1992.

## 5. Daytime Streetpeople

1. Selection bias may be operating here, but the direction is unclear. If the labor-supply curve is backward-bending, people who earn more per hour are less likely to be in our sample; if it is forward-sloping, higher earners are more likely to be in the sample. But if concern is with the colloquial homeless seen by the public, there is no bias.

2. The difference is significant at the 5 percent level.

3. The proportion in our survey is similar to the proportion of homeless people among those whom the New York Police Department Mendicancy Squad apprehended during the depression. Hopper (1987, p. 279) reports that between 70 and 80 percent of these people were homeless, although I'm not sure how the word "homeless" was being used in that context.

## 6. How to Think about Housing Markets

1. Most of the work on which this chapter was based is fairly mathematical. J. L. Sweeney (1974a, 1974b) was the first to develop an explicit model of filtering in the housing market, and I draw a good deal from his work. But in Sweeney's model there is no explicit provision for homelessness; the maintenance technology dooms every house to deterioration; and quality is a discrete variable rather than continuous. Discrete quality means that we can't make arguments about "just a tiny bit better": a unit is either the next step up—in both attractiveness and cost—or it is not. Treating quality this way makes it difficult to investigate how the abandonment quality is determined, since too much depends on the size of the step. Arnott (1987, pp. 971–981) provides an excellent survey of the many papers that were written in the Sweeney tradition in the first decade or so after it was published. The mathematical version of my chapter can be found in O'Flaherty (1995).

2. Strictly speaking, this dichotomy obtains only if maintenance is expensive relative to construction. If maintenance is cheap enough, a somewhat different situation obtains. No houses are ever abandoned. Instead, for the lower qualities, the quality-price schedule makes it just as profitable for owners to maintain as not. So lower-quality houses were originally built at higher qualities; they were not maintained for a while and so filtered down

to their current qualities; and they will be maintained at these current qualities forever. The lowest quality on the market is of substantially higher quality than homelessness because its price is substantially higher than the price of homelessness—this quality of house must still pay for both maintenance and operating costs—but it is not an "abandonment quality." It is simply the lowest quality that anyone is willing to buy.

In this situation, supply considerations alone determine the price-quality schedule for its whole length. That makes the determination of homelessness fairly easy: all that matters is the number of households whose income is below the standard for conventional housing, and that standard is determined by supply considerations alone. In particular, changes in income distribution don't change the price-quality schedule or the standard. Changes in operating costs and interest rates, since they are supply-side considerations, can therefore affect homelessness by changing the income standard. Increases in either will lift the entire price-quality schedule, which raises the income standard, the volume of homelessness, and the minimum quality on the market. These changes probably reduce the volume of both low-quality and low-rent housing. (Since the volume of each quality of housing adjusts passively to demand changes, more poor people above the income standard causes an increase in poor housing.)

I concentrate in the text on the situation where maintenance is expensive relative to construction because, in the cities where homelessness is most severe, abandonment has been an important activity. Explaining how both abandonment and homelessness can coexist is the major challenge of homelessness theory. A model like this, which implies no abandonment, is not helpful for this task. But I would not ignore the expensive-construction situation altogether. It may be useful in understanding cities like Toronto or London where demolition and abandonment seem negligible.

3. I ignore the possibility that construction quality can change. In fact it is likely to, but in either direction. Whatever the change, it will have little impact on homelessness. So for this and all the other comparisons, I pretend that construction quality doesn't change.

4. Sweeney (1974b) makes a similar point, concentrating on home-ownership subsidies.

5. Notice that the new abandonment quality is worse than the quality for which the old price equaled the new operating cost; that is, the new price-quality schedule is everywhere above the old one. This is an important property; the results described in the text depend on it. This property follows from the equal-demand requirement. To see how, suppose it didn't hold. The accompanying figure shows how the old and the new price-quality schedules would look. To save words, I labeled "the quality for which the old price equaled the new operating cost" as quality Q. Consider the households that demanded quality Q with the old price schedule. At the new operating cost, quality Q was more attractive than homelessness; so at the same price, the new abandonment quality must also be more attractive than homelessness. So the households that demanded quality Q will

not be homeless. Since the households that demanded qualities between Q and the new abandonment quality have higher incomes than this household, they won't be homeless either. Nor will any of these households demand housing of a quality in the range where the new price schedule is above the old. In fact, this is true of all households for which price has decreased. To see why, consider a household that demanded quality-A housing under the old price schedule. That was because this household found quality-A housing, all things considered, more attractive than quality-B housing and all other qualities of housing in the range where price was about to go up; otherwise the household would have demanded

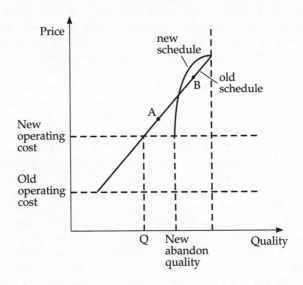

quality B instead of quality A. The price change, however, makes A even more attractive than it was and B ever less attractive. so the price change can't make a household that was demanding A shift to B, or any other quality for which price has increased. On the other hand, some households who originally demanded housing around B may shift their demand to somewhere around A. So demand for qualities where price has decreased must increase, and demand for qualities where price has increased can't increase. Since demand for both intervals was the same with the original price-quality schedule, the new price-quality schedule is unable to satisfy the equal-demand requirement.

## 7. Income Distribution

1. I fit (OLS) linear regressions: the income classes below the mode were the observations, and for each income class its midpoint was the independent

variable, and the height of the histogram (proportion of families per $1,000 income) was the dependent variable.

2. For Chicago there are three recent studies of SROs: a 1984–85 survey sponsored jointly by the Community Emergency Shelter Organization and the Jewish Council on Urban Affairs (1985), a study done by the city Department of Planning at about the same time but published later (1987), and a study by the Lakefront SRO Corporation (1991). I will refer to these as the CESO-JCUA study, the Planning study, and the Lakefront study, respectively. Hoch and Slayton (1989) rely mainly on the CESO-JCUA study. All studies include cubicle hotels within the class of SROs. The CESO-JCUA study is essentially a one-shot study. It uses a physical, not a price, definition of an SRO. An SRO is a hotel that (a) was not "listed on the advertising brochures of the Chicago Chamber of Commerce" or any local hotel associations and (b) either had a 24-hour desk clerk or provided free switchboard service (p. 76). It found 115 such hotels with a total of 11,800 rooms in September 1984. To estimate the decline in SRO units, the CESO-JCUA study cites an earlier draft of the Planning study (June 1985) that found a decrease of 22,600 "SRO units" between 1973 and 1984. The final version of the Planning study did not include this number.

The Planning study consists of two parts. The first is a one-shot study of various types of housing for low-income single renters; in fact SROs, as they defined the term, accounted for only 11 percent of the housing stock they studied. An SRO for this study was a hotel that had an office and a switchboard; offered linens and some maid service; had rooms with no cooking facilities; and rented some rooms for under $300 a month (p. 16). Despite this seemingly more restrictive definition, the Planning study found more hotels and more rooms than the CESO-JCUA study did: 161 hotels with 12,331 total rooms. I couldn't find the exact date for this study, but it appears to be approximately contemporaneous with the CESO-JCUA study.

The second part of the Planning study tried to estimate the number of units lost to conversion or demolition between 1973 and 1984: "A list of all demolition permits was obtained, compared with the master list, and scrutinized for SROs. Demolished buildings in urban renewal projects were identified, and buildings currently vacant and boarded up or under a demolition order were also considered to be removed from the supply. Other lost units were identified through a windshield survey in early November 1985. Finally, some units removed from the supply were found through the phone survey" (p. 45). The results that the Planning survey reports, however, are not about SROs (it is, after all, unclear how their retrospective techniques could have identified units that met their SRO definition). Rather, they conclude, "Between 1973 and 1984 nearly 18,000 units of housing in SROs *and other structures with small dwelling units* were removed from the housing supply" (p. 33, italics added). The executive summary uses similar language. Thus while it is not clear what kind of units these 18,000 were, they were not entirely SROs on the Planning definition, and clearly they were not SROs on the CESO-JCUA definition. And there were not 22,600 of them.

The Lakefront study is essentially an attempt to update the CESO-JCUA study to 1990. It starts with the 115 CESO-JCUA hotels and tries to find out what happened to them. In doing so, it implicitly changed the CESO-JCUA definition: an SRO for this study was a hotel that met the CESO-JCUA criteria in 1984, and charged less than $400 a month in 1990. Of the 11,800 CESO-JCUA rooms, Lakefront found that 615 had been demolished, 718 were in vacant buildings, 758 had been converted to other uses, and 1130 had been "upscaled"—were charging more than $400 a month now. On the other hand, four new SROs—including Lakefront's—had started up, although the criteria for a new establishment to be called an SRO were unclear. The net loss of SRO rooms was 2,837, and the 1990 total was 8,800.

By contrast, the SRO Owners' Association, using a more inclusive definition, had members in 1991 with about 15,000 rooms: this includes both roominghouses and YMCAs (Rubinstein interview, 1991).

Thus while it is clear that a large number of low-quality hotel rooms no longer exist and have probably not been replaced, the exact numbers are murky.

### 8. Interest Rates and Operating Costs

1. In particular, it appears that taxes are much more important for low-quality buildings, with labor costs much less important. Thomas and Wright (1990) provide 1988 expense data for several SROs in the south Loop of Chicago. For two of them, data are complete enough to compute shares. Fuel is just about as important for these buildings as it is in the New York City index (17.35 percent in New York, as opposed to 15.3 percent for one SRO and 20.8 percent in the other); so are utilities (12.4 percent in the New York index, and 10.2 percent and 12.5 percent in the two SROs). "Maintenance" costs in the two SROs are 10.2 percent and 12.5 percent of expenses, but labor costs (16.9 percent) and contractor services (15.4 percent) account for a much larger share of the New York index. On the other hand, "taxes, fees, and permits" have a weight of 18.4 percent in the New York index while property taxes alone accounted for 25.5 percent and 29.2 percent of expenses at the two SROs. This is consistent with Sternlieb's (1966) finding that property taxes accounted for a very large proportion of operating expenses for Newark tenements.

2. Rodda's results are actually just as supportive of the smaller-middle-class explanation as they are of the gentrification explanation. Rodda showed that, holding the distribution of income among poor people constant, an increase in the proportion of rich people increased the rents that poor people paid. But holding the distribution of income among poor people constant, the proportion of rich people can increase only if the middle class shrinks. So Rodda's gentrification is the same as my middle-class shrinkage.

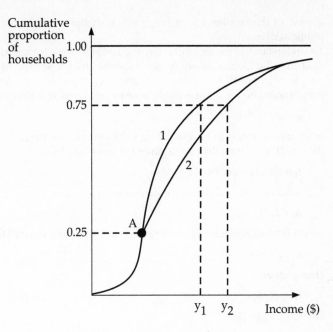

Looking at the cumulative distribution function for income lets us see the same point more specifically. The accompanying figure shows two cumulative distribution functions, 1 and 2. They are the same below point A, because Rodda controls statistically for differences in the amount of income poor people get. The variable he uses to represent how rich the rich are is income at the 75th percentile: $y_1$ for distribution 1 and $y_2$ for distribution 2. With A held constant, the only way income at the 75th percentile can go up is for the slope above A to decrease—which is equivalent to a smaller middle class. Rodda shows that distributions like 2, with a smaller middle class, are associated with higher rents for poor people.

## 10. Government and Housing

1. Park (1994) provides more detailed information about each of these possible explanations.

## 11. Income Maintenance

1. During most of the 1980s around 60 percent of New York's public-assistance households were constrained by the maximum, although on two occasions, right after the shelter maximum had been increased, the proportion fell slightly below half for a few months.
2. The high rate of recipiency for families does not stem from shelter efforts to get families enrolled. The first Eldred and Towber study found that

almost all the families trying to get into a shelter were already receiving public assistance.

3. To understand in rough terms why the LACH process is inconsistent with data like the Columbia study, let $a$ denote the proportion of homeless people who apply for public assistance every period, and let $f_t$ be the proportion who are getting public assistance in period t. Necessarily

(1) $a + f_t \leq 1$.

If we take a period to be about 6 months, and use the process implied by the LACH data, then the evolution of $f_t$ is governed by

$f_t = (1/2)a + (1/4)f_{t-1}$.

The solution to this difference equation is

$f_t = (2/3)a + 4^{-t}t$

which is monotonically decreasing and converges to a steady state where

$f_t = (2/3)a$.

Hence for all t

$f_t \geq (2/3)a$.

Substituting in (1)

$a + (2/3)a = (5/3)a \leq a + f_t \leq 1$,

and so

$a \leq 0.6$

and in the steady state

$f \leq 0.4$,

which is the Columbia study proportion, and smaller than the proportion in the Cuomo report. Thus the only ways the survey results can be made compatible with the LACH process are: (1) to assume that everyone not on welfare applies every six months, which is neither plausible nor in conformity with other survey data, such as SCG; or (2) to assume that the proportion on welfare is falling monotonically toward the steady state, but is not close to it yet.

4. SCG (pp. 208–209) provides some empirical support for this claim.

5. Hutchens, Jakubson, and Schwartz (1989) show that AFDC regulations do in fact change the proportion of single mothers who double up. They interpret the effect as small, but their criterion seems to be smallness relative to the total population of single mothers. The effects on the number of AFDC families who double up appear to be substantial.

## 12. Mental Health

1. The difference is even more striking when one corrects for population growth, since the elderly population grew faster than the rest of the adult

population. Table 12-2, though, would show an even greater increase in the institutionalized mentally ill population if we had included the elderly, because even though the elderly population of state and county mental hospitals went down by about 38,000 between 1975 and 1990, the elderly population of nursing homes went up by about half a million, and an increasing majority of people in nursing homes are mentally ill. Since Medicare started in 1965, it is curious that the reductions in the proportion of elderly people in state and county mental hospitals did not start until well after 1970. My guess is that very few people moved from one institution to the other. The number of nursing-home patients who were admitted directly from mental hospitals (of any kind) was only 84,600 in the 1973–74 nursing-home survey, 79,600 in the 1977 survey, and 34,000 in the 1985 survey. People probably were allowed to stay where they were, and new admissions were diverted.

2. Strictly speaking, this is the wrong criterion: the hospital policies that changed affect only inflows and outflows, and while flows eventually determine the stock of hospital population, in the short run what the population used to be matters a lot. Adjustment takes time, and the 1975 hospital population merely may have been adjusting to previous changes in inflow and outflow rates; population in 1990 might have been lower than population in 1975 even if no changes in procedure had taken place. I tested crudely to see whether this was the case, and it appeared not to be; turnover is so fast that most changes are almost fully reflected within a year. So I will continue to talk about levels as if they were representative of the inflows, outflows, and procedures in effect at that time.

3. But not all. State and county mental hospitals have always included a large number of people who could pay their own way. In some parts of the country, they are the only hospitals available. Even in 1980, a majority of people admitted could pay, although 46.5 percent did not (Rosenstein et al., 1986, table H).

4. New York state figures are derived from *Mental Health, United States, 1990* for working-age population in state and county mental hospitals in New York, and New York working-age population was derived by linear interpolation from *New York State Yearbook*.

5. Burt (1992, p. 120) estimates about 20,000 mentally ill homeless people in 1980. Jencks (1994, p. 17) estimates 121,000 homeless single adults in the same year. If the standard third were mentally ill, 40,000 mentally ill people would have been homeless in 1980. The 1975 and 1980 shelter populations were probably about the same, but in 1975 the street population may have been considerably smaller. (Chapter 4 showed that street populations barely existed in Chicago and New York in the late fifties and early sixties.) If the 1975 street population were half as large, and the standard third of homeless single adults were mentally ill, 26,000 mentally ill people would have been homeless in 1975. Estimates thus range from 20,000 to 40,000, with 30,000 looking like a reasonable guess.

6. A similar calculation, with decidedly different numbers but the same conclusion, can be found in Burt (1992, pp. 119–120).

7. I have no direct data on this question. The closest I can come is a comparison of the 1970 and 1986 age distributions of the entire mental-hospital population. During that time period, the number of inpatients between 25 and 44 declined by 27,000, while the number of inpatients between 45 and 64 declined by 127,000. Correcting for growth in the general population of each age group, the declines are 85,000 for the younger group and 137,000 for the older group. Data for general population are from U.S. Council of Economic Advisers (1994, table B-34); data for 1970 inpatients are from Kramer (1977, app. table 2); and data for 1986 are from *Mental Health, 1990,* table 2.4.

8. For instance, in Burt's 1992 national sample, 57 percent of single men and 53 percent of single women were between 25 and 44; 29 percent of single men and 25 percent of single women were between 45 and 64 (p. 14).

9. Holding someone responsible for the rise in homelessness plays an unfortunately large role in these discussions. When local officials argue that deinstitutionalization causes homelessness, they are in effect arguing that state officials are to blame and so the state should bear the cost of shelters. In New York, the city and state governments were already embroiled in a dispute over mental-health funding when shelter populations started rising in 1980, and the dispute was particularly vicious; but Stern (1984) observed the same dispute in Philadelphia. Thus vociferous local officials have also contributed to the association of homelessness with mental illness. (Similarly, vocal state officials have emphasized the loss of SROs as a cause of homelessness, since land-use regulation is a local responsibility.)

## 13. Substance Abuse

1. How much various intoxicants are substitutes for one another is an open question. Ornstein (1980) reviews the literature and comes to no conclusion.

2. Rouse (1991) provides evidence for the reliability of self-reports of drug use.

3. The high cirrhosis death rate among black men in the 1970s and 1980s raises again the question of why so few blacks were on skid rows in the two earlier decades, since they seem to have been suffering from both alcoholism and poverty at higher rates than whites.

4. Kleiman (1992) reported prices of $55,000 in the late 1970s, $30,000 in 1983, and $10,000 in the late 1980s. I interpreted these as nominal prices, and deflated according to the national CPI-U, taking 1977 as the late 1970s.

5. Numbers based on old releases are sometimes published for 1986 and 1987, but SAMHSA doesn't stand behind them.

6. Since many homeless people and extremely poor people smoke—and indeed spend considerable portions of their money income on cigarettes—raising cigarette taxes could increase homelessness. The distinction

between long-run and short-run responses in the two cigarette studies reflects the fact that rational decisions to become addicted take future prices as well as current prices into account. The difference between long run and short run indicates that the heroin and alcohol responses, by concentrating on the short run, may be understated. But even doubling the heroin response—doubling is what the cigarette studies indicate when you consider long run instead of short—does not change the basic conclusion.

## 14. Criminal Justice

1. According to Markel (1964, p. 5), section 1221 of the penal law, which prohibited public intoxication, was set aside in 1935 after Louis Schleicher, a once-promising assistant district attorney, was picked up, pleaded not guilty in night court, and moved to dismiss the complaint as "insufficient on its face," because the police alleged only that he was drunk in public, not that he was disorderly or that his conduct was a breach of the peace. The judge granted his motion. "Subsequently the chief magistrate had all the forms dealing with complaint and commitment on this count destroyed. Section 1221 has not been used since then in Greater New York." But through the 1960s, the New York police continued to make large numbers of arrests under "DC-2": disorderly conduct under section 722 of the penal code. This section prohibited acting "in such a manner as to annoy, disturb, interfere with, obstruct, or be offensive to others," and the example of objectionable conduct most frequently used by the police was: "annoying and disturbing pedestrians and others in the vicinity by lounging and loitering on the sidewalk while apparently under the influence of intoxicants."

2. In his study of panhandling in New Haven, Goldstein (1993) found the same policy: "The police considered panhandling at least as much a social and economic problem as a legal one, and generally finding the blunt use of arrest neither effective nor desirable, they regulated it largely by relying on their relationships with the panhandlers and on customary practices of control not always in accord with law. Arrest was an infrequent course of last resort: 'We're not using law to deal with [panhandling],' said New Haven Sergeant Arthur Alonzo."

3. For a description of this crackdown, see Markel (1964). The primary mechanism was more frequent and longer sentences for DC-2 offenses. The police, much in the manner that Bittner would have predicted, reacted by reducing the number of DC-2 arrests. They arrested men instead on closely related charges, such as DC-3 and vagrancy, which were much more likely to result in light or suspended sentences.

4. But not in or near skid row. I asked one police officer who worked near the Bowery in the 1950s how he dealt with panhandlers then. He replied that he rarely gave them money, preferring instead to arrange for meals. Begging was against New York law at that time.

5. Even in the unlikely event that the added 1,600 men who were in jail in New York in February 1964 would have been sleeping on the street if they had not been incarcerated, street homelessness in 1964 would still have been only a tiny fraction of its 1990 level. Since there is no evidence of greater street homelessness in 1963, in 1964, or in 1965, it doesn't seem likely that these men would have been on the street. Baker (1965) gives evidence that most of the Bowery men were back in lodginghouses by February 1965. The ticketman average numbers for March are:

|      |       |
|------|-------|
| 1962 | 1,662 |
| 1963 | 1,774 |
| 1964 | 712   |
| 1965 | 1,991 |

6. Some Bowery men even started using Irish names in the hope that Irish policemen would be more sympathetic to them, according to officers who worked then.

## 15. What We Should Do

1. Jagdish Bhagwati and I explore this issue at greater length (1993).
2. There is a large literature in economics and philosophy on this paradox, usually referred to as the time-inconsistency problem. Elster (1984) is perhaps the best known philosophical discussion.
3. There are quite a few studies on this question, from slightly different perspectives. The figure in the text is from Mayo et al. (1980) and O'Sullivan (1993).
4. Elster (1992) provides an extensive catalogue of different ways of approaching problems like this, but no definitive answers.
5. Jencks (1994) is another writer who dismisses therapy. There is nothing inconsistent in believing that pathology explanations are good descriptions of history and in rejecting therapy as the proper emphasis for policy.

# References

Anderson, Nels. 1923. *The Hobo: The Sociology of the Homeless Man.* Chicago: University of Chicago Press.

Apgar, William. 1988. "Rental Housing in the U.S." Working paper 88.1, Joint Center for Housing Studies, Harvard University.

Arbittier, J. S., and E. Winnick. 1976. "An Investigation of the Shelter Care Center for Men (SCCM) Operations and Clientele." New York: Human Resources Administration.

Arnott, Richard. 1987. "Economic Theory and Housing," in Edwin S. Mills, ed., *Handbook of Regional and Urban Economics,* vol. 2. Amsterdam: North-Holland.

———. 1989. "Housing Vacancies, Thin Markets, and Idiosyncratic Tastes." *Journal of Real Estate Finance and Economics,* 2:5-30.

———. 1995. "Time for Revisionism on Rent Control." *Journal of Economic Perspectives,* 9:99-120.

Bahr, Howard M. 1973. *Skid Row: An Introduction to Disaffiliation.* New York: Oxford University Press.

Bahr, Howard M., and Theodore Caplow. 1974. *Old Men Drunk and Sober.* New York: New York University Press.

Baker, Michael A. 1965. "An Estimation of the Population of Homeless Men in the Bowery Area, New York City, February 28, 1965." Mimeo, Bureau of Applied Social Research, Columbia University.

Barker, P. et al. 1992. "Serious Mental Illness and Disability in the Adult Household Population: United States, 1989," in National Institute of Mental Health, *Mental Health, United States, 1992.* Rockville: NIMH.

Baxter, Ellen, and Kim Hopper. 1981. *Private Lives/Public Spaces: Mentally Disabled Adults on the Streets of New York City.* New York: Community Services Society Institute for Social Welfare Research.

Becker, G. S., M. Grossman, and K. Murphy. 1994. "An Empirical Analysis of Cigarette Addiction." *American Economic Review*, 84:396-418.

Berlin, Gordon, and William McAllister. 1992. "Homelessness," in Henry Aaron and Charles Schultze, eds., *Setting Domestic Priorities: What Can Government Do?* Washington: Brookings Institution.

———. 1994. "Prevention and Population Dynamics: One Works, the Other Doesn't." Criminal Justice Research Center, City University of New York.

Bird, David. 1980. "Wilted Lives on the Fringe of the Garden." *New York Times*, September 26, p. B3.

———. 1981. "A Quiet Retreat for the City's Homeless." *New York Times*, pp. B1, B14.

Bittner, Egon. 1967. "The Police on Skid-Row: A Study of Peace-Keeping." *American Sociological Review*, 32:699-715.

Blackburn, McKinley L. 1993. "International Comparisons of Income Poverty and Extreme Income Poverty." Mimeo, Department of Economics, University of South Carolina.

Blank, Rebecca, and Maria Hanratty. 1991. "Responding to Need: Social Welfare Systems in the United States and Canada." Manuscript.

Blumberg, Leonard U. 1978. *Liquor and Poverty: Skid Row as a Human Condition.* New Brunswick: Rutgers Center on Alcohol Studies, monograph 13.

Bogue, Donald J. 1963. *Skid Row in American Cities.* Chicago: University of Chicago Press.

Braun, L. 1991. "Is a Lodging House a Home? Rent Protection for New York City Lodging House Residents." *Cardozo Law Review*, 12:1431-46.

Buchanan, J., and G. Tullock. 1975. "Polluters' Profits and Political Response: Direct Controls Versus Taxes." *American Economic Review*, 65:139-147.

Burt, Martha R. 1992. *Over the Edge: The Growth of Homelessness in the 1980's.* New York: Russell Sage.

*Callahan v. Carey.* 1979. Case no. 42582/79. New York Supreme Court.

Chaloupka, F. 1991. "Rational Addictive Behavior and Cigarette Smoking." *Journal of Political Economy*, 99:722-742.

Chicago Coalition for the Homeless. 1983. "When You Don't Have Anything: A Street Survey of Homeless People in Chicago."

Chicago Department of Human Services. 1990. "Title IV Comprehensive Homeless Assistance Plan." July 13.

Chicago Department of Planning. 1987. "Housing Needs of Chicago's Single, Low-Income Renters." Mimeo, December.

Chicago Housing Authority. 1980. "CHA Facts."

*Chicago Sun-Times.* 1983. "City-Funded Shelter for Homeless Opens." February 5.

Chicago Task Force on Emergency Shelter. 1983. "Homelessness in Chicago."

*Chicago Tribune.* 1982. "Chicago's Homeless Thousands." December 14.

Clines, Francis X. 1976. "About New York: Sidewalk World of Shopping Bag Women." *New York Times*, December 6.

Cohen, Carl I. 1992. "Down and Out in New York and London: A Cross-National Comparison of Homelessness." Mimeo, SUNY Health Center at Brooklyn.

Colwell, P., and J. Kau. 1982. "The Economics of Building Codes and Standards," in M. B. Johnson, ed., *Resolving the Housing Crisis*. Cambridge, Mass.: Ballinger.

—— and A. Yavas. 1992. "The Value of Building Codes." *Journal of the American Real Estate and Urban Economics Association*, 20:501-519.

Committee on Ways and Means, U.S. House of Representatives. 1993. *Overview of Entitlement Programs*. Washington: Government Printing Office.

Community Emergency Shelter Organization and Jewish Council on Urban Affairs (CESO-JCUA). 1985. "SROs: An Endangered Species." Chicago.

Conley, Dalton. 1993. "Street Corner Economy." Mimeo, Department of Sociology, Columbia University.

Cook, P. J., and G. Tauchen. 1982. "The Effect of Liquor Taxes on Heavy Drinking." *Bell Journal of Economics*, 13:379-390.

Cragg, Michael, and B. O'Flaherty. 1994. "Measuring the Incentive to be Homeless." Department of Economics, Columbia University.

Crystal, Stephen, and Merv Goldstein. 1984. "Correlates of Shelter Utilization: A One-Day Study." New York Human Resources Administration, Family and Adult Services.

Davis, Ann E., Simon Dinitz, and Benjamin Pasaminick. 1974. *Schizophrenics in the New Custodial Community: Five Years after the Experiment*. Columbus: Ohio State University Press.

Dawidoff, Nicholas. 1994. "The Business of Begging." *New York Times Magazine*, April 24.

Deitch, Joseph. 1993. "On Homeless Beat at the Bus Terminal." *New York Times*, New Jersey section, January 10.

Digby, Peter Wingfield. 1976. "Hostels and Lodgings for Single People: A Survey of Hostels and Lodging Houses Carried Out on Behalf of the Department of Health and Social Security." London: HMSO.

Dordick, Gwendolyn. 1994. "Friends Among Strangers: Personal Relations Among New York City's Homeless." Ph.D. diss., Department of Sociology, Columbia University.

Drake, St. Clair. 1962. *Black Metropolis: A Study of Negro Life in a Northern City*, rev. New York: Harper and Row.

Drapkin, Arnold. 1990. "Medical Problems of the Homeless," in Carol L. M. Caton, ed., *Homeless in America*. New York: Oxford University Press.

Dugger, Cecilia. 1993. "Search for Shelter: New York and Its Homeless." *New York Times*, July 4-6.

Eagle, Paula F., and Carol L. M. Caton. 1990. "Homelessness and Mental Illness," in Caton, ed., *Homeless in America*. New York: Oxford University Press.

Edin, K. 1991. "Final Report for Joint Statistical Agreement 90-16." Mimeo, U.S. Bureau of the Census, Washington.

Ellickson, Robert. 1990. "The Homeless Muddle," *Public Interest*, 99:45-60.

————. 1996. "Reclaiming Public Spaces: Panhandlers, Bench Squatters, and Skid Rows." *Yale Law Journal,* forthcoming.

Elliott, Marta, and Lauren J. Krivo. 1991. "Structural Determinants of Homelessness in the United States." *Social Problems,* 38(1):113-131.

Elster, Jon. 1984. *Ulysses and the Sirens,* rev. ed. Cambridge: Cambridge University Press.

————. 1992. *Local Justice: How Institutions Allocate Scarce Goods and Necessary Burdens.* New York: Russell Sage Foundation.

Faden, V. B., and H. H. Goldman. 1979. "Appropriateness of Placement of Patients in State and County Mental Hospitals." Statistical Note 152, National Institute of Mental Health.

Fallis, George. 1990. "The Urban Housing Market," in Alex Murray and Fallis, eds., *Housing the Homeless and Poor: New Partnerships among the Private, Public, and Third Sectors.* Toronto: University of Toronto Press.

Filer, Randall. 1990. "What Really Causes Family Homelessness?" *City Journal,* 1 (Fall):22-31.

————. 1992. "Opening the Door to Low Cost Housing." *City Journal,* Summer:37-46.

Food Research and Action Center. 1988. "FRAC's Guide to the Food Stamp Program." Washington: FRAC.

Freeman, Howard E., and Ozzie G. Smith. 1963. *The Mental Patient Comes Home.* New York: Wiley.

Freeman, Richard B. 1992. "Crime and the Employment of Disadvantaged Youths," in George E. Peterson and Wayne Vroman, eds., *Urban Labor Markets and Job Opportunity.* Washington: Urban Institute Press.

———— and Brian Hall. 1987. "Permanent Homelessness in America?" *Population Research and Policy Review,* 6:3-27.

Fuentes, Alberta B. 1989. Memorandum to Gail Gordon, New York Mayor's Office for Homeless and SRO Housing Services. September 29.

Gabriel, Stuart, and Frank Nothaft. 1988. "Rental Housing Markets and the Natural Vacancy Rate." *Journal of the American Real Estate and Urban Economics Association,* 16:419-429.

Goering, Paula, Donald Wasylenki, and Sylvia Grisonich. 1990. "Deinstitutionalization: Its Process, History, Impact and Implications in Canada." Mimeo, Clarke Institute of Psychiatry, Toronto.

Goldstein, Brandt J. 1993. "Panhandlers at Yale: A Case Study in the Limits of Law." *Indiana Law Review,* 27:295-360.

Goodwin, Michael. 1978. "Decline in Derelicts Hurting Bowery Flophouses." *New York Times,* March 27.

Greater London Council and London Borough Association Working Party. 1981. "Hostels for the Single Homeless in London."

Green, Paul A. 1991. "Informal Note for the Police Consultative Group Working Party on the Homeless." Mimeo, Holborn District, Metropolitan Police, London.

Guasch, J., and R. Marshall. 1985. "An Analysis of Vacancy Patterns in Rental Housing Markets." *Journal of Urban Economics,* 17:209-229.

*Guide to American Law.* 1984. St. Paul: West Publishing Company.

Hanratty, Maria, and Rebecca Blank. 1992. "Down and Out in North America: Recent Trends in Poverty Rates in the United States and Canada." *Quarterly Journal of Economics,* 107:233-254.

Hayes, Robert. 1979. "Trial Memorandum," *Callahan v. Carey (1979).*

Hess, John L. 1976. "Vagrants and Panhandlers Appearing in New Haunts." *New York Times,* August 1.

Hill, R., and M. Stamey 1990. "The Homeless in America: An Examination of Possesions and Consumption Behavior." *Journal of Consumer Research,* 17:303-321.

Hills, John. 1989. "Housing Subsidies, Taxation, and Benefits: An Overview," in Hills, R. Berthoud, and P. Kemp, eds., *The Future of Housing Allowances.* London: Policy Studies Institute.

Hirsch, Eric, and Peter Wood. 1986. "Squatting in New York City: Justification and Strategy." *New York University Journal of Law and Social Change,* 16:605-617.

Hoch, Charles, and Robert Slayton. 1989. *New Homeless and Old: Community and the Skid Row Hotel.* Philadelphia: Temple University Press.

Honig, Marjorie, and Randall Filer. 1990. "Policy Issues in Homelessness." New York: Manhattan Institute.

———. 1993. "Causes of Intercity Variation in Homelessness," *American Economic Review,* 83:248-255.

Hopper, Kim. 1987. "A Bed for the Night: Homeless Men in New York City, Past and Present." Ph.D. diss., Department of Anthropology, Columbia University.

———. 1988. "More Than Passing Strange: Homelessness and Mental Illness in New York City." *American Ethnologist,* 15:155-167.

———. 1991. "Monitoring and Evaluating the 1990 S-Night Count in New York City," *Final Report for Joint Statistical Agreement 90.18.* Washington: Center for Survey Methods Research, U.S. Bureau of the Census.

———. 1992. "Marginalia: Notes on Homelessness in the United States, 1992." Mimeo, published in M. Jarvinen and C. Tigerstedt, eds., *Hemloshet och Rusmedelsbruk* (Homelessness and Alcohol and Drug Use). Helsinki: NAD Publication 22.

——— E. Baxter, and S. Cox. 1982. "Not Making It Crazy: The Young Homeless Patients in New York City," in B. Pepper and H. Ryglewicz, eds., *New Directions for Mental Health Services: The Young Adult Chronic Patient,* San Francisco: Jossey-Bass.

Husock, H. 1990. "The Roots of Homelessness." *Critical Review,* 4:506-521.

Hutchens, Robert, George Jakubson, and Saul Schwartz. 1989. "AFDC and the Formation of Subfamilies." *Journal of Human Resources,* 24:600-627.

Jemelka, R., E. Turpin, and J. A. Chiles. 1989. "The Mentally Ill in Prisons: A Review." *Hospital and Community Psychiatry,* 40:481-491.

Jencks, Christopher. 1994. *The Homeless*. Cambridge: Harvard University Press.

Johnson, Ann Braden. 1990. *Out of Bedlam: The Truth About Deinstitutionalization*. New York: Basic Books.

Johnson, J. A., and E. A. Oksanen. 1977. "Estimation of Demand for Alcoholic Beverages in Canada from Pooled Time Series and Cross Sections." *Review of Economics and Statistics*, 59:113-118.

Jud, G. Donald, and James Frew. 1990. "Atypicality and the Natural Vacancy Rate Hypothesis," *Journal of the American Real Estate and Urban Economics Association*, 18:294-301.

Kadvan, A. 1993. "The Bowery Lodging House: The Forgotten Housing of the Poor." Mimeo, Columbia University.

Kemp, Peter. 1989. "Alternatives to the Housing Benefit," in J. Hills, R. Berthoud, and P. Kemp, eds., *The Future of Housing Allowances*. London: Policy Studies Institute.

Kennedy, C., and R. W. Manderscheid. 1992. "SSDI and SSI Beneficiaries with Mental Disorders," in *Mental Health, United States, 1992*. Rockville: NIMH.

Kessler, Warren. 1965. Memorandum to Grace Malone, October 11. Minutes of the Local Assistance Board, Newark.

———. 1966. Local Homeless Section Report, December 2. Minutes of the Local Assistance Board, Newark.

Kleiman, Dena. 1977. "Grand Central Tunnel People." *New York Times*, November 29.

Kleiman, Mark. 1992. *Against Excess: Drug Policy for Results*. New York: Basic Books.

Knickman, J. R. and B. A. Weitzman. 1989. *Forecasting Models to Target Families at High Risk of Homelessness*. Final Report, vols. 3 and 4. Health Research Program, New York University.

Kopperdahl, Richard. 1994. "In Memoriam: The Bowery." *New York Times*, January 16, city section.

Kramer, M. 1977. "Psychiatric Services and the Changing Institutional Scene, 1950-1985." Series B, no. 12. Rockville: NIMH.

Kreeger, David. 1992. "Economic Factors Affecting the Homeless in New York City." Mimeo, Department of Economics, Columbia University.

Lakefront SRO Corporation. 1991. "SRO Loss in Chicago 1985-1990: The Need for an SRO Protection Plan." Mimeo, Chicago.

Lav, I., S. Gold, E. Lazere, and R. Greenstein. 1993. "The States and the Poor: How Budget Decisions Affected Low Income People in 1992." Washington: Center on Budget and Policy Priorities and Center for the Study of the States.

Legal Action Center for the Homeless. 1993. "A Long Day's Journey into Night: Tracking Applicants Through the Entitlements Maze." Mimeo, New York, July.

Lelbach, K. 1974. "Organic Pathology Related to Volume and Pattern of Alcohol Use," in R. J. Gibbins et al., eds., *Research Advances in Alcohol and Drug Problems*, vol. 1. New York: Wiley.

Levy, Frank, and Richard Murnane. 1992. "U.S. Earnings Levels and Earnings Inequality: A Review of Recent Trends and Proposed Explanations." *Journal of Economic Literature*, 30:1333-81.

Liebow, Elliott. 1967. *Tally's Corner: A Study of Negro Streetcorner Men*. Boston: Little, Brown.

Liss, Jeffrey, and Carol V. Motaynes. 1982. "The Housing Gap: Deficiencies in Appropriate Housing for Ex-Psychiatric Patients." City of Toronto Department of Health and Supportive Housing Coalition.

Locke, B. Z., and D. A. Regier. 1985. "Prevalence of Selected Mental Disorders," in *Mental Health, United States, 1985*. Rockville: NIMH.

London Research Centre. 1991. *London Housing Statistics, 1990*. London: LRC.

———. 1993. *London Housing Statistics, 1992*. London: LRC.

L. B. Camden Housing Department. 1991a. "Housing Strategy and Investment Programme, 1992/93."

———. 1991b. "At Your Service: Camden Council's Annual Report to Tenants."

———. 1991c. "If You Are Homeless." Information packet.

Love, E. D. 1957. *Subways Are for Sleeping*. Toronto: Longmans.

Main, Thomas. 1983. "The Homeless of New York." *Public Interest*, 72:3-28.

Maloney, M., and R. McCormick. 1982. "A Positive Theory of Environmental Quality Regulation." *Journal of Law and Economics*, 25:99-123.

Manderscheid, R. W., and M. Rosenstein. 1992. "Homeless Persons with Mental Illness and Alcohol or Other Drug Abuse: Current Research, Policy, and Prospects." *Current Opinion in Psychiatry*, 5:273-278.

Markel, N. 1964. "A Preliminary Study of New York's Legal Agencies and Their Effect on Homeless Men and the Bowery." Mimeo, Bureau of Applied Social Research, Columbia University.

Maurin, Peter. 1933. "To the Bishops of the U.S.: A Plea for Houses of Hospitality." *Catholic Worker*, October.

Mayo, Stephen K., Shirley Mansfield, W. David Warner, and Richard Zwetchkenbaum. 1980. *Housing Allowances and Other Rental Assistance Programs: A Comparison Based on the Housing Allowance Demand Experiment*. Cambridge, Mass.: Abt Associates.

McCourt, Kathleen, and Gwendolyn Nyden. 1990. "Promises Made, Promises Broken. The Crisis and Challenge: Homeless Families in Chicago." Chicago: Travelers and Immigrants Aid.

McFarlane, G. 1993. Personal communication, Metropolitan Toronto Social Services.

McNeil, Donald G., Jr. 1978. "Drunks of Times Square Giving Area a Headache." *New York Times*, November 14.

Merrett, Stephen. 1979. *State Housing in Britain*. London: Routledge and Kegan Paul.

Michaux, William W., et al. 1969. *The First Year Out: Mental Patients after Hospitalization*. Baltimore: Johns Hopkins University Press.

Minkoff, Kenneth. 1978. "A Map of Chronic Mental Patients," in *The Chronic Mental Patient: Problems, Solutions, and Recommendations for a Public Policy.* Washington: American Psychiatric Association.

Miller, Norman S. 1991. Foreword, in Miller, ed., *Comprehensive Handbook of Drug and Alcohol Addiction.* New York: Marcel Dekker.

Mills, Edwin S., and Bruce W. Hamilton. 1994. *Urban Economics,* 5th ed. New York: Harper/Collins.

Moffitt, R. 1992. "Incentive Effects of the U.S. Welfare System: A Review." *Journal of Economic Literature,* 30:1-61.

Moritz, Owen. 1974. "They're Old, Alone, and Hungry: Women Derelicts on the Increase." *New York Daily News,* October 21.

Murray, Harry. 1990. *Do Not Neglect Hospitality: The Catholic Worker and the Homeless.* Philadelphia: Temple University Press.

Nash, George. 1964a. "The Bowery in the Small Hours of the Morning." Mimeo, Bureau of Applied Social Research, Columbia University.

———. 1964b. "Habitats of Homeless Men in Manhattan." Mimeo, Bureau of Applied Social Research, Columbia University.

——— and Patricia Nash. 1964. "A Preliminary Estimate of the Population and Housing of the Bowery in New York City." Mimeo, Bureau of Applied Social Research, Columbia University.

Newark Housing Authority. Various years. "Annual Report."

Nelson A. Rockefeller Institute of Government. Various years. *New York State Statistical Yearbook.* Albany: SUNY.

New Jersey Department of Human Services, Division of Economic Assistance. 1990. "Emergency Assistance for AFDC Recipients: A Sample Survey—September 1990." December.

New York City Commission on the Homeless (Cuomo Commission). 1992. "The Way Home: A New Direction in Social Policy."

New York City Housing Authority. 1962, 1990. "Annual Report."

New York City Housing Preservation and Development Department. 1979. "The In-Rem Housing Program: Annual Report." October.

New York City Human Resources Administration, Office of Special Housing Services. 1976. "Family Emergency Programs in Hotels and Other Facilities." June.

———. 1981. "Fiscal Year 1981 Management Plan."

——— Family and Adult Services. 1982. "Chronic and Situational Dependency: Long Term Residents in a Shelter for Men."

———. 1984. "The Homeless in New York City Shelters."

———. 1984. "A Comprehensive Plan for the Temporary and Permanent Needs of Homeless Families in New York." January 19.

———. 1986. "Homeless Families and Gentrification." PB 86.5.

———. Various years. "Monthly Shelter Reports."

——— Office of Program and Policy Development. 1987. "The Changing Face of New York City's SRO's: A Profile of Residents and Housing." October.

New York City Mayor's Office on Homelessness and SRO Housing. N.d. (1991 or 1992). "Laws and Regulations Affecting SRO Development."

New York City. Various years. "Mayor's Management Report."

New York State Office of the Comptroller. 1976. "Audit Report on Tenant Selection Operations of the NYC Housing Authority." NYC 31.75.

Nisbet, C. T., and F. Vakil. 1972. "Some Estimates of the Price and Expenditure Elasticities for Marijuana among UCLA Students." *Review of Economics and Statistics*, 54:473-475.

Oechssler, J. 1991. "Report on Homelessness in Hamburg." Mimeo, Department of Economics, Columbia University.

O'Flaherty, Brendan. 1993. "Abandoned Buildings: A Stochastic Analysis." *Journal of Urban Economics*, 34:43-74.

———. 1995. "An Economic Theory of Homelessness and Housing." *Journal of Housing Economics*, -4:13-49.

——— and Jagdish Bhagwati. 1993. "Does Free Trade with Political Science Put Normative Economists Out of Work?" Discussion paper 658, Department of Economics, Columbia University.

Ontario Ministry of Community and Social Services (ComSoc). 1992. "Income Maintenance Handbook." Toronto: Queen's Printer for Ontario.

Ontario Ministry of Housing. 1991. "Housing Statistics." April.

Orwell, George. 1933. *Down and Out in Paris and London*. New York: Berkeley.

S. I. Ornstein. 1980. "Control of Alcohol Consumption through Price Increases." *Journal of Studies on Alcohol*, 41:807-818.

Osterberg, E. 1982. "Alcohol and Economics," in E. M. Pattison and E. Kaufman, eds., *Encyclopedic Handbook of Alcoholism*. New York: Gardner Press.

O'Sullivan, Arthur. 1993. *Urban Economics*, 2nd ed. Homewood, Ill.: Irwin.

Park, J. 1994. "Why Are There So Many Vacancies?" Department of Economics, Columbia University.

Portney, P., ed. 1990. *Public Policies for Environmental Protection*. Washington: Resources for the Future.

"Pulse." 1994. *New York Times*, January 24, p. B1 (box).

Quigley, John M. 1990. "Does Rent Control Cause Homelessness? Taking the Claim Seriously." *Journal of Policy Analysis and Management*, 9:89-93.

Reid, Cecil. 1979. "Affidavit," *Callahan v. Carey (1979)*.

Rivlin, Alice. 1992. *Reviving the American Dream: The Economy, the States, and the Federal Government*. Washington: Brookings Institution.

Rodda, David T. 1992. "Rich Man, Poor Renter: The Relationship between High Incomes and Rents." Mimeo, Department of Economics, Harvard University

Rosen, Kenneth T., and Lawrence B. Smith. 1983. "The Price Adjustment Process for Rental Housing and the Natural Vacancy Rate." *American Economic Review*, 73:779-786.

Rosenstein, M. J., et al. 1986. "Characteristics of Admissions to the Inpatient Services of State and County Mental Hospitals, United States, 1980." Statistical Note 177, NIMH.

Rossi, Peter. 1989. *Down and Out in America: The Origins of Homelessness.* Chicago: University of Chicago Press.

Rouse, B. 1991. "Trends in Cocaine Use in the General Population," in S. Schober and C. Schade, eds., *The Epidemiology of Cocaine Use and Abuse.* Rockville: NIMH.

Salvation Army and Church Army. N.d. (c. 1975-1980). "Out in the Cold—The Future for Large Hostels for the Single Homeless." London.

Schooler, Nina R., et al. 1967. "One Year after Discharge: Community Adjustment of Schizophrenic Patients." *American Journal of Psychiatry,* 123:986-995.

Schwartz, R. 1988. "The Homeless: The Impact on the Transportation Industry." New York: Port Authority of New York and New Jersey.

Sen, Amartya. 1992. *Inequality Reexamined.* Cambridge: Harvard University Press.

Sheppard, Nathaniel, Jr. 1976. "City Subsidizes Six Hotels on the Bowery." *New York Times,* March 30.

Shlay, Anne B., and Peter Rossi. 1992. "Social Science Research and Contemporary Studies of Homelessness." *Annual Review of Sociology,* 18:129-160.

Silverman, L. P., and N. L. Sprull. 1977. "Urban Crime and the Price of Heroin." *Journal of Urban Economics,* 4:80-103.

Simpson, John H., and Margaret Kilduff. 1984. "Homelessness in Newark: A Report on the Trailer People." Mimeo, Newark Committee on the Homeless.

Smith, L. 1988. "An Economic Assessment of Rent Controls: The Ontario Experience." *Journal of Real Estate Economics and Finance,* 1:217-231.

Snow, D., S. Baker, L. Anderson, and M. Martin. 1986. "The Myth of Pervasive Mental Illness among the Homeless." *Social Problems,* 33:407-413.

Sosin, Michael R., Paul Colson, and Susan Grossman. 1988. "Homelessness in Chicago: Poverty and Pathology, Social Institutions and Social Change." Chicago: Chicago Community Trust.

Steadman, H. J., J. Monahan, B. Duffie, et al. 1984. "The Impact of State Mental Hospital Deinstitutionalization on the U.S. Prison Populations, 1968-78." *Journal of Criminal Law and Psychiatry,* 75:474-490.

Stegman, M. 1985. "The Model: Rent Control in New York City," in P. L. Niebanck, ed., *The Rent Control Debate.* Chapel Hill: University of North Carolina Press.

Stern, Mark J. 1984. "The Emergence of the Homeless as a Public Policy Problem." *Social Service Review,* 58:291-301.

Sternlieb, George. 1966. *The Tenement Landlord.* New Brunswick: Rutgers University Press.

University of Surrey, Department of Psychology. 1989. "The Faces of Homelessness in London: Interim Report to the Salvation Army." July.

Sweeney, J. L. 1974a. "Quality, Commodity Hierarchies, and Housing Markets." *Econometrica,* 42:147-167.

———. 1974b. "A Commodity Hierarchy Model of the Urban Housing Market." *Journal of Urban Economics,* 1:288-323.

Taube, C. 1973. *Utilization of Mental Health Facilities, 1971*. NIMH series B, no. 5. Washington: GPO.

Teplin, L. A. 1983. "The Criminalization of the Mentally Ill: Speculation in Search of Data." *Psychological Bulletin*, 94:54-67.

Thomas, Karen, and Patricia A. Wright. 1990. "An Assessment of Single Room Occupancy (SRO) Hotels in the South Loop." Technical Report 2.90, Nathaniel P. Voorhees Center for Neighborhood and Community Improvement, Chicago.

Toronto Commissioner of Community Services. 1992. "Report to Community Services and Housing Committee on Emergency Hostels for the Homeless." January 3.

Toronto Commissioner of Planning. 1974. "South of Carlton Report on Roominghouses." February 25.

———. 1977. "Skid Row: Population and Housing," November 4.

Toronto Department of Community Services. 1983. "No Place to Go: A Study of Homelessness in Metro Toronto: Characteristics, Trends, and Potential Solutions." January.

———. 1989. "Hostel Report FY1988."

Towber, R., and C. Flemming. 1989. "The Housing Alert Program: A One Year Evaluation." New York: Human Resources Administration.

Tucker, William. 1987a. "Where Do the Homeless Come From?" *National Review*, September:32-43.

———. 1987b. "Rent Control as a Cause of Homelessness." *New York Times*, November 14.

United Kingdom Office of Population Censuses and Surveys. 1991. "1991 Census: Preliminary Report for England and Wales: Supplementary Monitor on People Sleeping Rough." London: HMSO.

United Kingdom Home Office. 1980. "Future Fire Policy: A Consultative Document." London: HMSO.

U.S. Bureau of the Census. 1961. "Inmates of Institutions." PC (2).8A. Washington: GPO.

———. 1973. "Persons in Institutions and Other Group Quarters." PC(2).4E. Washington: GPO.

———. 1984. "Persons in Institutions and Other Group Quarters." PC80.2.4D. Washington: GPO.

———. 1991. "Census Bureau Releases 1990 Decennial Counts for Persons Enumerated in Emergency Shelters and Observed on Streets." Press release, April 12.

———. *Statistical Abstract*. Various years.

U.S. Council of Economic Advisers. 1994. *Economic Report of the President*. Washington: GPO.

U.S. General Accounting Office. 1985. "Homelessness: A Complex Problem and the Federal Response." GAO/HRD 85.40. Washington: GPO.

———. 1988. "Homeless Mentally Ill: Problems and Options in Estimating Numbers and Trends." GAO/PEMD.88.24. Washington: GPO.

U.S. Department of Health and Human Services, Federal Task Force on Homelessness and Severe Mental Illness. 1992. *Outcasts on Main Street.* Washington: DHHS.

—— Substance Abuse and Mental Health Services Administration, National Institute for Drug Abuse. 1987. "Trends in Drug Abuse Related Hospital Emergency Room Episodes and Medical Examiner Cases for Selected Drugs." Series H, no. 3. Rockville: NIDA.

——. 1991. "National Household Survey on Drug Abuse, 1990." Washington: GPO.

—— National Institute of Mental Health. 1990. *Mental Health, United States, 1990.* Rockville: NIMH.

U.S. Department of Housing and Urban Development, Office of Policy Development and Research. 1984. "A Report to the Secretary on the Homeless and Emergency Shelters." Washington: GPO.

"Voters' Awareness of Homeless." 1989. *New York Times,* June 20.

"Vouchers Successfully Provide Housing, but at Slightly Higher Cost, Report Finds." 1990. *Housing and Development Reporter,* July 9, pp. 148-149.

Wackstein, Nancy, director, New York Mayor's Office on Homelessness and SRO Housing. 1990. Memorandum to SRO Owners. August 15.

Waldmann, William. 1993. "A Special Report to the Legislature on General Assistance." April.

Walsh, Diane C. 1993. "Essex Shifting Funds from Hotels to More Stable Homeless Housing." *Sunday Star Ledger* (Newark), August 15.

Watkins, Conrad. 1990. "Mental Illness and Direct-Access Hostels." Mimeo, LSE Department of Social Science and Administration, London.

West Side SRO Law Project. N.d. "Know Your Rights." Leaflet, New York.

Welte, John W., and Grace M. Barnes. 1992. "Drinking among Homeless and Marginally Housed Adults in New York State." *Journal of Studies on Alcohol,* 53:303-315.

White, A. 1991. "Shelter Gridlock." *City Limits,* November, pp. 12-16.

Williams, John. 1988. "Temporary Accommodation for the Homeless in London: A Comparison of the Feasibility of Alternatives." Mimeo, LSE Department of Social Science and Administration, London.

Wright, James D. 1989. *Address Unknown: The Homeless in America.* New York: Aldine de Gruyter.

Yamahara, Tomoko. 1993. "Panhandlers in New York City." Mimeo, Department of Economics, Columbia University.

## Interviews

Matt Baggott, chief inspector, Metropolitan Police, Crime Prevention Service, London, October 3, 1991.

Thomas A. Banker, former assistant business administrator, Newark, June 1991.

David Baseda and Katherine Temple, Catholic Worker, July 30, 1992.

Brenda Beavers, director of social services, New Jersey Salvation Army, August 29, 1991.

David Boothby, superintendent, 51 Division Commander, Toronto Police Department, June 1991.

Bowery lodginghouse owners, August 19, 1993.

Frank Breeze, Toronto Department of Buildings, June 27, 1991.

Sue Brideweiser, Toronto City Planning Department, June 27, 1991.

Les Brown, former executive director, Chicago Coalition for the Homeless, August 1, 1991.

Jean Butzen, Lakefront SRO, Chicago, August 1991.

Jack Collins, Toronto Fire Department, June 27, 1991.

John Donahue, executive director, Chicago Coalition for the Homeless, August 1991.

John Dough, deputy chief, Newark Police Department, June 1991.

Sister Connie Driscoll, chairperson, Chicago Task Force on the Homeless, August 31, 1991 (telephone).

William Eimicke, former deputy commissioner for in-rem housing, New York City, September 1, 1992.

Karen Highsmith, manager, Newark Division of Public Welfare, April 1991.

Michael Hurley, Newark Archdiocese, September 5, 1991.

Sue Kelly, legal analyst, Chicago Police Department, July 30, 1991.

Father John Nickas, St. Rocco's Church, Newark, August 29, 1991.

Ray Rio, former hotel owner, Newark, May 15, 1991.

Eric Rubinstein, president, Chicago SRO Owners Association, July 30, 1991.

Joseph Ryan, detective, New York Police Department, July 18, 1991.

James F. Varn Hargen, McAuley Water Street Mission, New York, July 15, 1992.

Robert Widdowson, director of the London Housing Assistance Centre, October 8, 1991.

# Index